£25·00

STUDIES IN BRITISH ART

THE HOUSES OF PARLIAMENT

1. (over page) The Houses of Parliament from the south-west.

THE HOUSES
OF PARLIAMENT

Edited by M. H Port

Published for the Paul Mellon Centre for
Studies in British Art (London) Ltd., by
Yale University Press, New Haven and London, 1976

Library of Congress catalog card number: 76-3374

International standard book number: 0-300-02022-8

Designed by John Nicoll and set in Monophoto Ehrhardt

Filmset and printed in Great Britain by
BAS Printers Limited, Wallop, Hampshire

Published in Great Britain, Europe, Africa, the Middle East,
India and South-east Asia by
Yale University Press, Ltd., London.
Distributed in Latin America by Kaiman & Polon, Inc., New York City;
in Australasia by Book & Film Services, Artarmon, N.S.W., Australia;
in Japan by John Weatherhill, Inc., Tokyo.

Foreword

From its earliest days Parliament frequently met in the Palace of Westminster, and since the sixteenth century this has been its almost invariable home. The Palace, however, was originally constructed as a series of Royal apartments rather than as a meeting place for a national Legislature. When, therefore, in 1834 fire destroyed much of the ancient building Sir Charles Barry seized the opportunity to provide for the first time in this country a building expressly designed for the work of a Parliament, with legislative chambers, division lobbies, libraries, committee rooms and a record repository, all on the most splendid scale.

During the century that has since elapsed, Barry's New Palace has gained increasing recognition as the most remarkable example of secular architecture of the Victorian era. It was extraordinarily modern in the stress laid on functional planning and on efficient building services. It provided, moreover, by its elaborate decoration, vital encouragement to the revival of British craftsmanship, and the Houses of Parliament became a 'Palace of History and Art' with considerable influence on popular taste and knowledge.

The authors of the present volume provide a detailed and authoritative account of this whole process. They describe the collaboration of architects, engineers and craftsmen at Westminster, and emphasise the leading role played by members of the two Houses of Parliament themselves in the planning of the building and the choice of decorative details. The book should prove of great interest not only to those whose working days are spent at Westminster but also to all concerned with the history of Parliament and with the development of English architecture.

The Houses of Parliament were, as they remain today, a Royal Palace. Parts of the building are still in the charge of a great Officer of State, the Lord Great Chamberlain, The Marquess of Cholmondeley. Lord Cholmondeley desires to express his own commendation of the present volume, in which each of us as Speakers of our respective Houses, gladly join.

Elwyn Jones Lord Chancellor
George Thomas , Speaker

vii

Editor's Preface

The Houses of Parliament are a building of which the planning, construction and decoration touched many facets of nineteenth-century history. With today's high degree of specialization in scholarship one person could hardly do justice to such a theme. So this book, like the New Palace at Westminster itself, is a work of collaboration. I am grateful to my co-authors for their generous help and their ready co-operation.

We are greatly indebted to the Paul Mellon Centre for Studies in British Art (London) Ltd for making possible the publication of this work. The book could not have been written without the help of the authorities of the Palace of Westminster over a number of years. I am grateful to the Lord Chancellor and the Speaker of the House of Commons for their kindness in contributing a Foreword, and to the Lord Great Chamberlain for his goodwill. To Mr Maurice Bond, MVO, OBE, Keeper of the Records, House of Lords, I should like to express my personal thanks and those of my colleagues: his assistance and advice have been of the greatest value. For enabling us collectively and severally to visit the Palace on numerous occasions and penetrate its recesses we are grateful to the last two Speakers of the House of Commons (now Lord Maybrace-King and Lord Selwyn-Lloyd), the Gentleman Usher of the Black Rod, Admiral Sir Frank Twiss, KCB, DSC; Capt. Sir Kenneth Mackintosh, KCVO, RN, late Serjeant-at-Arms, House of Lords; Rear-Admiral Sir A. H. C. Gordon-Lennox, CB, DSO, Serjeant at Arms, House of Commons; Lt Col P. F. Thorne, CBE, Deputy Sergeant at Arms, and Cmdr D. Swanston, DSO, DSC, Assistant Serjeant at Arms; Brigadier N. E. V. Short, the Speaker's Secretary; Colonel C. L. Sayers, Yeoman Usher of the Black Rod; Mr A. J. Henshaw, sometime Resident Engineer; Mr Butler, Resident Superintendent (Engineering); Mr Matthews, sometime Clerk of Works; and the local staff of the former Ministry of Works, now the Department of the Environment.

Among the many who have assisted us in different ways we should particularly like to express our thanks to Lord Beaumont of Whitley, Professor S. T. Bindoff, Lord Bradwell, Mr John Charlton, Mr H. S. Cobb, Mr Christopher Cole, Mr Howard Colvin, Mr Alan Cook, Professor A. G. Dickens, Mr J. R. Ede (Keeper of the Public Records), Mr Patrick Feeny, Mr Denis Hall, Mrs M. P. Harper, Mr D. J. Johnson, Mr W. A. Kellaway, Mr C. J. Mabey, Mr R. J. Mamlok, Dr Colin Matthew, Mr R. Phaendler, Professor E. Rawstron and the Department of Geography Technicians (Mr P. Newman and Mr A. Gillard) Queen Mary College, Mr A. A. Slaney, Lord Sudeley, Mrs P. B. Stanley-Evans, Sir John Summerson, Mr R. J. B. Walker, Mrs H. M. Wedgwood, and Miss G. Wild.

M. H. Port
Queen Mary College, London

March, 1976

ix

Contents

Acknowledgments

To the Controller of Her Majesty's Stationery Office for permission to publish Crown copyright records in the Public Record Office; to the Trustees of the Broadlands Archives for quotations from the Palmerston and Cowper Papers; to Lady Lucas for that from Lord de Grey's MS memoir; to The Johns Hopkins University for quotations from Pugin letters in the Fowler Collection; to the Librarian, Birmingham Reference Library for those from the Hardman Archives; to Professor Phoebe B. Stanton for those from her transcripts of letters formerly in the possession of the late Sebastian Pugin Powell and from her London University Ph.D. thesis, 'Welby Pugin and the Gothic Revival'.

The following drawings, paintings or photographs are Crown copyright: Reproduced by permission of the Controller of Her Majesty's Stationery Office: III, V, VI, X; 5, 18, 26, 30, 34–9, 54, 62–4, 67–71, 73, 81, 83, 88, 95–7, 102–4, 107–10, 115, 118, 119, 121, 122, 128, 129, 132, 134–7, 152, 155, 156, 158, 166, 179–84, 186, 187; Pl. 33 from *History of the King's Works*, vol. vi; Royal Commission on Ancient Monuments, Scotland: 31, 49, 80; Victoria & Albert Museum VIII, 28, 41, 42, 48, 57, 58, 84, 85, 140, 165.

To each of the following for kind permission to reproduce drawings, paintings or photographs in their ownership or possession, as indicated: Mr L. Blair-Oliphant (31, 49, 80); the Curators of the Bodleian Library (159); the Trustees of the British Museum (50, 94); the British Architectural Library, Royal Institute of British Architects (17, 24, 25, 27, 29, 32, 44–7, 52, 55, 56, 65, 82, 154, 163, 164, 170, 172–4); Cole & Son (wallpapers) Ltd (86, 87); Country Life Ltd (21); Courtauld Institute of Art (19, 178); the Governors of the Schools of King Edward VI in Birmingham (46); Greater London County Record Office (93); the Keeper of Prints and Pictures, Guildhall Library (16, 23); the Clerk of the Records, House of Lords (IX, 113, 127, 133, 149, 153, 157, 167–9, 171, 176, 188–92, 194, 196–9); Interfoto MTI Hungary (205); National Monuments Record (43, 79, 206, 207); National Portrait Gallery (4, 22, 40, 72, 76); Philadelphia Museum of Art, John McFadden Collection (XI); M. H. Port (II, IV, VII, 141, 177); Public Archives of Canada (201); Royal Academy of Arts (195); Denis Smith (123–6, 141, 146); Mrs P. B. Stanley-Evans (61, 170, 172, 174); Lord Sudeley (19, 20); Westminster Public Library (13, 14, 208).

List of Plates

Colour Plates

Monochrome Plates

List of Abbreviations

BM	British Museum
HLRO	House of Lords Record Office
ICE	Institution of Civil Engineers
IMech.E	Institution of Mechanical Engineers
PRO	Public Record Office (see note below)
q.	question
RA	Royal Academy
RIBA	Royal Institute of British Architects
Sess.	Session
V&A	Victoria and Albert Museum

Art-Architect	E. W. Pugin, *Who was the Art Architect of the Houses of Parliament?* (1867)
A.Barry, *Life*	*The Life and Works of Sir Charles Barry* (edns. 1867 and 1870).
—*Reply*	*The Architect of the New Palace at Westminster. A reply to the statements of Mr E. Pugin* (1868)
AR	*Architectural Review*
B	*The Builder*
BN	*Building News*
CE	*The Civil Engineer and Architect's Journal*
CJ	*Commons' Journals*
GM	*The Gentleman's Magazine*
H.d.b	*Hardman day book*
Holmes, *Illustrations*, (1865)	E. N. Holmes, *Illustrations of the New Palace of Westminster*, Second Series (1865)
ILN	*Illustrated London News*
King's Works, vi	J. M. Crook and M. H. Port, *History of the King's Works*, vol. vi, *1782–1851*, ed. H. M. Colvin (1973).
Parl. Deb.	*Parliamentary Debates* (see note below)
PP	*Parliamentary Papers* (see note below)
Reply	See above, A. Barry, *Reply*
RIBA Drawings	RIBA Drawings Collection
Ryde, *Illustrations*, (1849)	H. T. Ryde, *Illustrations of the New Palace of Westminster*, First Series (1849).
Walker, 'Catalogue'	R. J. B. Walker, 'A Catalogue of Paintings, Drawings, Sculpture and Engravings in The Palace of Westminster', 7 parts (duplicated, Ministry of Works, 1959 ff.)—annual supplements in HLRO.

Note:

For the collections at the Public Record Office, the call-references are used: T. is Treasury papers; Works, those of the former Office of Works. Works 29 is a series of more than 3,000 drawings and tracings relating to the Houses of Parliament.

Parliamentary Debates (Hansard) are referred to as *Parl.Deb.*n.s. (new series), or *3 Parl.Deb.* (third series), followed by the volume and column numbers. For *Parliamentary Papers* (printed) references follow the convention recommended by Professor P. G. Ford. For House of Commons Papers, the year of the session is given, followed by the sessional number in brackets, and the number of the volume in which the paper occurs. An additional reference to 'p.' indicates the printed pagination of the individual paper; or 'q.', the question number in Minutes of Evidence. If neither 'p.' nor 'q.' is used, the final number refers to the MS pagination of the volume in the British Museum. For printed House of Lords Papers which were not printed also as Commons Papers, 'HL' precedes the year, and no volume number is given, as the British Museum volumes differ from those preserved in the House of Lords. Where the paper is a Command Paper, the Command number is given in place of the sessional number, but in square brackets: this is a series continuing over many sessions, and subsequently re-started from time to time with 'C.', 'Cd.', 'Cmd.' etc. preceding the number.

I

Introduction

A mystery and a paradox: that in a nutshell is what this book is about. The Houses of Parliament were the first great Victorian building—indeed the first great modern building, 'the initial letter in the chapter of our architectural history which the age has been composing',[1] as a critic wrote in 1869—the first and greatest. We think of it as 'the Houses of Parliament', but to the men on the job it was 'the New Palace at Westminster'. The name itself is significant; its connotations of vast size and lavish expense did not escape attack. It was no longer the classical 'British Senate House' of the eighteenth century, but a sublimer concept: a palace worthy of the world's greatest nation, great in moral achievement and the lesson it could teach mankind—

> A land of settled government,
> . . .
> Where Freedom slowly broadens down
> From precedent to precedent

—as great in its economic hegemony and naval supremacy, and in the extent and wealth of its imperial sway. Fittingly, such a palace, affording instruction to the populace in art as well as in government, should excel the palaces of kings. That experienced builder William Cubitt could declare in 1850 that there was 'no building in Europe, whether ancient or modern, which could compete with that which was deservedly termed the New Palace of Westminster.'[2]

But the 'swelling splendour of the imperial theme' is by no means the only Victorian characteristic of this structure, 'the largest and most elaborate architectural work ever perhaps undertaken at one time in this or any other country', as its architect asserted.[3] The purpose of this book is to explore the significance of the Palace in terms of why and how it was built, and as the focal point of argument about professional rights and status. These problems have been obscured by two factors. The Victorian obsession with the historic succession of styles, and the fact that the revived Perpendicular Gothic fashionable in 1835 had ceased to please refined palates of the 1850s meant that by the end of its lengthy period of gestation the New Palace was condemned as a stylistic travesty, and a grossly expensive one at that:[4]

Of what it pleases Mr Ruskin to call *reticulation*, there is such a superabundance in Mr Barry's river front, that a good deal of money must have been sifted away through it. Excess of cost has been rendered still more excessive by very needless decoration,—by so much of it, in fact, that it amounts to fritter, it being unaccompanied by anything of that breadth and repose which would give it value . . . The employment of means excessive in proportion to the end and to the effect obtained does not, in our opinion, evince any very extraordinary artistic power or skill.

Nevertheless, when British architects were called upon to design other public buildings of great size, they still turned to Westminster for guidance on composition, as in the New Law Courts competition of 1866. Thus paradoxically what was technically the most advanced large building of its day was commonly written off for stylistic reasons: 'nothing more than a metropolitan asylum for birds' nests and soot'.[5]

The other factor that has obscured the significance of the New Palace is the mystery associated with the authorship of the design. From the very beginning, the story of the design was clouded by misgivings and suspicion; there was some deceit. This belief was fostered by the prevalent distrust of public works as a 'job', an arrangement contrived for the benefit of individuals at the expense of the public. 'Who but a fool', asked Tennyson, 'would have faith in a tradesman's ware or his word?' And architects were commonly regarded as tradesmen. Mistrust could thrive, too, because circumstances were changing over the thirty or forty years of building. Commodity and labour prices fluctuated. Changes in society at large involved Parliament more closely in every aspect of national life. Accordingly Parliament's own needs grew. These changes meant increased expenditure, on which the architect claimed commission. So suspicion of jobbery grew. It was but a short step to suggestions that the whole exercise was a gigantic fraud, and that the real designer of the Houses of Parliament was not Barry but Pugin: whose allure as romantic hero and victim was enhanced because he died young and mad.

The idea of rebuilding the Houses of Parliament was not new in 1834. The post-Napoleonic era in particular had seen much building or re-building of public offices; and in an age when Parliament had been reformed, there was a cry that it needed comparably improved accommodation. The Westminster fire came so pat that there were rumours of arson. But how was the rebuilding to be organized? It was an age in which old restrictions were being abolished. Monopolies, deprived of accustomed protection, were withering away. This was true not only in commerce or industry, but in architecture as well: public opinion would not tolerate giving the job to a governmental favourite. Britain's architectural community afforded a considerable amount of talent, and the idea of competition was congenial to the public and sufficiently familiar to the profession. So designs were obtained and one selected for execution. Such a mighty work required an unexampled collaborative effort. Far from being surprised, like some contemporaries, at the slowness of the building, we may reflect on the impressiveness of the achievement that Barry master-minded, one that could only have been accomplished in so short a time by a high degree of teamwork, making full use of recently developed techniques. Though the Palace contained little structural innovation, it did employ the most advanced technology in such important features as the process of selection of the building stone, use of concrete foundations, all-timber nailed scaffolding, machinery for carving. In the actual process of construction, new techniques were devised on the site, notably for the three great towers that excelled all since the most daring accomplishments of the Middle Ages. In the organization of the men working on the building, too, from the initial process of design to the final decoration, the New Palace represents the most advanced technique of the day. *The Builder* even hoped that it would be 'made morally influential for the advancement of the working builders, and through them, for general building art.'[6] The comfort of the users was considered, and experimental schemes of ventilation, warming and lighting introduced.

Charles Barry had not merely to conduct a large orchestra: he had also to perform to a critical audience able to call the tune. It was not, however, a singleminded audience, and it tended to go to sleep during the *allegro*; so that Barry could generally get away with his selections so long as the *scherzo* was not too elaborate. Unfortunately the audience was sometimes roused by expert players who wished to interrupt the concerto with extended solo cadenzas. Barry's success may be measured by the degree to which the New Palace coped with the hugely enlarged activities of Victorian parliaments and their members. But such a task demanded qualities not to be found in the golden book of professional ethics, in which *Architect* was seeking then to enrol his title. In pursuit of his ideal Barry, an 'artist whose religion was his art', was prepared to trample down obstacles and ignore prohibitory notices; and if a gate were too heavily barbed for climbing over, then he would crawl under to get through. If this tale has a moral, it is perhaps that a set task should not be hedged around with impossible conditions. Some of the ministers responsible for public works at that time recognized this, giving Barry a free hand and their backing; others took a different view. But 'Parliament had never effectually committed the responsibility . . . to the Executive Government'.[7]

His struggle affected Barry's practice as well as his health. He was 'called upon to do more than is usual or could have been anticipated'. Not only had he the 'labour and anxiety' of meeting Dr Reid's structural requirements for a system of 'warming and ventilating the entire edifice to an extent never before attempted . . . and much beyond what I [Barry remarked] considered to be necessary', but—let him speak:

I have also been called upon to remodel the internal fittings of the Two Houses and to vary from time to time the arrangement and appropriations of the Offices, the Division Lobbies &c of each House owing to the changes made in the mode of conducting the business of Parliament and the vagueness and insufficiency of the information afforded for the preparation of the original design which information upon being reconsidered by committees appointed from time to time during the progress of the works has been found in many instances to be altogether at variance with the requirements . . . The entire plan and construction of the building has had to be modified and recast over and over again . . .[8]

Legal conferences on contracts, claims and threatened proceedings, negotiations about government workshops, abortive planning for the public records and the like might perhaps be considered incidental to such a commission, but beyond that were exhausting interrogations by parliamentary committees, attendance upon the Fine Arts Commission, reports and drawings for these bodies, voluminous returns to orders of the House, 'one of which occupied myself and clerks for nearly 4 months'.

The result of winning this splendid commission was quite the contrary of Barry's expectations: 'I have been obliged to give up more than two-thirds of a lucrative practice', he wrote in 1849, 'and have to my knowledge been deprived of employment to a very considerable extent from a prevalent feeling which has existed that it was out of my power to attend to any other work'. His reward up till then had worked out at the net rate of £1,500 *p.a.* For this he had 'devoted almost exclusively the best period of [his] professional life' to the New Palace, at a period when leading men in other professions—law, medicine, civil engineering—were 'well known' to earn £12,000–£20,000 a year and even more.[9] Born into very modest middle-class circumstances, Barry had his sights set high. Moving in high Whig circles before he was forty, the thousand a year that represented comfortably more than the middle-class average[10] was far below his measure,

> Who makes by force his merit known
> And lives to clutch the golden keys.

For let us not be too sorry for Barry: he left £80,000—true, not so much as Scott, but not bad for a self-made man who had long given up two-thirds of his practice. Of course, the labour told on his health: he was seriously ill in 1853 and again in 1857–8; and death took him suddenly on 12 May 1860. But private clients too have been known to drive architects near distraction; and at 65 Barry was past his prime.

Unpleasant though some of Barry's characteristics may have been, there can be little doubt that it was his 'cool determination to act without leave' that built the New Palace at Westminster. Had it not been for his steely resolve, oiled with a superficial agreeableness and pliability, the machinery of public building would once again have failed. The Houses of Parliament, as *The Architect* remarked in reviewing Alfred Barry's life of his father, was a monument to public stupidity and official mismanagement:[11]

The story . . . shows up the whole career of an architect who was not only one of the very ablest and one of the most successful of modern times, but who, in these respects, was especially a typical man; and it exhibits also the whole process of development of an architectural work, not only a marvellous production in itself, and a *chef d'œuvre* of English design, but a landmark in artistic history and a remarkably characteristic example of English procedure.

II

The Old Houses of Parliament

THE Houses of Parliament were burned down during the night of 16 October 1834, thereby offering English architecture its finest opportunity since the Great Fire of London. It was, too, an opportunity to mend matters long awry: the old Houses were cramped, ill-ventilated, inconvenient. John Wilson Croker, who had been an MP for a quarter of a century, in 1833 described the offices of the House of Commons as:[1]

notoriously imperfect, very crazy as buildings, and extremely incommodious in their local distribution. I know of no advantage whatever that attends the present adjacent accommodation or the accesses to the House. They are not well disposed for the transaction of business; they are not symmetrical with the House of Lords; they are not symmetrical with Westminster Hall; there is no proper access for Members, although we have the misfortune to see the Prime Minister . . . murdered in the Lobby; and, on several occasions, Members have been personally insulted in going to the House. A Member who does his duty in Parliament is sometimes liable to offend individuals; he must pass every day of his life up a series of narrow dark, tortuous passages, where any individual who wishes to insult him may have the certain and easy opportunity of doing so.

It would, after all, have been 'very surprising if an apartment of the most ancient palace in England, applied accidentally in the lapse of ages to a purpose for which it was not originally intended, should now be found to be, by some strange accident, the most convenient of all possible places.'[2]

The ancient palace of the English kings next St Edward's abbey at Westminster was a rambling conglomeration of buildings used, often indiscriminately, for a variety of purposes, ceremonial, judicial, financial as well as residential, with its own once-magnificent chapel (Pls 2, 3). When Parliament met, it was often at Westminster; and in 1547 the king gave the Commons the use of the royal chapel, St Stephen's. There for nearly three hundred years they were habitually to meet, though not without grumblings of discomfort.[3] Alarmed by cracks, the Members persuaded Wren to demolish the clerestory and lower the roof in 1692 (cp. Pl. 5); and into that reduced space Wren inserted side galleries after the Act of Union had added 45 Scottish MPs. Wren's designs for a general rebuilding were never carried out, and discomfort drove Members to press for a new House in 1733. The Office of Works

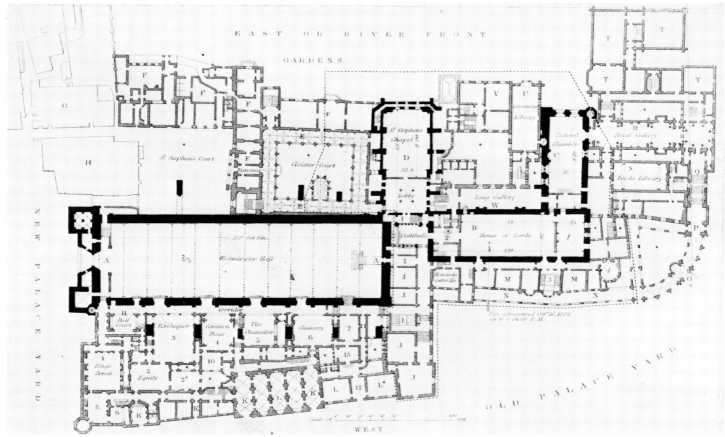

2. Plan of the Old Palace of Westminster, 1834. The dotted line marks the extent of the fire of 16 October 1834.
Key: C, Painted Chamber; D, House of Commons; B, House of Lords (from 1801); 1–11, Law courts.

prepared plans for new Houses in the Palladian style.[4] Kent offered a choice of forms
for the Commons' Chamber—circular, oval, or square with a semi-circular end—
ideas that were to be taken up nearly a century later. The outbreak of war with Spain
in 1739, and with France in 1740, doubtless explains why no action was taken. Then
Members' attendance fell off, only reviving in the political struggles of the 1780s. In
1789 the Commons called fourteen architects to report; many of the Westminster
buildings were found to consist at least partly of timber, and some were covered
with nothing more than tarred sailcloth.[5]

Then the Lords demanded fresher air and in 1792 suggested a move to a larger
chamber. A competition of architects was mooted, but it was the official architect in
charge of the palace, John Soane, whom the Lords asked for plans. His characteristic
neo-classical designs for new Houses along the river front (with St Stephen's restored
for worship) were doomed by war again, as well as by the intrigues of James Wyatt,
surveyor-general of Works from 1796, who obtained the management of the Lords'
improvements in 1799.[6] This proved stylistically significant: neo-classic was de-
throned in favour of another antiquarian style, Gothic. Commonly believed to be of
English invention, this struck a responsive chord at a time of desperate national struggle against the hereditary foe. Gothic was favoured as the appropriate style for Westminster, both symbolically, for the generally received political theory of the day

6

3. Old Palace of Westminster: River front after the fire. In the foreground is the Painted Chamber (Temporary House of Lords, 1835–46); in the middle distance the ruins of St Stephen's Chapel (Old House of Commons), with the cupola of Westminster Hall rising above it; and beyond lie Speaker's House and the old Exchequer Offices.

looked back to a golden age of Gothic (or 'Saxon') liberty as the real basis of England's glorious constitution and the rights of freeborn Englishmen; and also physically, as harmonizing with the existing buildings, Hall and Abbey in particular, and a St Stephen's of which the ancient glories were being rediscovered.[7] Wyatt gave a semblance of order and cohesion to the palace by erecting façades of a collegiate Gothic towards the river (for the Speaker's residence) and to Old Palace Yard, where he provided ancillary accommodation for the Lords.

When the British and Irish legislatures were united in 1801, 100 Irish MPs were added to the Commons and twenty-eight Irish peers to the Lords. Wyatt devised expedients: the Lords moved to more spacious quarters in the old Court of Requests (Pl. 2); and crowded, hot, fetid St Stephen's was stretched for the Commons by the cutting of recesses in the medieval arcading of the walls.[8] Increased numbers were not, however, the only problem. Parliament responded to the need to take a more active part in the life of the nation at large as the dynamic economy of the industrialized state developed. The volume of legislation was growing steadily from the 1790s, much of it concerned with enclosures, various forms of transport, and, as time went on, with conditions of work. The parliamentary select committee was perfected as a means of exposing abuses and proposing remedies. All this activity required large numbers of committee rooms: in 1824 as many as forty-four bills were sometimes under con-

7

4. Joseph Hume, MP (1777–1855). Detail of portrait by J. W. Walton.

sideration by committees on a single day.[9] James Wyatt's additions were of little help.

During the 1820s, accordingly, Soane (back in favour) built new offices and committee rooms for the Lords and libraries for both Houses, with a new Royal Approach. The exterior of these new buildings was discreetly Gothic, the royal *porte cochère* in a Perpendicular version 'improved' by the king himself (Pl. 16). The Commons' library, too, was Gothic. Previously, from 1809, large sums had been voted for the restoration of the nearby Henry VII's Chapel under the direction of James Wyatt's eldest son, Benjamin; and from 1819 for that of Westminster Hall, conducted by Soane. The accumulation of centuries was cleared away from the Hall: coffee shops and tenements from the exterior, the Courts of Law and Equity from their ancient seats inside (cp. Pl. 2). In building new Law Courts immediately west of the Hall (opposite the Abbey) Soane determined to avoid any comparison between modern Gothic and the much-admired ancient structure—even though most of its surface was the work of himself or his coadjutors. But the *cognoscenti* insisted that his 'outlandish' neo-classical façade for the Law Courts, a 'monument to posterity of the bad taste of the present age', must come down, despite the inconvenience thereby caused to the administration of justice. The government was compelled by the

8

Commons to spend £9,000 on rebuilding the façade in Gothic to harmonize with the Hall and set back so as to give a better view of it (see Pl. 93). The new Goths had won.[10]

But Gothic art presented no obvious solution to the most pressing of Parliament's domestic problems. The stench of the Commons was an old story,[11] but the struggle over the Great Reform Bill gave it a new poignancy. When more than 600 members took part in divisions they experienced acute discomfort. Colonel Frederick William Trench in 1831 chaired a select committee to consider how St Stephen's could be made 'more commodious and less unwholesome'.[12] Trench was an intriguer mixed up in several architectural projects. He had taken a leading part in the attack on Soane's Law Courts, and had published a scheme for embanking the Thames in which his collaborators were Benjamin Wyatt and his brother Philip.[13] His committee took evidence from Benjamin and his cousin Sir Jeffry Wyatville, then converting Windsor Castle into a modern palace, and from Robert Smirke, an accomplished 'doctor' of other men's constructions. Smirke merely referred to enlarging the Lobby and improving the ventilation of the House; the other two recommended building a new House in preference to any more tinkering with the old. Wyatt proposed the deceptively simple solution of throwing the Lobby into the House, re-uniting St Stephen's Chapel as a single room. This not only deprived members of their Lobby, but would have necessitated other complicated alterations. Wyatville preferred building a new House in the garden between the chapel and the river.

This idea was one that found much favour with those architects consulted in 1833, when after the passing of the Reform Act Joseph Hume (Pl. 4) called for further consideration of the Trench committee's recommendation for a new building. Hume, a brawny, obstinate, common-sensical Scot, once an army surgeon, now Radical Member for Middlesex, was invariably in his place when the House was sitting. Such unremitting attendance, sustained on a diet of pears, made him peculiarly aware of the inadequacies of the Chamber. The committee of which he was chairman took evidence from thirteen leading architects. Sir John Soane (as he had become) stated with uncharacteristic forthrightness that having considered the subject for some thirty years he believed that 'it was totally impossible, by any means whatever, to enlarge the House of Commons sufficiently.'[14]

The difficulties confronting any attempt to alter the existing structure may be most readily grasped by looking at the plan of the old palace (Pl. 2) and at the section prepared by the Office of Woods and Works at the committee's behest (Pl. 5). The jungle of rooms and passages was made yet more confused by the complete lack of a uniform floor level: to go from the House of Commons to the House of Lords members had to 'go down 14 steps and come up seven'. If a new Chamber were ranged with the floor of the old House of Commons, therefore, the approach to the House of Lords would involve a change of level. While it seemed perhaps the most obvious and simple solution to build a new House as a continuation of the old towards the river, that too was not without its pitfalls: it removed the Commons further from the Lords' House (which they attended on state occasions) as well as from facilities such as library and smoking room that the longer sittings made it desirable to have as close as possible to the House itself. So sited, it would also block the windows of the Speaker's Dining Room in the so-called crypt of St Stephen's, and would darken the other rooms of his house. Its protusion would, moreover, break what little measure of cohesion Wyatt and Soane had given to the river front. In many ways a more convenient site would have been to the south or south-east of the old, close to the library, and permitting a direct communication with the House of

9

5. The Old House of Commons buildings: Section from west to east, showing committee rooms to west of Westminster Hall, and the chapel of St Mary Undercroft, the House of Commons, Lobby, ventilators and roof space (used as a Ladies' Gallery) in St Stephen's, 1834. The line CC shows the floor level of the old House of Lords.

Lords. Unfortunately this site was occupied already by the house of the Clerk of the Commons, who refused to give it up.

The architects who appeared before the Hume committee in 1833 nearly all advocated a new building on one or the other of these sites. But one, Thomas Hopper (1776–1856), who had made his reputation long before with a Gothic conservatory at Carlton house for the Prince Regent, preferred altering the old House. He proposed to take down the side walls, building them some 13 or 14 ft further north and south. Business might go on in the old House while the new was built around it. 'The roof itself might be kept on,' he suggested, 'and the new part of the roof so formed as to support the present roof, and to make it as strong as a new roof.' This economical mode of proceeding, he explained, saved 'two-thirds at least of the basement storey, the Speaker's Dining-room and the walls attached to it, and the floor, except the new pieces; the ends are retained, the roof is preserved, and there are many other things connected with a new building which it would be difficult to explain.' But in Soane's view it would have been impossible to remove the side walls without removing the roof likewise and in fact 'building an entire new House'.[15] Among the witnesses was John Wilson Croker, former Tory minister, who suggested building a new House immediately north of St Stephen's (Pl. 6); and the hirsute MP Rigby Wason, a strong advocate for the improvement of the Westminster district. Charles Hanbury Tracy (Pl. 19), a member of the committee who, himself an amateur architect, had built his own great Gothic mansion at Toddington in Gloucestershire (Pl. 20), submitted a plan on the lines of Hopper's proposal.[16]

The designs put forward by the various architects consulted were mostly for new Chambers internally of a Classical character, often nothing more than the vernacular of the day (Pls 7, 11), though some of them proposed a more elaborate architectural treatment, and one, Bardwell's, was a full-blown Gothic design.[17] The principal reason for this restraint was undoubtedly financial: Lord Grey's administration was pledged to economy. A new House of Commons could be built for something like £20,000 or £30,000 according to the architects' estimates. But certain members of the committee had wider views, and some questioning was directed towards the possibility of building new Parliament Houses on some other site, perhaps that of

St James's Palace: the old parliamentary buildings would then be applied to the use of various government departments such as the Ordnance Board which occupied a valuable site in Pall Mall.[18]

It was a mark, however, of the development of English taste and even of architectural scholarship, that the architects' common voice declared in 1833 for the preservation and restoration of St Stephen's be it as library, lobby, or chapel for the House. The richness and beauty of the ancient architecture of the chapel had been pointed out in a detailed description from John Carter's drawings published in 1795 by the Society of Antiquaries, with additional plates based on the discoveries made when the House was enlarged in 1800, published in 1807.[19] At the same date J. T. Smith published his *Antiquities of Westminster*, also with plates of the chapel. Carter wrote an account of the palace in the *Gentleman's Magazine* in 1810, in which he remarked of the chapel:[20]

In this building every trial of the arts of architecture and painting is brought to the utmost stretch of human ability; and while our wonder is excited at those who wrought its completion, our disgust is at the same time raised against the savage hands that . . . have either mutilated its divine attractions or hoarded up the beauteous relics still in being, with common wainscoting.

In the early nineteenth century the Gothic Revival had moved into an archaeological phase, to which the draughtsmanship of Capon and Carter at Westminster contributed. Rickman produced a viable classification of English Gothic architecture;

6. J. W. Croker (1780–1857): Plan for new House of Commons, 1833.

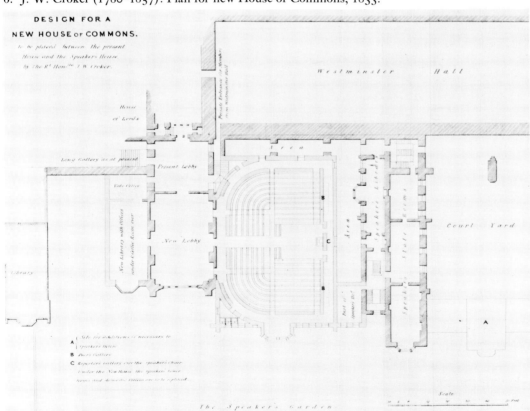

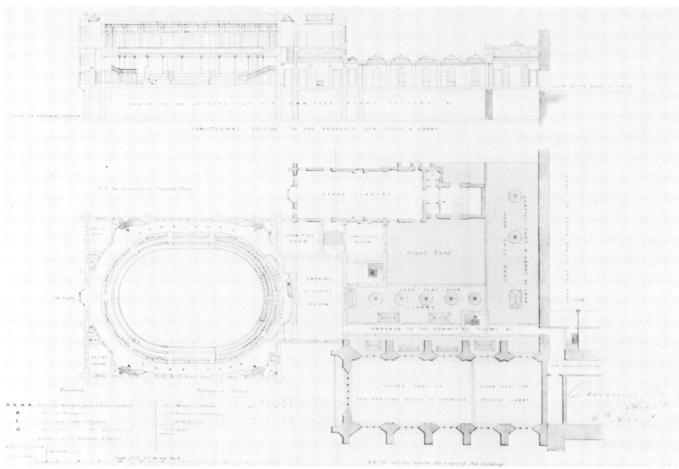

7. Decimus Burton (1800–81): Plan for new House of Commons, 1833.

8. James Savage (1779–1852): Plan for a new House of Commons, 1833.

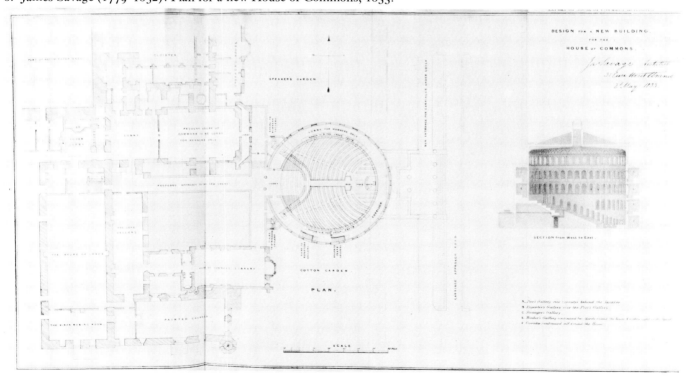

the publications of Auguste Pugin and E. J. Willson gave accurate details for architects who wished to employ the Gothic style. Opportunity was provided by the great wave of church building set in motion after 1818 by the Church Building Commission, and the readiness of the landed interest, liberated from war taxes, to build or rebuild country houses.[21]

Style, however, was of less concern to Hume's committee than atmosphere. Attempts to improve the bad air of St Stephen's had been many and ineffectual. Opinion among the architects consulted favoured the use of open fires for assisting ventilation, whatever form of heating might be adopted for general warmth. The committee hoped that a more pleasant atmosphere might be maintained in a new chamber, largely isolated from other buildings.

Even more of the committee's time was devoted to acoustics. 'There is no point of natural science', declared Croker, 'that has been brought to so little practical certainty.'[22] James Savage (1779–1852), architect of St Luke's church, Chelsea, asserting the superiority of a circular room (Pl. 8), compared the motion of sound with that of water in a circular basin. But Croker, drawing on his recollections of the old Irish House of Commons, a circular chamber, as well as his experience of the Chamber of Deputies in Paris, a semi-circular one, rejected both forms as reverberatory. Soane thought that a circular end (Pl. 9), as in Palladio's *Teatro Olimpico* and 'all the ancient theatres, both Greek and Roman', was 'peculiarly favourable to hearing'; but George Basevi (1794–1845) suggested that while a semi-circle was best if speakers addressed members from a tribune, as in Paris, it was not successful if members spoke from their places, as at Westminster. He recommended an oblong room like the Concert Room in Hanover Square, rather than a square one of the same area, a view shared by a fellow-architect, Francis Goodwin (1784–1835) (Pl. 10). Rigby Wason, MP, like the fashionable architect Edward Blore, preferred an octagon, on the principle of some chapter houses (Pl. 12), 'a form which our scientific ancestors uniformly adopted for deliberative assemblies, where it was necessary that each member should deliver his sentiments from his place, sure of being heard equally well by all present.'[23]

Acoustics were also a factor in deciding the best size for the prospective Chamber. Hume's committee stipulated that it must accommodate 600 Members (out of a total of 658), allowing 2 ft to each Member and 3 ft 4 in between the benches. The architects pointed out that such a room would necessarily be very large unless some seats were provided in galleries. The deleterious effect of projecting galleries on the transmission of sound was evident in the existing House; accordingly some witnesses preferred galleries that receded, possibly with shutters to close off back seats when they were not in use, as at the English Opera.[24]

Nor were members alone to be accommodated. The House in session was one of the sights of London. Peers might be found a place on the floor, beyond the bar of the House, but for the public a separate gallery with direct access from the outside was desirable. Soane suggested seats for 400, but most of his colleagues thought about 150 would be quite enough of the public. Ladies in recent years had listened to debates concealed in the roof space, peering down through the central ventilator in the ceiling of the House: the ease with which they heard was used as an argument against such a method of ventilation, as 'the great draft . . . carries off a great portion of the sound.'[25] The ladies, then, must have new accommodation. Reporters, too, were to have a special place—in 1828 Macaulay had declared: 'The gallery in which the reporters sit has become a fourth estate of the realm.' Now they should have a separate gallery, which most proposals placed behind the Speaker's Chair, as the

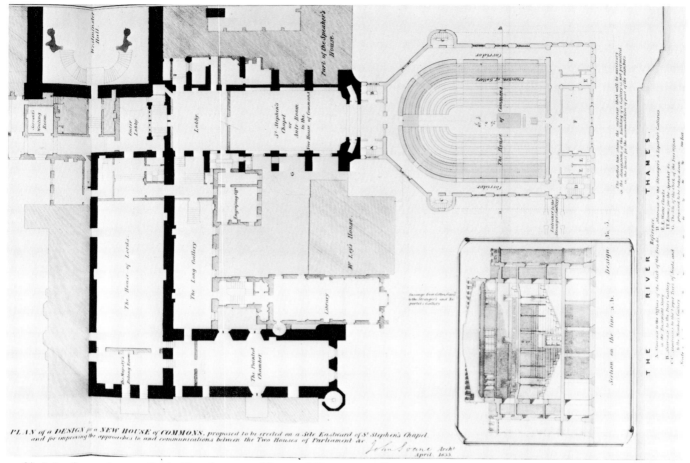

9. Sir John Soane (1753–1837): Plan for a new House of Commons, 1833.

10. Francis Goodwin (1784–1835): Plan for a new House of Commons, 1833, with principal approach from Margaret Street in line with St Stephen's Chapel, restored as a lobby.

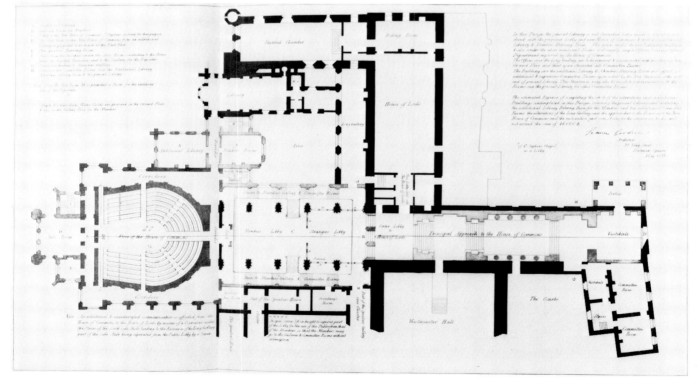

11. Francis Goodwin: Designs for a new House of Commons, 1833.
 (left) St Stephen's Chapel restored as Lobby to new House.
 (right) New Approach Gallery from Margaret Street.

12. Design for a new House of Commons, 1833, recommended by Rigby Wason, MP and drawn by William Bardwell, architect.

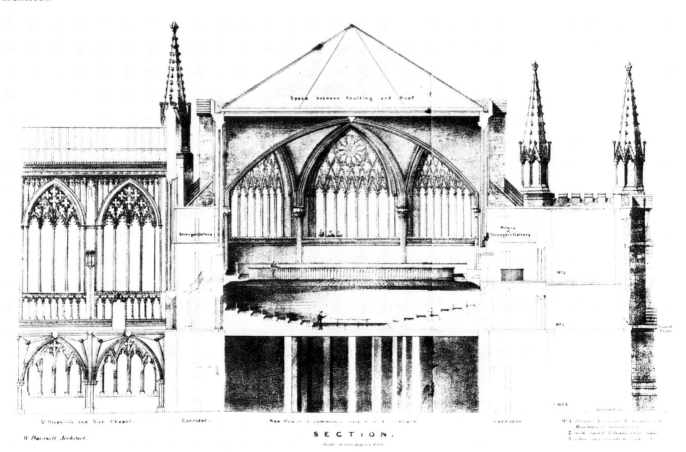

point to which most Members directed their speech. For this was the Reformed Parliament: 'I know how anxious the constituency are to know what their representatives are doing, and as the reporters are the channel of conveying that information, it appears to me desirable that they should have the best means afforded to them', remarked Hopper.[26]

In the 1834 session, other problems preoccupied Parliament. Hume, supported by only a minority, would have had a hard struggle to win anything from the Whig ministry that was faced with a depression in the economy, a falling revenue and mounting expenses. But fate stepped in. A new court of Bankruptcy was required at Westminster, and the Treasury ordered that part of the Exchequer Offices should be temporarily fitted up, including the Tally Office.[27] Though the use of wooden tallies in accounting had been entirely discontinued in 1826, a considerable quantity of the foils remained in the Office. Ordered to burn them in the Exchequer Yard, the clerk of the works, Richard Whibley,[28] objected that such a blaze would alarm the neighbourhood and the police would stop it. He decided instead that the stoves of the House of Lords would be 'a very safe and proper place to do it'. On 16 October 1834, from seven in the morning until about five in the evening, two labourers fed the two furnaces with the tallies. There were two cart-loads in all. The flues had not been cleaned for a year, and the constantly-open doors of the furnaces created a fierce draught. The clerk of the works looked in three times during the day, to make sure that the men were not embezzling the tallies: but he had no fear of their over-loading

13. Contemporary news-sheet, with wood-cut of Old Palace Yard on the night of 16 October 1834.

DREADFUL FIRE!

And total destruction of both Houses of Parliament.

On Thursday evening, between six and seven o'Clock, a fire broke out in the House of Lords. The flames spread very rapidly, and great alarm immediately prevailed. Detachments of police out of the different offices, &c. where they were deposited, and put into all sorts of vehicles—hackney-coaches, cabs, waggons, &c. which were put in requisition for their conveyance to of Commons fell in, three firemen and one of the Life Guards were buried in the ruins; but they were got out alive. Many persons were seriously injured; but we have not heard of Tower, at the south end of the building, totally destroyed. The Painted Chamber, totally destroyed. The north end of the Royal Gallery abutting on the Painted Chamber destroyed from

14. The Houses of Parliament on fire, 16 October 1834, seen from the Chapter House. Contemporary lithograph by M. Gauci.

the furnaces. During the afternoon, however, visitors taken over the House of Lords by the deputy housekeeper, Mrs Wright, noticed smoke and felt the heat of the stone floor, covered with matting. Mrs Wright complained to the workmen, who retorted that they had their orders, and that they would be finished in about an hour. About five o'clock they put out the fires and went off for a pint of beer. Mrs Wright locked up the House about the same time. At six, a door-keeper's wife who was coming in called out 'Oh, good God, the House of Lords is on fire.' Mrs Wright thought that it was the matting, which had smouldered once before, but she found Black Rod's box (which stood over the flues) in flames. Running for help, she met Whibley who 'seemed perfectly petrified' at the news; then into the street 'without bonnet or shawl', closely followed by her maid 'with the lead running on her shoulders'.

The wind blew briskly from the south-west, but became more southerly as the night advanced; the moon was near the full and shone with radiance; but occasionally vast masses of cumulus clouds floated high and bright across the skies, and as the fitful glare of the flames increased, were illumined in a remarkably impressive manner, which gave great interest to the busy scene that was passing below.[29]

For ministers, members and firemen struggled to save the ancient Palace from the flames, while crowds gathered to see London's worst fire since 1666 (Pls XI, 14). The veering of the wind doubtless saved Westminster Hall. But the House of Lords, together with the adjacent offices, the ancient Painted Chamber, St Stephen's

17

Chapel and part of the Cloisters were burned out (Pls 2, 3, 13). It was not until about three in the morning that the fire was 'sufficiently subdued to remove apprehensions of further danger', and it burst out again the next day and 'burnt furiously for two hours'.[30]

That one of the labourers employed on burning the tallies was a jailbird, the other an Irish papist, was sufficient to arouse suspicion in the mind of an excited public. Rumours were strengthened by a strange tale told by one James Cooper, a master ironfounder: he alleged that at Dudley, 127 miles from London, he had heard, soon after ten o'clock in the evening of the fire, that the House of Lords was burned to the ground. His testimony was, upon searching inquiry, found to be 'wholly unsupported'. 'It would be very difficult', reported the Lords of the Privy Council, 'to point out a case of fire which could be more clearly traced than this has been to its cause, without suspicion of evil design.'[31]

15. (left) St Stephen's Chapel (Old House of Commons) after the fire, from the north-west.

III

The Houses of Parliament Competition

1. The Preliminaries

THE fire need not have entailed an entirely new legislative building. The nearly-finished Buckingham Palace was immediately offered for Parliament's permanent home by King William IV.[1] But Parliament after intense scrutiny had decided it should be finished as a royal residence;[2] it would have required vast alteration for legislative use; its position, even less fashionable than Westminster, was not hallowed by the tradition of centuries. That force proved stronger than the commonsense of those bold innovators who recommended the superior advantages of Charing Cross, or of St James's with its cleaner air and propinquity to gentlemen's houses and clubs.[3] The juxtaposition of law courts and Parliament then considered desirable also argued for Westminster, as did the facility which the Thames offered for escaping from inflamed mobs.[4]

With a new session in the offing, the immediate need was to provide temporary accommodation. The simplest course was to patch up the old buildings. The Prime Minister and the First Commissioner of Woods and Works called in the only effective surviving member of the old trinity of architects 'attached to the Board of Works', Robert Smirke. He reported that the walls of the House of Lords were sound enough to permit its fitting-up as a temporary House of Commons. The Lords for their part could be given a temporary home in the medieval Painted Chamber, of which the walls had similarly withstood the fire. So successful were Smirke's arrangements that the Whig *Morning Chronicle*, viewing the Commons at the start of the 1835 session, remarked: 'We do not conceive that there will be any necessity to erect a new building.'[5]

It would indeed have been open to the government, since extensive and quite new parts of the parliamentary complex had been saved from the fire (Pls 2, 16) to carry out a work of repair and restoration. There was, as Smirke pointed out, ample space between the old palace and the river to build new Chambers.[6] The decision would need to be made by Parliament itself,[7] but before the king dismissed Lord Melbourne's administration in November 1834, Hobhouse, the Whig First Commissioner of Woods and Works, had already directed Smirke to prepare plans for rebuilding the Houses of Parliament on a 'moderate and suitable scale of magnitude'. Peel, hastily recalled from a Roman holiday, in a situation 'wholly unforeseen and un-

16. The Parliamentary Buildings after the fire, 1835, showing the gutted House of Lords re-roofed for use by the Commons, with Soane's King's Entrance and Royal Approach on the right. Drawn by Samuel Russell, 'pupil to Thos. L. Walker, Archt.'

expected', confronted with this among many other pressing problems, saw no cause to interfere.[8] Smirke drew up designs[9] (Pl. 18) in the collegiate Gothic of James Wyatt's work at Westminster which, approved by the king and given to Peel, were submitted to committees of both Houses.[10]

Rumours that the new building was to be entrusted to Smirke were hardly reassuring to a public critical of recent official works. Already the main contract for Smirke's temporary Houses had been given to his brother-in-law. Were the old monopolies to endure in the Age of Reform?[11] After all, this was not merely a domestic matter to be settled privately among MPs. Even the purity of Smirke's character could not compensate for the poverty of his taste. The opportunity, it was generally agreed, must not be lost. 'Mother of Parliaments', England must have a parliamentary building to do justice to her place in the world, 'worthy of being the palace of the [Reformed] constitution which its authors boast of having effected so great an improvement on the old English government.'[12] This was an 'opportunity of redeeming the age from the obloquy to which it has become exposed from the gaudy attire and ephemeral character of its metropolitan edifices, and erecting at least one structure worthy of being placed beside the noble monuments of St Petersburg and Paris, in the architectural race of the nineteenth century.'[13]

> No longer shall forsaken Thames
> Lament his Commons' House in flames;
> A pile shall from its ashes rise
> Fit to invade or prop the skies.[14]

21

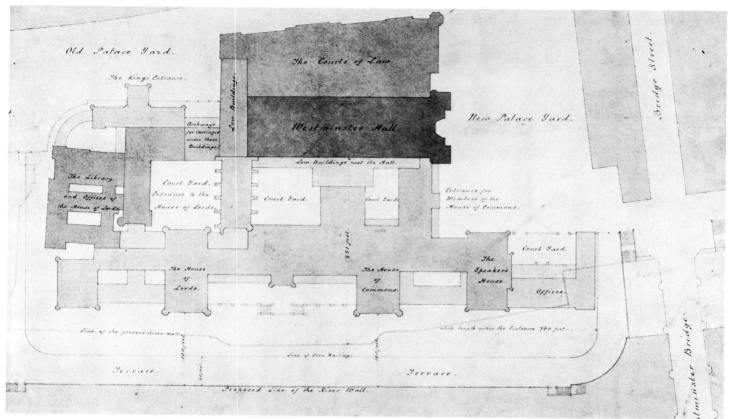

The Courts of Law.

Old Palace Yard.

The Kings Entrance.

Low Buildings.

Westminster Hall.

New Palace Yard.

Bridge Street.

Archways
for Carriages
under these
Buildings.

Low Buildings next the Hall.

The Library
and Offices
of The House of Lords.

Court Yard.
Entrance to the
House of Lords.

Court Yard.

Court Yard.

Entrance for
Members of the
House of Commons.

251 feet.

The House
of
Lords.

The House
of
Commons.

The
Speaker's
House.

Court Yard.

Offices.

Line of the present River Wall.

Line of Iron Railing.

Whole length within the Enclosure 760 feet.

Terrace.

Terrace.

Proposed Line of the River Wall.

Westminster Bridge.

17. Sir Robert Smirke (1781–1867): Plan for new Houses of Parliament prepared by orders of the government, 1835.

18. Sir Robert Smirke (1781–1867): Design for new Houses of Parliament, prepared by orders of the government, 1835.

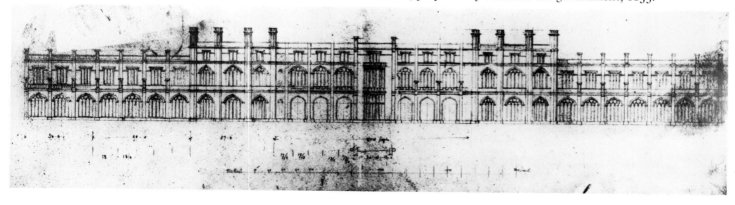

The result would 'in great measure determine the rank which the Arts of this country must take in relation to other civilised states.'[15]

The building . . . which is to be the most important in its destination, and the largest in size, of any which this island can boast, is to supply the means of transacting the legislative business of this vast empire, and will be daily and hourly frequented by the elite of our countrymen, in every class of society . . . will be regarded as a part and parcel of the intellect of the age, as the model par excelence, the example in character, art and decoration, of what is to come after.[16]

On the very morrow of the fire, *The Times* had called for deliberate planning to 'ensure the erection of a noble Parliamentary edifice worthy of a great nation', spelling out the cardinal objects: 'space, form, facility of hearing, facility of ventilation, facility of access, and amplitude of accommodation for *the public* as well as for the members themselves, and for those who have immediate business with them.' A week later the radical *Spectator* took up the theme, pressing for a comprehensive rebuilding on Reform principles: no jobbing, precipitancy or secrecy.[17] 'The Palace of the Legislature, where the laws are propounded and settled, and the interests of a whole people are discussed, should include every accommodation that past experience and forethought of the prospect of future improvements may show to be required. It is a structure to endure for ages; and as such should anticipate, as far as may be foreseen, future wants.' The principal considerations should be ample accommodation, a suitable site, and an appropriate architectural character. 'The cost is not an object: money is not to be wasted, but it is not to be spared.' The two Houses should decide what accommodation they required, the site should be determined by the space needed, and a design should be obtained by 'a competition, open to all, foreign as well as native artists.' Similarly, the Utilitarians' *Westminster Review* declared that 'the entire arrangements . . . for the despatch of business require to be reviewed' in the light of recent experience.[18] 'The calamity may be regarded as peculiarly fortunate', for otherwise only the mere palliatives proposed in 1833 could have been effectuated. What was needed was 'a powerful machine of nicest force . . . of wondrous power but composed of a multitude of parts adjusted to a thousand special functions, yet combining for the production of one grand general effect.' 'The building of a new House of Commons is not . . . a question of four walls placed here or there, built by this architect or that, in this or that style; but the question by what machinery shall the legislative functions be best performed.' 'Let the House then pass resolutions as to the general nature of the objects to be accomplished, and afterwards cause the plan to be the subject of competition, by all the skill the country can supply.' 'The British people intend [to have the] choosing of the architects', the influential conservative *Morning Herald* warned the government. 'By public competition *alone*' could architects' abilities be discovered and used.[19]

The very general criticisms of recent governmental architecture and the common belief in the virtues of a competitive society make this loud and persistent demand unsurprising, but in the Commons' committee appointed in 1835 to consider rebuilding, Joseph Hume was at first almost its only advocate. Yet this was not a demand voiced by only one party. We expect to find the Benthamite *Westminster Review* in sympathy with the *Spectator*; but *The Times* was not a Radical mouthpiece, still less the *Morning Herald*; and a former Tory MP, Sir Edward Cust, was also in the van of the campaign. Long an active critic of the achievements of the Office of Works, Cust published an Open Letter to Peel calling for a new system.[20] His principal

19. (left) Charles Hanbury Tracy (1777–1858), cr. Lord Sudeley 1838. Miniature by C. J. Basebe, 1842.

20. (right) Toddington, Gloucestershire. Designed and built by C. Hanbury Tracy from 1819.

recommendation was the setting up of a commission of gentlemen interested in architecture who should organize and judge a limited competition for designs for new Houses of Parliament, and subsequently superintend their erection. He proposed that these commissioners should be unpaid, and to show his perfect disinterestedness offered his own services as one of them. Cust's arguments, based on the failures of official architecture in the 1820s and incorporating features already approved by the House of Commons, appealed to the spirit of the times: there can be little doubt that they were supported by Radicals like Sir John Cam Hobhouse and Henry Warburton or the connoisseurs Ridley Colborne (Pl. 76) and Charles Hanbury Tracy (Pl. 19), all of whom were members of the 1835 Commons' committee.

In face of the press campaign, Cust's arguments and Hume's persistence, the committee yielded its first inclination to accept Smirke's scheme, and agreed to recommendations clearly based on Cust's but differing in one major respect.[21] Cust had urged that the executive government should make the decisions: that it was unwise and unprofitable to leave them to the 'chance-medley' of debate in the House. This characterized the difference between the Tory Cust and the democratic protagonist Hume. The Radicals intended to keep the operation under parliamentary control, and Peel's minority government was in no position to impose decisions even had it wished to. A year or two before, a committee had pointed out that an irresponsible commission, like that for re-furnishing Windsor Castle, might serve simply as a cloak for irregular acts.[22] The 1835 committees on rebuilding—for Lords and Commons adopted a joint policy—accordingly narrowed the role of the proposed commission. A competition for architectural designs was to be invited, but anyone would

be free to submit an entry so long as it was in either Gothic or Elizabethan style. Certain requirements of accommodation were specified (Appendix II). The author's identity concealed by motto or pseudonym, the entries were to be judged by a commission of amateurs of architecture, who were to select between three and five designs for Parliament's consideration. A premium of £500 was to be awarded to each of the selected designs, and the first prizewinner would receive an additional £1,000 if not appointed to superintend the building. Other conditions specified that all entries were to be executed on the scale of 20 ft to an inch—chosen because it happened to be that of Smirke's plans. 'No coloured Drawing of any Kind' would be accepted, and only three sepia-tinted perspectives taken from points (chosen by Hanbury Tracy) specified on a lithographic plan (Pl. 26) supplied to competitors on payment of £1. They were also to be supplied with the resolutions of the Rebuilding Committee and the evidence presented to it.[23]

These conditions were intended to meet criticism of past practice, and C. R. Cockerell thought the competition 'a model in most respects'. There was no general confidence in the abilities of the senior architects of the day, and limited competition would have smacked too much of jobbery to be acceptable. The real prize, the building of new Houses of Parliament, was one to tempt even the most eminent architect, and the premiums of £500 (described by 'An Old Artist' as 'the most munificent I ever heard of') represented a fair recompense for three months' work for all save the leaders of the profession.[24]

The government had then to find members for the Royal Commission to judge the designs. Only amateurs were considered: professional men were suspected of

professional jealousies—and few were then authorities on medieval architecture. In this period, 'when most professional architects were indifferently "ambidextrous"... two or three convinced amateurs were the most authentic exponents of the period's aspirations.'[25] Charles Hanbury Tracy (1777–1858) was one; 'than whom', wrote John Britton, 'I know not a better judge' of Gothic architecture. His great house at Toddington (Pl. 20), begun in 1819, was designed with no more professional assistance than that of an architectural draughtsman.[26] Being an MP, Hanbury Tracy acted as chairman of the commission. The Hon. Thomas Liddell (1800–56), Lord Ravensworth's son, another Gothic enthusiast and amateur architect (cp. Pl. 21) was another of the government's choices.[27] The other two active commissioners were Sir Edward Cust, who could hardly have been ignored after his campaign, and George Vivian (1800–73) (Pl. 76) of Claverton Manor, Bath, author of pamphlets on the architectural improvements of London and 'The Prospects of Art in the future Parliament House', who was something of an authority on the Picturesque.[28]

No doubt this was as strong a team of amateurs as could have been assembled. There was some confusion over one man of taste, Samuel Rogers, who was appointed but declined to act. Two other eminent amateurs refused the appointment: Lord Aberdeen, celebrated as a connoisseur of Grecian antiquities, and Lord De Grey, the first president of the Institute of British Architects, who was engaged in rebuilding Wrest Park in a forward-looking revival of eighteenth-century French style.[29] John Britton, who hinted at his own qualifications, lacked the social cachet for the appointment. And there lay a problem. The commissioners were of an old-fashioned cast, characteristic of the 'noble owner' of past centuries; they were to clash with the representatives of the new class of 'clients', Joseph Hume at their head, and with those of the new type of architects keen to establish their professional status, who resented the intrusion of 'superficial amateurs' and claimed that only a professional

21. (left) Beckett House, Shrivenham, Berkshire. Designed by Hon. Thomas Liddell for Lord Barrington, 1834.

22. (right) Lord Duncannon (1781–1847), later 4th Earl of Bessborough, First Commissioner of Woods and Works, 1831–4 and 1835–41, by Landseer.

could properly judge architectural designs.[30] There was also another ground on which competitors might take exception to this team. Cust had notoriously made use of Charles Barry's assistance in attacking Wilkins' National Gallery two or three years before, had employed him in enlarging his house in Spring Gardens, and had too vigorously recommended him for such undertakings as the new Westminster Hospital and the Fitzwilliam Museum.[31] Some of the commissioners were supposed to be over-friendly with J. C. Buckler, Hanbury Tracy's assistant at Toddington. Vivian had allegedly 'excited more than suspicion of his candour' by misquoting Thomas Hope's *History of Architecture* in a *Quarterly Review* notice, in which he had also advocated the use of the Roman style for public buildings.[32] The minister responsible for nominating the commissioners, Lord Duncannon (Pl. 22), contended that any favouritism among them would cancel out, and that anyway the final choice of designs lay with Parliament.[33] Cust himself took care to have no dealings with Barry during the period of the competition. Hanbury Tracy declared that as a member of the Commons' committee he had sought to guard against favouritism, and that as a commissioner his few guesses at the authorship of designs had proved incorrect.[34] But to avoid such charges in subsequent official competitions, judges were not named until the entries had been received, a procedure recommended by the *Spectator* in March 1835. That could obviate the likelihood of competitors seeking to please a given individual, but could not be the complete answer in a society in which leading amateurs were closely associated with particular professionals. The exclusion of favouritism can really only depend on the integrity of the judges.

A more realistic criticism levelled at the arrangements was that they afforded inadequate time for preparing an entry, a common fault of competitions of that day. Here, all competitors should have been at an equal disadvantage; but official delay in publishing the requisite details, including the map of the site, bred rumours that favoured competitors were being fed with advance information.[35] The short time allowed was said to be deterring young artists. Ministers did not show much understanding of architects' problems: they claimed that four clear months was ample; and in a work of such importance, 'young artists were not the most desirable persons . . . It would be much better to make the selection from the plans of able and experienced artists', who would, it was implied, need less time for preparation.[36] But clearly for many it was a rushed job. The strain was said to have killed Francis Goodwin, whose proposals for rebuilding the Commons in 1833 had been much admired (Pls 10, 11); he told his doctor that 'so intense had been his studies . . . that . . . he was unable to obtain any rest at nights—so completely engrossed were his thoughts upon the plans he was engaged in drawing out.'[37] James Savage, having urged an extension of time, submitted an unfinished entry; and Barry's assistants were at work on his designs until the last possible moment. But doubtless there would have been as much last-minute haste had another month or even three been allowed. Cockerell's principal criticism was not of the shortness of time, but of the decision to require no estimates although cost is 'the paramount consideration in architecture'.[38]

2. The Competition

Competition for architectural designs was no new device. In the early fifteenth century 'competitions for public works were a regular feature of Florentine life.' In England in 1835 an observer commented on the prevalence of the practice, especially for public buildings. Professor Collins has suggested that the open competition derives 'from the type of judgement exemplified by the annual Salons of academies of painting'.[39] But in England these exhibitions were scarcely competitive in form. Here it was the client—and above all the multiform client, the committee—not the artist, who fostered architectural competitions, whether with the genuine intent to get the best value for money, or in order to conceal jobbery. It was, as Loudon recognized, a consequence of the market economy. By the early nineteenth century such competitions were common, many architectural commissions coming from middle-class clients often acting not individually but in committees on behalf of bodies of subscribers. Such men neither possessed nor had the time to acquire an amateur's skill in architecture: they 'know not nor care not whether a column is on its capital or its base.' But they were not fools: they wanted buildings that would 'work' for them. Architects were having to contend with not merely the shifts of fashion but also the specific requirements of experienced clients demanding new sorts of buildings: public buildings of various sorts for growing towns, banks or commercial offices, warehouses, chapels. And clients expected value for money: often interpreted as showy designs at low prices. Competition was their way of life, and they looked to it to produce the best results in architecture too.[40]

This attitude of mind had penetrated the House of Commons by 1815. A committee considering a projected new General Post Office called for competition for designs for all major public building, and the House itself so resolved in 1819. But after an unsuccessful trial, the government fell back on its old method of nomination.[41] The disasters of public building in the 1820s, however, made it unlikely that this 'monopoly' system could persist in the Reform era. Competitions in the early 1830s that attracted notice included Fishmongers' Hall and King Edward VI Grammar School at Birmingham.

Although it was so common a practice, not all architects favoured the competition

for designs. Busy practitioners might well grudge time and effort spent on so uncertain an endeavour. Many, with good reason, suspected the way competitions were
conducted. Yet there were always plenty to come forward. It has been suggested
that architects' attitudes to competition can be identified with two prevalent philo-
sophies of architecture, viewing it as an art or as a profession.[42] But the hostility of
'professionals' was directed principally against abuses of the system. Strictly, it is
true, the professional ideal might seem to offer little scope for competition, since
it adumbrated providing on a basis of trustworthiness expert services sought by a
client in return for a standard fee. Newly-emerging professions were establishing
governing bodies with a greater or lesser measure of control to regulate entry, stipulate fees and maintain high standards of business decorum. On the other hand, romantic concepts of artistic autonomy married well with laissez-faire attitudes opposing
control by any professional body. The architectural writer W. H. Leeds, pointing out
that in no other of the liberal arts was it a stigma for a man to be self-taught, argued
that the self-taught architect might possess more talent than plodding professionals,
pilferers from others' unoriginal designs. Loudon declared: 'Let knowledge be
free; and let all who have acquired skill and knowledge enough to practise professions be free to exercise them, whether they have acquired their knowledge in the
regular manner or not', save only where human life was concerned. Genius would
carry a man further in his chosen profession than accidental circumstances of training
or education. For men with this philosophy competition offered a platform from which
they might legislate for the world. This aspiration 'to bend the public to their fancy'
was attacked by Cust in his pamphlet.[43] Cust devolved judgment upon the amateur,
a policy obnoxious to artist and professional alike. Both groups agreed on the necessity for the practitioner's eye in judging. For professionals, no more than artists,
could eschew the competition for designs. Entrepreneurial and professional ideals
clashed, but faced with the widespread belief in the inherent virtues of competition
as universally beneficial, confronted with the businessman's insistence on getting
what he wanted at the lowest price, 'professional' architects welcomed architectural
competitions as affording, in the ill-regulated profession of that day, the best means
for exhibiting their functional efficiency, thereby establishing merit as the prime
factor in the selective process. But that merit, they argued, could be judged effectively
only by other professionals.

Thus for both characters of architect, competition was an acceptable means.[44]
But in practice it posed a dilemma, for it was commonly judged by the client, the
despised layman, 'ignorant and conceited'. This encouraged fraud and made
competition too speculative. Committees innocent of architectural knowledge chose,
all too often, not designs that recommended themselves to a trained eye, but those
tricked out in pretty perspective drawings heightened by attractive colouring, or those
of some backstairs intriguer favoured by a powerful committee-member. Frequently
competition was nothing more than a cloak for jobbery. An architect, even if he won a
competition, might find the building entrusted to another, for it was seldom clear
whether the purpose was 'to choose an ideal design, or to choose an ideal designer.'[45]
Nevertheless, market pressures were irresistible. There were too many would-be
architects; competition was one way in which a young architect could make his
name; and prestigious buildings were a lure to trap even leading practitioners.

There was seldom, then, any shortage of entrants for competition on the client's
terms. His sharp nose discerning in the winter air of 1834–5 a whiff of the greatest of
conceivable competitions, that for new Houses of Parliament, the Solon of the
profession pushed his own idea for regulating it. In his Royal Academy lectures

(widely reported in the press), Sir John Soane urged that 'the best and most certain means to procure designs for all great public works is by a well-regulated competition.' He recalled his recommendation of 1818 to the newly-appointed Church Building Commissioners. He advocated competition, open or limited, for designs drawn to a common scale, 'finished in India ink without any colour whatever'; the entries to be exhibited and then referred to a 'committee of artists to determine on the relative merits' by giving reasoned written opinions. The designs would then be exhibited again. Such a scheme, carried into effect by commissioners appointed by Parliament after approval of the designs by the Treasury, offered the surest hope of obtaining the 'best designs and most satisfactory execution' for public buildings. This was similar to contemporary French practice recommended by other practitioners.[46] But professional assessment, a solution for both 'artists' and 'professional architects' to the dilemma of competition, was not yet one acceptable to the still socially-exclusive Reformed Parliament. Nor was the professional pressure yet sufficiently strong: the lure was too great, and during 1835 only rumbles of dissatisfaction were expressed in the professional press. It was not until this competition had been judged that criticism reached a crescendo.

What did, however, start a paper war that raged before the adjudication as well as after was Parliament's stipulation that the designs were to be in the Gothic or Elizabethan styles. The arguments in favour of this requirement may be reduced to three, the natural, the national, and the associative, but we may consider the two designated styles separately, as each had its advocates. The stipulating of Gothic indeed aroused little surprise, though much opposition. Contemporary aesthetic theory regarded the associative qualities of architecture as of major and perhaps of paramount importance.[47] Westminster was where Britain's constitution had been moulded of old, and where the antique majesty of the law held visible sway. The style was 'adapted to the Gothic origin and time-worn buttresses of our constitution', dating from a 'time when classic architecture was unknown in this country'. It was therefore appropriate to build the new palace of the legislature in Gothic, the forms of which, associated with the tales that charmed childhood, were a link in the great chain of associations that bound Englishmen to their country.[48] The belief that new building at Westminster must be assimilated to the hallowed Abbey and Hall had been expressed forcibly in 1824, as has been recounted above. Now the influential *Quarterly Review*, hailing assimilation as 'one of the principal elements of beauty', declared that dissimilarity between objects brought into contact, 'and the discordant ideas they suggest, are . . . a source of positive pain to the beholder.'[49]

Moreover, Gothic, commonly thought to be a British invention, struck a note of national assertiveness pleasing to the age. 'Derived from our ancestors', Gothic was 'eminently English . . . by its early adoption and very general use for ages, and by its having been brought to the greatest perfection in this country.' Even such an architectural scholar as E. J. Willson, who derided the English claim to have originated Gothic, referred to it as 'our old English architecture.'[50] The sombre sublimity of Gothic against a stormy sky was better suited to the 'German character' of the British nation than was the graceful elegance of Grecian.[51]

Gothic, furthermore, was a 'natural' style. Not only was it adapted to the climate of Northern Europe, its very forms were derived from nature. Even if the theory deriving the Gothic vault from the meeting branches of trees framing a forest walk were discounted, it was 'in the botanical works of nature only' that the germ of the 'endless variety of beauty' in the style's ornaments was to be found.[52]

It was not difficult, then, to justify the choice of Gothic. But what of 'Elizabethan'?

Though popularized in the early nineteenth century by landscapists and novelists, Elizabethan architecture had received little close study, and it was only about 1830 that serious works on the subject began to appear.[53] Thus it was a new enthusiasm at the moment of the great competition. Loudon regretted the predilection for the style that 'unfortunately' prevailed 'among many liberal patrons'; and Pugin remarked on 'the fashionable rage for this architecture (if so it may be called)'.[54] But the *Quarterly Review* in 1831 denied that it was the 'bastard offspring of an unnatural connexion': it was rather a *tertium quid* between Tudor Gothic and Italian, with[55]

a general character much more exclusively *English* than either the correct Palladian which succeeded [it], or the pure Gothic of the preceding age, which at the same period was common to France and Germany as well as England . . . There is something in the rich irregularity of the Elizabethan architecture, its imposing dignity, gorgeous magnificence, and quaint and occasionally fantastic decoration, reminding us of the glorious visions that flitted across the imagination of the immortal bard of the same age.

The association with Shakespeare, Bacon, and other national heroes was sufficient to justify its possible use at Westminster. But scholarly knowledge was restricted to a narrow circle, and to most Elizabethan was scarcely distinguishable from Henrician. Indeed, the *Spectator* suggested that the intention in specifying 'Gothic or Elizabethan' had been to direct competitors to the Tudor rather than the earlier Gothic styles.[56]

It has been suggested that this stylistic choice represented a victory for the middle classes, the aesthetic equivalent, as it were, of the 1832 Reform Act.[57] But the patrons of Gothic architecture in the early nineteenth century had been largely aristocrats or gentry. It is true that popular novelists such as Scott fostered a medieval vogue at lower levels of society too, but there is little evidence that Gothic was 'peculiarly attractive' to the middle classes—that archetypal middle-class figure Joseph Hume certainly disliked it. Anyway, the choice did not lie with them.

But Goths and 'Olden Time' folk were forced to defend their position. Many of their arguments could be applied as effectively and ingeniously to classical architecture. Grecian was 'more expressive, from its associations, of the character of the institutions of a free people' than a style derived from feudal times. A further appeal to a free people lay in its being 'infinitely more economical', its beauty depending on 'bold and pleasing outline, and just proportions' rather than on a 'multitude of petty details', quickly begrimed by London's soot.[58] Truth as well as cost told against Gothic in the argument of W. R. Hamilton, the most vociferous and able critic of the committee's choice: the adoption of by-gone styles, 'confounding times and usages', 'would convert our public buildings into architectural romances'. His theory of cyclical progress in British architecture was rooted in a concept of Graeco-Roman civilization contrasted with 'Gothic barbarism', science with ignorance, 'true principles of knowledge' with superstition. Based on science, architecture culminated in art, and the highest art was that of ancient Athens.[59] The prescribing of 'Elizabethan' at Westminster showed that it was not essential for the new work to harmonize with the old, he argued. When the old palace was erected, the style of the time had been employed. The excessively ornamented Gothic, offspring of the 'overgrown wealth of the Romish hierarchy', was ultimately non-christian in origin. In simple grandeur and massive proportions it was inferior to Norman, 'which derived these qualities from the Greeks' (also non-christian!). Though gorgeous, Gothic was based on 'no true principles' and therefore had 'no real hold upon the enlightened intellect'; with moral, political and scientific progress, its allure was destroyed. As for

31

the claim that it related to the period of the establishment of the British constitution, that epoch could be placed anywhere between the Witanagemot and the Reform Act.

At a period of time, when the greatest exertions are making to get rid of all preconceived notions handed down to us from a Gothic ancestry, when we are told that everything Britons have held sacred for centuries, in law, morals, religion and philosophy, are to give way to the march of intellect, and are to be tested by the public opinion of the day, we are to be consoled by the reflection that in one department of reason at least we may go back to, and glory in an humble copy of the gloomy mansions of our forefathers.

Yet, crowning irony, Gothic was no more English than it was French or German.[60]

In the *Quarterly Review* George Vivian had already advocated a quite different model for modern purposes: Roman architecture.[61] Good taste in England was stultified by a 'decided inclination to adopt a disordered in preference to a beautiful and an orderly system of architecture.' 'We see no other salvation', he asserted, 'than in acknowledging the whole range of classic architecture, whether in Greece, in ancient or in modern Italy, to be the legitimate source of knowledge . . . Thus may a truly national style be created, as uniform in principle, as capable of endless variety in practice.' But 'the whole range of classic architecture' even was no longer sufficient to satisfy the eclecticism of clients and critics primarily concerned at heart with the visual effects of the Picturesque. The collapse of the rule of taste was exhibited in the competition entries.

3. The Field

The site allotted for the building of new Houses of Parliament (Pl. 26) was of awkward shape—a rectangle nearly 800 × 350 ft out of which was excised a large north-west quadrant composed of New Palace Yard and Westminster Hall, reducing the depth of the site at its northern end to about 180 ft. At the southern end a further rectangle approximately 200 × 350 ft could be taken in if competitors so chose. To the east flowed the unembanked Thames, to the north a busy thoroughfare leading to Westminster Bridge formed a natural boundary. Although the Westminster Improvement Commissioners had lately cleared some buildings in Margaret Street, St Margaret's Church and King Henry VII's Chapel barred any extension to the west, and indeed stood uncomfortably close, suggesting rather the desirability of contracting the parliamentary site.

On this site the competitors had to provide the two Chambers and a great deal of ancillary accommodation. Each House has been called 'the best club in Europe', and it was precisely the accommodation of the great clubs then rising in and about Pall Mall that Members looked to have for themselves: refreshment rooms for themselves and their guests, smoking rooms, waiting rooms and the rest. The old standards were no longer acceptable; it was only in 1818 that a room had been set aside for the Commons' library, but now three rooms of 60 × 28 ft were specified, as well as apartments for the librarian. All this was over and above the needs of the basic services: the departments dealing with elections, bills, fees and the like, storage for the journals and papers of the Houses, rooms for the officers and residences for those who must always be on call. That of the Speaker of the House of Commons must befit the first commoner in the land. And public interest in parliamentary proceedings was an acknowledged fact: so galleries had to be provided in the Chambers, lobbies where constituents might speak to their Members. The increasing use of committees made indispensable an ample supply of rooms in various sizes, and for the considerable numbers attending in connexion with those committees—witnesses, lawyers, interested spectators—facilities had to be furnished. Frequent divisions of the Commons, inescapable in a lively two-party system, called for additional lobbies adjoining the Chamber.

In a purpose-built legislative seat there was a real opportunity of providing adequately and rationally for these various needs. So, as the Utilitarians argued, Parliament must decide on its functional needs: 'ample and explicit directions . . . even to the most minute details, are essential for the guidance of the architect.'[62] The select committees of the two Houses did their best to draw up such guidance for the competitors, listing the number and size of the rooms required for particular purposes, and indicating general desiderata, such as quietness for libraries and committee rooms (and these last to be conveniently accessible for witnesses and public), and their being so disposed that the library might be extended if necessary. Refreshment facilities must be close to the Chambers, which themselves must be effectively ventilated.[63]

So the task of a competitor in 1835 was much more complex than the rather academic exercises in parliamentary planning of Kent, Adam and Soane in the previous century, being governed by detailed specifications from the clients as well as by the exigencies of the site. Not all the leading men were willing to put so much effort into so uncertain an operation, but many were. Although the great majority of their designs are now lost to view, most were exhibited in 1836 and the catalogue entries, penned by the competitors themselves, provide an insight into their intentions.[64] The exhibition produced, too, many comments in the contemporary press. Thus it is possible to make some analysis of the entries.[65]

One major distinction that may be drawn is between those who treated their composition as a unity and those who produced an agglomeration of more or less separate elements. Excellent examples of each type are furnished, curiously enough, by the two designs in which Pugin is known to have had a hand, Barry's unitary composition, and the agglutinative concept submitted by Gillespie Graham (Pl. 31). The experienced James Savage was concerned to combine the features of his design 'so as to appear one building, with a definite purpose, and not an aggregate of different buildings grouped together by accident'.[66] J. Dowson, who aimed at a 'compact and convenient plan', 'caused his structure to rise upon the view to its very centre, from whatever point of view it may be seen' in order to achieve a sublime effect. Unity of composition was the declared aim of H. E. Kendall (1805–85), and appears to have been that of E. C. Hakewill (1812–72), while Thomas Hopper (1776–1856) claimed to have treated 'the entire mass of buildings . . . as a single edifice', though his success is open to question (Pl. 23). There were many more competitors, however, who like T. L. Donaldson (1795–1885) preferred to compose in distinct units and varied styles in order to 'avoid a series of the same effects', or as L. N. Cottingham (1787–1847) put it, 'the all-round-alike monotony of ditto repeated' (Pl. 24). Foster and Okely of Bristol adopted the functionalist principle of making 'the external features of a building indicative of its uses, and internal arrangements', seeking a 'rich and cloistered effect' in the entrance front, but a 'castellated effect' in the river front to give dignity and strength to the two Houses, 'appropriate characteristics of these two bulwarks of our liberties'. Others achieved heterogeneity by economically preserving the unburnt work of Soane in their reconstructions, and Lewis Wyatt stretched the principle to its limit, recommending the employment of four architects simultaneously.

OLD PALACE YARD.

23. Thomas Hopper (1776–1856): Competition design for New Houses of Parliament, 1835, with St Stephen's restored and duplicated. Hopper published his designs.

24. Lewis Nockalls Cottingham (1787–1847): Competition design for New Houses of Parliament. Perspective of River Front.

This general preference for variety may be accounted for partly on aesthetic grounds, but probably arose chiefly from practical problems. The awkward shape of the site, and the brooding presence of Westminster Hall with its enormous roof, a building too sacred to destroy, but difficult to make use of. The 'vomitory of the Law Courts' (Poynter) had no other obvious function: its position was far from convenient for an entrance to the new Houses, whether as royal entrance, or for members, or for the public, as competitors variously suggested. The building of Soane's Law Courts alongside and the abandoning of the Coronation Banquet robbed the Hall of its traditional functions. It became a white elephant—and such it has remained. The difficulties of integrating it functionally with new Houses and of constructing a uniform and coherent building while it stood encouraged many competitors to follow principles of diversity and irregularity. 'No grand pervading idea' could be adopted (Fowler).

A similar problem that encouraged loose planning and stylistic diversification was the survival of the walls of St Stephen's Chapel and adjoining medieval buildings (Pls 3, 15). So highly renowned now were the beauties of the 'glorious edifice of the third Edward' (Lee), that a majority of competitors wished to restore it. Nevertheless, as the *Gentleman's Magazine* pointed out, 'restoration as a prominent and valuable feature of the general design has been almost entirely overlooked'. Not only was there the question of what to do with a restored chapel; even more difficult was the require- ment of a House of Commons larger and necessarily—for practical and symbolic reasons alike—more dominant than the old. Wilkins made his new buildings of 'moderate elevation' as 'an harmonious appendage', rather than 'as attempting to rival or eclipse' the old (Pl. 25), but few dared be so moderate. Other solutions ran into practical objections: the Lords disliked their cramped temporary quarters in the Painted Chamber where Donaldson wished permanently to immure them for the sake of a balanced composition, with the Commons in St Stephen's Chapel on the opposite side of a central court. There was little point in restoring the chapel's magnificence if it were to be concealed by other buildings, but to insulate it could work, as in Buckler's design, to the detriment of the planning.

Uncertainty how to treat a river front of anything up to a thousand feet in length was a third factor with a similar effect. English architects had no experience of giving a monumental character to façades of more than 250 or 300 ft. When Nash had tried to design a palace—and he was one of the architects most experienced in large-scale

25. William Wilkins (1778–1839): Competition design for New Houses of Parliament, 1835. Elevation of River Front.

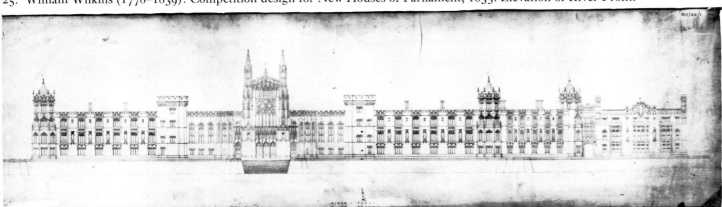

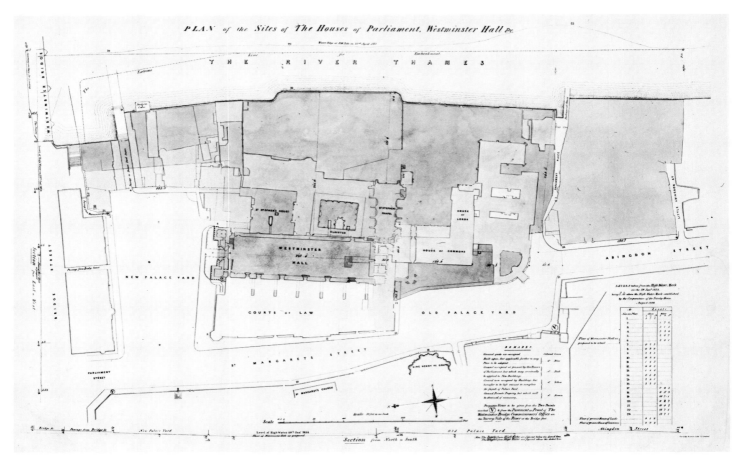

26. The lithographed plan sold to entrants in the New Houses of Parliament Competition, 1835. Perspectives were allowed only from the two viewpoints marked Ⓥ and from the Surrey end of Westminster Bridge. The ground on the right between Abingdon Street and the river was available if architects wished to use it.

building—he was heavily criticised for the pettiness of his conception. At Westminster, some competitors made economy their excuse for not using the whole available extent of river front, thereby reducing the façade to more manageable proportions. Barry himself in his competition design did not use the extra hundred or so feet to the south. Another device was to use the long, narrow north-eastern rectangle between Hall and river for a distinct Speaker's House. 'The projection of the Speaker's residence', wrote Kendall, 'conceals the heterogeneous and discordant buildings in the rear'. Cottingham (Pl. 24) employed the same arrangement. Others cloaked their inability to handle a long front by vigorously attacking the 'tedious monotony' of 'extensive buildings characterized by the same external features' (Brees and Griffiths), while the feeble efforts of such as David Mocatta (1806–82) afforded justification for their charge (Pl. 27). Yet other solutions were to employ a receding centre, as Cockerell did in a design avowedly based on Greenwich (Pl. 29), or to emphasize the centre. Thus Harrison introduced a central tower with supporting lateral towers as did Alderson—adding spires—and J. T. Knowles (Pl. 28). Oriels offered a cheaper alternative for those like G. R. French, conscious of cost, as well as a more practical one: what might towers be used for?

With the material available it is difficult to make more than the most generalized comments on the planning exhibited in the entries. The two Chambers were frequently treated as distinctive elements composing picturesquely with existing features. The libraries' requirements of quiet and light led many competitors to place them in the river front, though some employed blind walls and top-lighting.[67]

36

27. David Mocatta (1806–82): Competition design for New Houses of Parliament, 1835. Elevation to Old Palace Yard.

28. J. T. Knowles, Sr. (1806–84): Competition design for New Houses of Parliament, 1835. Perspective of River Front.

29. C. R. Cockerell (1788–1863): Competition design for New Houses of Parliament, 1835. Perspective of River Front. This was one of the few designs not in Gothic style. 'Elizabethan architecture cannot be defined, the Examples all differing', claimed Cockerell, who based his design on Greenwich.

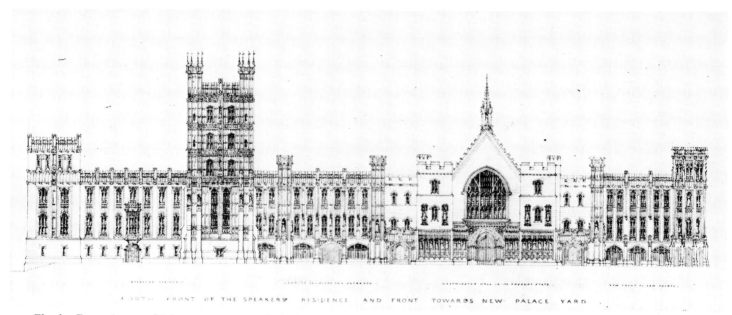

30. Charles Barry (1795–1860): copy, watermarked 1843, of competition design for New Houses of Parliament 1835. Elevation of North Front looking on New Palace Yard.

31. J. Gillespie Graham (1777–1855): Competition design for New Houses of Parliament, 1835, drawn by A. W. Pugin. River Front perspective.

The airiness of the river front also pointed it out for committee rooms, though the bustle of witnesses, counsel and similar concomitants of committees persuaded some entrants to place these rooms close to points of public access. But if the commotion of committees made them unwelcome neighbours for libraries, traffic noises might make committee rooms themselves almost unusable. One common solution to this dilemma was to establish different systems of circulation for different classes of person, as Barry did (Pl. 33).

The difficulty of providing enough entrances, or sufficiently noble entrances was resolved in a number of designs by embanking the river to provide a wide road forming the principal access to the palace (Pl. 28).[68] One influential plan upon which several entries appear to have been based was that which Francis Goodwin had prepared for Hume's select committee of 1833 (Pls 10, 11). In this, St Stephen's

32. Thomas Rickman (1776–1841): Competition design for New Houses of Parliament, 1835. Perspective of Old Palace Yard front.

Chapel formed the culmination of a line of approach from an entrance in Margaret Street, past the south end of Westminster Hall, to a new House of Commons constructed immediately to the east of the Chapel. This sort of plan was all very well for providing a new Commons' Chamber within the old palace. But it was not satisfactory, as Goodwin himself obviously realized, for an entire rebuilding of the Houses of Parliament. Unless an irregular plan such as Gillespie Graham's (Pl. 31)[69] were adopted, a Commons' Chamber east of St Stephen's called for a Lords' Chamber in a corresponding position, so complicating the provision of convenient communication between the two. The simplest basic plan was to dispose the two Chambers on a common axis. Barry and Railton both hit on an adaptation of Goodwin's plan which preserved the attractive notion of a grand line of approach through St Stephen's Chapel by continuing that as a minor axis communicating with the river front and intersected east of St Stephen's by a major axis along which lay the two Houses (Pls 33, 38). The intersection of the two axes provided an obvious opportunity for some display, and a central hall (frequently octagonal), surmounted by a tower or lantern, was often a feature of the axially-planned designs: perhaps the outstanding example was Bunning's 200 ft lantern in the 'florid architecture' of Henry VII's Chapel.

Turning to considerations of style, we find few entrants who availed themselves of the Elizabethan option. Of these, however, the designs of David Rhind, a young Scot, with the motto 'Pro patria semper', were hailed by the *Gentleman's Magazine* as the star of the exhibition: the composition 'decidedly magnificent, the style pure, the ornaments well selected and admirably arranged, and the different constituent features finely proportioned and harmonized'. Turrets and domes resembled those of Audley End, but were 'superior in detail'; while the 'beautiful decorations of the parapets' were largely derived from Hatfield. Cockerell (Pl. 29) imposed his own interpretation on the terms: rejecting English work of Elizabeth's time as 'puerile imitations', he sought to unite the 'legitimate proportions' of the great Italian architects with 'the English mode of the sixteenth century—the commodious and luminous bay-window, elongated turret, and vertical tendency of lines'. The result gave the judges to pause, but they rejected no entries purely on stylistic grounds.[70]

Cockerell's view of British work was a common enough one, however. The exhibition, reported the *Gentleman's Magazine*, afforded 'a convincing proof that the architecture of their own country has formed no part of the study of our present race of architects.'[71] Gothic features were often borrowed from foreign models. Thus Morgan, once Nash's assistant, had copied gables and pinnacles from old German domestic architecture and adorned his Houses with the spire of an *hôtel de ville* and a lantern tower which failed to harmonize with the flat, square character of his design. Donaldson, again, incorporated a 260 ft tower and spire avowedly based on Brussels and Bruges.

It was Pugin's wish to substitute a tour of old English architecture for architectural students' visits to classical sites, but as yet his father's publications and those of Britton commonly served them in lieu of personal knowledge. Most of this material was ecclesiastical, and this was reflected in the entries. Competitors expressed some awareness of the danger of giving their designs too ecclesiastical a character,[72] but there were few surviving secular buildings earlier than the fifteenth century (other than castles) that might serve as models. This lack was hailed as an advantage by J. C. Loudon: 'Where will you find ancient examples for the customs, comforts and improvements of modern times?' Ancient buildings should be used as words to compose new sentences.[73] One of the few who really tried to do this was E. B. Lamb. But it is not surprising that most competitors favoured Perpendicular and Tudor. Hampton Court, East Barsham and Wingfield Manors, Hengrave Hall, Oxburgh, and Thornbury were generally requisitioned. There was the further advantage that those styles responded to nationalistic prejudice: even if 'gothic' were not an English invention, these forms were. Cottingham described Perpendicular as 'the invention of a noble-minded race of men, who dared to look at hill and dale—at rise and fall—advance and recess; and by imitating nature, introduced into their designs beauty and grandeur, by powerful contrast, without encroaching on utility and convenience'.

Nevertheless, it was almost universally agreed that the competition designs in general had too ecclesiastical—or at best, too monastic—an air.[74] Lack of personal knowledge and lack of secular models failed to stimulate invention, but set men ransacking the available publications: hence many designs like 'the elongated side of a cathedral, with transept-ends interspersed to vary the line.'[75] Hopper's, indeed, was a congregation of English cathedrals (Pl. 23), while that of Pennethorne (Nash's professional heir) was not only cathedral-like, but foreign to boot.[76]

Naturally the competition entries included the inane and the ludicrous. Wilkins complained that 'carpenters, bricklayers, house-agents, artisans, and even amateurs, submit their plans with the same confidence as the proved and experienced architect'. The clouds of professional mystique were not yet swirling sufficiently thickly to dissuade the untrained. William Buckland, 'Amateur', admitted that he had 'never received any instruction in drawing or design'. The *Morning Chronicle* remarked that one exhibitor who had submitted a Corinthian composition had been found to be insane, and wondered whether a similar excuse could be made for poor Buckland.[77]

Peter Thompson, carpenter and builder of Osnaburgh Place, who did not send his plans to the exhibition but published them instead, was more conscious of his lowly status as 'a *mere* carpenter'. John Tertius Fairbank perhaps deserved a prize for ingenuity: he saw the key problem of the plan as the need for ready access to 'multifarious important offices', and thought a great corridor 800 ft long the solution—but 'to abridge this distance, and to approach the parts by the most compact form, it is proposed to convert the line into a circle', with an inner court of 110-ft diameter. As the problem of the elevation was for dignity 'to announce externally the seat of government', he proposed to erect on the walls of his corridor 'a colossal circular tower, 220 ft in diameter; upon the external abutment-walls . . . battlements, statues, flying buttresses, pinnacles, and pierced windows, raise up in regular gradation a vast and ornamental object'.

4. The Winners

After protests that 1 November was impossibly soon, the closing date for entries was fixed as 1 December 1835. Then the commissioners for the selection of designs set to their task in the abandoned rooms of Speaker's House. On 15 January, with only five days left before they were to announce their decision, they too asked for an extension of time until the end of the month: ninety-seven entries, involving twelve or fourteen hundred drawings, had to be examined.[78] From these, the commissioners selected only four; they were apparently unable to agree where to bestow the fifth premium.

The first place went to Charles Barry (Pls 30, 33):

Although a difference of opinion may exist between us [reported the commissioners] respecting the Ground Plans separately considered, we are all unanimous in our opinion, that the one delivered to us, marked 64, with the emblem of the Portcullis, bears throughout such evident marks of genius and superiority of talent, as fully to entitle it to the preference we have given it . . . and we have no hesitation in giving it as our opinion, that the Elevations are of an order so superior, and display so much taste and knowledge of Gothic Architecture, as to leave no doubt whatever in our minds of the Author's ability to carry into effect Your Majesty's commands . . .[79]

Putting together ground plan and general design, Barry's entry was, declared Hanbury Tracy, 'far superior to any other plan that has been submitted'. But when questioned by a parliamentary committee, he found it difficult to particularize its merits.[80] Contemporary comments might lead one to suppose that Barry's design was distinguished by some unique feature. When the awards were announced the *Spectator* reported that Barry's design had been seen by many while preparing, and that 'it was recognised by one of its grand features, a tower, 170 feet high, richly decorated, which forms the centre of the façade of the River front.'[81] It was true that Barry's entry was dominated by a great tower (his northern tower being comparatively low), but this concept was a common one; the Pugin-Graham design (Pl. 31), for instance, being dominated by an elegant lantern tower resembling St Ouen, rivalling the 280 ft high towers of Westminster Abbey. Nor was Barry's more remarkable in its function as an entrance tower or glorified *porte-cochère*. Knowles had three towers through which carriages passed to the foot of staircases (Pl. 28). In Rickman's project (Pl. 32), 'The King's entrance is under a tower, by which he is set down at the foot

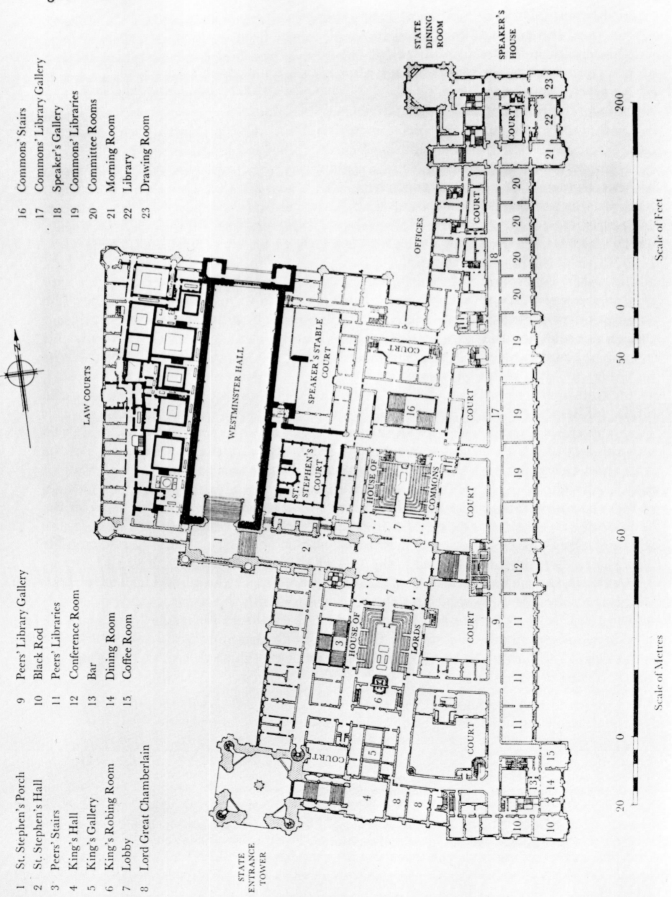

1 St. Stephen's Porch
2 St. Stephen's Hall
3 Peers' Stairs
4 King's Hall
5 King's Gallery
6 King's Robing Room
7 Lobby
8 Lord Great Chamberlain
9 Peers' Library Gallery
10 Black Rod
11 Peers' Libraries
12 Conference Room
13 Bar
14 Dining Room
15 Coffee Room
16 Commons' Stairs
17 Commons' Library Gallery
18 Speaker's Gallery
19 Commons' Libraries
20 Committee Rooms
21 Morning Room
22 Library
23 Drawing Room

LAW COURTS

WESTMINSTER HALL

STATE ENTRANCE TOWER

ST. STEPHEN'S COURT

SPEAKER'S STABLE COURT

HOUSE OF LORDS

HOUSE OF COMMONS

OFFICES

STATE DINING ROOM

SPEAKER'S HOUSE

COURT

Scale of Metres

Scale of Feet

33. Charles Barry: Competition design for New Houses of Parliament, 1835. Plan of principal floor, from a tracing of the lost original (redrawn).

of a magnificent staircase.' Bardwell had the king pass beneath 'a lofty Norman tower into the cloistered court . . . [to be] set down beneath a second tower in the river-front'; while Ferrey more simply would have had him alight beneath a 'gatehouse on the plan of such appendages to ancient noblemen's residences'. Whether derived directly from medieval gatehouses or from the towered porch which Nash had made a common feature of the Picturesque country house, some variation on this theme was a frequent enough feature of the competition.[82]

As one looks at the available evidence it becomes clear that what distinguished Barry's design was a skill and a mastery in the handling of features common to many entries, a mastery public opinion was quick to acknowledge. The *Gentleman's Magazine* was convinced of 'the soundness of the judgment'.[83] *The Times* thought Barry's 'undoubtedly a splendid design . . . one of the completest as a whole, and one of the most artist-like and scientific in design and arrangement';[84] while the *Athenaeum* declared that he had 'entered into the spirit of our national style . . . and made an original and effective palatial elevation, having every required variety of light and shade to give it life and expression, without destroying the character of the style by horizontal projections, and without breaking it up into detached masses, which would have prevented the simplicity and harmony that now pervade it.'[85] Almost alone the *Morning Herald* kept up a campaign of vilification against the decision.[86] Contemporary comments referred chiefly to Barry's elevations, but we may note the efficiency and logicality of his planning (Pl. 33), hallmarks of an architect experienced in designing buildings used by large numbers of persons of differing condition. Even an unsuccessful rival acknowledged his 'sterling merit' in terms that gave short shrift to rumours of favouritism.[87]

The other awards, however, received less acclaim, one correspondent suggesting in *The Times* that they had been selected merely as foils to Barry's.[88] Such a comment stresses his outstanding quality, but does the others less than justice. John Chessell Buckler (1793–1894), no. 14, using the too-obvious rebus of an R inside a buckle, was placed second for a design (Pl. 34)[89] showing the skills and familiarity with Tudor buildings to be expected of a professional antiquarian draughtsman, 'one of the best informed, and most skilful Gothic antiquaries of the age.' It exhibited, said *The Times*, 'in the most apparent manner, the difference between the architect and the architectural draughtsman . . . a cento composed of a series of anybody's old mansions that belong to one of the prescribed styles'. Yet another reviewer was struck by its originality as a composition: he did not observe 'that imitation of particular examples' which characterized some entries.[90] Charmed as they were by his pencil, the judges confessed that they were uncertain whether the much-broken river front would prove pleasing if built.[91] The plan (Pl. 35) was dominated by St Stephen's Chapel. Buckler evidently realized that there would be little point in restoring it only to hide it again in a maze of buildings, so, extending Old Palace Yard towards the river, he created a 200 ft wide court ranging the whole length of the chapel, which was to be used as a library, with others placed round the restored cloisters. This arrangement drastically narrowed the available space, ruling out the internal courts employed by Barry. Even so, Buckler gave over the centre of his building to twin staircases. Twin corridors on either flank of the two Houses were the principal thoroughfares.

The entry of an elderly Scotch architect, David Hamilton (1768–1843), number 13, 'King, Lords and Commons',[92] called down some contempt: 'What in the name of all fine art is the style of this?' Objectors protested that it was too late in date, for although in its roof balustrading and towers somewhat reminiscent of Longleat, the elaborate columned porches and corbelled-out window surrounds were of a Scottish Jacobean

34. J. C. Buckler (1793–1894): Competition design for New Houses of Parliament, 1835, awarded the second prize. Perspective of River Front.

character (Pl. 36).[93] Hamilton achieved sufficiently palatial elevations, but treated the various parts almost as distinct buildings even where, as in New Palace Yard, they adjoined. In Old Palace Yard he offered a mansion block, its differing west and south faces anchored by the Vanbrughian device of uniform corner pavilions. The river front, with Speaker's House, libraries and committee-rooms, was a monotonous composition, its external articulation exhibiting little relevance to the significance of its internal elements. But the plan (Pl. 37) was intelligible, providing for the needs of the several categories of user, and ample internal courts ensured good light and plentiful ventilation throughout. The *scala regia* in the Old Palace Yard front, and twin staircases for Lords and Commons, one at either end of the central spine which contained the two Chambers, were, however, space-consuming. Between the two Houses was an octagonal conference chamber, where a subordinate east-west axis crossed the main north-south axis. In general outline Barry's revised plan (Pl. 58) had resemblances to Hamilton's—which did not escape contemporary notice. But libraries and committee rooms in the river front and a central octagon were not exclusive to Hamilton. And the differences are quite as significant as the similarities: Hamilton placed the two Houses back to back, which would have complicated the Commons' access to the Lords; his staircases are far more conspicuous features than Barry's; he made no use of Westminster Hall, and his east-west axis was of less importance.

William Railton (c. 1801–77), number 42, marked with a Winged Orb,[94] won the fourth prize (Pl. 38), the judges stressing the merits of his plan.[95] Like Barry, he arranged his main blocks at an acute angle to Westminster Hall and borrowed Goodwin's idea of a major cross-axis from the south end of the Hall to the river front. The principle of the plan, however, was an arrangement of corridors around courts, with a main corridor or gallery linking the two Chambers. It had a clarity on paper that might well have proved less satisfactory in use. The committee rooms, distant from the Chambers, were exposed to the traffic noises of Old Palace Yard. An imperial staircase for the Lords was awkwardly placed in the south front. In the elevations (Pl. 39) Railton showed a certain facility with Picturesque devices: all his

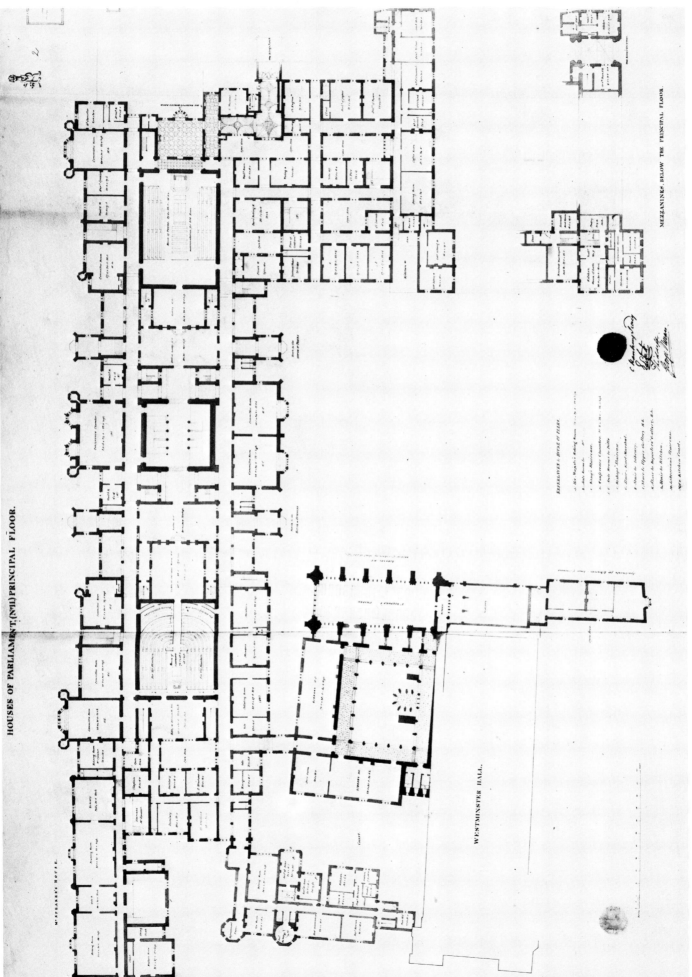

35. J. C. Buckler: Competition design for New Houses of Parliament, 1835, awarded the second prize. Plan of principal floor. Note Buckler's competition device (Buckle around R) at top right, and the signatures of the judges.

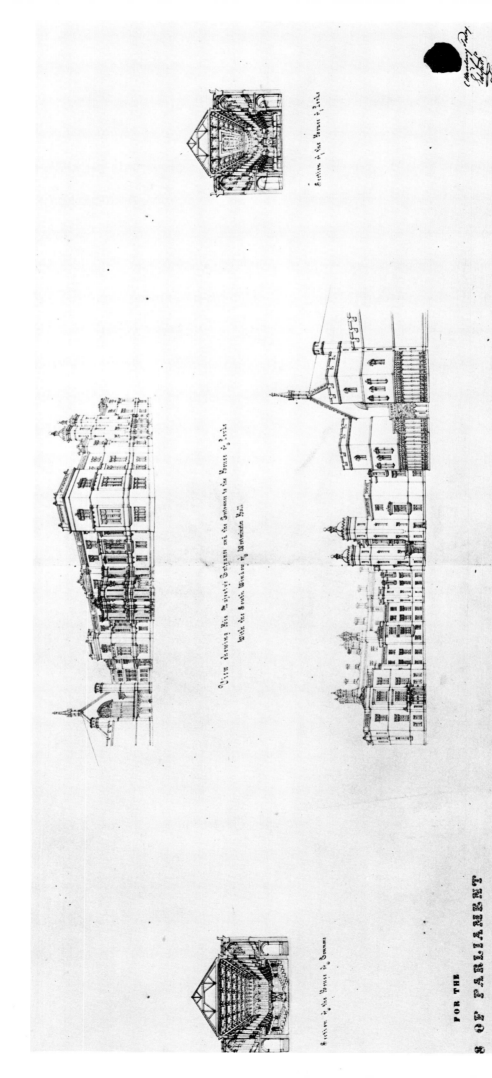

36. David Hamilton (1768–1843): Competition design for New Houses of Parliament, 1835, awarded the third prize. Perspectives of Old and New Palace Yard fronts, and interior sections of the two Houses.

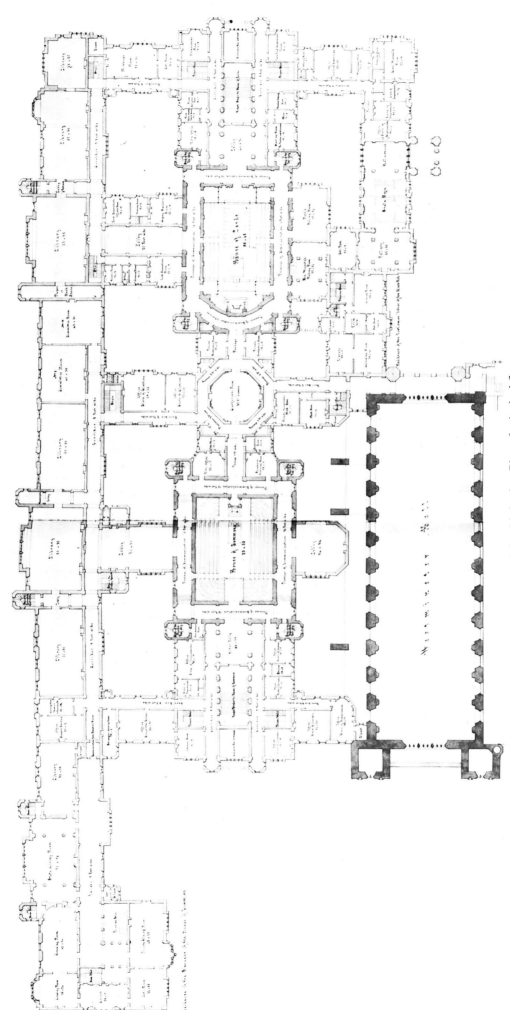

37. David Hamilton: Competition design for New Houses of Parliament, 1835, awarded the third prize. Plan of principal floor.

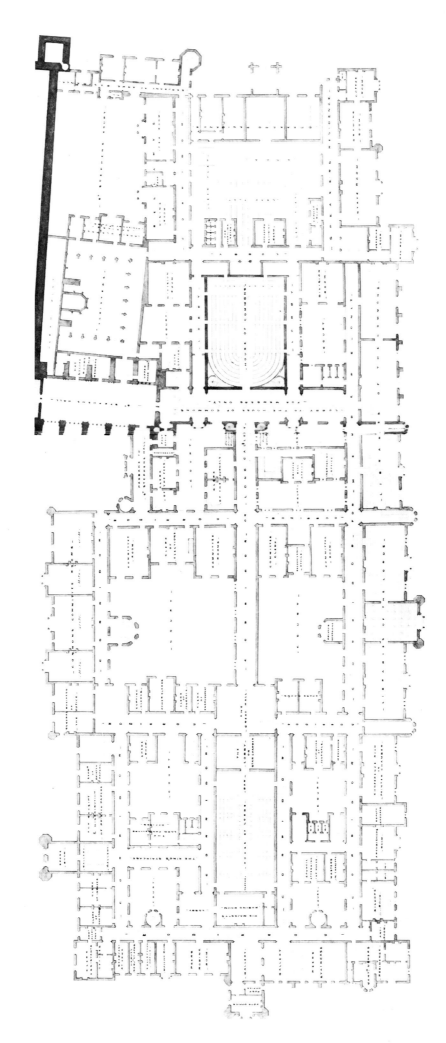

38. William Railton (*c.* 1801–77): Competition design for New Houses of Parliament, 1835, awarded the fourth prize. Plan of principal floor.

39. William Railton: Competition design for New Houses of Parliament, 1835, awarded the fourth prize. Perspective of Old Palace Yard front.

fronts were asymmetrical assemblages of symmetrical units, one section in the Old Palace Yard front reminiscent of Wyatville's York and Lancaster Towers at Windsor Castle. The East Barsham gatehouse was pressed into service as a Gothic alternative to a portico, in the manner of Nash or Wilkins. The House of Lords, resembling a Tudor royal chapel, the corner turrets with heavily crocketed ogival terminations, rose well above the surrounding buildings. Railton's charming perspectives, perhaps, even more than the apparent straightforwardness of plan, may have been decisive with the judges.

Naturally the judges were influenced by their own predilections. Vivian with his avowed fondness for Roman architecture would seize on the sympathetic points of Hamilton's entry. Hanbury Tracy doubtless appreciated the familiar skill of Buckler's drawing, for as James Savage observed, in all good faith a judge might favour a design in a known hand and 'actually believe that the owl so much resembling the darling bird of his own nest was the fairest object of the creation.'[96] It was claimed for the amateur that he was free of the jealousies of rival 'schools' of professionals; but, at this time, when amateurs were in the forefront of the aesthetic battle, that was not true. Gentlemen sufficiently prominent in the world of the fine arts to be acceptable as competition judges were bound to have become associated with some party or other in current stylistic controversy. But it was less their prejudice than their inadequacy that roused professional ire. It was almost a dictum of the métier that only a trained—meaning a professional—eye could read architectural drawings meaningfully. The fondness of the amateur for the pretty perspective drawing was a fact of life. In this particular competition there was an admitted failure of the judges to check in detail whether the entries provided the accommodation stipulated. Disgruntled competitors were thus able to use that as a pretext for upsetting the awards. Another handle for criticism was provided by the judges' recommendation that Barry's working drawings should be 'submitted from time to time to competent judges of their effect', a proposal appearing to contradict the prior assertion of their utter confidence in his ability to carry out his design.[97]

5. Conclusion

The subsequent adventures of Barry's design are considered below. There too belongs the story of the disgruntled competitors' attempts to upset the award. But it is appropriate to conclude this chapter with some consideration of the effect of the Houses of Parliament competition on English architectural practice and its relation to the development of the architectural profession.

In the 1830s that body may only loosely be described as a profession, though many contemporary 'artists' habitually used the term of themselves. Not only was entry unregulated (an 'eminent and opulent brassfounder and gas-fitter', quoted in *The Times* as remarking that one only needed a 'few bits of paint and a sheet or two of paper' to set up as architect, had reason for his assumption);[98] there was no systematic education and many thought there should be none; the precise functions of the architect were ill-defined; the ideals of professional conduct as fostered by the IBA were observed strictly by few who claimed the title of 'architect' and there was no means of imposing discipline; remuneration was not infrequently a matter of arrangement, though a tradition of a five per cent commission on executed works had been enforced by the courts; whether the architect was commissioned by a patron or a client, whether he was an 'artist' or practitioner was uncertain. The architect was still too closely associated with the builder, at least in the public's mind, for much respect to be accorded to him; and unless he lent himself to improper practices, his earnings were commonly less than those of his peers in other professions. Government for its part tended to treat him with contempt.

Some of the discord in the profession was heard in the pamphlet warfare to which the competition gave rise, the first such English public architectural controversy. At first conducted on the high ground of style or the mode of conducting public works, it sank into personal polemics. Wilkins, outraged at his lack of success in a competition he had fiercely opposed, attacked his old critic Cust as a '*maître charlatan*' who misrepresented the truth and was out to reward Barry for former help—but at the public expense.[99] Wilkins in his turn was 'Savaged': 'a gigantic monopolist [who] is much enraged at the departure from the old system . . . His unsupported assertions will not be accepted as proofs that the servile copying of details, and parts of Classical buildings, will compose a building which shall emulate those of ancient Greece.'[100]

Savage made a more valuable contribution to the controversy than mere mud-slinging. He offered an analysis of the faults of the competition and of the architect's role.[101] If the amateur possessed the technical knowledge to enable him to construct a building, then he entirely superseded the architect, Savage argued. But without that skill, he had no role to play in building: the professional was a better judge of design even. The most splendid works were produced by the most masterly constructors, who could achieve a boldness exhibiting the most valuable qualities of design: originality and simplicity. If the architect were to be under any control, it should be that of the man of business who was to use the projected building: a person who required no amateur knowledge of fine art. But to 'derive the proper advantage' from the architect's 'skill and talent' he must be treated with the 'liberal confidence' too often denied him by 'modern boards of management'. Similarly, Hopper argued that a man must be architect or builder to judge the effect of a building, and 'must have been long in the habit of comparing drawings with buildings, to be able to determine whether a fine drawing is a good design'. Cockerell advocated a jury of architects or artists for the design, scientists for the technical services, and a majority of intending users of the proposed building.[102] Given the wide range of education and skill in the ranks of avowed architects, it was not surprising, however, if leisured gentlemen who had devoted themselves to the study of architecture should feel quite as competent to judge designs. Disappointed competitors might claim that 'professional study and technical knowledge . . . are indispensable requisites for judging of their labours';[103] but if they aspired 'beyond the mere exercise of a trade' to rank with the fine arts 'whose predominant merit is the influence they possess over the feelings and imagination of man', then, argued George Vivian, architecture must like its sister arts be subject to general laws, 'and its best prize of admiration awarded by an unprofessional tribunal.'[104] The help of architects might be necessary in devising accommodation, but amateurs could assess the beauty of an elevation quite as well. It might even be suggested that the amateur, free of professional jealousies, was a better judge. For, although an elderly practitioner like Hopper might argue that the architect's business was 'to understand all styles, and to be prejudiced in favour of none',[105] observers saw the profession as being in a state of war: Greeks v. Goths.[106] Pugin made that evident enough in his *Contrasts* (Pl. 54), published in 1836.

Nevertheless, there was a school of thought which deprecated the stress laid on purity of style and accuracy of detail. 'In architecture . . . the expression of mind is the great essential', wrote Savage. The styles of the ancients grew out of their turn of thought and the demands of the subject, so to dictate a style was absurd: 'the imitation of styles is a valuable discipline for a pupil, but it is a confession of incapacity in a professor.'[107] 'Precedents drawn from ancient buildings', argued E. B. Lamb, 'should be considered merely as the foundation of a new style.'[108] Here already was the kernel of the early Victorian argument about copyism.

We have seen that there was much controversy about the actual conduct of the competition, but there was nevertheless a strong opinion that competition (properly organized) was the way to achieve as near perfection as man might hope for. 'Competition is the proper stimulus', Savage declared, echoing Soane. Yet even this was not universally accepted. Eminent architects were reluctant to spend their time and energy on such a lottery, as Cockerell pointed out to a select committee. Peel had had to bow to public opinion, but he maintained his own view, that 'if the most eminent architect of the day were directed to undertake the task, there would be a much greater likelihood of obtaining a plan which would secure accommodation and do credit to the architectural taste of the country.' A writer in the *Athenaeum*, perhaps Cockerell, who shared Peel's distaste for open competition suggested a solution: limited competition.[109] The same periodical commented, after another ill-managed competition, that for a new Royal Exchange (1839):

However, out of evil comes good. Though public faith may be shaken in the presumed advantages to be derived from competition, through these strange and repeated failures; yet every one of them directs attention to some weak point to be guarded against in future. In one instance, the judges were notoriously incompetent; in another, the instructions were obviously defective; in some, the conditions have been strictly enforced; in others, largely and loosely interpreted. Now, these errors suggest at once their remedy. Let the instructions for the future be drawn up by a professional man, the conditions strictly abided by and the arbitrators . . . men of high character and known ability.

Let there be fewer competitors, but those more careful.[110]

For not only the judges but too many of the entrants were incompetent. The *Gentleman's Magazine* commented that the exhibition of designs afforded 'convincing proof'

51

of the failure of contemporary architects to study the architecture of their own country. The *Spectator's* reviewer did not find, among the seventy-eight designs first exhibited, one 'that we should particularly desire to see carried into effect, [but] many we should be very sorry to see erected.'[111] British architects could muster a passable vocabulary of Gothic ecclesiastical detail, but their use of that vocabulary was clumsy and unidiomatic. There were few who showed themselves capable of organizing and planning a large-scale building on an awkward site. Would they have done much better tramelled by the classical rules? *The Times* thought they would,[112] but the evidence is wanting. It seems unlikely that a free choice of style would have given a finer building than that Barry and Pugin devised.

These controversies however influenced not only the future character of architectural competitions but also the arrangements under which the Houses of Parliament were to be built. Cust's proposals for continuing a commission to supervise the architect and take the responsibility for taste in public building found support in Parliament but ran into a storm of professional opposition; and Parliament rose for the summer. The contemporary practice of the Office of Woods and Works was accordingly adopted and Barry, once appointed, obtained (despite what Wilkins termed his 'known ductility') full responsibility—at any rate until Parliament took up in the mid-1840s that lively interest that Peel had seen as the likeliest obstacle to Cust's proposals.[113]

IV

Barry and Pugin: A Collaboration

THE building that Barry devised in 1835 developed in a sequence of phases. Early 1836 saw changes before the design was approved; between August 1836 and January 1837 detailed drawings were made for estimates; the complex, time-consuming preparation of the site followed; after 1840 during construction there was continuous revision of the design and its rich external and internal ornament. From the outset of his work on the design in 1835 Barry used the services of Augustus Welby Pugin (1812–52) (Pl. 40), then virtually unknown. In 1836–7 he assisted Barry with the great number of drawings required for making out estimates. He then devoted himself to his own practice. In 1844 when Pugin returned to assist with the work he was famous as the architect of Roman Catholic churches, for his work on a number of unusual country houses, and above all for his bold, truculent and exciting publications on architects, architecture and inferentially the society which produced them. His conversion to Catholicism in 1835 was inseparably linked with his personality, theories, designs and artistic philosophy. After his apparent mental illness and premature death in 1852, Pugin became in memory a tragic figure, isolated even in death by his devotion to his faith and the splendour of his genius. Between Pugin's death and his own, Barry was confronted by a posthumous Pugin, more myth than man. The *dénouement* did not come until 1867–8 when, Barry and Pugin both dead, their heirs fell to disputing the nature of the association between the two men which had produced the new Palace at Westminster. The assertions made in this quarrel, made public by newspaper controversy and pamphlet warfare, the partiality of the evidence produced and the implications of dishonesty which emerged clouded the attribution of the building. Certain information then brought forward, however, clarified the otherwise confused record.[1]

The competition for New Houses of Parliament was announced on 3 June 1835. The first phase of Barry and Pugin's work ended with the submission of their design on 1 December 1835. The history of their earlier collaboration and their activities in these months, and a description and assessment of the capabilities of each at this stage in their careers will cast light on the authorship of the competition drawings.

Amid thousands of onlookers, Barry and Pugin each saw the fire on the night of 16 October 1834 (Pls XI, 14). Returning from Brighton, Barry saw 'a red glare on

53

40. Augustus Welby Pugin (1812–52), by J. R. Herbert, R.A.

the London side of the horizon' and learned 'that the Houses of Parliament had caught fire'. He spent the night in the crowd, 'absorbed in the grandeur and terror of the sight'.[2]

Pugin, who then lived in Ramsgate, was in London when the event occurred that was to bring the largest and most prolonged of his professional responsibilities. Three weeks later he wrote idiosyncratically to a friend:[3]

You have doubtless seen the accounts of the late great conflagration at Westminster which I was fortunate enough to witness from almost the beginning till the termination of all danger

54

as the hall had been saved which is to me almost miraculous as it was surrounded by fire. There is nothing much to regret and much to rejoice in a vast quantity of Soane's mixtures and Wyatt's herasies [having] been effectually consigned to oblivion. Oh it was a glorious sight to see his composition mullions and cement pinnacles and battlements flying and cracking while his 2 [s]. 6 [d.] turrets were smoking like so many manufacturing chimneys till the heat shivered them into a thousand pieces. The old walls stood triumphantly midst the scene of ruin while brick walls and framed sashes, slate roofs etc. fell faster than a pack of cards. In fact the spread of the fire was truly astonishing from the time of the house of commons first taking fire till the flames rushed out of every aperture it could not have been more than 5 or 6 minutes and the effect of the fire behind the tracery was truly curious and awfully grand. What is most to be regretted is the painted chamber the curious paintings of which I believe are totally destroyed. I am afraid the rebuilding will be made a compleat job of as that execrable designer Smirke has already been *giving* his opinions which may be reasonably supposed to be a prelude to his *selling* his diabolical plans and detestable details. If so I can contain myself no longer but boldly to the attack will write a few remarks on his past work and if he does not writhe under the lash his feeling must be harder than his cement as if I spare him I hope to sink myself. His career has gone on too long and this will be a capital opportunity to show up some of his infamous performances.

In October 1834 Pugin was twenty two, he had a small family to support and he aspired to establish himself as his father's heir as an expert on Gothic architecture and draftsman. The years 1832 and 1833 had been difficult and tragic: within twelve months his young wife had died in childbirth and both his parents had died. With such business of the Pugin drawing office, bookshop and publications as remained after his father's death still to manage and his infant daughter to care for, Pugin married for a second time in 1833, and a son, Edward Welby, was born in March 1834. Burdened as he was, Pugin endeavoured to reorganize his life and launch a practice comparable to his father's. He negotiated with E. J. Willson, his father's collaborator, that together they might complete *Examples of Gothic Architecture*.[4]

Pugin's training in architecture had not been orthodox. His father, A. C. Pugin, had trained his pupils in drawing, but not in the rigorous disciplines of architectural construction. A. W. Pugin was never to obtain that experience provided by the prolonged pupilage in an architect's office normally the basis of an architect's education. In 1827, aged fifteen, he had moved from his father's office into the design of furniture and thence, in 1830, into the manufacture of furniture from his own designs, an enterprise that failed financially and threw him back on the support of his father who, because of failing health, required assistance in the campaigns of study and drawing in preparation for *Examples*. The younger Pugin had a second string to his bow, for he had worked with some success at the creation of settings for the theatre and in the summer of 1832 the manager of an opera house in Paris offered him a permanent position which he refused.

At this time of personal crisis, in late 1832 or early 1833, Pugin changed his drawing style. He discontinued the blue ink and coarse line of his early furniture designs,[5] and began to work exclusively in the delicate, even microscopically fine, pen and black ink which would distinguish his drawings of 1833 to 1836. At the same time he began to compose volumes of drawings of imaginary buildings and their accoutrements of which *Le Château* is typical (Pl. 41).[6] These abrupt changes in technique and subject matter coincide with and surely derive from the decision Pugin recorded in February 1833 to 'give up my theatrical connection altogether and to devote *myself entirely* to the pursuit of Gothic architecture.'[7]

In the spring of 1834 Pugin had at least the ten volumes of drawings of fictitious

Une partie de la longue Gallerie

41. (left) A. W. Pugin,
Le Château, 'Une partie de la longue
Gallerie'. Pen drawing, 1833. This
exhibits the 'foreign' character in
Pugin's work complained of by
contemporaries.

42. (right) A. W. Pugin:
St Marie's College, The Great Hall.
Pen drawing, 1834.

buildings—bird's-eye views, plans, elevations, interiors—all in his new style, which
today survive (Pls 41, 42).[8] Here were more than three hundred drawings, dazzling
evidence that their maker could compose on paper buildings in a late Gothic style,
embellish them with architectural detail which, though extravagant, was logical and
derived from study of medieval models, and supply them with interiors decorated
and furnished to the last tapestry and door plate. In addition to these, Pugin could
show a prospective employer books of sketches made on travels in England and on
the Continent in 1832 and 1833, and sequences (also bound into pretty volumes)
of pen-and-ink studies for metalwork and furniture from which he would later
develop the plates Ackermann published. Though Pugin would probably not have
showed it to an architect whom he wished to impress, he had also a complete first
series of 'contrasts' which he would in 1836 improve, sharpen, add to and publish.
His religious conviction and his architectural partisanship had begun to crystallize.

56

interior of great hall.

Pugin was, however, already accustomed to collaborative work, and from 1829 he had been occasionally employed by James Graham (later Gillespie-Graham), an Edinburgh architect. The continuation of this association indicated the usefulness of Pugin's talent, his capacity to understand and adapt to the ideas of another, and an ability to produce designs that were practical.

At the start of 1834 Pugin visited Lincolnshire and Norfolk, and in the summer made a major expedition to Europe:[9]

I have seen and learnt more in the last 3 months than in the 3 past years . . . Only conceive of entering a church at Nuremburg where I saw 13 Gothic altars (even the candlesticks original), a tabernacle for the Holy Sacrament 50 feet high containing hundreds of images and all perfect . . . I have ascended the spires of Strasbourg, Chartres, Antwerp and the great tower of Malines.

43. Charles Barry: St Peter's, Brighton, 1826–8, an early competition success in Gothic style.

Only a few weeks after his return his aunt Selina Welby died suddenly, leaving him a modest estate. At the end of the year he was negotiating to buy land near Salisbury, and declaring that he had:[10]

seen the fallacy of the new sects and trust ere long I shall be united to the original and apostolick church which suffers no change or variation. I trust no man will attribute my motives solely to my love for antient architecture for although I will allow the change has been brought about in me owing to *my studies of antient art* yet I have still higher reasons.

This, then, was the state of Pugin's affairs and beliefs on that night in October 1834 when he watched the old Houses of Parliament burn.

Charles Barry first employed Pugin early in 1835. Barry himself at forty was an accomplished architect whose practice was then prospering as a variety of commissions in both the Renaissance and Gothic styles came his way. He had built Gothic churches in fashionable Brighton (Pl. 43), in Islington and Manchester, and restored that at Petworth. An assiduous entrant in architectural competitions, his success in that for the Travellers' Club in Pall Mall (1829) had confirmed his position as a leader among the rising younger architects. In February 1833 his Gothic design had won a competition for the King Edward VI Grammar School, Birmingham

58

44. Charles Barry: King Edward VI Grammar School, Birmingham, 1833. Elevation of end bays of main façade.

(Pl. 44). As well as work in the leading industrial and commercial cities, he was acquiring clients among the Whig aristocracy, and 'appreciated the higher class of society into which he was thrown'; invitations to dine at Holland House were acknowledgements of his talent and social graces which offered an opportunity to meet persons of influence.[11]

The Birmingham Grammar School had by 1835 reached a point at which Barry could use services of the kind Pugin had been rendering Graham: drawings were needed for its decorative details and such fittings and furniture as were part of the contract. Pugin himself was looking for work which would help pay for his new house near Salisbury and broaden the base of his acquaintance in the architectural community. How the two met is not known—possibly through the furniture manufacturer and dealer Edward Hull.[12] Pugin's books of drawings would have been enough to impress even a man as informed and fastidious as Barry. On 18 April 1835 Pugin dined with Barry, and on 28 April began drawings for him. They met again on 9, 20 and 27 May. On 9 and 15 June, Pugin, who was then in Salisbury supervising the building of St Marie's Grange, noted the despatch of drawings to Barry.[13]

No mystery surrounds the arrangement for the Birmingham school. The drawings and tracings of drawings for it now in the Royal Institute of British Architects and the House of Lords Record Office give, with the information in Pugin's diary, a reasonable picture of what took place.[14] Pugin listed approximately 127 drawings of details and furniture he designed for the school;[15] of these, sixty may now be recognized in drawings or tracings in the two collections. Barry signed and dated only a few of his own drawings and those of others that are extant; the earliest identifiable as by Pugin is one labelled 'Pateras on parapet over doorway', signed by Barry and dated 18 May 1835, a large-scale drawing sufficiently detailed for carvers to work from directly. This was surely one of the drawings Pugin delivered to Barry when they met on 9 May in London. Other orders followed, for though most of the drawings recognizably by Pugin are not signed and dated by Barry, those that are indicate that at first intensively, then occasionally and as late as August 1836, Pugin was doing bits and pieces of design for the school. The headmaster's ceremonial chair, details of the coat-of-arms for the library, and the bookcases, screens and panelling for library and schoolroom, the desks and chairs, are among the undated and unsigned Pugin drawings that survive. James Murray while employed as an assistant in Barry's office in the 1840s traced many others.

Pugin's hand is not difficult to recognize. His drawings for Scarisbrick Hall, made a few months later, may be used for comparison (Pl. 45). His characteristic lettering and technique of drawing details in broad strokes of ink wash were faithfully transcribed by Murray. The distribution of elevations, moulding profiles and sections on a sheet did not follow the form usual in Barry's office. In his designation of points at which sections were taken Pugin employed a personal set of letters; these, too, Murray recorded. He also traced Pugin's handwriting when it appeared on the original from which he was working.

With the exception of the details of ornament, such as the study of pateras of May 1835, the original drawings are rather more difficult to attribute than the tracings. Murray may have been asked to trace the more intricate and valuable drawings in the office, while he and others were perhaps allowed to carry away casual sketches. In some, Pugin appears to have drawn in only the decorative portion, the surrounding architecture having been laid in by another member of Barry's staff. Others are ephemeral sketches on the back or in the margin of drawings.

None of the drawings from which Murray made his tracings can now be found, but it would appear that the best of Pugin's work was kept in a reference collection in Barry's office where Murray was able to work with it as late as 1847.

In the summer of 1835 both Barry and Pugin travelled on the Continent, Barry to see the town-halls of Belgium, 'especially those of Brussels and Louvain'.[16] Pugin returned from France on 3 August; en route for Salisbury he stopped in London where he met Graham and spent a day working on drawings ordered and discussed at this encounter. These may have been the preliminary studies for Graham's competition proposal. Conferences with Barry on 6, 10 and 11 August and the preparation of 'working drawings' and 'large drawings' were surely devoted to the Birmingham school.

Pugin's participation in the design of the school has tended to obscure other equally important relationships between it and Barry's competition proposal. In the course of the charges and counter-charges over the authorship of the Houses no one was ever to say that Pugin was or was not the 'art-architect' of the school or that he rather than Barry was its architect. No one claimed that Pugin's role in the preparation of the design had been hidden to bring credit to Barry. If the school was mentioned it was only in passing and as an obligation which could account for a part or the whole of Pugin's employment by Barry in 1835. The Birmingham Grammar School is, however, important to the history and attribution of the Barry competition

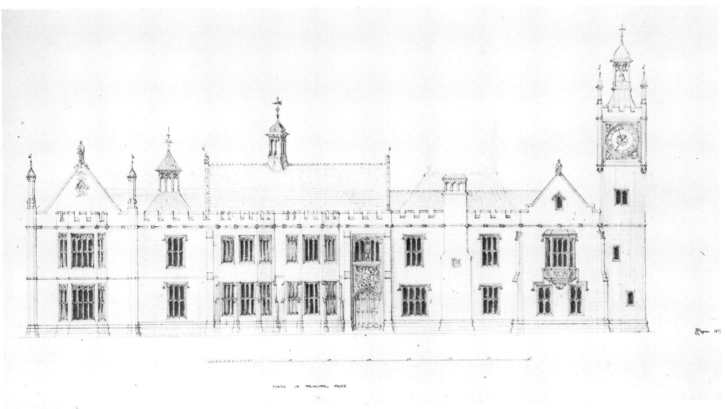

45. A. W. Pugin: Scarisbrick Hall, Lancashire, 1837. Elevation of principal front, showing the clock tower thought to have been the prototype for Westminster.

drawings, because it included in a smaller, experimental form many of the ideas developed in large scale and with assurance in the new Houses of Parliament and, presumably, in the now-lost competition drawings.

In his design for the Travellers' Club in 1829 Barry had attained a personal style and artistic maturity. He was at ease with the Renaissance palace form, for its stately simplicity accorded well with what M. Digby Wyatt was to describe as 'his resources in planning, and refined perception of just proportion, both in detail and general distribution, in which he has scarcely ever been rivalled.' Without discounting the importance of Barry's stylistic preferences and his capacity to design and organize refined detail, it was, finally, in the masses of his buildings, particularly in the relationship between height and length of façades, and in his plans—in the distribution of rooms around a court, the exploitation of the first floor front and rear as long large chambers for communal use, the situation of smaller rooms for service and residential purposes in the ends of the building—that his characteristic 'resources in planning and general distribution' emerged.

The difference of architectural style which appeared to separate the Travellers' Club and the Birmingham school was but superficial, for common principles governed their external organization and their internal planning. The club was 67 ft long, two storeys high and divided into five bays on its street front. The school, more than twice as long as the club, was composed of eleven bays, nine in the central portion and terminal wings set slightly forward (Pl. 46). Presumably aware of the cumbersome

61

length of the street façade, Barry had proposed an enriched central bay with oriel which was dropped from the design in December 1834. In others of his buildings he eschewed a central feature as a 'mere excrescence'. The choice of a late Gothic style assisted the composition, for the large windows, the repeated verticals of the buttresses, the crested battlements, and the gable and oriel of the end features successfully qualified what could have been an oppressive horizontality (Pl. 44). The school was taller than the club to accord with its greater length.[17] Barry's design for the Birmingham school well represents his preoccupation with and capacity to solve problems of proportion, and its relationship to decoration, which would stand him in good stead in the creation of his design for the Houses of Parliament.

Similarities between the plans of the club and the school (Pl. 46) reappear in Barry's later buildings. The inward orientation around a court was both a personal preference and a useful adaptation to modern urban necessity. The unified first floor spaces at front and rear appeared in the school after they had been a notable success at the Travellers'.

In one significant feature the two buildings differed. Expenditure of space on an elaborate staircase and corridor system had not seemed necessary in a private club; in a school, ease of circulation was a requirement, for hundreds of boys would come and go at regular intervals. Staircases and ample corridors were a necessity. Barry placed his main corridor across the width of the court and took part of the courtyard for the principal staircase. It was both reasonable and aesthetically logical to line both the corridor and staircase chamber with Gothic detail similar to that of the exterior, for stone panelling and an elaborate groined ceiling would be not only elegant but durable. A public area so decorated would also relate the exterior to the interior.

46. Charles Barry: Birmingham Grammar School, 1833. Plan of first floor, from the contract drawings (redrawn).

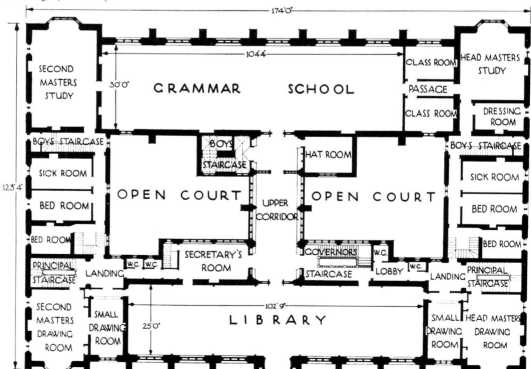

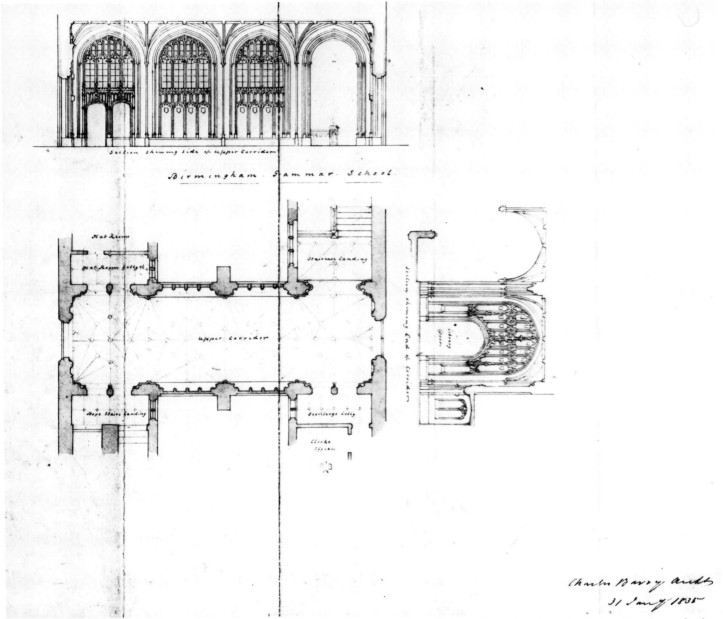

Section shewing side of Upper Corridor

Birmingham Grammar School.

Hat Room

Hat Room Lobby

Staircase Landing

upper corridor

Boys Stairs Landing

Secretarys Lobby

Clerks Offices

Charles Barry archt
31 Jany 1835

47. Charles Barry: Birmingham Grammar School. Plan, elevation and section of Upper Corridor, signed and dated '31 Jany 1835'—
Barry's work before Pugin came on the scene. The use of stone vaulting at this date is noteworthy.

The design of this corridor (Pl. 47) is critical, for more than any other part of the
school it was to be an important source of the relationship of architectural mass and
decoration with which Barry would work in the Houses of Parliament. The stone
panelling, the rich roof with its bosses, the lighting from windows which open onto an
interior court are characteristics of the corridor which reappear infinitely repeated
but in no major way altered in their style or handling at Westminster. Fortunately,
when the school building was demolished, this corridor was preserved and moved
to the new site in Edgbaston, and there re-erected as the school chapel. Even a
cursory examination of it convinces one of its importance to the Houses of Parliament
design.

Establishing the authorship of the corridor is, therefore, the first step in examining
the extent and kind of collaboration that produced the competition drawings and the

new Houses as they were built. A series of drawings for it exists (Pl. 47).[18] Unmistakably by Barry, they are dated 31 January 1835, several months before he acquired Pugin's services. In the course of his work on the school Pugin was to draw various of the carved enrichments for the staircase; those for its spandrels and pendants are among the Murray tracings. The idea for the corridor and many of the details of its design were, however, complete when Pugin arrived on the scene.

The first phase of co-operation was limited to specific tasks, such as bosses, heraldic compositions, furniture, a variety of carved details—nothing as large even as an oriel. At a late stage Pugin may have been asked to try his hand in the organization of the elaborate entrance on the street front. The remaining Pugin drawings give some idea of the relationship's character: they are carefully, even boyishly, prepared, often titled in Pugin's best Gothic script, as though the young assistant had set out to satisfy his employer. Pugin was impressed by Barry and pleased to be working for him.

From such a working arrangement it was easy to slide into similar cooperation on competition drawings for the new Houses of Parliament. Pugin was available, and Barry had learned that he was useful, discreet, knowledgeable about Gothic and marvellously able in pen-and-ink drawing, a necessity in the competition submission and a skill in which Barry was not particularly adept. Though his drawings show Barry to have been a remarkable artist, he worked in pencil. His few drawings in ink lack the brilliance of his pencil sketches and are even coarse and clumsy. Pugin's little volumes of drawings, each page an achievement of the highest order of draftsmanship, would have been a recommendation even had Barry not already found him imaginative and responsive, sympathetic to guidance, and capable of filling blank spaces with ornament that was historically accurate and yet somehow original. To retain Pugin and use his services wisely was an intelligent decision, and Barry made it; it was to prove both fortunate and fateful.

*   *   *

The question what part each played in the work which Barry and Pugin shared between the end of July and 1 December 1835, though apparently simple, is almost impossible to answer unless one fills with suppositions the gaps that separate one genuine fact from another. However, a realistic reconstruction of events is necessary, for at issue is the authorship of the premiated design and, ultimately, of the notable building developed from it.

A small amount of useful evidence was brought forward in the course of the quarrel between the Barry and Pugin families in 1867–8.[19] Most of what then emerged was, however, either casual memories of events that had taken place thirty years earlier in circumstances not sufficiently dramatic to inspire accurate recollection, or partisan statements which distorted facts or added nothing to the argument. But Pugin's diary entries were written without guile or malice aforethought. Edward Welby Pugin's errors in transcription did not advance his cause.

There is nothing to make one suppose that Pugin worked with Barry on the Parliament House design before 1 September 1835. This is not to imply that either was uninterested in the competition. From early June its general terms, including the style requirement and the closing date had been public knowledge, though the details were not available before 18 August. Barry had certainly resolved to compete. Pugin must have begun to dream of what he might do as soon as he heard that Gothic was proposed, and he must have realized that one way or another he would play a part.

Pugin's diary shows that immediately he returned from abroad he settled to work on the Birmingham school, for the 'working drawings' he designated would be unnecessary for a competition. Only at the end of the month, from 24 to 27 August, is work for Barry recorded, but without any description of its nature. Pugin was, however, in Salisbury on those dates and he had not seen Barry since 10 August, so it seems reasonable to conclude that he was completing work for the school. But for 1 September the entry reads, 'Mr Barry all day composition'; that for 2 September, 'sent of Drawing of Ding [sic] room to Mr Barry' (Pl. 48). This last must refer to the Master's house at the Birmingham school. On 11 September Pugin 'first drew at St Marie's Grange', and noted sending drawings to Barry; the next two days he simply noted 'Mr Barry', but on 16–18 September he was 'on composition for Mr Barry', sending off more drawings on the two days following. The 23rd is again 'Mr Barry', but on the 24th 'Mr Barry came'. This was confirmed by Alfred Barry, who quoted his father's diary: 'arrived at Salisbury from Bowood at half past four. Mr Pugin at the White Hart to receive my directions as to designs for the furnishing of Dr Jeune's house'—the Birmingham headmaster.[20]

Meanwhile another architect, Talbot Bury (1811–77), had been at Salisbury since 11 September, working for Pugin on drawings for Graham; he assisted Pugin in drawing and etching in several periods of heavy work. In 1867 Bury volunteered testimony in support of the Barry family, stating that 'A. W. Pugin did not make any plan or design for this building [the Houses of Parliament] until I went to his house in Salisbury to assist him in Mr G. Graham's set of drawings.'[21] If William Osmond, Pugin's confidant in Salisbury, remembered with accuracy in 1867, then Bury was established in his drafting room rather than at St Marie's Grange.[22] At all events, he left on 4 October. Whether he knew of Barry's visit on 24 September is doubtful, but the event may have been crucial, for on the 27th Pugin noted 'Parliament H'—the first explicit reference. On the 29th he 'Sent to Mr Barry 14 drawings' (and another twelve at a guinea apiece on 3 October), and on 30 September he noted 'central portion'. Similarly, Alfred Barry's quotations from his father's diary include one for 27 September, 'commenced design in detail for the New Houses of Parliament'.[23] Barry was in London that day, Pugin in his new house: they were not working together, but Pugin's comments can only mean that he was working on a competition design for one or the other of his clients, and that probably Barry's, for Graham's had no 'central portion' comparable with Barry's river façade (Pls 31, 53). The Birmingham school had long before progressed beyond the design for its street elevation, and may be disregarded. At the White Hart meeting, Barry may have asked for assistance in his Parliament House design. There are no facts which establish Pugin's earlier participation. The drawings charged at a guinea must have been large and complex; they could well have been studies of elevations and interiors for the new Houses developed from preliminary plans and sketches Barry gave Pugin and discussed with him at the White Hart. Pugin could well have decided that it would be prudent to keep his own counsel in the matter of competition drawings: composing one set and assisting in another was lucrative, but perhaps not entirely fair to the architects who would be submitting drawings in the same hand. It is unlikely that Barry was aware that not far from the White Hart work was under way on a set of drawings which could come from 'north of the Tweed' (Pl. 49).

Thereafter, we have more explicit evidence: 6–8 October, 'Mr Barry S.E. view' and 'elevation'; and 12–18 'Drew at Mr Barry's'. Returning to Salisbury on 19 October, two days later Pugin 'Began Mr G elevations'.

The drawings Pugin made in the last days of September and early October may

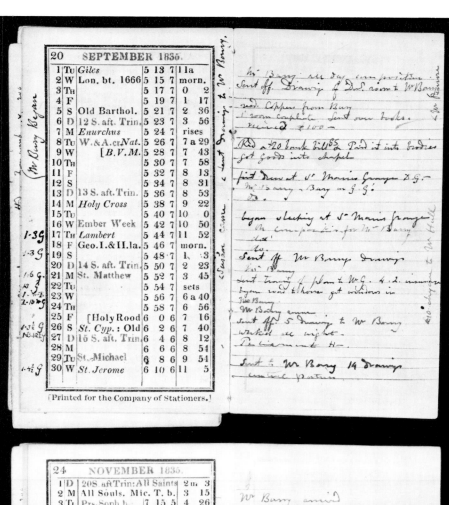

SEPTEMBER 1835.

1	Tu	Giles	5 13	7	11a	
2	W	Lon. bt. 1666	5 15	7	morn.	
3	Th		5 17	7	0	2
4	F		5 19	7	1	17
5	S	Old Barthol.	5 21	7	2	36
6	D	12 S. aft. Trin.	5 23	7	3	56
7	M	Enurchus	5 24	7	rises	
8	Tu	W. & A. cr Nat.	5 26	7	7 a 29	
9	W	[B.V.M.	5 28	7	7	43
10	Th		5 30	7	7	58
11	F		5 32	7	8	13
12	S		5 34	7	8	31
13	D	13 S. aft. Trin.	5 36	7	8	53
14	M	Holy Cross	5 38	7	9	22
15	Tu		5 40	7	10	0
16	W	Ember Week	5 42	7	10	50
17	Th	Lambert	5 44	7	11	52
18	F	Geo. I. & II. la.	5 46	7	morn.	
19	S		5 48	7	1	3
20	D	14 S. aft. Trin.	5 50	7	2	23
21	M	St. Matthew	5 52	7	3	45
22	Tu		5 54	7	sets	
23	W		5 56	7	6 a 40	
24	Th		5 58	7	6	56
25	F	[Holy Rood	6 0	6	7	16
26	S	St. Cyp.: Old	6 2	6	7	40
27	D	15 S. aft. Trin.	6 4	6	8	12
28	M		6 6	6	8	54
29	Tu	St. Michael	6 8	6	9	54
30	W	St. Jerome	6 10	6	11	5

[Printed for the Company of Stationers.]

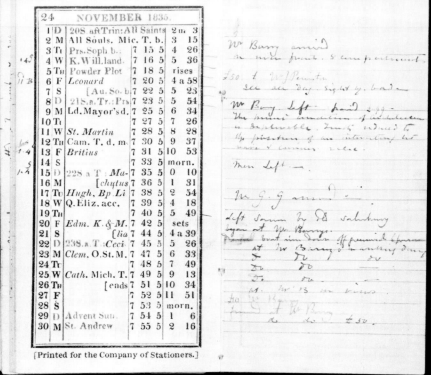

NOVEMBER 1835.

1	D	20 S. aft Trin: All Saints			2 m	3
2	M	All Souls. Mic. T. b.			3	15
3	Tu	Prs. Soph b.	7 15	5	4	26
4	W	K. Will. land.	7 16	5	5	36
5	Th	Powder Plot	7 18	5	rises	
6	F	Leonard	7 20	5	4 a 58	
7	S	[Au. So. b.	7 22	5	5	23
8	D	21 S. a. Tr.: Prs	7 23	5	5	54
9	M	Ld. Mayor's d.	7 25	5	6	34
10	Tu		7 27	5	7	26
11	W	St. Martin	7 28	5	8	28
12	Th	Cam. T. d. m	7 30	5	9	37
13	F	Britius	7 31	5	10	53
14	S		7 33	5	morn.	
15	D	22 S. a. T: Ma-	7 35	5	0	10
16	M	[chytus	7 36	5	1	31
17	Tu	Hugh, Bp Li	7 38	5	2	54
18	W	Q. Eliz. acc.	7 39	5	4	18
19	Th		7 40	5	5	49
20	F	Edm. K. & M.	7 42	5	sets	
21	S	[lia	7 44	5	4 a 39	
22	D	23 S. a. T : Ceci	7 45	5	5	26
23	M	Clem. O. St. M.	7 47	5	6	33
24	Tu		7 48	5	7	49
25	W	Cath. Mich. T.	7 49	5	9	13
26	Th	[ends	7 51	5	10	34
27	F		7 52	5	11	51
28	S		7 53	5	morn.	
29	D	Advent Sun.	7 54	5	1	6
30	M	St. Andrew	7 55	5	2	16

[Printed for the Company of Stationers.]

48. A. W. Pugin: Diary for
September and November 1835.

have been those J. L. Wolfe described when he ransacked his memory during the controversy of 1867.[24] They could have been, as Wolfe said, 'foreign', but they were certainly not 'coarse' and 'ill proportioned', for Pugin's drawing books show him incapable of such errors of judgement or technique. The possibility that Barry discarded them does not eliminate Pugin, but rather instals him firmly as a kind of partner in the process of trial and error through which Barry devised his final design. Pugin's quick hand and mind, his powers of improvisation and sensitivity to Barry's directions and intentions could have saved the latter hours, indeed days, of struggle with drawings. Once Barry had seen the design Pugin had made in a siege of day and night work in which he gave body to the building Barry had visualized, it was possible to know where first conceptions had gone wrong. Pugin was thus not 'making' Barry's competition drawings, but he was making it possible for his employer to produce a better design in the limited time allowed than he could otherwise have done. I am, of course, suggesting that Pugin's drawings converted Barry's plans and tentative sketches into a picture of the building which Barry could then study. They were used as a model often is today, one step among many in the refinement of the design of a building.

It is probably to Pugin's mid-October visit that we should assign the conversation Talbot Bury recalled as taking place in London: Pugin, he said,[25]

told me that he had seen 'a very remarkable design, the plan being most ingenious and comprehensive, and the elevations treated in a very original and effective manner'; he added that 'Mr Barry had sought to give an Italian outline to Gothic details, and, though he probably should not have treated the composition in that manner, the general effect would make a noble work and he anticipated a decision in Mr Barry's favour'.

Pugin may well have been both startled and chastened, for the drawings he had prepared for Barry had not been finally influential, though instrumental, in the form Barry's competition proposal was assuming. Until he arrived in London Pugin could have assumed that Barry, like Graham, would accept his suggestions and drawings without revision. Instead, he found they had been absorbed and reworked in fundamental ways. Pugin's statement also suggests that he recognized quality when he saw it, for slowly and deliberately Barry had composed the first version of an entry in a composite style that Pugin found puzzling but 'effective'. The Graham–Pugin entry was, of course, well advanced, so when he admitted that he 'anticipated a decision in Mr Barry's favour', Pugin was saying candidly and somewhat sadly that Barry's design was better than his own.

The London visit was certainly devoted to another group of studies in which Pugin's details and Barry's revised plans and elevations were united. This may have been the moment when Barry's design first reached maturity.

Pugin's diary (Pl. 48) shows that Barry visited him from 2 to 8 November.[26] During this visit, Pugin suffered the first recorded attack of the recurrent eye inflammation which would lead, after years of pain and despair, to his premature death in 1852. If Barry was relying on him to do the final ink drawings, then 6 and 7 November must have been days of panic. Barry paid Pugin £99 and returned to London. The day after his departure Pugin wrote the sullen comment: 'The present condition of architecture is deplorable. Truth reduced to the position of an interesting but rare and curious relic'. Why he did so, we do not know.

After a visit from Graham on 17 November, Pugin went to London to resume at Barry's on 20th. The diary entry for 22 November appears to read: 'at Mr Barry on

working drawings'. As Alfred Barry pointed out, working drawings were not at that juncture needed in the competition submission; his conclusion was that Pugin was engaged on another project.[27] But the Birmingham school was long past the working drawing stage, and Pugin had for some weeks been involved with Barry in preparing the Parliament Houses design. The word may possibly be read as 'making', or Pugin may have used 'working' loosely to indicate the elevations and sections, rather than the 'views'—the three required perspective drawings—he mentioned on 26 November.

On 28 and 29 November, Pugin noted 'finished at Mr Barrys'. The technician who mounted the drawings, J. Hogarth, in 1867 recalled the last frenzied hours:[28]

Graham's designs [he wrote to E. W. Pugin] were revised by your father up to five or six of the evening they were to be sent in and when he left he was most anxious that I should follow him to Mr Barry's as quickly as possible, which I did; and it was past 11 before I had the drawings finished, and the corrections were made in the office up to the last minute.

Pugin, who was not above a swagger or two when in a self-congratulatory mood, was reported to have said, 'I made Barry's designs for 400 guineas, and Graham gave me 300 guineas for his'; and 'Is this not a regular joke? Here are two rivals competing

50. A. W. Pugin: St Mary's Roman Catholic Church, Derby, 1839. Pugin's etching shows a spire, steps and terrace that were never built.

for one prize, and I am making the designs for both', remarks which set off the discussion of his clandestine part in the creation of the winning design.[29] The amounts Barry paid Pugin in 1835–6 relate to the quantity of Pugin's contribution in time and labour and the store Barry set by his assistance. Pugin charged a little under £70 for his work on the Edward VI Grammar School.[30] In 1835, however, Barry paid him sums totalling some £171. Pugin's diary for 1836 records on 17 February '£105 from B to House', which Alfred Barry confirmed was a payment from his father; and on 22 June, 'Mr Barry paid me', which Alfred Barry identified as a sum of £160.[31] Pugin did no work for Barry from the night the competition drawings were submitted up to 4 June 1836. The conclusion, therefore, is that Charles Barry paid Pugin £265 for his assistance in the competition design.

*   *   *

The nature and value, however, of Pugin's services to Barry in the preparation of the competition design cannot be identified by the amount of money Barry paid for these services. When the quarrel over the attribution of the design broke in the public press diligent persons went out to study Barry's earlier Gothic churches and returned assured that if these buildings were alone evidence of his knowledge of Gothic Barry could not have accomplished the Parliament Houses design unassisted. Because the Barry family had acknowledged that Pugin had a hand in it no one looked carefully at the history of the design of the Birmingham school. Nor did either party in the argument ask another and equally logical question: could Pugin, who in 1835 had built only his own house at Salisbury, and who would in 1838–9 design St Mary's Derby (Pl. 50), have designed the competition drawings single-handed? Dramatic and evocative of Gothic though that church is, its weaknesses lie precisely in its plan and in an uneasy accommodation between ornament and exterior masses and interior space, the features in which Barry's Parliament Houses scheme excelled. St. Mary's is the work of a gifted and exotic young man. Pugin possessed an extraordinary talent but he lacked the practical training and sense for the architectural whole and command of complexity in planning which Barry had demonstrated long before 1835.[32]

The Travellers' Club and the King Edward VI Grammar School, rather than his churches, are the antecedents of Barry's premiated design for the new Houses. Parliament required an enormous club, replete with service quarters, meeting rooms, restaurants, libraries, chambers of state, corridors and offices (Pl. 33) and circulation through and between these varieties of useful spaces presented, much magnified, the very problems that Barry had solved with such finesse in the Birmingham school.

The answer to the riddle of the authorship of the competition design lies, first in the recognition of Barry's accomplishment in the management of planning, second in his superb sense for the composition of external masses and surfaces. Finally there was the working relationship with Pugin: begun tentatively for the completion of the school, it was expanded and made infinitely more complex in the head-long rush to produce, in an impossibly short time, the sensible, useful and ornamentally complex building which Barry first visualized for Westminster in 1835 and to which he was loyal through the rest of his life.

Barry was able to compose in Gothic, as his drawings for the corridor at Birmingham show, but Pugin's skill and imagination in the use of the ornaments of the style were better than anything Barry or anyone else could produce in 1835. Pugin was also an incomparable master of architectural drawing in ink. His mind was a glossary of medieval details. He could weave a tissue of decoration. These, and the ability to draw, in record time, illustrations of the building that could result from a plan were the talents that Barry bought and for which he paid well.[33]

The attribution of the competition drawings and hence of the distinguished building which was ultimately built, must rest upon a definition of what is important in architecture. In the battle between the Pugin and Barry parties the success of the plan, the conception of the vast fronts on the river and Abbey sides, and the composition, bulk and placement of the towers in relation to the whole, were not considered. Yet they are the building, and Barry was solely responsible for them.

It was also Barry's idea to cover the interior and exterior of the structure with a repetitive pattern of ornament which would suggest Gothic without imposing on the occupants of the building an ecclesiastical environment in which to conduct the business of a modern government.[34] An exterior of the sort he proposed would accord well with the Abbey and the walls of the Chapel of Henry VII and so fit the new building into its site. Despite its great size Barry perceived that the Palace must neither be subordinate to nor dominate its architectural environment. He seems also to have perceived that the new building should possess an identity as a nineteenth-century monument.

The compartments of decoration which Barry proposed imparted human scale and comprehensibility to the expanses of wall and offered an opportunity for legible heraldic enrichment in which the political purpose of the structure would be underscored. The legislative palace was to be a great book of national history. Parapets and a variety of finials would break up what otherwise would have been oppressively long and massive roofs. Barry understood and exploited the possibilities inherent in the observation Pugin later made in *True Principles*: 'In pointed architecture the different details are *multiplied with the increased scale of the building*: in classic architecture they are only magnified.' In the vast and windy reaches of the new capital city of Washington a Neo-Classical legislative palace could rise like a monument and await its environment. London was another matter. The style requirement of Gothic or Elizabethan had not been Barry's but it had been wise. Within its limitation Barry composed a work which was original, aesthetically successful and at the same time a deliberate statement of the times from which it came.

For Pugin Barry's request that he assist in the preparation of the studies and final drawings for the competition meant an opportunity to create the greatest of his fictitious buildings. The new Houses of Parliament may have been conceived on the day that Barry first saw Pugin's remarkable books of drawings and found in them a decorative excitement which could be related to his own refined but muscular sense for architectural form.

Critics of the new Houses of Parliament as well as the participants in the row over its authorship suffered from a variety of myopia which caused them to define the building as its decoration and attribute its design to its stylist. The character assumed by the Gothic Revival in the years between 1835 and 1860 encouraged such an approach for it became increasingly preoccupied with the accurate reproduction of the medieval styles, developed loyalties to one or another of them to the exclusion of the others and raised hopes that duplicates of the monuments of the Middle Ages would benefit not only the art of building but the life and spirit of England. This was a quest for the impossible which Barry skilfully avoided. In the revivalists' view—and this included Pugin's—the Houses of Parliament was old fashioned before its time, and yet, in its pragmatic use of architectural style it was more modern than most of what was to be built in the years while it was being completed.

Architects were still identified with other artists, so that a building not entirely by the hand of one man was considered, somehow, not his. The necessity for collaboration was not acknowledged, even when, as in the case of the new Houses of Parliament, the project was large and complicated and the time allowed for the preparation of drawings so short that employment of assistance was the only way to accomplish the tasks of design.

In its great size and its purpose, in the character of the clients with whom the architect would cope, in the feeling that it was necessary to establish an accommodation between it and its existing urban site, in its initiation in a public competition, in the political symbolism of the style requirement the new Houses were a modern building. It elicited a modern working arrangement from Charles Barry, who was, however, himself not ready to accept the significance of the system of delegated tasks he had devised. Even less were Parliament and the public prepared to understand the need for limited and controlled collaboration. Nor was Pugin, as his remark about 'making' Barry's design indicates. This conflict was to linger on unresolved to burst forth in the claims and counterclaims of 1867. E. W. Pugin expressed the older idea of single genius and the Barrys, who half agreed with him, answered his challenge poorly with tepid claims for their father's sole authorship. The master-and-staff or group-design idea had not taken hold even in the 1860s. Teams of architects are today arranged to prepare competition proposals and to meet demands for large, complex, and technically elaborate buildings such as the new Houses. Now we would say that the competition design emanated from the office of Charles Barry.

V

Select Committees and Estimates:
The Collaboration Continued

1. Committees and Competitors

PUBLIC interest in the great competition remained lively. Once it was under way attention turned to the judging, and proposals were aired in the press advocating a public exhibition of the designs.[1] A meeting of competitors was held on 4 February 1836, almost as soon as the judges' report was signed, under the respectable chairmanship of P. F. Robinson, vice-president of the recently-formed Institution of British Architects.[2] Welcoming the competition as 'beneficial to the Artists of this country' and praising the judges' ability and impartiality, this meeting nevertheless agreed to petition Parliament (the government having refused assistance) to provide for the public exhibition of all the plans to 'allay any apprehension in the public mind, with respect to the propriety of the decision.' Barry's triumph seemed to confirm the common rumour that it was all a 'job'. Further study of the award went in the same direction: Buckler's too-easily identified rebus (Pl. 35) was commented upon, as was his sometime role as Hanbury Tracy's architectural draftsman at Toddington.[3] But dissatisfaction's opportunity to bite was at hand: the commissioners' award had to be considered by committees of both Houses, which would then report to the Houses themselves. Thus in committee and on report critics could make themselves heard, and possibly overthrow the award.

A campaign to achieve this was waged both in and out of Parliament. When the Commons appointed a committee (almost identical with that of 1835 which had prescribed the competition) to consider such plan as might be 'most fitting and convenient' for new Houses, Hume gathered 43 supporters in an attempt to have the site reconsidered—but 141 voted against him (9 February). Next, he alleged that Barry's plans among others had been seen by many during their preparation, and criticized the announcement of judges' names before the entries were received.[4] The implications were obvious. His friend Hawes' motion instructing the committee to review all the entries and receive estimates from the architects was defeated 48–120. Then Benjamin Hall, a radical MP whose name was later to be closely associated with the Houses of Parliament, moved for a public exhibition of the plans before the Commons' committee considered them, to enable the voice of the public to be heard before a decision was made. Ministers objected that this would reopen the whole question of which was the best plan: they did not object to an exhibition, but to a

51. Charles Barry (1795–1860), by J. Linnell, 1839.

delay they would not consent.[5] The commissioners' report was laid before Parliament on 29 February 1836, and committees of each House subsequently reported concurring in the judges' preference for Barry's plan, but recommending that there should be further inquiries both as to its cost and as to procedure (15 and 17 March).[6]

The commissioners had attended the Commons' committee on 10 March, when questions were asked about any possible breach of competitors' anonymity, the bases of the judges' choice, and in particular about the winning design. Hanbury Tracy explained that the commissioners had established guide lines for determining the merits of each plan:[7]

74

52. Charles Barry: North Front, New Houses of Parliament Competition, 1835. Preparatory pencil sketch, published by H. Heathcote Statham in *Builder*, 5 Jan. 1901 as 'Sir C. Barry's First Elevation Study for the Houses of Parliament Competition'.

the general disposition and convenience of the several entrances, and of the different communications of the interior; the situation of the different offices; the situation of the Houses with respect to each other; the communications between them, private and public; the situation of the libraries, committee and refreshment rooms, and the various conveniences required . . . After examining a plan and weighing the objections to it, we decided upon its general merits as a design compared with those of other competitors.

Joseph Hume pressed Tracy uncomfortably about the specific merits of Barry's entry and introduced important practical questions: ventilation, acoustics, light, and the durability of Gothic ornament. He argued that Barry's small, irregularly-shaped courts immediately behind the river front (Pl. 33) would be ill-ventilated and offer little light to the surrounding rooms, while the great King's Tower would cast long shadows. When he pointed out that the ornamental stonework of King Henry VII's Chapel, restored in 1809–22, had rapidly decayed, he was met with a fusillade of arguments: if a plainer style were desired, then it should have been called for when the committee specified the style; Gothic buildings in a ruinous state retained their beauty, whereas Grecian ones lost theirs; a durable stone would no doubt be found—in any case it was the right directional laying of the stone that mattered. And, a last sneer from Cust, 'As Gothic architecture is the creation of the severer climates of Europe, it is a fair inference that it is not ill-calculated to endure the weather'.[8] But Peel made the useful suggestion, later acted upon through Hume's and Barry's initiative, that the Office of Works should inquire into the relative merits of various building stones. He also proposed that a model of the design should be prepared.[9]

This interrogation revealed that the commissioners had permitted, even encouraged the prizewinners to revise their designs. Barry had altered the position of his Commons staircase and moved the House away from the central lobby for instance

53. Charles Barry: New Houses of Parliament, adopted design. Perspective of River Front. Lithograph by T. Kearnan.

(Pls 33, 58), while Hamilton had turned his principal axis from north–south (Pl. 37) to east–west. But Tracy made it clear that he knew what he wanted from the competition—to find the best architect: 'there is no such thing as perfection in architecture; Mr Barry may go on improving this plan, and I do trust that if it is adopted it will be improved from time to time . . . until the building is completed.'[10] On 22 April Barry himself was called before a joint meeting of the Lords' and Commons' committees to explain what he was about. By this time he had considerably recast his plan to meet Hume's objections, of which he had clearly appreciated the force (see Pl. 58). He advanced the north-east corner (near the Bridge) into the river to square off the irregular internal courts, and to enlarge them extended the building southwards in the direction of Millbank. The lengthened façade had to be modified. The two lateral towers were altered, the Speaker's reduced in area, and given a clock surmounted by a spire; the King's increased in height to some 200 feet, probably to maintain its compositional importance in a lengthened building (Pl. 53).[11] Barry, a taciturn witness, skilfully minimized the real scope of his changes. He drew attention, however, to the reduction of cost by the 'omission of niches, statues, panelling of parapets'. He managed questions on style particularly well, though the committee which had been assured it had procured an 'English' building was later told something quite different:[12]

Sir Robert Peel: Is there any authority for a building of this style, except as applicable to ecclesiastical buildings?—Yes, I should say the Town-halls in the Netherlands.
Sir Robert Inglis: The town-hall of Brussels?—Yes.
Sir Robert Peel: Are there towers there also?—It has one tower.
Are there buttresses?—There are angular projections between the windows which may be called buttresses.

Improved though the plan might be by these changes, the elevation suffered. Tracy had remarked that 'it is quite impossible to consider internal arrangements but with reference to the elevations, and that an architect must occasionally make some sacrifice in one or the other, or in both, in forming his design'.[13] In order to meet the practical requirements of his brief, Barry was obliged to sacrifice the unity of his composition.

The Lords' committee made its second and final report on 28 April 1836, recommending the adoption of Barry's plan but expressing the trust that: 'considering the Magnitude of the Expense to be incurred, such Arrangements will be made by Government, as will secure the greatest Vigilance and Economy in carrying the Object into effect, both with reference to the just remuneration of the Persons to be employed, and the Details of the work itself.' But the Commons' committee, as was appropriate, held a final session on 29 April largely devoted to the question of cost— some solace to Hume for its exclusion from the terms of the competition. Barry was accompanied by his quantity surveyor, Henry Arthur Hunt (1810–89), and by Thomas Chawner (1774–1851), surveyor of the Office of Woods and Forests. The architect explained that his estimate of £724,986 (exclusive of site, embankment, furniture and grates) was calculated upon the basis of his Birmingham Grammar School, then nearing completion. He had adopted, he said, the same architectural character and amount of decoration as in that building. Having the cost of that school (a lump-sum contract), and the prices at which all the materials were charged, he had added what would make them equal to London prices for labour and materials. Chawner had carried out a mere mathematical check, but Hunt had gone into the matter more thoroughly. He had dissected various parts of the Birmingham calculation and applying the components to corresponding parts of the Houses of Parliament he had found Barry's figures correct. As a further check he had considered the cost of the Carlton Club House for which he had been the quantity surveyor. Multiplying its cost per cubic foot by one and a half to cover the extra ornament of the New Houses, he arrived at a figure of one shilling per cubic foot, including contingencies.[14]

Welcoming Barry's recent alterations as 'calculated materially to improve' his plan, the committee recommended Parliament to adopt it (9 May). But, still doubtful about the cost and doubtless remembering Nash's Buckingham Palace and similar public works where expenditure had slipped out of control, they advised caution. Hume's warnings were not entirely unheeded, and his colleagues recommended that Barry's plan should be adopted

only on the express understanding that it can be executed for a sum not exceeding by any considerable amount the estimate submitted ... by Mr Barry ... It does not appear ... that it would be safe or expedient to engage in a work of such magnitude and importance until a due and accurate estimate, founded on detailed specifications and working drawings, shall have been made and carefully examined, and approved by competent authority.

Therefore Barry should forthwith prepare such drawings so that a 'close estimate' could be ready by the next session. Even these preparations were not to commit the 'Public in the slightest degree to the ultimate adoption of the Plan'; though if the figures were satisfactory, there was 'every probability' that Barry would get the job. He was to be paid a distinct fee for the necessary plans and specifications, the question of the architect's remuneration for 'superintending the execution of the Plan in the event of its ultimate adoption' being reserved.[15] Barry replied laconically that he 'placed himself in the hands of Government'.[16] He was not yet home, but he had taken a long step towards becoming architect of the New Houses of Parliament.

On one important matter the Rebuilding Committee made no specific recommendation. Peel suggested making some arrangement for conducting the great work; it might be better to appoint 'persons permanently to superintend it, rather than leave it merely in any department of Government'. Tracy referred to the commissioners' recommendation that the architect's drawings should 'be submitted from time to time to competent judges of their effect'; and Cust reiterated his criticism of the executive's inefficient control of public building in late years.[17] Draft resolutions of the committee offered a scheme that might have obviated much subsequent argument: Barry was to be appointed architect, to make an estimate, and to state the mode in which he proposed finishing the interior; the royal commissioners were 'to take charge of and superintend the work in conjunction with the proper officers of his Majesty's Government'. No alterations were to be made unless approved by two commissioners. The architect was to receive five per cent commission on the outlay if within his estimate, or otherwise four per cent on his estimate, except for approved alterations.[18] But these proposals were dropped from the adopted report. Lord Duncannon (later Earl of Bessborough) recalled in 1844 that one or two of the commissioners were going out of town and 'declined altogether themselves to be responsible for what was going on', sensibly enough, as they had no authority, having discharged their function.[19] Cust revised his pamphlet on control of public building.[20] But the moment for changes had passed: Radical influence in Parliament was failing; and the Whigs had already made changes in the management of public works. Duncannon, the minister responsible, had decided to replace the former government architects by commissioning some leading architect for each particular job.[21] This did little effectually to break up the monopoly aspect, as the government tended to stick to the same few men. But as in private works, the architect was now charged with the full responsibility for his work; his was the design and his the superintendence. The success of this system depended upon the accuracy of estimates, and the degree to which the House of Commons felt inclined to indulge in architectural criticism. Had the Houses of Parliament been built within the time expected there would probably have been little parliamentary interference. Barry rashly told the 1836 committee that the job would take about six years: but in 1842 he was only setting the foundations of the Houses.

*   *   *

Of these proceedings, Joseph Hume was the most notable and most persistent critic. Initially, he had been alone on the Rebuilding Committee, save for Warburton, in advocating open competition.[23] With outside help he could claim to have won that victory, but thereafter little fell out as he desired. With each step taken along the path to building, he became more convinced that they were going awry. Many of his proposals were adopted in subsequent competitions for public works, but their history was to show that there was no infallible receipt—the outcome was likely to be controversial, however carefully considered the conditions. Even Hume's apparent success in having the Rebuilding Committee hedge a disagreeable prospect with prophylactic conditions was illusory, and his prophecy that Barry's design would cost £1,800,000 was not very far from the mark. His criticisms however made their impact on Barry and, as described above, influenced the plan of the new Houses.

Hume's limited successes and major failures have to be seen against a background of discussion both within and without Parliament. Within, Peel, even in Opposition, was Barry's most powerful advocate, and he induced the Commons to reject Hume's arguments, declaring that the only fate worse than that of being a judge in such a business was to be the successful competitor: if, as Hume wanted, they were to start all over again, they would have neither competition nor judges.[24]

Naturally there were disgruntled spirits among the competitors, who were willing to work with Hume, and many more who were keen for an exhibition. Official men were often pretty contemptuous of architects, and while numbers of influential persons had viewed the competition designs in the Speaker's House, where they had been set out for the judges, professional men were rigorously excluded until the competitors were invited to collect their entries. Then the government agreed that the newly-completed east wing of the National Gallery could be used by competitors who wished to mount an exhibition of their drawings. The premiated entries, however, were withheld for Parliament's use. So on 24 March 1836 the exhibition opened without the prize-winners' plans. 'The public must be the more inclined to believe the reports of jobbing and unfairness which are so current', declared the ministerial Whig *Morning Chronicle*.[25] Within a month, the Rebuilding Committee agreed to release the four designs, but their exhibition only stirred the critics' wrath. 'It was apparent', declared the disappointed Hopper,[26] that Buckler, Hamilton and Railton

were inferior to many in the exhibition; no. 64 [Barry] although pronounced surpassingly beautiful and greatly superior to all the rest, was discovered upon examination to be merely a drawing made for effect, but which could not be executed; many essential parts of the elevations being omitted, and several important apartments, accommodations and conveniences being left out of the plan, and the elevations and sections not agreeing with it.

It was contended also that Barry had contravened the instructions in other particulars, such as including eight 'minute drawings' illustrative of his skill (cp. Pl. 54). The commissioners had reported that the success of his proposal rested upon 'evident marks of genius and superiority of talent' and the brilliance of his detail: then he should be called upon for large-scale drawings to show how he intended to handle the ornament he had used so liberally. Many of his competitors were highly suspicious of the alterations made in Barry's plan before it received final approval and claimed that their own designs had been raided for ideas.[27] And the failure to allot the fifth award was seen as a slur on the profession, the more puzzling in that Tracy could comment in Parliament on the high quality of drawings submitted: 'particularly . . . one which came from the North of the Tweed [Pugin's for Gillespie Graham, Pls 31, 49, 80], in point of execution, never has been, and I believe never will be surpassed'.[28] To architects it was evident that the judges should have had professional assistance.

A sub-committee of the exhibiting architects then organized a petition, signed by thirty-four of them headed by C. R. Cockerell and presented in the Commons by Hume, asking for the appointment of a commission of inquiry before the final choice was made.[29] They protested that the judges had made their selection by elevation instead of by plan, that Barry's plan contravened the instructions, that the other awards were not judicious, that the failure to award a fifth prize was an imputation 'to the prejudice of the character of the profession', and that professional expertise was required in selecting designs. This sub-committee also issued a lithographic print of Barry's plan to show the commissioners' incompetence, and put their case personally to the Chancellor of the Exchequer and to Sir Robert Peel. Hume followed this appeal with a motion for a new competition without restriction as to style, but limited as to expense, the entries to be exhibited before judges were appointed.[30] He repeated the specific allegations about Barry's deficiencies, which Tracy had little difficulty in showing to be largely unfounded: for instance, that Barry, instead of providing a lobby of 1800 sq ft and one of 1100 sq ft, had allowed an area of only 1028 sq ft for both. This assertion was based on the 'private passage for members' or division lobbies at either side of the House, whereas the required lobbies Barry had provided at either end of the Chamber, each of 1738 sq ft.[31]

The failure of Hume's motion was followed by a meeting of the exhibitors at which a minority criticized their sub-committee's activities as having been directed against Barry personally instead of against the management of the competition generally. Simultaneously with a final general meeting, the minority, led by T. L. Donaldson, put a notice in the papers attacking misuse of the exhibition gate-money by the sub-committee and objecting to all its proceedings as 'tending to produce disunion among the members of the profession, to lower the standards of professional courtesy, and to lessen its members in the public estimation'.[32] The eleven signatories included Angell, Kendall, Robinson and Hakewill. But the great majority at the meeting (chaired by Cockerell) condemned their action. The remaining proceeds of the exhibition, £794, were shared out, instead of being applied 'in the promotion of the art' as the minority wished.[33] This coda to the competition, amplified by press comments and such pamphlets as those of Savage and Hopper noticed above, shows how slow to emerge was an architectural profession with defined standards of conduct even after the foundation of the Institute of British Architects.

Outside, the general feeling was that the commissioners had, by luck or judgement, made the right choice. The *Architectural Magazine* might declare that upon sober reconsideration it felt the site was ill-chosen and the competition should be scrapped; the *Westminster Review* might deride it as an ecclesiastical plot; the widely-read *Morning Herald* denounce Barry's 'very much ornamented abbatial Gothic' chosen by the incompetence of amateurs; a *Gentleman's Magazine* correspondent point out flaws in Barry's entry and conclude that it was 'in fact, a *Grecian* design overlaid with *Gothic* ornament'.[34] All in vain. Public opinion liked Barry's synthesis.[35]

2. A Hidden Hand

Pugin's anonymous participation in preparing the competition drawings lies behind many of these events. The fate of the designs in which he had had a part appears not to have interested Pugin. There are but two references in his letters: one is a recommendation to E. J. Willson to read his contribution to the debate, *A Letter to A. W. Hakewill, Architect, in Answer to His Reflections on the Style for Rebuilding the Houses of Parliament*, which, he remarked, had been 'much read and will I trust be productive of good'; the other a statement relating to the autumn of 1835: 'I have been fully occupied by important business for some time past and have been working early and late.'[36]

Reticence about his achievements and charity towards others practising in his field were not among Pugin's characteristics. He normally enjoyed recounting his exploits. The silence about this 'important business' suggests that Pugin had agreed to keep his employment secret. A hand in two entries was tribute to his talents.

When at long last they were permitted to study the prize drawings the disappointed competitors may have perceived similarities that suggested Barry and Graham had shared an assistant, an observation that could only confirm their doubts as to the credibility of Barry's 'skill' and right to the job he had won. The critics who asserted that Barry had presented a 'drawing for effect' had been correct. Pugin had been

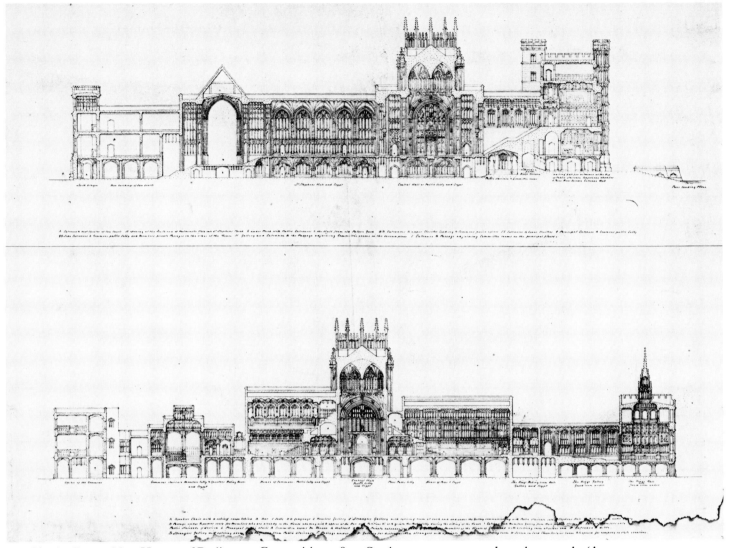

54. Charles Barry: New Houses of Parliament Competition, 1835. Sections west to east and north to south. (A copy on paper watermarked 1844.)

co-author of the 'effect' so much admired and so persuasive to the commissioners. If there were indeed mistakes in Barry's design they could have resulted from collaborative effort as well as from haste.

Barry's willingness to temporize may have arisen from his awareness that the design he had proposed would inevitably undergo continuous revision. He seems to have been assured that Pugin would be on hand to prepare drawings for the estimates; after that, there would be time to work out the details as they were required. He would have acquired a reasonably complete programme for the architectural ornament and the interior decoration. From that point he could, at least for a time, go on alone.

On 28 April 1836, when the prize designs joined the others at the National Gallery, Pugin went up to London to see the exhibition, the first manifestation that he shewed of interest. The rooms were crowded and the atmosphere must have been rather tense, for early in the day all purchasers of the catalogue received also a pamphlet by Wilkins which contained 'matter of an extremely personal nature'. At the same time

81

were exhibited earlier designs for new Houses, including Kent's of 1739, Soane's (1779, 1794 and 1796), Gandy's (1833 and 1835) and twelve from the Hume Committee of 1833 (Pls 6–12), one of which had been the work of Charles Hanbury Tracy.

The competition drawings of Buckler, Hamilton and Railton (Pls 34–9) are among the thousands of those connected with the Houses of Parliament now in the Public Record Office. As Barry's cannot now be found, it is necessary to reconstruct them from such evidence as remains in preliminary sketches, written descriptions, and a copy of parts of the original set.[37]

Since the commissioners stated that they had examined about 1200 or 1400 drawings, the average set must have contained about thirteen sheets. Buckler's portfolio contains sixteen, Hamilton's nine and Railton's fifteen (including revisions). 'Eight minute drawings' were reported to have been part of Barry's set. The scale of these drawings and their inclusion to illustrate Barry's skill in ornament suggest that they were by Pugin, whose responsibility for the three 'views' or perspective drawings has been discussed above.

A review of the exhibition in *The Times* is of tangible assistance in reconstructing the lost Barry entry.

Mr. Barry's is a splendid design, gorgeous in decoration, tasteful in arrangement and combination, replete with good taste and sound knowledge of our best national style of architecture, and more palatial than we could have expected from the ecclesiastical style required by the committees. As drawings they are artist-like, but architecturally not more so than Mr. Cockerell's, but like that gentleman's have all the appearance of autography about them that many of their competitors want, whose drawings are evidently polygraphical in every respect, the buildings being by one hand, the skies by another, and the figures by a third.

It would appear that, as the drawings were 'autographical', Pugin drew all but the plans.[38]

Another incomplete but tempting glimpse of what these drawings must have been may be recovered in the two sheets of copies in the Public Record Office (Pls 30, 54).[39] In the early 1840s portions at least, and perhaps the whole, of the competition set were copied, by a third person. They show interiors which resemble those Pugin had provided for 'St Marie's College' (Pl. 42). The small size and the delicacy which are preserved in the copies make Pugin's authorship of the originals virtually incontrovertible.

The most balanced statement among the many outpourings on the competition, the *Athenaeum*'s article of May 1836, included Barry's description of his original design—that is the competition design as distinct from the first revision, of which the river front view and block plan were reproduced from the committee's report (Pls 53, 58). In view of the common emphasis on the richness of Barry's entry and the knowledge of Gothic ornament it displayed, it is interesting to note that Barry himself said not one word about ornament. Instead he discussed the reasons which dictated his arrangement of the plan, the massing of the building in relationship to what was already on the site and adjacent to it, the practical necessities of ventilation, heating and circulation of persons, and the adjustment he proposed for the south end of Westminster Hall in the creation of St Stephen's Porch. These were the fundamental matters with which he had been engaged as Pugin drew the ornamental details. Barry had definite ideas about the appearance of the building, as his choice and supervision of Pugin demonstrated, but his primary concern was purely architectural. Ornament would enhance the 'sound healthy and well proportioned body' which Cockerell had said was essential to architecture; ornament must, however, always play a secondary

55. Charles Barry: New Houses of Parliament, adopted design, 1836. Elevation of the North Front.

role. On this fundamental the views of the commissioners and the public differed from those of the architect. Barry's description of his plan explains why he was willing to accept curtailments in decoration. It could be replaced. Loss of quality in the plan or in materials would be irreplaceable.

The parliamentary lithograph of the river front and the block plan reproduced in the *Athenaeum* introduced the public to the revised design (Pls 53, 58), which could be compared with the competition drawings exhibited at the National Gallery. *The Times* was saddened by the changes: it referred to the 'denuded, altered, and in fact newly-made design, now in hand, or completed, by order of the committee for rebuilding the two Houses of Parliament', implying that a wealth of external ornament which had graced the competition proposal had been wiped away in the interest of economy (cp. Pls 30, 55). One commentator said that the revised building resembled the King Edward VI Grammar School; but Barry himself had made this point to the committee.

The character and qualities of Barry's competition entry may thus be reconstructed from descriptions and from the expressions of disappointment that greeted the revision. The Barry-Pugin drawings had been a *tour de force* of draftsmanship, appealing in the same ways that distinguish those for 'St Marie's College'. They were probably small, complex and delicate, and they illustrated an effect rather than a building. With the exception of the plans they were, certainly, all drawn by Pugin. The

56. A. W. Pugin: New
Houses of Parliament.
Pen, ink and wash
drawing of Royal Arms,
c. 1836.

building, however, was Barry's. The drawings may have assisted him to win the contest, but it was he who would make the imaginary palace a reality.

Pugin had none of Barry's worries. He was in and out of Salisbury, working for Graham, travelling to the north and west of England. At Easter, just as the finishing touches were being put on the plates for *Contrasts*, Pugin received his first communion. In July he went to France, but was back in London by 2 August, when he saw Barry. For the last ten days of August he was working intensively in London for both Barry and Graham. Into 1837 he was to work prodigiously for both men.

Although on 9 September 1836 Pugin merely noted 'Mr Barry's drawings' in his diary, he was sometimes more specific. Thus, 12 September, 'sent fireplaces to Mr Barry 4.4'; 14th, 'sent working drawing of Lamp to Mr B 2.2'; 27th, 'sent Mr Barry doors and framing'. These entries relate to one in Barry's diary for 23 September: 'Forwarded to Pugin tracings of the three floors complete, and sections to enable him to proceed with the details of the interior. Letter to him thereon.'[40] This letter survived to be printed by E. W. Pugin:[41]

Dear Sir,
As a measure of precaution for the safe delivery of a parcel of tracings, forwarded by the Exeter Mail this evening to your address, I write by post in order that if it should not be duly delivered, you may know where and how to make enquiries for it. They will furnish you with the necessary data for the preparation of a large batch of internal details, including the two Houses complete, the King's Robing Room, Gallery, and Staircase, and the Entrance Vestibule, all of which I shall be obliged to you to set about immediately and send them to me from time to time as each subject is completed. The drawings that I should be glad to have first, and as soon as possible are a collection of doors, archway openings to corridors etc., and a series of designs and details for wall framings. The door openings to the smaller rooms need not exceed 2 ft. 10 ins. in the clear, and those for the Committee and other large rooms should not for practical convenience exceed 3 ft. 6 in. The great folding doors, wherever they occur, may have a clear opening of 5ft. 8ins.

The plans (which I should tell you are all prepared to a scale of 10 feet to one inch) will furnish you with the several thicknesses of walls for the door jambs. The wall framings in the the great rooms are to be 6 ft. 9 ins. in height, in the second class rooms 4 ft. 9 ins., and in the smaller or third class rooms 4 feet. All to have frieze panels from 6 to 7 inches in height, and long panels beneath them ranging from 12 to 13 inches clear width. Eight different sorts of doors (all to be set in stone) and double that number of jambs will suffice. The sections of the stonework may be tinted brown, brickwork red, and plaster purple; the scale may be half an inch to a foot excepting when doors, windows, turrets etc. are drawn out separately, when I agree with you it would be desirable to adopt a scale of inch to the foot. The sheet of fireplaces came safely to hand, and will answer the purpose exceedingly well, many of them are excellent. Perhaps it would be as well to do one or two more *rather* richer for the Speaker's House, but remember the motto "simplex etc". I shall be able very soon to send you the data for the grand approach through the "Noble Hall of Rufus", by St. Stephen's Porch, St Stephen's Hall, Central Hall, Committee Rooms, Staircase to the great waiting Hall for witnesses, but I think you now have enough to do for some little time to come, notwithstanding your *50 horse power of creation*. Let me hear from you on the receipt of the parcel, and believe me ever,

Yours very faithfully etc
Charles Barry

The tracings comprise the whole of ground floor, principal floor and second floor.

There can be little doubt about the meaning of this letter. Pugin was sent plans for which he was asked to supply drawings of details. The direction about colour means that Pugin was redrawing any sections that were sent and composing others from the information given on the plans.

In response to this letter, Pugin on 10 October 'Sent 3 drawings to Mr Barry £15.15[s.]', and on the 20th 'Sent 5 drawings to Mr B. K.Staircase. Robing Room. Lords 2.' The price of five guineas each for the first three drawings was high: they may have been tinted sections showing internal details. Acknowledging receipt of the second group, Barry wrote again on 22 October.[42]

Being from home yesterday I could not acknowledge, by return of post, the receipt of the drawings of the House of Lords, King's Stairs, etc., which came safely to hand last night, and afforded me a rich treat. They will in all respects answer the purpose most admirably. I can easily imagine the great labour they must have cost you, and, knowing all the difficulties, I cannot but wonder that you have been able to accomplish so much in the time. I am not much surprised to hear your health suffers from excess of application. Do not, however, I beseech you, carry too great a press of sail, but take in a reef or two if you find it necessary in *due time*. I send by this morning's mail a packet containing tracings of the grand public entrance and approach to the Houses and Committee rooms. They are most wretchedly made by a youngster who is as dull and destitute of feeling as the board on which he draws. They will, nevertheless, I have no doubt, afford you all the data you require. The groining and interior generally of the King's or Record Tower Entrance you may make of any design you think proper. You need not be shackled as to height, but the groin should, I think, be concentric with the arch of the opening of the vestibule at the foot of the King's stairs, which you already have. The *design* of this part of the building should, I think, be in a simple and massive character, and a pillar in the centre of the tower must be avoided. I am much flattered by your hearty commendation of the plan, and shall know where to look for a champion if I should hereafter require one. Truly it has cost me many an anxious thought and an extraordinary degree of perseverance.
With many thanks for your glorious efforts in this cause.

Believe me, in haste, dear Sir
Yours most truly etc

The 'difficulties' Barry referred to were the birth of a daughter, Agnes, on 13 October and the angry response which the publication of *Contrasts* (Pl. 57) had evoked. Pugin was evidently also pleading ill-health, but he did not record any in his diary, where he habitually noted even minor indispositions. He was not ill; but he was disturbed by the intemperate response to his book; and he was busy with a vast programme of drawings for the restoration of Holyrood Chapel ordered by Graham. Entries in his diary for 26 and 29 October list no fewer than thirty-four drawings for this project. But then he settled again to Barry's work: 'all week on Mr Barrys drawings', he noted on 5 November. The next day Barry came, and the next entry thereafter is for 12 November: 'Sent 11 drawings to Mr Barry'.[43] A letter from Barry dated only 'November, 1836' seems to refer to this parcel:[44]

My dear Sir,
I am sorry you have had to endure a moment's suspense concerning the safe arrival of the box containing the last *set of exquisite details*, which on my arrival from the country where I have been for the last three days, I have just received. I can only say "Go as you have begun and prosper," for nothing can be more satisfactory than the result of your labours hitherto. Ever yours, most truly, etc.

Then Pugin himself went to London on 26 November to work at Barry's. On the 27th he noted 'for Mr Barry 4 ceilings'; on the 28th, 'Compt. Land front do. Center

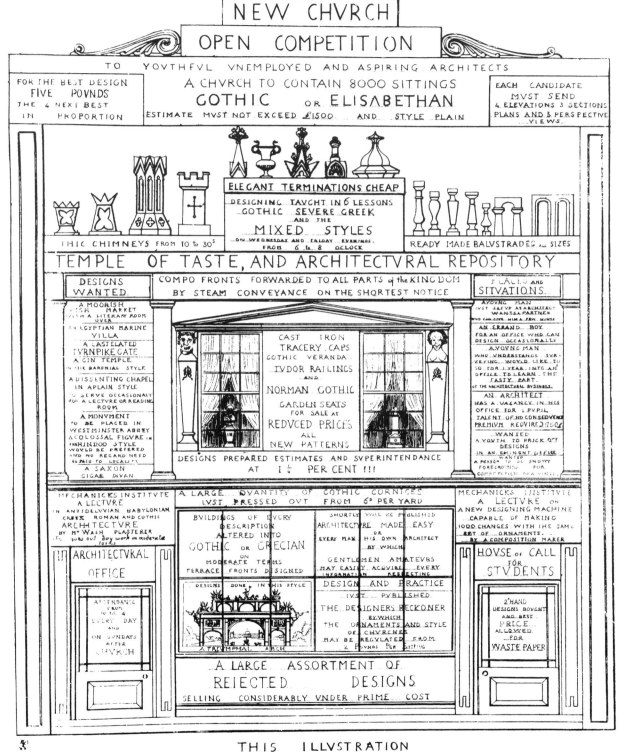

57. A. W. Pugin: *Contrasts* (1836). Dedicatory page, attacking contemporary architectural practices.

front upper part of do.'; on the 29th, 'turrets upper part of return towers'; and on the 30th, 'Commons entrance speakers court entrance'. Then he went into Kent for a few days, and on 5 December 'recommenced at Mr Barry's'. No further details of this work are given in the daily record, doubtless because in the space between November and December is a list entitled 'Drawings done at Mr Barry's'.[45] On 7–9 December Pugin was working on Graham's drawings, and on 21 December he returned to Salisbury. On 28–30 December he was working on the Commons entrance hall, Black Rod's and the Speaker's houses. Then he turned to finishing his book on timber houses as well as the Holyrood Chapel project. Another visit to London followed, when he was working at Barry's for at least part of the time: 'January 9. 1. Compt of new river front began Lodges'. Similar entries follow for the next two days. Then Pugin was ill for three days, and Barry does not reappear until 26 January when Pugin 'returned £10 to Mr Barry'. On the last day of the month he wrote, 'finished at Mr Barry's drawings sent', which suggests he had been at work there on days for which no entries were made. On 4 February he returned home with further orders to execute, for a few days later he 'finished chapel for Mr Barry' and made a list of drawings and etched a plate for him. He and Barry did not meet again until 14 August 1837, and after that Barry disappears from the diary until 1839.

3. The Estimates Drawings

Thus by the end of January 1837 Barry had sufficient drawings ready for a start to be made on the official examination of measurements and quantities. In this task of preparing working drawings, Pugin's assistance had been vital. The quantity surveyor, Hunt, had warned that the drawings alone would take a year, and then it would take him four months to work out the estimate. Now, thanks to Pugin's '50 horse power of creation', months had been saved and as Barry fed in data the examination proceeded.[46] The government surveyors, Chawner and Henry Hake Seward, engaged no fewer than seven assistants, of whom the senior, John Richardson and William Corderoy, gave their services at the specially low rate of 27s.6d. per day. Investigations went beyond a mathematical computation: they queried, for instance, Barry's failure to take cornices and string courses through the walls to form a connecting bond, the slight scantlings of his timber, the lack of iron girders to support the receding parapets of the river front towers and wings, and the inadequate bonding of ashlar and brickwork. The question of a quite small reduction in brickwork was closely investigated. Hunt (as Barry's surveyor) was called in to make a revision with Richardson so that the 'whole underwent a double checque'. In late March consulting Barry almost daily, by early April they had checked the prices and to Barry's estimate of £654,710 for the building had added works valued at £38,300. Barry rejected most of these as unnecessary, but to meet an additional £13,000—principally for wood ceilings and oak wainscoting—he substituted deal for oak joinery in servants' rooms and offices in the residences to be provided for parliamentary officers, as well as reducing the prices for wood and stone carving, which he considered excessive. Finally on 12 April 1837 a figure of £707,104 was agreed, from which £14,000 were deducted for old materials, making the £693,104 that was approved by the Rebuilding Committee. This was exclusive of architect's fee (at the conventional five per cent nearly £35,000), £40,000 for embankment and coffer dam, £70,000 for land purchases, £10,000 for ventilation and warming, and £17,000 for fittings and furnishings, making a total of about £865,000, a figure that for some reason was never put before Parliament.

Barry on 17 April 1837 informed Pugin, to whom he was in debt for drawings, that the government had not yet reached a decision about his 'heavy expenses', and he had not, so far, 'received one farthing'. But matters were looking up, for 'the Board of Works people have finished their examination of my detailed estimate and will report to their superiors tomorrow that they are perfectly satisfied with its accuracy and liberality.'[47] Pugin was politely being asked to wait his turn. Sometime in 1838, according to Alfred Barry, a payment of £120 terminated Barry's debt to Pugin, a total of £229.6s. for the working drawings.[48] For Pugin's part in the first phase of what Barry called 'the great work' he had received in all £494, only £6 short of the prizewinner's award.

There are few surprises in this account of Pugin's participation in the competition and the transformation of an idea into a precise programme in the estimate drawings. The Houses of Parliament have long been attributed to Charles Barry and A. W. Pugin; most historians have used the term collaboration in acknowledgement of Pugin's contribution.

The innuendoes and charges of dishonesty raised in the dispute of 1867–8 posed questions that have never been fully answered. The work Pugin performed after returning to assist Barry in 1844 has also been confused with his earlier, different employment. To the extent that the attribution of the building to him has been queried, Barry's reputation has suffered, whereas Pugin's has been enhanced by the implications of mystery and the exploitation of his talent. The history of the careers of the architects and of the building they together designed must however be based on facts rather than on suppositions, and on definitions of the part each played rather than on the fictitious image of Pugin as the shadow architect whose brilliance Barry appropriated.

Though there were to be innumerable modifications after 1837, the substance of the design for the New Houses of Parliament was established by the drawings for the estimates. The lineaments of the building were refined and its proportions stabilized. Drawings had been prepared for every important exterior and interior part and surface then planned. Barry had worked out techniques for the repetition of standardized details which would reduce the cost and supply the building with the decorative continuity which was one of its attributes.

The history of the making of the Houses, therefore, consists of two parts, the design—1835–7—and construction—from 1838 onwards. To what extent was Pugin responsible for the former?

A first part of the answer to this question lies in the recognition that Pugin drew the competition drawings: but the distinction between *drew* and *designed* must be emphasised. Thanks to the character of the commissioners' training and interests, Pugin's drawings may have had a good deal to do with Barry's success. But their standards of judgement should not be the criteria by which the building as a work of architecture is today appraised. It is to Barry's credit that he had the perception to acquire Pugin as his artistic partner and the strength, as a designer, to marshal and manage his talents so that the decoration never wagged the building. That the commissioners and the public failed to perceive this subtlety is a commentary on their taste rather than on Barry's design.

In the discussion of the estimates drawings and Pugin's role in design at that more advanced stage, the parliamentary block plan (Pl. 58) is of positive assistance. On the plan the rooms were identified in a numbered key by which the terms Barry and Pugin used in the diary and letters may be comprehended today. Starting at the King's (later the Victoria) Tower, then moving along the south front to the east or

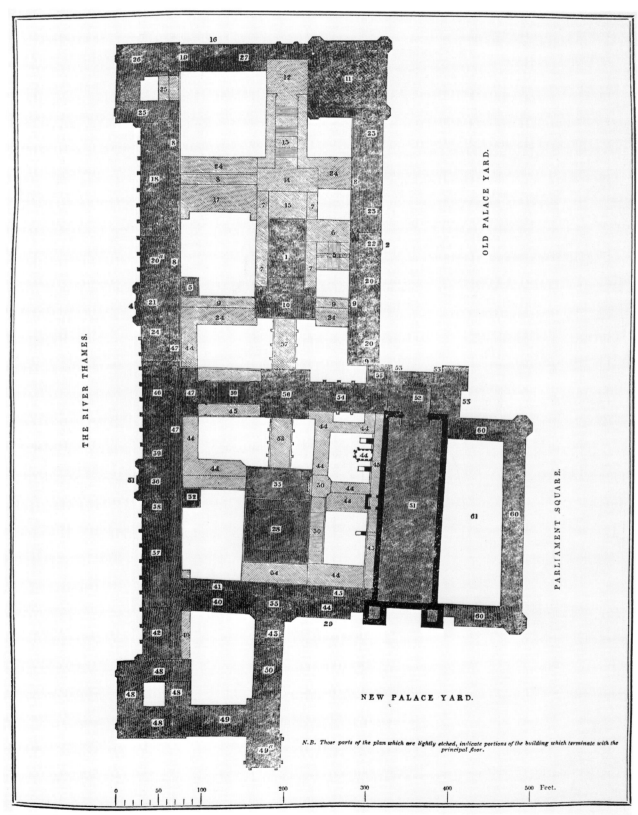

58. Charles Barry: New Houses of Parliament, adopted design, 1836. Block plan of principal floor, showing the leading principles of the arrangement.

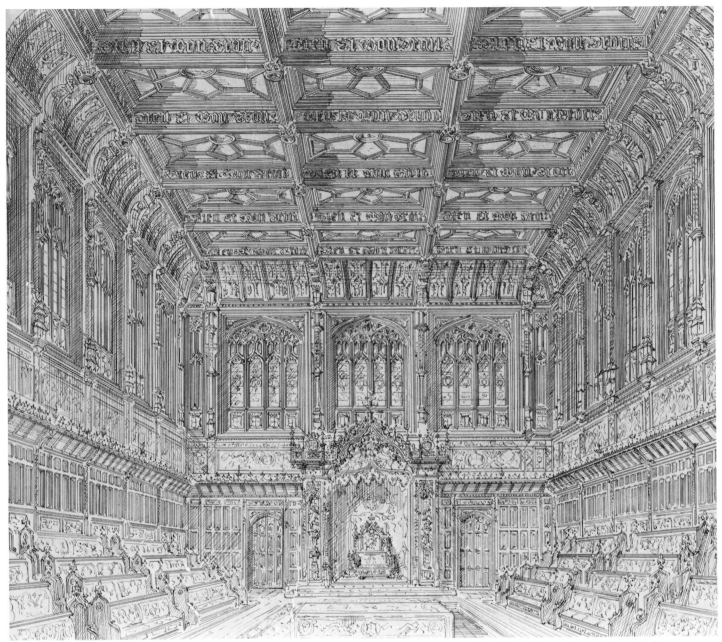

59. The House of Lords: 'Estimates' design. Perspective of the interior, 1836–7, traced by John Gibson from a drawing by A. W. Pugin.

river front, the record shows that Pugin made detailed drawings of the exterior of the Tower, the return and corner towers, compartments of the river front and oriels and the higher central portion. Returning west along the north front, he drew studies for the Clock Tower and the entrance to the House of Commons next to Westminster Hall. Moving past the Law Courts, to Old Palace Yard, he drew a proposal for the south end of Westminster Hall, specimen compartments of the west, land front and the Peers' entrance. This sequence of drawings omits the south curtain between the King's Tower and the river front, and the façades on New Palace Yard. Barry had the prototypes to compose the sweep of building that he envisaged rising from the

60. The House of Commons: 'Estimates' design. Perspective of the interior, 1836–7, traced by John Gibson from a drawing by A. W. Pugin. The square shape was stipulated by the 1835 Rebuilding Committee. Barry later reduced the width.

river. He could handle the remaining façades exactly as the compartments on the river front. This explanation would account for the painstaking trial-and-error and devotion to detail which went into the preparation of the river front compartment designs—done over at least twice, as the diary shows. In allowing Pugin a free hand in the drawings of the King's and lantern towers, Barry was asking for his fullest thought on these important features, knowing that the drawings would serve for the estimates, yet could be worked over and modified later should his suggestions prove too ornate and expensive. What Pugin would design Barry would adapt to practicality. Similarly for the interior Pugin furnished a huge sequence of rich rooms and passage-ways from the King's Entrance in the great tower, up the Royal Stair through the Gallery and Robing Room into the Peers' Chamber. St Stephen's Porch, the Central Hall and the great staircase to the Witness Room formed another suite of public chambers. The designs for the two Chambers prepared by Pugin in 1836 formed the basis of their ultimate appearance. All the subsequent debate about revisions in the Throne design (Pls 80–82), though interesting, merely proves that Barry reworked, or asked Pugin to rework, almost everything before it became architectural fact. Gibson's tracings of Pugin's 1836 drawings for the interiors of the Chambers (Pls 59, 60) are proof of the advanced stage attained in the estimates designs.

Nor were these major ranges of rooms all that Pugin was asked to decorate. The residences of the Speaker and Black Rod, the Lords' Library and Refreshment Room were the subjects of another group of studies. As for the exterior, Pugin prepared enough specimens of the interiors of the principal floor so that the parts he did not draw specifically could be composed. Of the sixty-one identified parts of the principal floor which appear on the block plan, Pugin made drawings for the decoration of all except the corridors, minor rooms such as Committee Rooms, the Librarian's and Housekeeper's residences, messengers' rooms, rooms for the Clerk of the Commons. He did not work on chambers nos. 33–42 in the plan, which were offices and other facilities for the Commons. Once he had established the requirements for comparable rooms for the Lords, estimates could be made without drawings for the Commons' part of the building.

This draft on Pugin's taste and skill for the decoration of complex portions of the interior is impressive, but the careful directions for the design of doors and wall framings which are contained in Barry's letter of 23 September 1836 are, though less spectacular, equally interesting. The corridors and minor rooms were to be enriched only with doors and wall framing. The doors would be chosen from the eight types Pugin was asked to design. Using these patterns the draftsmen in Barry's office could compose those parts of the interior not mentioned by Pugin; the same process would be used for fireplaces, wall-framing, and ceilings.

The conclusion that in making the drawings for the estimates Pugin did, indeed, design the first full set of interior and exterior decorations for the building is unavoidable. Without corroborating evidence it would remain another of those suppositions that have lingered about the history of the Houses of Parliament. However, the many tracings and some drawings in the volumes that James Murray collected in Barry's office, those in the House of Lords and Public Record Offices substantiate the evidence of the diary and the assessment which has been made here.[49]

What had begun, in the preparation of the competition drawings, as a relationship between employer and employee had evolved as the drawings were made into a true collaboration on which Barry relied as he consolidated his idea of the building. The details of the competition design displayed a superb knowledge of late Gothic decoration and a singular ability to compose an original mesh of ornament unlike anything seen previously. In the detailed drawings the design must take positive form: Pugin was then a necessity. To lose the commission then would have been professional disaster.

When on 31 January 1837 Pugin wrote 'finished at Mr Barry's drawings sent'. Barry and he had carried the building another major step forward. There were still great passages that would require further detailed and exacting development. There were, for example, no drawings for metalwork, for carved panels in Pugin's doors, for the details of the brattishing of the woodwork, for the heraldic devices and figures in which the building was to abound, for stained glass, wall coverings, tiles, and carved furniture. Step by step the two men had been drawn by circumstance and their own talents into the quagmire of constructing one of Pugin's imaginary buildings. No one but Pugin could do the decorative part. Only Barry could supply the control of composition, the sense of the whole, the technical knowledge of building without which there could be no building. He, too, would handle the boring business of dealing with government, committees, contractors, and the advisors forced upon him—such as Dr Reid. Pugin could have done none of these things. Nor could he have managed his own talent as Barry did for him.

Contrary to E. W. Pugin's statements, there is nothing in the surviving documents to suggest that Pugin and Barry parted enemies. They appear instead to have drifted apart; Pugin to the development of his own practice, which grew enormously in 1837 and 1838; Barry to the competition for the Reform Club, to Highclere and Trentham, and the preparation of the site at Westminster. The need for further collaboration was years away. Barry had paid Pugin extremely well for the work he had performed. Had he wished, Pugin could have withdrawn from the association after the competition. The charges of dishonesty were made by E. W. Pugin, not by his father; and they came too late for explanations of the creative collaboration which had produced one of the most remarkable buildings of the nineteenth century.

To Pugin the work with and for Barry was of the greatest importance. With it, his architectural practice began. He acquired the opportunity to assist in the construction of his earliest and largest decorative scheme. The Houses of Parliament, completed long after his death, represented to perfection his tastes and decorative capacities as he entered his career. Barry managed to restrain Pugin's ebullience, he provided the building for Pugin to ornament. What Pugin could do alone was to be apparent in the interiors of Scarisbrick Hall, composing rooms which boil with decoration, having none of the prevailing sense of order through repetition and immaculate scale and sound planning which Barry supplied.

4. The Fairy Palace

'C'est un rêve en pierre', said Tsar Nicholas I of Barry's and Pugin's achievement. 'Seen . . . in a fine moonlight, or under certain effects of clouds . . . it is a fairy palace, a marvel of the Thousand and One Nights', remarked a French architect, Lassus, in 1852. Lately, Lord Clark has called the Houses of Parliament 'a triumph of the Picturesque', in the sense that 'no painter can resist them'.[50] We have seen how the design came to realization. We may here properly ask what the relationship of this great work is to the aesthetic and architectural theories of its time. Does it mark the end of one phase of the Gothic Revival, the culmination of a period of picturesque experimentation?[51] Pugin's famous comment—'All Grecian, Sir; Tudor details on a classic body'[52]—springs out of his own view of Gothic as highly articulated forms and implies an acceptance of the Picturesque theory of the irregularity of Gothic architecture such as that expressed by Lassus in complaining of the despotic reign of symmetry. As Hussey pointed out, however, 'Gothic architecture in its complete expressions, is as symmetrical as any other kind . . . Irregularity is not inherent in Gothic.'[53] The New Palace at Westminster is Picturesque in the terms of Hussey's definition: a 'building and design conceived in relation to landscape, whether as a setting, or as the source of certain qualities and features reflected in the architecture.'

One of the tests of the presence of the picturesque is the degree to which frontality has been eliminated. The academic principle of considering a building as made up of one or more façades to be seen from a distance on an axis perpendicular to the plane of the façade, gave way, in the fully developed picturesque, to a desire to have the building seen in the round and from many points of view, from each of which the various masses would compose differently.[54]

The choice of styles, after all, was prescribed on Picturesque principles, because of the vicinity of Hall and Abbey, and of the associative qualities of the styles designated.

Contemporaries were sharply aware that the Houses of Parliament, then closely surrounded by buildings, could be seen only obliquely. There was no Albert Embankment on the opposite shore to provide a frontal view. So each competitor had to submit not one but three perspectives, from viewpoints chosen by Hanbury Tracy, each giving an oblique view (Pl. 26). Competitors were thus guided to construct a Picturesque composition. Barry's composition took specific account of the low-lying site, overlooked by the high-standing Bridge (rebuilt in 1854–62 on a lower curve, as Barry recommended) and dominated by the brooding mass of the Hall (Pl. XI). It was essential to master these features.[55]

Yet a façade of three storeys, 800 ft long, was not a promising prescription. Barry disliked advancing 'the centre of an architectural composition' because he considered the perspective effect was to diminish the apparent size of the building. Here, where he sought grandeur, such an effect must be avoided. Similarly he objected to raising the centre of a façade because that split its unity into three small parts. He preferred 'a central mass with two slightly elevated angles', the form adopted at Westminster, though the length of the front was such that he was obliged to raise the centre. 'If the length of a front was too great for its height he admitted flanking towers', remarked his friend Wolfe. 'These did not destroy the unity of the mass.' To protect the unity of the river front with its small angle towers, at Westminster the great lateral towers were set well back. The design may be regarded as Picturesque in its asymmetry and movement—both in the changing relationship of its own elements, and also as seen in juxtaposition with the towers of the Abbey. 'Care in the grouping of masses and the treatment of the skyline in connection with landscape effects' was highly important here, as Cottingham too realized (Pl. 24), so that the towers, thought

61. Charles Barry: The New Houses of Parliament, adopted design. Perspective of Old Palace Yard front, showing the sovereign's arrival. Water colour signed 'T. P. Neale 1836', handed down in the Barry family.

Barry, had to be 'set in positions where they would form natural and prominent features, without interfering with each other', and so placed that they 'should be seen from their parapet to their base'.[56] The Palace rose cliff-like, too, sheer from the water, another Picturesque feature much admired by Tracy. But bearing in mind the complexities of the site, we may distinguish at Westminster Barry's predilection for 'symmetry, regularity and unity'. After Barry's death, M. Digby Wyatt recalled his insistence on 'the indispensability of symmetrical arrangement, [and] sustained tranquillity of effect obtained through reduplication of similar parts.'[57] This is a quality opposed to that 'variety' distinguished above as one of the basic elements of Picturesque architecture; perhaps derived from Barry's classical grounding, perhaps from his examination of town-halls in the Netherlands, the 'reduplication' was eventually accepted as authentically Gothic even by Pugin.[58] But it was also forward-looking. Aesthetically, the New Palace at Westminster marks a transition; its controlled massiveness, its calculated asymmetry, the stupendous verticality of its great towers, its high roofs, and its all-over ornamentation are characteristic of the Victorian period that was about to open. Yet the Victorians with their obsession about historical styles could regard the Perpendicular Gothic of the Palace as old-fashioned when in the 1850s its features became distinct. Some could see that 'Mr Barry is leaving a grand autograph for posterity to read', and others praised 'the grandeur of the whole and the beauty of the parts', creating an impression 'before which all theories of aesthetics hold themselves in subjection'; or the 'rich beauty of detail and elegance of design' which made the Palace 'unequalled, by any other building in the world'. Yet the same critic could uphold a common objection that 'the extent of florid architecture is too great; that it wearies the eye'.[59] In 1836, however, Members of Parliament could make their own assessment of the projected building's qualities only from the drawings.[60]

VI

Problems of Building in the 1840s

WE have seen how Parliament's caution over Barry's estimate made for delay. Other necessary preliminaries to a start on the New Houses included an embankment, a sewer, clearing sufficient of the site,—and the choice of a good stone, for London's coal-burning had already affected stone buildings. Barry seized Peel's idea of an investigatory commission, and the government appointed him with Sir Henry De la Beche and William Smith, the leading geologists of the day, and Charles Harriott Smith, a distinguished stone carver.[1] During the summer of 1839 they visited many old buildings and quarries. Their attention was focused on limestones for their general uniformity, homogeneity and easy use. On the advice of Professors Daniell and Wheatstone of King's College London, they preferred the most crystalline. Of all those they examined, the magnesian limestone or dolomite of Bolsover Moor and its neighbourhood was, they thought, 'the most fit and proper material to be employed in the proposed new Houses of Parliament.' This stone, they inaccurately believed, had worn well at Southwell Minster, and their recommendations were strongly influenced by the evidence of ancient buildings. Magnesian limestone had in fact been used for Westminster Hall and St Stephen's Chapel since the fourteenth century. Though their choice was not to prove a success, the publication of the commission's researches was hailed as an important advance in building technology.[2]

When, however, the contractors came to sink shafts at Bolsover Moor, they found the stone could only be obtained in small pieces: none was ever used in the Houses of Parliament.[3] C. H. Smith and Barry decided that the search must recommence. Smith went to Yorkshire on the recommendation of the contractors' agent to look at Anston stone, which 'appeared in every respect suitable' and was approved by the other commissioners. But finding a harder stone at a neighbouring quarry, Stones End, they had 'a good many barge loads' sent to London, where it was used in the plinth at either end of the river front. As it proved full of vents (irregular joint-planes involving cleavage of the stone), arrangements were then made to use a more compact and crystalline stone from new quarries at Mansfield Woodhouse, Nottinghamshire. Once again, it proved impossible (perhaps because the quarry was not sufficiently explored) to get large enough blocks for the base moulding of each buttress or for window or door jambs, the best being only 10 cu ft. So resort had finally, after five or six months' delay, to be made to the Duke of Leeds' Anston quarry, where the stone was similar in hardness to the Mansfield Woodhouse, but blocks up to four feet thick could be obtained, the ordinary bed being about 18 inches thick. It was also cheaper.[4]

It was a sad irony that so much effort to select the best stone should have resulted in the choice of one characterized by jointplanes running through the beds, leading inevitably in time to extensive lamination and consequent failure of the stonework. The unmarked stone was frequently not laid in its natural bed, so that decay set in rapidly.[5]

For the interior of the building, softer stones were used. For the exterior walling of the courts, Steetly was originally specified. The contract price for the main building was calculated with Bolsover stone for the outside walls, Steetly for the rest, but 'Norfal' was substituted for the whole of the exterior in the contract. This would appear to be an alternative name for the stone from Anston. For the inside of the Palace, Painswick was specified, but from 1843 Caen stone was used very extensively.[6]

Meanwhile, work had begun on the river embankment on New Year's Day, 1839, in the shelter of a giant coffer-dam. Barry was later criticized for beginning with the river front instead of commencing with the two Houses.[7] This was, however, a logical resolution of the difficulties of building on the partly-occupied site. The work of Parliament was continued all through the building of the new Palace: the Commons sat in the old Lords' Chamber, the Lords in the former Painted Chamber, ancient buildings the walls of which had resisted the fire. The Speaker's House was used for committee rooms for a time, as were parts of the Royal Approach, and near-by houses, too, were hired. Later, temporary rooms were put up in New Palace Yard and the Cloister Court. All these buildings lay towards the Abbey: the river side offered the greatest facility for new building. The vast quantities of materials required could be landed there and stored on the new embankment, itself an essential preliminary to building the river front. This block was to contain the committee rooms, libraries and kitchen services essential to Parliament's smooth functioning. To have built the central block with the two Chambers first would have been more difficult, and the efficient working of the Houses scarcely possible (cp. Pl. 62). The limited area available ruled out the alternative of starting both sectors simultaneously—even had the funds and the work force been available, the men and materials would have got in each other's way. With 700 men on site in 1844, Barry insisted that he was employing as many as practicable, and previously he had complained of the want of space.[8]

The contract for the embankment was won by Messrs John & Henry Lee of Chiswell Street, Lambeth (contractors for a number of churches and for Barry's Travellers' Club), the work to be completed within eight months. Although in November 1837 Lees obtained the second contract, for the foundations of the river front building, they proved unsatisfactory: inexperience in dam-building and casualties among their men were their excuse; but after the closing of the coffer-dam in December 1838 progress was no more rapid. Barry blamed their 'want of proper management and the non-employment of a sufficient number of hands.'[9] Accordingly the advantages of retaining the on-site contractor seemed few. Lump-sum tenders were invited in June 1839 from nine metropolitan general builders for contract no. 3, the carcass of the river front.[10] Although employing twice the usual number of quantity surveyors, these firms found it impossible to prepare their bids in the month allowed. They were reluctant either to assume the quantities or to give in only a schedule of prices; so the Office of Woods and Works extended the time to noon on

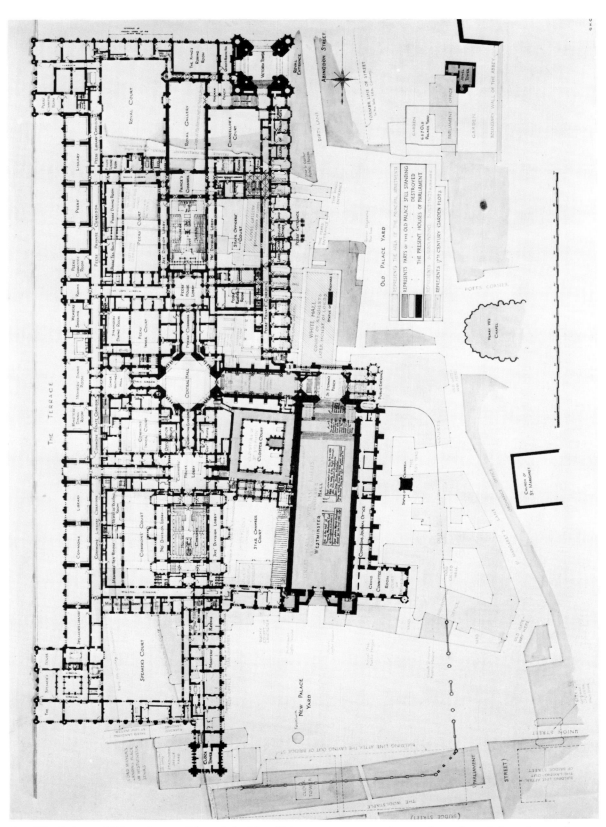

62. The Palace of Westminster: Plan of the New Palace, *c.*1930, superimposed on plan of the palace as it existed in the 18th century.

26 September. It appears that the Commissioners had gone home by that hour: the bids were left unopened till the next day, that of Grissell and Peto arriving an hour late. All were then opened at the same time—except Lees', returned unopened as lacking the required schedule of prices for calculating any variations from the specification—so the Commissioners felt justified in accepting Grissell and Peto's, at £157,615 the lowest for Bolsover stone, though some £9,000 more than Barry's estimate. To bring down the actual cost Barry suggested using a cheaper stone on the less exposed parts.[11]

Grissell & Peto were to have started their operations on 1 January 1840: Lees not having finished, it was agreed that they should take over the whole site progressively, including completion of the second contract. They were to complete their own by 31 March 1843, a date that proved ludicrously unrealistic.[12] Contractors in the end for the larger part of the New Palace, Grissell & Peto were among the greatest of the new entrepreneurial general builders who had emerged in London since the Napoleonic Wars. Successors to their uncle, Henry Peto, whose building of the Custom House had been a notorious scandal during the Regency, they were already employed by the government on the stables at Windsor Castle, the model prison at Pentonville and at Woolwich. Soon they were to be officially employed under Barry simultaneously at Westminster, the government offices (now the 'Old Treasury') in Whitehall, and in Trafalgar Square. The Westminster operations were entirely under the management of Thomas Grissell (1801–74), his partner concentrating on railway construction and retiring from the partnership in 1845 in order to enter Parliament.[13] Impressed by their work and arrangements, Barry recommended in November 1840 that the foundations for the south front and the two Houses should be added to their contract at their scheduled prices—probably lower, he thought, than those obtainable by a new competition. Employing another builder simultaneously would create confusion on site, and Grissell's arrangements could not be matched, argued Barry. Thus contract no. 3, for the river front, was a lump-sum contract (then advocated as an economical way of building), but contract no. 4, for the south front and foundations of the Houses, like Grissell's contracts no. 5 (carcass of the two Houses), no. 6 (public approach and St Stephen's Hall) and no. 9 (continuation of towers to height of 160 ft) was a contract for prices—so the total expenditure would only be ascertained on completion.[14]

The first stone of the superstructure, 'the angle of the plinth of the Speaker's house nearest the bridge', was laid without ceremony by the architect's wife on 27 April 1840.[15] One wonders whether this was to avoid drawing attention to the apparently slow rate of progress. The contract drawings for the river front were not signed until 5 February 1840; but even then Barry's itching pencil, which had already reworked the front in 1838, had to revise the design, so that new contract drawings were dated between 5 and 13 January 1841 (Pls 63, 64).[16] The effect of this revision was to re-introduce a horizontal emphasis by means of continuous bands of panelling and lettering extending across the bays, which in the earlier design had been to a much greater extent self-contained units demarcated by the strong vertical accent of polygonal turrets. These turrets had themselves replaced the original buttresses, a change which Alfred Barry explained as intended to 'elevate and break the skyline, and . . . relieve the flatness of the front . . . The "castellated" form [given in 1836] necessarily disappeared at once, the parapet became subordinate . . . an upward tendency was given to the whole.' Such enlivening of the skyline appealed to contemporary taste. The new alterations however created an ambiguous reticulation over the whole façade. A feature of Barry's aesthetic theory that may be observed here is the

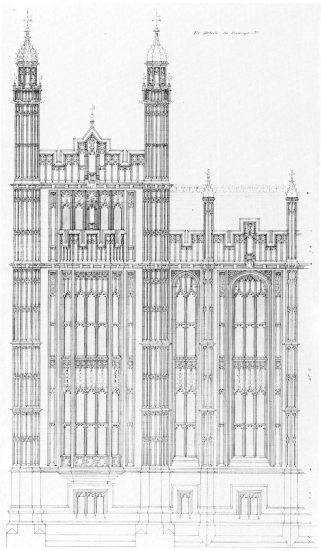

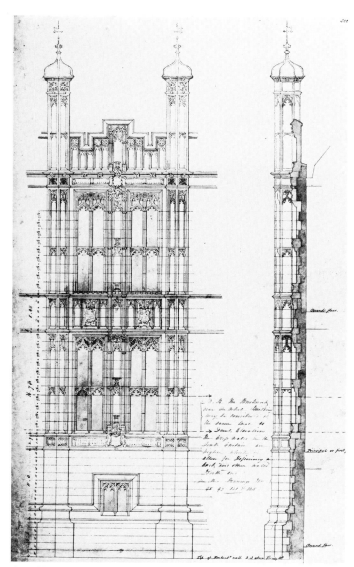

63. Charles Barry: New Houses of Parliament, contract drawings. Part of detail elevation of North and South Wings of the River Front. Dated '5/2/40' and signed by the contractors, T. Grissell and S. M. Peto, and by four quantity surveyors.

64. Charles Barry: New Houses of Parliament, revised contract drawings. Part of elevation of North Return of South Wing of the River Front. Dated '5th Jany 1841'. Note the emphasised horizontality of this version, compared with Pl. 63, as well as the alterations in the battlements and the termination of the buttresses.

progressive enrichment of a façade proportionately to its height above ground;[17] to this richness the high roofs (a feature of the Birmingham school, too) that made their appearance in the first set of contract drawings also contributed.

With the commencement of the building proper there came what was to prove the worst of the architect's many problems: that of ventilation.[18] The temporary House of Commons' ventilation was directed by Dr David Boswell Reid (1805–63), a teacher of chemistry from Edinburgh (Pl. 142). In October 1839, with building about to begin, Barry asked Lord Duncannon, head of the Woods and Works, to appoint a practical engineer 'to direct, superintend, and be responsible for the proper execution of all the works that may be requisite in carrying out the details of the system that may be agreed upon.'[19] Barry also notified Reid, whom he regarded as a theoretician. But Reid saw his chance and pushed, hastening to Ireland to see Duncannon, who— unfortunately for all concerned—placed the ventilation of the New Palace entirely in Reid's hands from 1 April 1840 until the end of the first session after the occupation of both Houses. This was subject only to an instruction to defer to the architect in respect of 'either the solidity or the architectural character' of the building.[20] Barry had warned Duncannon that Reid did 'not profess to be thoroughly acquainted with the practical details of building and machinery', and he was subsequently found to be unable to read architectural plans and drawings. This lack of skill, coupled with his inability to make up his mind, his megalomaniac demands and his readiness to take offence, made it impossible that he should prove a satisfactory colleague, and by 1845 Barry was refusing to communicate with him save in writing.

Though Reid was to cause prolonged delays in the great work, slow progress was in part due to Government and to Parliament itself. Parliamentary decisions—over Works Department opposition—to give residences to several parliamentary officers obliged Barry to make several changes in his plan.[21] Then, faced in 1841 with an estimate of £65,000 for the ventilating system and another £21,000 for a fire-proof floor between the principal and upper storeys, Melbourne's ministry, clinging to office and financially in deficit, referred the proposals to a select committee in the hope that they would be rejected. Meanwhile Barry was allowed to put in stronger foundations. After a general election brought Peel to power a further committee decided in 1842 that Reid's scheme should be tried as an experiment. This entailed erecting a central tower as a great chimney for both vitiated air and smoke from open fires, i.e. as a purely functional addition. Barry made it also an ornamental addition, designing it as a spire to contrast with the lateral towers, placed over the Central Hall (Pl. 71). His first design had something of a Gothick quality (Pl. 65); a loftier version of 1846 resembled Wren's pagoda-like spire in the Warrant Design for St Paul's, or perhaps that of Brussels Town Hall; the form finally built, with inner dome and outer cone, may also have been inspired by Wren's construction at St Paul's.[22]

Yet another factor in delay was a masons' strike that began in October 1841, breaking up the skilled force of some 220 men already employed at Westminster.[23] Barry estimated its effect as a six-week delay, but its repercussions were felt for a longer period. It was caused by a dispute between the masons and Grissell's blunt Derbyshire foreman, George Allen.[24] Known even as a journeyman for 'a proud and overbearing disposition', Allen acquired a bad reputation for giving workmen the rough side of his tongue, sacking them on the least provocation. Masons were said to have struck against him at Birmingham in 1837, and this may have been the root of the strike that began at Westminster in September 1841, for the masons were said all to be members of the Birmingham Union of Masons. Another underlying factor was a dispute over supplying beer, and even water, to the men on site. Allen was a martinet, but his men 'had minds too enlightened to be brought under anything like the discipline of an army.' He saw himself as a defender of the laissez-faire principle, resisting union attempts to limit the rate of output. The men saw it differently; one recounted how Allen

kept the men working about small jobs, until he had as many stones up as would enable all to work regularly on, all round the building, calculating that by this arrangement, the men being spirited, would work against each other, and makes slaves of themselves to enrich the masters; but the men, with but few exceptions, resolved not to do so, yet, a few were such fools as to work like horses to beat their fellow-workmen. These got their work done sooner, and Allen when he found this resolved to compel the other workmen to work at the same rate; he there-fore 'sacked' a number who had not produced the same quantity, and bullied and blustered about the works.

The mass of the masons resolved to fine the 'chasers', those who worked too fast:

65. Charles Barry: An early design for the Central Tower, 1842. Pencil drawing.

'they did not mind a reasonable difference in the quantity . . . they only wished to restrain that excessive spirit of rivalry'—though according to another version, a 'chaser' was fined five shillings for finishing his work roughly and failing to put a head mark on it. Allen threatened to discharge a hundred men, so they struck work.

A self-justificatory letter from Allen received wide publicity.[25] He declared that after searching inquiry into the men's allegations his employers 'were fully satisfied that the bitter persecution of me by the Union arose from my bringing before them the limitation of the amount of labour by the Unionists . . . I will never submit myself to a system which levels the good man with the bad.' But Cubitt's foreman, who gave work to some of the strikers, asked another foreman from the Houses of Parliament for his view: 'He said that there was no question as to their being perfectly justified in striking against him; they would never have done it if Allen had conducted himself as a man ought to do.' The strike was soon joined by other masons working for Grissell, at Woolwich and on Nelson's Column, and it even spread to the Cornish granite quarries. Nationwide support was expressed in workmen's resolutions, often accompanied by cash.

'Necessary severity is often mistaken for tyranny.' Grissell, a believer in strict discipline, backed his foreman, and advertised all over the country for '150 good hard-stone masons'. The strikers alleged that he had to employ 'butchers, shoemakers, and others, merely to keep up an appearance, in order to hoodwink the Commissioners of Woods' (who supported him), and that the great majority of the blacklegs were paid only 3s.6d. per day—itself a comment on their capabilities when the rate for a trained mason was five shillings. 'They have been several nights seen engaged in taking down work which the architect had condemned', reported one paper in February 1842.

Of the strikers, many soon found employment in London, others further afield. The strike committee was wound up at the end of May 1842 and the score then without work given a small cash bonus. Although unsuccessful in its object, the strike did not collapse. It may even have had some success in curbing Allen's harshness.

*   *   *

To manage successfully the increasing specialization that flowed from the growing complexity of knowledge, and to exploit the possibilities offered by industrialization for the execution of works on a new scale of magnitude, an architect needed to develop a new quality of office organization. By 1835 Charles Barry was already a successful architect whose 'lucrative practice' required the support of a staff and attracted pupils. His chief assistant was Robert Richardson Banks. In mid-1835, with the competition looming up, Barry took as a pupil John Gibson, who remained until 1844. Immediately after obtaining the 'great work', he engaged W. Wright: as 'superior clerk of the staff employed . . . to get out the working drawings of the New Houses', Wright prepared from Barry's drawings 'detail workings, drawings [sic], plans, sections, and elevations to the same scale as his own'.[26] Edward Pugin later suggested that Wright was the youngster 'dull and destitute of ability' for whose wretched drawings Barry had apologized to his father; but Barry's articled clerk, William Hayward Brakspear, engaged in June 1836, is another contender for that distinction.[27] We find the office staff augmented to handle the prize commission, but Barry himself always in close control.

In August 1839 Frederick Humphrey Groves succeeded Wright, remaining as superintendent of the office and works at Westminster until April 1845. Under him on the site he soon had three 'practical' clerks of the works, Paulby (d.1846), Lowry and Parsons, for Barry divided the work into three sections (as Nash had done in rebuilding Buckingham Palace). Groves himself inspected the works daily or even twice a day, spending the rest of his time in the office making out drawings to be issued to the contractors. When work started on the river front, Barry again increased his office staff, his son Charles (who acted as his confidential secretary) and George Somers Clark both joining him in 1840. For his first three years Clark was Barry's amanuensis. Octavius Barrett was a draughtsman at this time who, like Clark and

James Murray, made his own collection of office drawings. Without this highly organized staff, progress on the works could not have been maintained.[28]

The change from a lump-sum contract to a contract at agreed prices for the south front obliged Barry to measure the work done before making up the accounts. This required skills superior to those of ordinary clerks of works, and Barry employed first Banks and then added T. H. Webster (1841) and Alfred Meeson (1844), paying them up to £200 *p.a.* from his own pocket in addition to their official salaries. Webster headed the on-site hierarchy until his death from cholera in July 1849, when his place was filled by R. Quilter. The precise relationship, however, with the superintending clerk of the works is not clear. When F. H. Groves resigned in April 1845 to set up his own surveying practice, he was succeeded by Meeson (described by Charles Barry jr in 1857 as 'long my father's chief assistant in his office'), a trained engineer on whose skills Barry leaned heavily, and who probably could not long be spared for routine duties. At any rate, he handed over his supervisory duties on 30 September 1846 to Thomas Quarm, 'chief superintendent at the building', who also worked on measuring. 'No one', said Quarm, 'could give instruction to any one on the building unless it came through myself.' He retained his position until the end of 1860, when he was succeeded by Daniel Ruddle, 'assistant to Sir C. Barry' and author of the text to E. N. Holmes' *Illustrations of the new Palace at Westminster*. Meanwhile Edward Middleton Barry, Sir Charles's second son, had joined the office in place of his brother, who in 1847 set up his own architectural practice in partnership with R. R. Banks. An office clerk who was promoted to be a measuring clerk of works in 1849 was J. Strudwick. Among the office staff under Quarm in the 1850s were Edward C. Pressland, who joined in 1852 to work on the Old Palace Yard front, and P. G. Smith.[29] Meeson took over responsibility for the heating and ventilation of the Palace for a time upon the dismissal of Reid in 1852.

Much light is thrown on Barry's problems by the inquiries conducted in the 1840s by select committees. While the Commons' temporary accommodation was generally comfortable enough, the temporary House of Lords was inconvenient and often hot. Barry had not known of an undertaking to give the Lords priority; but fortuitously site difficulties had resulted in the Lords' Chamber being a twelvemonth in advance of the Commons.[30] Criticism in the Upper House led to the appointment of a committee in March 1843, by which time the river front should have been finished, whereas the roof was not even begun. Barry reported that with a wooden instead of a plaster ceiling and with temporary fittings, the Lords' Chamber might be made ready for the session of 1844. He was very much of an optimist, and the hopes he held out were delusory. Indeed, no special effort was made to complete the Lords, because the committee's report was not communicated to the government. Meeting again in their narrow Chamber for the 1844 session, the Lords appointed a new committee which examined Barry on 21 March, 26 April, 29 April, 2 May and 6 May. During its investigations, Lord Sudeley (the former Hanbury Tracy), aided by a plan published in the *Illustrated London News* (Pl. 66), brought to light changes in the Royal Approach that Barry had made on his own responsibility without consulting any authority. Sudeley particularly objected to an unbroken flight of 25 or 26 steps on the Royal Stair (Pl. 110), and to the Queen's Robing Room being separated from the Lords' Chamber by the Victoria Gallery, which was raised to the same height to the detriment of the light and air of the Chamber (Pl. 67).[33] The peers in general, however, were more disturbed by Barry's making alterations without specific authority. His claim to 'the privilege of an artist, to work up his ideas as he goes along, to touch and retouch where he considers it necessary, and to improve upon his first

THE NEW HOUSES OF PARLIAMENT.

We here present to our readers the plan of the principal floor of the New Houses of Parliament, as now definitively decided on for completion. The original bears the signature of the architect; and we are assured that no deviation will be made from this arrangement.

1. Earl Marshal
2. Sealer
3. Dressing room
4. Lord Chancellor's office
5. Messengers' room
6. Lord Chancellor
7. Dressing room
8. Clerk of Parliament
9. Peers' robing room
10. Dressing room
11. Chairman of committee
12. Secretary's room
13. Counsel room
14. Unopposed committee room
15. Select committee room
16. Doorkeeper
17. Royal staircase
18. Parliament office stairs
19. Court
20. Cabinet room
21. Housekeeper
22. Deputy Speaker
23. Members' stairs
24. Court
25. Proxy room
26. Dress room
27. Yeoman Usher
28. Staircase
29. Vote office
30. Peer's private corridor
31. Private room
32. Waiting room
33. Clerk of Parliament

34. Clerk assistant
35. Witness room
36. Witness room
37. Witness room.
38. Master in Chancery
39. Witness Room
40. Counsel
41. Ventilating office
42. Messenger
43. Waiting room
44. Clerk's office
45. Lord Great Chamberlain's room
46. Lord Great Chamberlain's dressing room
47. Writing room
48. Ante room
49. Archbishops room
50. Bishops room
51. Reading room
52. Doorkeeper's dressing room
53. Peers terrace stairs
54. Refreshment room
55. Office
56. Office
57. Office
58. Sergeant at Arms
59. Witnesses waiting room
60. Witnesses waiting room
61. Doorkeeper's room
62. Public petitions
63. Public petitions
64. Messenger
65. Copying office

66. Public stairs to committee rooms
67. Stationery room
68. Messenger
69. Black Rod's dining room
70. Black Rod's stairs
71. Witness in Chancery
72. Court
73. Librarian's stairs
74. Librarian's ante-room
75. Black Rod's drawing room
76. Black Rod's library
77. Librarian's drawing room
78. Refreshment
79. Public courts
80. Clerk of Committees
81. Passage
82. Clerk's office
83. Examiner and Speaker's court
84. Clerk's office
85. Examining office
86. Clerk of private bills
87. Examining office
88. Court
89. Public office for Deputy Inspector of Plans
90. Engrossment office
91. Commons private entrance
92. Messenger
93. Cloak room
94. Clerk's office
95. Vote office
96. Court
97. Refreshment

98. Chaplain
99. Secretary
100. Trainbearer
101. Speaker's official room
102. Court
103. Store room
104. Messenger's lobby
105. Committee clerks
106. Committee Clerks
107. Private bills
108. Doorkeeper's room
109. Clerk's office
110. Commons terrace stairs
111. Court
112. Sitting room
113. Dining room
114. Tower
115. Clerk of the House—dining room
116. Clerk of the House—study
117. Clerk of the House—drawing room
118. Librarian's residence—drawing room
119. Librarian's residence—study
120. Librarian's residence—dining room
121. Librarian's residence—bed room
122. Air shaft
123. Messenger
124. Gallery
125. Offices for votes and proceedings of the House
126. Division room
127. Speaker's room
128. Clerk assistant
129. Clerk assistant
130. Clerk assistant
131. Clerk assistant
132. Deputy Sergeant
133. Refreshment
134. Business room
135. Dining room
136. Drawing room
137. Speaker's staircase
138. Writing room
139. Writing room
140. Drawing room
141. Library
142. Speaker's gentleman's room
143. Waiting room

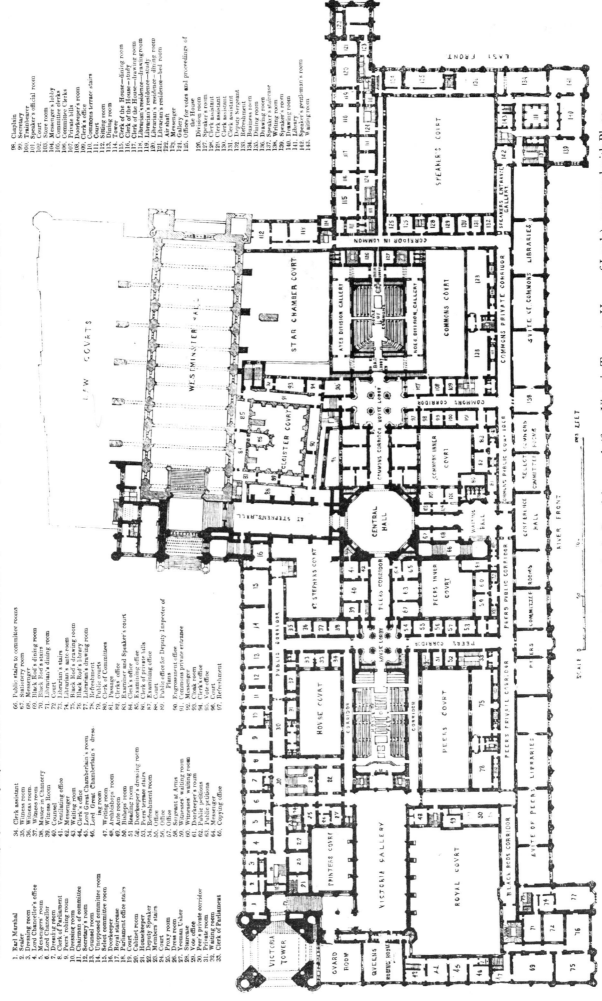

66. The Houses of Parliament: Plan of principal floor, 1843. Note the alterations in the Royal Approach (from Victoria Tower to House of Lords), compared with Pl. 33.

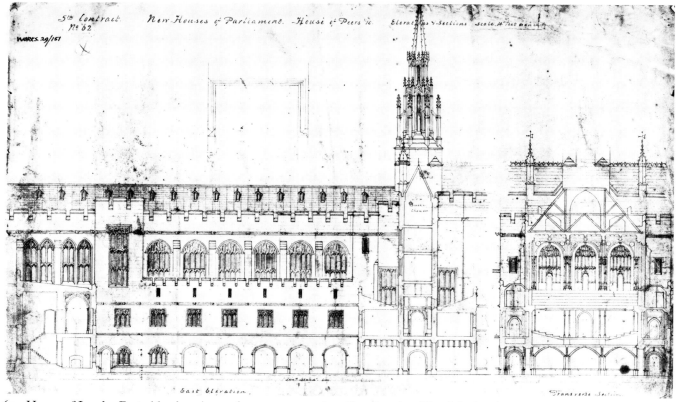

67. House of Lords: East side elevation and transverse section. Pen drawing 'No. 62', dated 12 June 1844, showing window of transverse corridor at the end of the Royal Gallery next the Lords' Chamber, as in Pl. 66.

68. House of Lords: East side elevation. Pen and wash drawing, dated 4 July 1844 and annotated 'This Drawing supersedes No. 62 June 12th 1844'. This shows the introduction of three low 3-light windows, marking the Prince's Chamber, inserted by Barry between the Royal Gallery and the Lords' Chamber in response to criticism from Lord Sudeley and other peers.

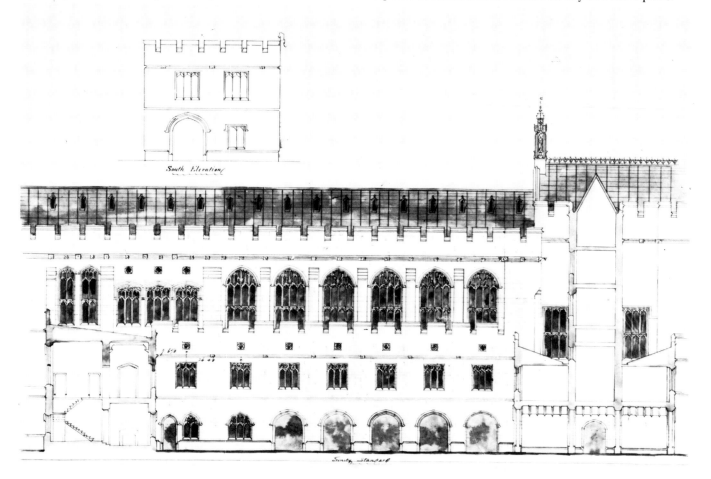

ideas, instead of being tied down to them too strictly', which had been asserted, in effect, in his 1843 report to the Fine Arts Commission, had won support in the professional press, but was unpalatable to these clients.[34]

In consequence of the Lords' criticisms Barry stopped the works. After discussions with ministers and Prince Albert he compromised with his critics, substituting the small 'Prince's Chamber' for a passage-way across the Gallery, next to the Lords' Chamber (Pls 67, 68). He was supported powerfully by Peel, who told Sudeley: 'My own opinion is decidedly in favour of the Victoria Gallery being appropriated to the encouragement of the Art of painting—and to such an arrangement of the Royal Robing Room as shall enable the Sovereign to pass through the Victoria Gallery direct to the House of Lords in the Robes of State.'[35] Barry's excision of an elaborate spire proposed above the Lords' Lobby was doubtless an economy consequent upon the alterations. But this explanation does not serve for revisions in the design of the north elevation of the Royal Court (Pl. 69).[36] Barry could not leave his designs alone, even in those parts hidden from public gaze.

More important than these changes in detail was a modification of the general plan. In his original competition plan (Pl. 33) Barry ranged the central spine containing the two Chambers parallel to Westminster Hall. In his revised plan (Pl. 58) the spine was slightly angled to the Hall. Between 1836 and 1842 he shifted the spine again, making it parallel to and nearer to the river front so as to make the courts more regular and more equal throughout, and shorten the route from the Chambers to the refreshment and committee rooms (Pl. 66). In his interior planning, by sacrificing grand stairs and unnecessary passages, he succeeded in providing 'great additional accommodation' in the same space. In elevation the two Chambers no longer stood above the other buildings but formed part of a continuous range (Pls 68, 71). In 1843 he proposed extensive additions, enclosing New Palace Yard and hiding the discordant bulk of Westminster Hall (Pl. 70).[37] At the same time he had been re-elaborating his external façades. In 1844 he exhibited two general views at the Academy: 'Sculptural decoration, niches, canopies, figures, devices, and armorial bearings have been unsparingly applied, where nothing of the kind was originally "proposed".' Additional towers had shot up, and if Utility might justify the central ventilating tower, this was not true of a clock tower 'when almost every mechanic carries a watch in his pocket'.[38]

Of authorised changes introduced by Barry the most important related to the ventilation (notably the central tower) and to providing storage for the public records. The legal records were scattered in repositories spread across London, and there was considerable pressure for better care and easier public access.[39] Barry had from the outset intended his great 'King's Tower' for the records of Parliament, including the great collection of original Acts, stored principally in the Jewel Tower of the old Palace. Warned of great fire risks to which the legal records were exposed, Melbourne's government saw the cheapest solution in transferring them all to Barry's fireproof building. There was talk of storing them in the basements or in the roof spaces, but the Master of the Rolls, their official custodian, objected; so it was determined to raise the great tower another fifty feet to take the judicial records.[40]

The Lords' concern at slow progress and unauthorised changes spread to the Commons, who in May 1844 appointed their own committee, chaired by Lord Lincoln (Pl. 72), First Commissioner of Woods and Works.[41] This was probably designed to rescue Barry from the hot water into which he had tumbled. It contained, however, Members who 'showed that they acted with great suspicion'

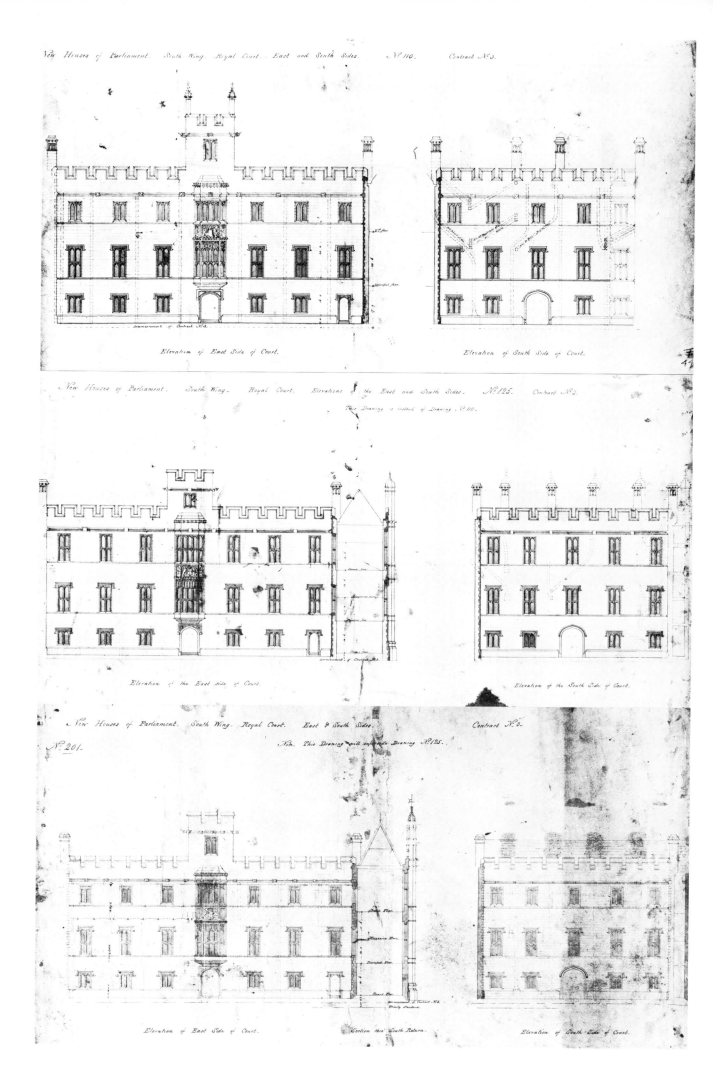

New Houses of Parliament. South Wing. Royal Court. East and South Sides. Nº 110. Contract Nº 3.

Elevation of East Side of Court.

Elevation of South Side of Court.

New Houses of Parliament. South Wing. Royal Court. Elevations of the East and South Sides. Nº 125. Contract Nº 3.

This Drawing is instead of Drawing Nº 110.

Elevation of the East side of Court.

Elevation of the South Side of Court.

New Houses of Parliament. South Wing. Royal Court. East & South Sides. Contract Nº 3.

Nº 201.

Note. This Drawing will supersede Drawing Nº 125.

Elevation of East Side of Court.

Section thro' South Return.

Elevation of South Side of Court.

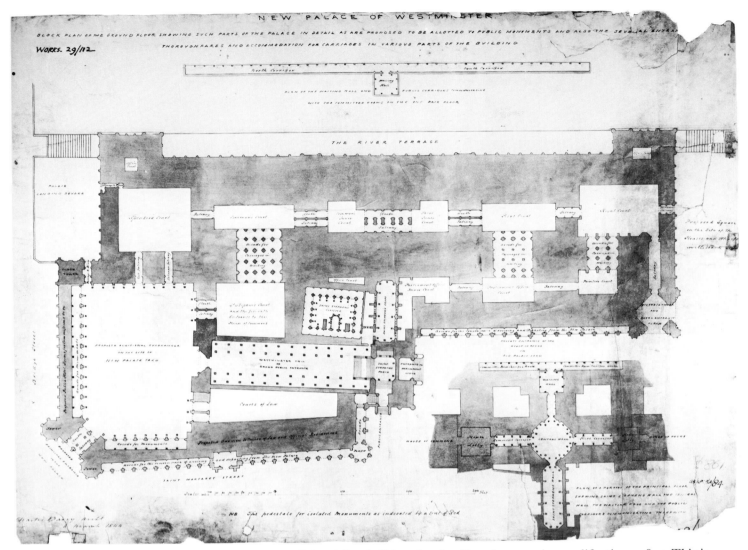

69. (left) Royal Court: Elevations of East (Black Rod's) and South Sides, showing Barry's successive modifications, 1844. This is typical of the elevations of the internal courts throughout the Palace.

70. (above) Charles Barry: New Palace of Westminster. Plan dated 4 March 1844, showing additional buildings around New Palace Yard, proposed by Barry in 1843; and the parts he proposed to allot to public monuments.

towards him. Only after 'a most minute examination' (on four occasions in June and July) did they exonerate the architect for making alterations without specific authority.[42] 'Looking to the misapprehension that appears to have prevailed as to these proceedings hitherto', their report recommended that Barry should in future make a half-yearly report to the Commissioners of Woods, and should submit to that Board any proposed alterations, with plans.[43] The total cost of the building was to be re-estimated. They warned that an early occupation of offices or committee rooms (Pl. 73)—urgently needed as parliamentary business increased—might impede the satisfactory completion of the whole; it was clear that arrangements for ventilation could not be ready before 1847 anyway. But a rapid increase in business, notably the great wave of railway bills, made the need for better accommodation urgent. Nineteen committee rooms in the river front were pressed into use, partly finished, in the exceptionally busy session of 1846.[44]

An important principle discussed in the committee was the nature of the authority Government should exercise over the architect. Lord Lincoln, Conservative head of the Office of Woods and Works, differed from Lord Bessborough (formerly Duncannon), his Whig predecessor. Lincoln, a firm Barry supporter, regarded his

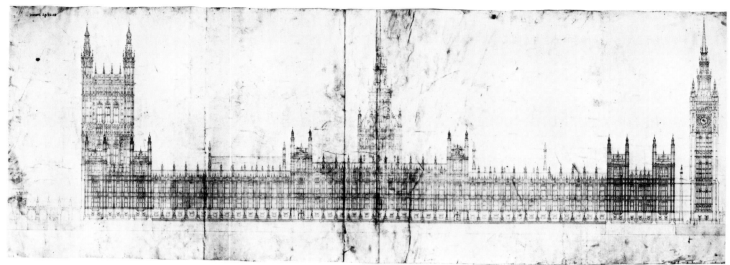

71. Charles Barry: New Palace of Westminster. Design after addition of a Central Tower for the purposes of Reid's ventilation scheme, 1842. At this early stage, the Lords' and Commons' Chambers were still free-standing. All three towers were modified in execution, and the Chambers connected at roof level with their adjoining buildings.

own duty as 'wholly ministerial', merely superintending the 'conduct and execution' of contracts and requiring from the architect only an estimate of any increased expense resulting from proposed alterations:[45]

The plans for the new Houses of Parliament having a special regard to those bodies which are supposed to be interested, namely, the Members of the two Houses, having been sanctioned by them in the first instance, and laid before them at subsequent periods, when alterations were suggested by the Committees of the two Houses, stand in a totally different position from other public buildings, with the details of which Parliament [he stated inaccurately] has in no instance interfered.

Lincoln expressed a laissez-faire philosophy of administration: let the expert have a free hand to get on with the job that he knows more about than any minister or civil servant can. Lincoln declared that as First Commissioner, 'I neither did, nor conceive I ought, to have exercised any official cognizance or control over those alterations in architectural detail which have not entailed any additional expense on the public.' He explicitly rejected any analogy with a private individual employing his own architect, and repudiated the notion that he was 'to exercise a control of architectural taste and design over the architect who is selected to carry this national building into execution'.[46]

I conceive [he remarked] the position of a private gentleman with reference to his own house, and the position of an officer of Government with reference to a national building, to be so dissimilar, that it is impossible to compare them or to guide one's conduct by one case with reference to the other; . . . my opinion is, that it would tend neither to the advantage of the building nor to the public service, that either any Commissioner of Woods, or I will go further, any Member of either House of Parliament, who conceives himself to be as good an architect as Mr Barry, should interfere in these matters in details of taste . . . It is possible that a better architect than Mr Barry may be found, but Mr Barry has been employed by the Legislature itself, . . . and I hope that no Committee of the House of Commons will sanction any interference . . .[47]

72. Lord Lincoln, MP (1811–64), later 5th Duke of Newcastle, First Commissioner of Woods and Works 1841–6, detail from a drawing by G. Richmond, 1856.

Lord Bessborough, on the other hand, held a low view of architects: a contract was intended to bind architect as well as builder; he was to report any alteration, and was precluded from making any without obtaining written authority from the Commissioners.[48]

Despite Lincoln's efforts the committee naturally asserted the principle of responsibility: the ordinary back-bencher readily accepted the analogy of a private gentleman and his house as the criterion appropriate for public works. The architect must refer alterations to the Office of Woods and Works; the First Commissioner could answer in Parliament for his Board's decisions.[49] The extent to which ministerial intervention should be carried still remains contentious, however.

Meanwhile, after further examinations of Barry on 21 May and 6 August 1844, and of Grissell, Reid and Lord Lincoln, the Lords' Committee had made a second report:[50] works on the House of Lords should be 'advanced with the greatest possible speed', but temporary fittings should not be used. The state rooms apart, the interior should be completed in 'the most simple and solid manner consistent with the character of the general building' by April 1845. Some censure of Barry was implied rather than uttered for his failure to hasten the work. But the Treasury, heeding the Commons' committee and the architect, decided against trying to

complete the Lords by 1845, though it was to be pushed on with all practicable speed. Though Barry had announced that henceforth he would make no alteration of any kind without the previous written authority of the Woods and Works, Lincoln declined to exercise 'any control in matters of architectural criticism over Mr Barry which may have the effect of relieving him from that responsibility which . . . ought to attach to the architect.'

The newly-established professional press supported Barry in his struggle for power. 'We think he was perfectly right', declared the *Civil Engineer and Architect's Journal*, on the basis of the reports of 1844. 'He was substantially right in reserving to himself the conception and execution of the details.' His proposition that 'all great undertakings are best accomplished under an undivided responsibility' was 'almost incontrovertible'. The *Builder* thought that had he been an older man who felt more firm in his position, Barry would have withstood the Lords' pressure for earlier completion: he had neither wasted time nor spared effort.[51]

In such a work as the Houses of Parliament, every superficial yard demands the closest thought, and requires as many detailed drawings as for the whole of an ordinary dwelling-house. Every ornament, every moulding, every line, must be produced and delineated; and over all these does Mr Barry's own pencil pass. An architect careless of his reputation may get through any amount of work, *by deputy*; but if determined to execute it to the best of his power, strive as he may, he can only produce a certain quantity, and we will venture to say that the architect of the Houses of Parliament finds little time for other occupations or recreation from early on Monday morning till late on Saturday night. The wear and tear must be immense . . . We do not ourselves wish to throw any blame on Dr Reid; the whole is an experiment . . . but it is too bad that an architect's operations should be suspended, his designs altered, and his views interfered with; and then that he should be blamed for what has been done against his will.

Similarly, Barry enjoyed the support of the comparatively mass-circulation illustrated press. The *Illustrated London News* hailed him as 'the only directing mind in the whole business . . . the only fixed point', and condemned the inadequacy of his remuneration. In the daily press, *The Times* supported the architect somewhat coolly until 1847–8, reserving its passion for sustained attacks upon Reid, a quack, an 'aerial Guy Fawkes' capable of blowing up Parliament. 'It would be fearful indeed if Mr Barry should give in to Dr Reid's ventilating whimsies.' Later, *The Times* became almost lyrically pro-Barry. Both men were butts for the wit of *Punch*, but Reid afforded the more amusing target (Pls 74, 75).[52]

It was when the internal arrangements of the new House of Lords had to be settled that the difficulties with the ventilator had come to a head. Differences between him and Barry caused significant delays from April 1845. Pugin was privately telling the metal manufacturer Hardman that they would 'have another year for the House of Lords', though warning him: 'this is quite secret and only my supposition'.[53] Early in the following year these differences halted work on the House. Yet another select committee heard Barry and Reid on 23 February, and later other experts in ventilation.[54] Barry complained that Reid would not produce drawings of his requirements; Reid, that the architectural drawings were not adequate for his purposes. 'If I [said Reid] had complete plans of what was intended, and of such modifications as might be made, then I would shape my system without any communication with the architect.'[55] That cannot have helped matters. Then three summer nights of fierce debate on the repeal of the Corn Laws brought the peers to the pitch of exasperation with the ventilator, whom they grilled on

14 August 1846. The whole history of the dispute, with its unsuccessful reference to an arbitrator, Joseph Gwilt, was related to the committee.

Gwilt (1784–1863), author of a respected *Encyclopaedia of Architecture*, reported that: 'for want of detailed drawings, such as are usually furnished by ventilators, an extraordinary number of flues have been introduced into the building, whereby it has been rendered less solid.' It was 'the impolicy . . . of having two separate directors of works independent of each other, on the building' that had produced delays. He suggested leaving the air conditioning to Barry, assisted by a specialist of his choice.[56]

The *Builder* thought the evidence gave 'an additional and heavy blow to the doctor's system'.[57] The committee agreed: having first laid all round them with a brush heavily laden with criticism, they reported that Reid's scheme was 'the only impediment to the preparation of the new House of Lords, for the commencement of the session of 1847' (*Third Report*). They recommended accepting Barry's offer to carry out the ventilating and warming of the new House.

Simultaneously the Commons had been conducting their own inquiry.[58] Satisfied, more or less, with their spacious temporary chamber, they were always readier than the Lords to give Reid the benefit of the doubt, though *The Times* complained of stifling heat in June 1845, and reported, 27 May 1846, that 'a disinclination to take any more of the draughts he prescribes was visible from the manner in which the allusion to his system was received in the House of Commons.' The first report of the Commons' committee (1 April) suggested arbitration. Lord Lincoln appointed three experts—Robert Stephenson, Andrew Graham and Michael Faraday: but Reid proved as hostile to their investigation as to Gwilt's. Clearly he was an impossible man to deal with. But the Commons' committee, having heard him, called attention to his success in the temporary House and advised that Lincoln's three 'eminent scientific persons' should resolve the problem. This, of course, was not acceptable to Reid.

Mindful of Reid's supporters and of the hard fact of his contract, Lord John Russell's Whig government followed Solomon's judgment: dividing the body, it entrusted the Lords to Barry (as the peers wished) and the Commons to the doctor. This merely added zest to Reid's invective. The Office of Woods had to act as intermediary between the two disputants, a role it discharged with little enthusiasm and some strong criticism of Reid.[59] Meanwhile, until the ventilator's intentions could be elucidated and accommodated in the architect's designs, much of the internal work remained at a standstill. Barry promised a Lords' committee in July 1846 that the libraries, refreshment rooms and ancillary accommodation would be ready for the next session, but they took another two years, though they were under his control. Reid, for his part, remained as indecisive and querulous as ever.[60] 'To a very large portion of the building nothing whatever has been done *for four years*', reported the *Builder* in February 1850.[61]

II. (right) The House of Lords, looking towards the Throne. An interior largely designed by A. W. Pugin under Charles Barry's supervision. Barry indicated the general form of the Throne (cp. Pls 80–2) and modified the details of the gallery railing (Pl. 174). The original windows of kings and queens designed by Pugin (Pl. 168) have been replaced since 1945 with heraldic glass, and the lighting arrangements have been changed, but Pugin's great standing candelabra remain in place.

A NEW VERSION OF "THIS IS THE HOUSE THAT JACK BUILT."

This is the house that BARRY (ought to have) built.

This is the money laid out on the house that BARRY (ought to have) built.

This is the REID that wasted the money laid out on the house that BARRY (ought to have) built.

This is the architect that snubbed the REID that wasted the money laid out on the house that BARRY (ought to have) built.

This is the BROUGHAM that worried the architect that snubbed the REID that wasted the money laid out on the house that BARRY (ought to have) built.

This is the press with its newsman's horn, that took up the BROUGHAM that worried the architect that snubbed the REID that wasted the money laid out on the house that BARRY (ought to have) built.

This is the peerage, all forlorn, that appealed to the press with its newsman's horn that took up the BROUGHAM that worried the architect that snubbed the REID that wasted the money laid out on the house that BARRY (ought to have) built.

This is the report, all tattered and torn, presented to the peerage all forlorn that appealed to the press with its newsman's horn that took up the BROUGHAM that worried the architect that snubbed the REID that wasted the money laid out on the house that BARRY (ought to have) built.

This is the chairman, all weary and worn, that brought up the report all tattered and torn, presented to the peerage all forlorn that appealed to the press with its newsman's horn that took up the BROUGHAM that worried the architect that snubbed the REID that wasted the money laid out on the house that BARRY (ought to have) built.

This is the witness not to be borne, who tired the chairman all weary and worn, that brought up the report all tattered and torn, presented to the peerage all forlorn, that appealed to the press with its newsman's horn that took up the BROUGHAM that worried the architect that snubbed the REID that wasted the money laid out on the house that BARRY (ought to have) built.

This is the Counsel as sharp as a thorn, that bothered the witness not to be borne, who tired the chairman all weary and worn, that brought up the report all tattered and torn, presented to the peerage all forlorn, that appealed to the press with its newsman's horn that took up the BROUGHAM that worried the architect that snubbed the REID that wasted the money laid out on the house that BARRY (ought to have) built.

This is the Clerk who at early morn woke up the Counsel as sharp as a thorn, that bothered the witness not to be borne, that tired the chairman all weary and worn that brought up the report all tattered and torn, presented to the peerage all forlorn, that appealed to the press with its newsman's horn that took up the BROUGHAM that worried the architect that snubbed the REID that wasted the money laid out on the house that BARRY (ought to have) built.

74. (above) Contemporary comment on the situation in 1846, when mounting criticism of the delays was voiced.

75. (right) Brougham and Reid. Lord Brougham was a leading critic of the slow progress made on the House of Lords.

BROUGHAM AND REID.

"I DON'T WANT EXPLANATION. I WANT AIR."—*Brougham on Ventilation.* *Vide Times.*

In the Commons' lobby the scaffolding is standing exactly as it was eighteen months ago, and there are no orders yet given for building it. In the Commons' library there had not been a man at work for two or three years till last week, when three or four joiners were sent in to—take down some pedestal presses which had been put up.

The delay, asserted the paper, was the responsibility of the House of Commons: let Barry have the money and the authority to finish the job. 'He owes it to himself and the profession to make a stand and maintain his right position as architect.' Soon after, the architect commenced an inconclusive action against Reid for defamation.[62] However, by this time contracts for the main heating and ventilation equipment had been placed. By July 1851 Nasmyth Gaskell and Company's boilers were installed in the basement of the Commons. Reid wisely sought to test them during the parliamentary recess, lest necessary alterations should involve him in 'labour and exposure in January weather'. Unfortunately, even then the noise of the primitive engine drowned speakers in the Chamber, and Reid was obliged to send post-haste to Manchester for one less noisy. By 1852 he had spent nearly £58,000 and had three assistant engineers; but MPs were still complaining of the draughts, the heat and the smells.[63]

Another factor making for delay was the problem of the internal decoration of the building. Lord Lincoln had told the 1844 select committee that the fitting up of committee rooms (urgently needed) was awaiting the determination of the Royal Fine Arts Commission (Pl. 76): a decision to employ fresco would considerably delay their completion.[64] In 1841–2 Barry's office had been tracing Pugin's designs for the interiors of the Chambers, but the appointment of the Commission implied a different character of decoration. The Fine Arts Commission, whose work is discussed in Chapter XII, was one outcome of a campaign led by such Utilitarian Radicals as Hume, Hawes and Ewart to elevate the intellectual and moral standards of the working classes and thereby to improve the standard of British manufactures so that they should be superior in design to those of foreign competitors: free libraries, free access to public monuments, Sunday opening of galleries and museums without charge, adult education classes, government schools of design, all form part of a great pattern of national instruction, together with the use of the New Palace at Westminster for the encouragement of art.[65] Here was a heaven-sent opportunity to develop the arts to a new peak of perfection: lost skills, such as fresco-painting, might be revived and perfected; and there was an unrivalled scope for mounting a permanent exhibition of national art-craftsmanship in the form of the numerous artifacts required for common use in the building: metal or wood or tile. Few questioned whether the scale of public access envisaged was practicable.[66] The notion struck a responsive chord in the queen's young husband, an art-loving prince inspired by high ideals. Prince Albert became chairman of the new Commission to supervise the decoration of the New Palace, a body which like the commission to select designs for New Houses of Parliament, was composed purely of gentlemen: amateurs and connoisseurs, not professional artists. There was no place on the commission for the architect of the building intended to be decorated. But Barry had his own ideas which he set forth in a report to the Fine Arts Commissioners. And Barry was in a position to obstruct any proposals varying seriously from his own: 'He said whether anything were done or no, he would leave the Hall and House of Lords, so that they would be in a mess if painting was not introduced.' His exclusion from the commission made only for friction.[67]

With all the works to be pressed on as fast as practicable and with the House of

76. Meeting of the Royal Fine Arts Commission, 1846. Key to painting by J. Partridge showing Barry exhibiting a model of the palace to the Commissioners. Those seen here include Lord Canning, who succeeded Lord Lincoln as First Commissioner of Woods and Works in February 1846, and the Whig Lord Morpeth, who succeeded Canning in July. George Vivian had been one of the judges in the Parliament Competition, and Sir R. H. Inglis was chairman of the 1846 select committee on the completion of the palace.

Lords to fit up and decorate, Barry had in June 1844 turned once more to Pugin. The renewal of their collaboration is discussed in the next chapter. Pugin's association with the work was publicly recognised by his appointment as superintendent of woodcarving at a salary of £200 p.a.[68] This had for Barry the advantage, at a time when he was exhausting the fee to which the government had decided to limit his remuneration, of paying Pugin from public funds rather than entirely from his own pocket. The title, however, was deceptive: Pugin's functions being to furnish Barry with designs for internal fittings and furniture, and to provide casts of medieval work for the carvers to use as models. The resident superintendent of the government workshops at Thames Bank was Richard Bayne; there was also a 'woodcarver in chief', one Potts, described by Barry as an 'artist-workman'; and Jordan of carving-machine fame was employed from April 1845 at £200 p.a. to superintend 'the moulding and carving of the wood fittings'.[69]

With Pugin hard at work on the interior designs, Barry at the end of 1844 negotiated a short-lived contract (number 7) with Grissell for the ordinary finishings.[70] He struck a good bargain, at prices often lower than the Office rates for common repairs, though least favourable for plasterer's, painter's and slater's work. Wainscot, from 'best Crown Riga wainscot, in the logs, and from pipe staves of the best quality, in equal proportions', was charged at 6½d. per square foot for one-inch boards steam-seasoned—atmospheric seasoning cost an additional 7½ per cent. Such 'extremely moderate' prices were grounded on the great extent of the work and the consequent opportunity to save labour by using machinery. For the preparation of the joinery Barry recommended that the government should lease 'extensive premises' at Thames Bank just west of Vauxhall Bridge.[71] The workshops, described below, were soon enlarged and equipped with Jordan's patent carving machinery. This, though not as successful as had been hoped, was used for much of the woodwork.[72] Some 200–300 men and occasionally more were employed there in 1845–8. But Grissell soon found his contract 'so entirely unsatisfactory' financially that after only ten months he gave notice of termination. Barry checked his prime costs and agreed that revised prices would only yield eight or nine per cent profit, a conclusion confirmed by Thomas Cubitt. As an example of the revised prices (contract number 8), the discount on Office of Works' prices for carpenter and joiner's work was cut from 22 to 6 per cent.[73]

Signing the new contract was delayed until October 1850, however, first by Grissell's refusal to accept responsibility for fire risk, then by Barry's insistence on controlling sub-contracting. Grissell objected to the architect's determining without appeal what works were comprised in his contract and what were not. Professor Bowley has commented on the general builder's dependence on 'the traditional craft organization of the building industry' with his sub-contracting the work of those trades which he required too seldom to specialise in himself. This is a pattern discernible in Grissell's handling of the Houses of Parliament contracts, notably for ironwork. It is further interesting to note the resistance of one of the principal English general builders to the architect's attempt to diminish the 'contractor's control of the building process'. Grissell's suggested compromise, that in the event of a difference between himself and the architect, the New Palace Commissioners might decide, was finally accepted by Barry.[74]

This problem had first assumed significant dimensions in 1845, when certain specialised works were put out to separate tender.[75] Grissell had on Barry's recommendation been awarded the contract for iron roofs over the two Houses and the Royal Gallery (though at £21.11s. a ton his was not the lowest), partly because this avoided the difficulties of another employer's workmen on the site. Grissell in fact sub-contracted the job to his nephew Henry of the Regent's Canal Ironworks. But he failed to secure the glazing contract, won by John Foord and Sons against five others. Most extensive of these minor contracts was that for the metal window-frames throughout the Palace, secured by James De Ville (succeeded on his death in 1846 by William Matthews trading under the same name).[76] With regard to ornamental metalwork there could be no hesitation: Hardman's manufactory, Barry insisted, was 'the only one in the kingdom where such work is properly executed'. This enabled Pugin to collect commission on his designs, as is explained in the next chapter. Similarly, the ornamental painting and the encaustic tiling were allotted to other protégés of Pugin, Crace and Minton respectively, without competition—though these two firms had in fact been recommended by the Fine Arts Commission. Barry asserted that he had the 'greatest faith in [Crace's] artistic skill to carry out my views, in the most effective and workmanlike manner'.[77] A furniture contract was awarded to Gillow, though Barry had proposed that it should be made in the government workshops.[78] Other firms were employed on specific works, and the great building on the bank of the Thames gave employment to a wide range of craftsmen in various parts of the country.

VII

The Collaboration Renewed: Barry and Pugin, 1844-52

THE Palace at Westminster, as contemporaries observed, had been designed and was being constructed in the glare of public interest. At the beginning of 1844 the building itself was not sufficiently advanced to attract much comment. Behind a mass of scaffolding, the river and south fronts were pretty well up (Pl. 77), though their interiors had not yet been begun, and the base of the Victoria Tower could be seen. 'Many years may elapse before even the mere shell of the structure will be completed.' The Palace had however become fashionable, thanks to the activities of the Royal Commission on the Fine Arts which had set out to determine which artists and craftsmen were capable of preparing the decorations: 'The exhibition of [their] cartoons contributed not a little to give vogue to whatever was connected with the building.' Accounts of the character of the proposed interior, presumably founded on the estimate drawings, gave promise of an unusual and exciting 'splendour of embellishment'.[1]

The Lords, as we have seen, unwilling to endure further delays, had appointed a select committee in 1843 to inquire into progress. At its hearings Barry experienced considerable unpleasantness, and was pushed to promise that after Easter 1844 he would lay before the committee 'the whole of the drawings for the fittings of the House'. But he added that he could not be certain that the House would be ready for the next session.[2]

Prompted by the publication of the committee's report, *The Times* described the state of the building in September 1844. The river front was being roofed in; its exterior presented 'a rich display ... which, whilst they strike astonishment to the beholder, must raise in his heart a high admiration for native genius.' The two great towers were scarcely begun, standing but 35 feet high; the west front had not been started. In the midst, the new House of Lords loomed up, its roof virtually completed. The account concluded with a 'tribute to the genius of the able architect'.[3]

Nevertheless, Barry was in trouble. The Lords' 1844 committee had set April 1845 as a reasonable date by which Barry must finish the House.[4] Barry had been, as his many drawings of the exterior and its details show (see Pls 67-9), revising and working with the possibilities, including the ideas Pugin had provided in the estimate drawings (see Pls 80-2). The composition of the Victoria and Clock Towers was

77. The River Front under construction, showing the new type of framed timber scaffolding, travelling cranes, masons' sheds, and the chimney shaft of Reid's steam-engine for ventilating the Temporary Houses, June 1842.

especially on his mind. This is the work to which Banks, Barry's chief assistant, alluded when he said that Barry had never intended to build from Pugin's drawings and that 'every part of the building was designed and re-designed, when the time for its execution arrived, by Sir C. Barry—in some parts, I should think, ten times over.'[5] Banks was a partial witness, but what he said was true. The collaboration had moved one step further: for a second time Barry was reworking Pugin's suggestions, organising and refining them. The impatience of the Lords' committee was, however, a blow, for if the surviving drawings are a reliable indication Barry had devoted himself largely to the structure. The interior, which in 1836 had been designed (Pls 59, 60) but not worked out in every detail, was still under consideration. So matters stood in June 1844, when Barry again sought Pugin's assistance.

*   *   *

Pugin's fame had grown since Barry had last dealt with him. He was now known as England's leading Catholic architect, with a huge practice of his own. In 1844 Pugin was at the crest of his powers; it must have seemed that no end of opportunities lay ahead. Extensive travel on the Continent and in England had enhanced his knowledge of medieval architecture and the decorative arts. Along the road to success which Pugin had travelled so rapidly, he had acquired deep convictions about the stylistic revival which he served, and he had gained some enemies as powerful as his friends. In addition to the two editions of *Contrasts* and the four volumes of plates on medieval decorative arts, he had published three books, *The True Principles of Pointed or Christian Architecture*, *The Present State of Ecclesiastical Architecture in England* and *An Apology for the Revival of Christian Architecture*, as well as a number of pamphlets. His books had made their mark, although they had infuriated many. Pugin had found that without undue expenditure of time he could through writing extend the influence of the ideas he had evolved in study and the practice

78. The Lords' Staircase. Hardman's armorial glass and Minton's tiles contribute to the rich effect.

of design. He had also participated in acrimonious debates in the public press. His magnificent *Glossary of Ecclesiastical Ornament and Costume* was about to be published.

The *Builder* declared: 'Acknowledged or not acknowledged, he is the virtual pope or chief pontiff in these matters, and his bulls are received and deferred to as the canonical ordinances of the orthodox.' But it criticised his 'overweening vanity and an imperious spirit', and the 'unmeasured—the cruel—the opprobious and unjust outpourings of his pen' which damaged the cause in which he believed. One critic spoke of 'Welby's notorious naughtiness'; others were not so charitable.[6] 'Intolerant' was the word most often used to describe him, for he had by 1844 trodden on the feelings of so many people that he was no longer the silent, anonymous partner Barry had earlier enjoyed. The merest whiff of gossip that Pugin was to be formally employed in any capacity in the already controversial business at Westminster was bound to generate disturbance.

The years between 1837 and 1844 had not only changed Pugin's reputation, they had changed Pugin. His family responsibilities had grown: when Barry first hired him he had been the boyish father of two; in the spring of 1844 there were six children, and Pugin was preparing to move into a capacious new house he had built in Ramsgate. Financially, his professional life was rewarding. In his best years Pugin appears to have earned as much as £4,000, receiving from his practice not only the normal architect's percentage and payments for his designs from manufacturers in the decorative arts, but also a share in profits. His partnership with John Hardman in the production of metalwork had begun to prosper, orders to the value of £3,284 being taken in 1844: and Pugin received ten per cent on the profits, in addition to payment for his drawings. In the decoration of his new house Pugin was relying on the London firm of Crace, the beginning of another relationship that would be profitable artistically as well as financially. Because he was unhappy with the craftsmen in stained glass with whom he had worked and with whom he invariably quarrelled, Pugin would in 1845 add stained glass to Hardman's manufacturing programme. And with his role of 'virtual pope' of the Gothic Revival, of which his prosperity was the visible manifestation, came a personal satisfaction.

Charles Barry was thus seeking in 1844 to join forces with a highly educated, famous, assertive practitioner. The prodigy had become a public figure and an assured artist who knew his own worth and sensed the almost boundless power of his own capacities.

Only a few letters are known in which Barry and Pugin settled the terms for Pugin's return to work on the Palace. In June 1844 Barry wrote asking for Pugin's assistance, but we have only Pugin's reply.[7] Barry had evidently asked Pugin to participate in the design of a part of the Palace, doubtless the House of Lords. There is no other explanation for Pugin's remark that 'it is next to impossible for me to design any abstract portion of a great whole in the same spirit as you have conceived the rest.' His comment, 'Remember, I never made a drawing which was of any real use to you yet, and it is a dreadful loss of time to me, incessantly occupied as I am with Church work, to attempt it', must refer to the revisions Barry had in the past imposed on Pugin's work. It also expresses Pugin's unwillingness to forgo the kudos of authorship.

Pugin proposed an alternative which would assist Barry, yet preserve Pugin's newly-won position as an authority on Gothic art and architecture. He said 'I can do you no good except in actual detail, and in that more by ferreting out the fine things that exist than in composing new ones.' Pugin no longer wished to design

79. (above) House of Lords: The Lobby. Pugin's hand is everywhere here: the great brass gates to the Chamber (made by Hardman), Minton's tiles (with brass inlay for the central design), the chairs, desk, and cloakroom furniture.

80. (right) J. Gillespie Graham: Competition design for New Houses of Parliament, 1835. The House of Lords, interior perspective, showing the Throne, drawn by A. W. Pugin.

Elevation of the Throne

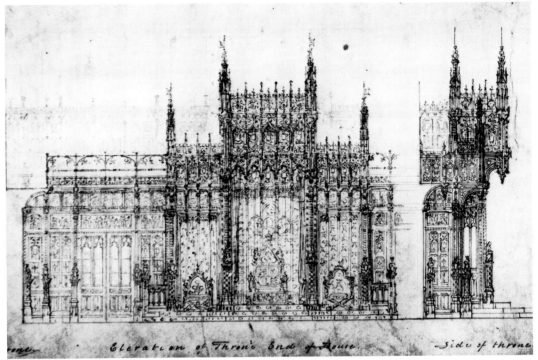

81. (left) House of Lords: Elevation of the Throne. Tracing dated 'Dec 8/42', from an 'Estimates drawing' of 1836–7 by A. W. Pugin, retaining monogram and arms of William IV.

82. (above) House of Lords: Elevation of Throne end. Tracing dated 17 Dec. 1844, from a drawing by A. W. Pugin.

imaginary Gothic; what he called his 'authorities' had replaced his earlier, youthful willingness to extemporize. Barry's building would be completed in a 'good' style if Pugin had anything to do with it. To this end he suggested that Barry himself might profit from a journey to Antwerp and Louvain!

No further correspondence in the summer of 1844 survives. Pugin was energetically pursuing other commissions when in August Mrs Pugin died suddenly. On 3 September Barry wrote again. In all that he had to say Pugin's earlier refusal may be felt. The House of Lords was for Barry a crisis. If Pugin would collaborate, he could have the new working arrangements he had suggested. Barry invited Pugin to visit him in Brighton for a few days of work together to make the 'drawings in question' and to consult so that they might 'enter into some permanent arrangement that will be satisfactory to you, as to occasional assistance for the future in the completion of the great work, as well as for the discharge of my obligations to you for what you have already done.' Barry also stated that he had decided 'as to the principles' of his design, assurance to Pugin that everything they did would not be altered. If he and Pugin could spend time together, Barry felt sure that they could 'make out definitely every portion of the design of the House of Lords fittings, etc., in general drawings, so that you might be able to supply me with the details subsequently, from time to time, according to your own leisure and convenience.'[8]

Pugin then visited Barry at Brighton from 12 to 16 September. One reason for the urgency of Barry's request may be found in the coarse, ugly water-colours for sculptural details now in the House of Lords Record Office.[9] Barry had tried without

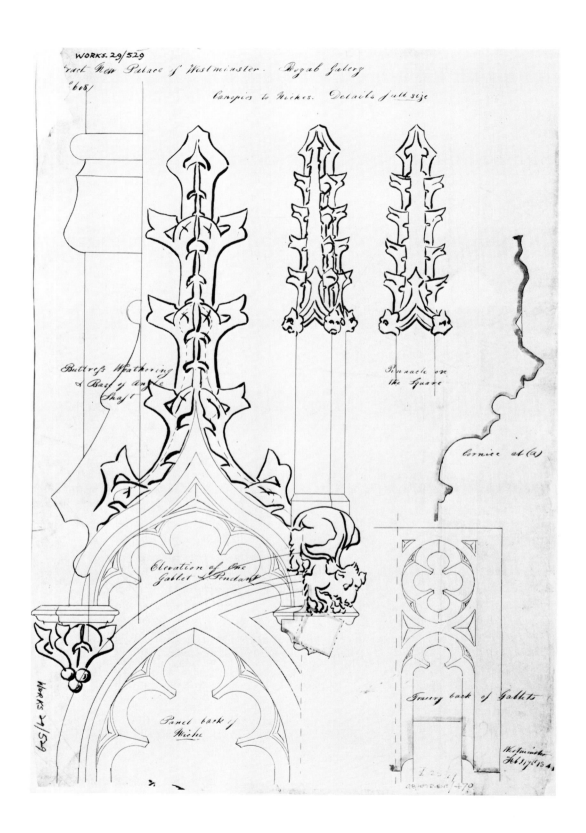

83. Royal Gallery: Details of canopies to niches for statues, ?1847. (Reduced)

success to find adequate assistance to pick up the work Pugin had laid down in 1837. For decorating the interior with requisite richness Pugin's aid was essential. In all the thousands of drawings in the various archives of work for the new Palace at Westminster there is not one study or drawing for a detail that in any way equals the quality of those produced by Pugin.

After visiting Pugin in Ramsgate between 7 and 10 November 1844, Barry in December completed arrangements with the government for the appointment of Pugin to superintend the works of woodcarving at the new Palace.[10] The third of the letters in which the renewal of their collaboration was discussed is the most important, but a precise date cannot be assigned it. When Alfred Barry quoted the letter he reported that it was post-marked 'Amiens',[11] yet in 1844 and 1845 Pugin's only visit to that city was in May 1844, earlier than the tentative refusal of June 1844 discussed above. The content of the letter would seem, however, to point to a date after the establishment of the government contract for Pugin's services: the amount of Pugin's salary is mentioned, and so is the arrival of John Hardman Powell as assistant in the drafting room at Ramsgate.

... First, for the 200£ a year, I agree to furnish drawings and instructions for all the carved ornaments in wood that may be required. Secondly, that all travelling expenses whatever connected with the above work are to be paid extra to that sum. My residence being at Ramsgate, my journeys to London must be considered as travelling expenses, and paid accordingly, unless I am compelled to take the journey for other purposes not connected with the work. Thirdly, I am empowered to send persons to collect squeezes, etc., and all expenses connected with that object, or the purchase of original models, to be paid from time to time according to the accounts I will furnish you, and all journeys which I make for the purpose of finding out proper models. Fourthly, all drawings for glass, metal works, and tiles, etc., will be paid for in the estimates for the same, according to the rates we agreed, Fifthly, you must include the expense of preparing these detail drawings in the estimate of the fittings, and I will furnish you with the cost of them as you may require. Sixthly, I am only responsible to you in all matters connected with the work. I act as your agent entirely, and have nothing to do with any other person.

Pugin remarked finally that he knew the amount of work he had contracted to perform was enormous, but that he was prepared to move full steam ahead.

Superficially this arrangement seemed satisfactory. Pugin would collect the price of drawings from the craftsmen who made the stained glass, metalwork, tiles, etc. His £200 salary would pay for his drawings for woodcarving and the supervision of the workmen. Travelling expenses for Pugin and for the men he would send forth to procure models would be extra, as would the cost of the collection of casts.[12] Pugin would not be required to appear for any of those painful sessions in which Barry explained himself to committees. Responsibility solely to Barry would set Pugin apart from Bayne or any other of the supervisors of the work.

There were, however, hazards, not the least of which were the activities of the Royal Commissioners on the Fine Arts, who had industriously encouraged artists and craftsmen to prepare specimens of their skill to be considered for employment in 'the great work'.[13] Among those who exhibited stained glass was Warrington, a man with whom Pugin had already had disagreements. Were he, for example, to receive a contract for stained glass Warrington would surely refuse to comply with any arrangement to use Pugin's cartoons and write into his fee a percentage to cover their cost. Minton & Company and F. & J. G. Crace presented specimens of their work; of the latter's painted heraldic panel it was noted that though the design was magnificent it would profit from the 'chastening of the architect'.[14] Public exhibitions of the works submitted were arranged in the late spring of 1844.[15] There were therefore a number of firms and artists in the decorative arts who had a right to feel that they might be called upon to assist at Westminster.

However Barry thought he might both meet the Fine Arts Commissioners' intentions and also have Pugin prepare drawings for 'glass, metalwork, and tiles etc.' for which he would be paid, the arrangement of December 1844 certainly brought Pugin back as the prime designer in the decorative arts for the Palace (Pls 84–7). Pugin had provided for the financial good health of Hardman's firm, which would certainly execute the metalwork (discussed in Chapter XII), and for a small salary for himself to which payments for drawings would be added. He had, however, sold his talents for a long time to come. Delays in payment by the government would be passed on to him by Barry. The volume of work undertaken would confuse his life and increase his irascibility. His enemies and those of Barry would rise up to complain about his appointment. Pugin was locked into a collaboration which had begun years earlier; he would assist in the completion of a building for which he felt some but not great sympathy.

Inevitably news of Pugin's employment brought his detractors into action. The *Artizan* had attacked Pugin in 1843 for the 'hateful intolerance' of *An Apology for the Revival of Christian Architecture in England*.[16] In 1845 the *Artizan* struck again in an article entitled 'Charles Barry and His Right-Hand Man'. It accused Barry of silence over Pugin's employment, and Pugin of 'publishing the fact in the most cock-crowing tone'. It wondered whether Barry had been forced to accept this assistance; he was surely not overwhelmed with work at the new Palace, for he had entered an unsuccessful design for the Carlton Club competition.[17] Pugin was accused of proclaiming 'the matter to the world at the same time modestly insinuating that he is the only person in the world—at least in this country, who possesses the requisite taste and knowledge.' There was much more in the same tone.

Insignificant as this paper might be, the attack hurt. Pugin suggested that he might publish a statement describing his role. He assured Barry that he had never said anything which might be misinterpreted, adding that he wished to serve Barry 'in this work with the greatest fidelity; no one can better appreciate your skill and judgement than myself'.[18] He then drafted a short statement which he proposed to send to the *Builder* if Barry agreed. But it did not appear, Barry apparently deciding that it would be best to let the challenge go unanswered.

In the summer of 1845, however, it appeared that the matter would not disappear of its own accord. Pugin had himself provided material for further attacks when he chose inopportunely to join in a discussion of the merits of English craftsmen in the decorative arts, failures in the curriculum of the School of Design and the paucity of English talent for the decorative works at Westminster. In July, the *Builder* repeated a report in the *Spectator* that, though the Fine Arts Commission had recommended English artists to carry out these works at the House of Lords,[19]

certain it is that the most skilful and experienced practical workmen among the carvers and painters thus recommended have not been engaged; and what makes this still more extraordinary, is the statement of Mr Pugin, who superintends the interior decorations, that for want of competent assistance from Englishmen he is compelled to send for foreigners.

Undaunted, Pugin allowed a letter he had written on the School of Design to be published. It contained an intemperate attack on contemporary sculptors.[20]

84. A. W. Pugin: Cartoon for tiles for the New Palace at Westminster. The lion pattern was used extensively at Westminster, notably in the Peers' Lobby (Pl. VII).

85. A. W. Pugin: Cartoon for tiles for the New Palace.

On 6 September 1845 further letters from Pugin and Crace appeared in the *Builder*. The immediate occasion was a letter of criticism in the *Builder*, but there is said to have been also a reference in a Lords' debate to Pugin as 'joint-architect' of the Houses of Parliament.[21] In many and interesting ways Pugin's letter was stronger than that he had drafted in June.[22] Whereas that had stated that Pugin was 'superintending the practical execution of the internal details and decorations of Mr Barry's design', the published letter underlined Barry's role as initiator of all designs and Pugin's as executant. If these statements are compared with the 'Amiens' letter, a portion of which has been quoted above, it will be obvious that that in the *Builder* did not describe the situation. Barry had hired Pugin and his associates, which by September 1845 meant Crace as well as Hardman, to complete the decoration of the House of Lords.[23] Pugin was preparing drawings for these men as well as for the carvers. Whenever the tenders for Crace or Hardman were challenged by the Office of Works, Barry responded by saying that no other firms were capable of executing the work properly.[24]

At first glance this partnership seems to have been entirely to Barry's advantage: he could relax and let Pugin carry the burden. Such was not the case. Barry's diary for 1845 shows that he was working as hard and as much as Pugin and that the duties he performed were always intricate and sometimes trying.[25] When Barry told Pugin that he had made up his mind about the 'principles' of the design he meant what he said, for nothing was too small to pass unnoticed. The diary shows days spent in revision of details, reconsideration and study of larger elements such as the Throne in the Lords' Chamber (Pls 80–2), the masonry working drawings for the House of Commons and studies for whole rooms—the libraries, lobbies and the Royal Gallery (Pl. 83). It is significant that Barry refers to models of parts of the building with which he was working in design revisions.

Barry also bore the onerous weight of parliamentary and public pressure. It cannot have been pleasant to hear that Lord Brougham had said he was 'not only a Gothic architect, not only a dilatory man, but the name of delay itself', and that his promises were 'not worth the paper they were written on'.[26] Articles such as that in which Pugin was entitled his 'right-hand man' might be dismissed, but were nonetheless annoying. Moreover Barry had endless ceremonial and supervisory duties. Prince Albert (on 7 and 10 March 1845) was only the most distinguished of visitors to escort over the site. There were regular visits from Lord Lincoln of the Woods and Works. Commissions and committees met with tiresome frequency. The problems raised by Dr Reid had become acute. There were conferences and site consultations with Pugin. Barry also visited the building yards and factories where the materials were being prepared. He turned up periodically at Hardman's in Birmingham. On 2 October he met Pugin at Stoke to 'settle the tiles' for the Palace at Mintons (Pls 84, 85); then on to see St Giles Cheadle, the Hospital and works at the castle in Alton, reaching Alton Towers for dinner.

Before we describe the final phase of the work that Barry and Pugin shared, some assessment of Barry's intention in founding the partnership and his role in maintaining it is called for. Barry was a perfectionist and a man of persistence to the point of stubbornness. From the day the competition drawings were submitted until his death he fought to preserve intact his conception of the building he had designed and to improve it in detail without compromising its integrity. Had he accepted the directions and suggestions of the various bodies that beset him the new Palace would have ended in an artistic muddle. Barry would have had to supervise a variety of artists and craftsmen including some of meagre talent, who knew nothing of the origin and character of the design. This gratuitous intervention by governmental bodies, their nomination of artists because they represented native talent, and the fact that such artists felt they had a right to work at Westminster because they had been so nominated were unhappy features of the modernity of the building. E. W. Pugin's irresponsible attack in 1867 was also symptomatic of the problems that building with a rising democracy as patron could entail. These were some of the costs of the change in patronage which occurred in the early nineteenth century. If Barry had been responsive to the suggestion of every self-appointed or quasi-governmental authority he would have lost the character of his building along the way. His stubbornness was providential.

Had Barry been an acquiescent type Pugin's talent would not have been acquired by the government. Pugin would not compete, nor would he allow Hardman to do so. His Catholicism and especially his books were enough to alarm committee

86. (left) A. W. Pugin: 'Tudor' wall paper for the New Palace, printed from the original blocks by John Perry Ltd. A cartoon for this pattern is in the V & A (Prints and Drawings, D 719–1908).

87. (above) A. W. Pugin: Wall paper for the New Palace, printed from the original blocks by John Perry Ltd, and used in the Bishops' Rooms.

members and raise a storm of protest in the architectural press. But Barry's good taste told him that Pugin was the best, he and the building belonged together and, in spite of his mercurial temperament, Pugin was brilliantly able to see the end for which its architect was aiming.

Between 1844 and 1852 a kind of collaboration came into being as Barry fitted his building together and Pugin designed the parts of the decorative portions. Barry was the architect, Pugin and he shared the decoration.

For Pugin too the work meant laborious days. It is true that it brought money: statements that Pugin was oblivious to money are wrong, for his letters abound in references to it, and the bargain he drove with Barry in 1844 was self-interested to a degree. He had a large family to maintain and his heart was set on the expensive project of building St Augustine's Church beside his house in Ramsgate.[27] West-minster was added to heavy commitments which included the completion of churches at Kirkham and Cheadle, the castle at Alton and other architectural projects in England and Ireland, and the large business in ecclesiastical metalwork and stained glass of the Hardman firm. But in the search for new work Pugin was beginning to encounter disheartening difficulties. The new Palace kept him busy at a time when his church practice was declining thanks to the appearance of other Catholic architects; to be incessantly active was a necessity for Pugin. And, though he grumbled about him, Pugin liked and respected Charles Barry and recognised his skill and talent.

Nevertheless the new work brought Pugin difficulties. He was in Ramsgate, Hardman in Birmingham, the building in London. So the business was carried on largely by mail, and entailed much travel. It was the subject of many of the hundreds of letters Pugin wrote between 1844 and 1852. The creation of a staff of assistants at Ramsgate was not a change to which Pugin accommodated gracefully, for he shouted and worried when things went wrong, writing to Hardman of one disaster in the studio, 'If I had not the spirit of a lion with three tails I should never get over all my difficulties.' Pugin also was a perfectionist; in February 1845 he wrote, 'I have been with Mr Barry today to see [the panels] at St George's, Windsor, and they beat mine hollow. I have got a person taking rubs of them which will be of great service.' Barry's capacity to revise designs, furthermore, seemed endless: 'I now find that we shall have to begin quite afresh with the railing for Mr Barry altered all the rose work at the bottom and we must start quite a new pattern. He is aware of the great loss of dies etc. for I explained it to him and he says it cannot be helped for he must have it perfection to his mind.' The government was often late in paying for services rendered: 'The delay in the parliamentary commission is monstrous. At this moment I have actually expended between 4 and 500 pounds for casts and carvings etc. and not recieved back a penny. The railing delay is scandalous and then there will be all hurry and driving.'

Pugin's letters to Crace and Hardman, Barry's to Hardman and Pugin, the Pugin and Barry diaries, and drawings and tracings show the collaboration at work. Late in 1846 Pugin wrote to Crace:

Things will be very active at the new Palace forthwith. I am preparing sketches which Mr. B. will forward to you . . . and I have strongly urged the necessity of getting all the patterns ready for the cove in the house . . . you will be obliged to draw out full size the various shields that are to be painted about the throne and the sooner they are done the better . . . the ceilings etc. in the chamber next the House of Lords will be next done. I mentioned to Mr. Barry about your making the carpet for the throne which he seemed to approve of and I will send you a sketch to get out a coloured drawing full size for him to see.

The next letter from Ramsgate included the pattern for this carpet. At the same time, Pugin was preparing pattern locks for Westminster using old ones on a chest in the museum at Oscott as sources; he was working on cartoons for the Lords' Chamber and Peers' Lobby windows and attempting to match at long distance the heraldry in these windows with that which Crace was drawing in London. Quarm was asking Hardman for the vanes for the Lords roof and the metal railing, mentioned above, and metal gates to the Chamber. Barry wanted hands and dials manufactured by Hardman to Pugin's designs so that Vulliamy, the clock maker, could devise 'the best mode for attaching them' to the works of the interior clocks. All this while Pugin was confined to his bedroom with a severe attack of eye disease for which mercury in large quantities was being prescribed, and young John Hardman Powell was writing letters for him. In 1847 Pugin reported, 'I am getting on with the cartoons as fast as I can but Mr Barry has brought in all the details for the House of Commons to do so it seems I shall die in harness.'[28]

It is clear that Barry usually worked over each design himself:[29]

I have sent back the door plates by this evening's train. When applied to the doors they look too large. I should like them therefore to be reduced and modified in design, in accordance with the enclosed sketch. The screws for fastening them to the doors may be arranged to take up with the design as obvious in the sketch. With the same papers I send a sketch for the iron vane and stem for the octagon turret in the Royal Court for which you already have the screw. Let it be prepared immediately and sent up as soon as you can for galvanizing. Amongst the screws in the parcel I have sent is one that we have in town which I prefer to yours as the head is regularly punched and not burred as yours is to the risk of injury to knuckles.

He was equally careful about the stained glass, concerning which he had positive ideas:[30]

In the draperies there is a great prevalence of a dirty flannel colour which is very disagreeable to the eye. I wish you could get rid of it.

I have put in such lines and touches as will, I think, give the best effect to the canopies for the House of Lords windows as seen from the floor of the House and the lights will be forwarded to you by your man this evening. I have also made up my mind that it will be best to have the canopies of clear white glass partially stippled and relieved with yellow.

The character of the working relationship between Barry and Pugin is best conveyed by a letter of 14 June 1851:[31]

In my note of this morning, I forgot to ask your opinion of the mode of filling up the pannels flanking the open galleries between the windows of the Victoria Tower. I do not think that statues would do at so great a height as that of the galleries but it struck me that crowned shields and supporters below, as shown in the enclosed tracing, would be appropriate and have a good effect. If you are of the same opinion will you have the goodness to send to me, in the quaint and knowing way of which you are so great a *maestro*, a good-sized sketch thereof, for a model. The crowns might project boldly out and be cut through to prevent heaviness.

Pugin for his part blew hot and cold about Barry. Sometimes he was a 'man who does not care for anybody beyond his own interest. He could see you and me ruined with the most perfect apathy.' Sometimes he was a helpful contriver: 'I got an order for £2,000 for Hardman. Mr Barry has got Hardman now appointed by the government so there is no competition or humbug of any kind'. Pugin complained about the many alterations in his designs only because he was annoyed by the resultant delays; he never expressed anger that his artistic prowess and taste had been questioned.

The House of Lords was an impressive success. 'The whole glitters with colours and gilding,—carvings in stone, stained glass, encaustic tiles, and fine work in metal.' Items over which great care and much anguish had been lavished emerged in dazzling array: 'the elaborate brass gates' of the Chamber (Pl. 79), the beautiful tiles (Pl. VII) with 'lions, on a red ground, and initials on a blue ground', and the panels about which Pugin had worried after his Windsor trip.[32]

Having completed the House of Lords, Barry moved on to finish the committee rooms (Pl. 73) and the House of Commons. Then suddenly in mid-1848 the government began to require stringent economies. Barry proposed to rush through orders before restraints could take effect. Pugin was asked to make drawings for furniture to be made in the government workshops at Thames Bank, an idea which was

88. The House of Lords in Session: F. Sargent, 1880. Lord Beaconsfield is addressing the House. The Prince of Wales is conspicuous on the right of the cross-benches.

dropped, but which was threatening because Pugin would have lost the money he had been receiving for his drawings.

Among other economies, Pugin was informed that his salary might be terminated.[33]

I swore that if it was I would never draw another line for the job. It is infamous. I worked for 2 years, the whole money was swallowed up in expensive training . . . I am disgusted with everything for I get shamefully treated on all sides and miserably paid . . . you must put the House of Commons windows in at such a price as to have them remember there is no chance of making any more money . . . they keep all the rascals who are paid for doing nothing and the deserving ones are turned adrift . . . a man is a slave for four years for a miserable pittance like that then to kick him out because that infernal rascal, that double hypocrite, humbug, thief, that imposter Cobden, who has got £100,000 to his own whack makes a trade of crying out against a little carving and painting.

As the record of Barry's payments to Pugin shows, the years of greatest activity on the new Palace were drawing to a close in 1850, when Pugin's salary was reduced.[34]

The rascally Commissioners have reduced my salary at Westminster to 100 a year, just half and no man has worked harder or better than I have. It is almost an insult to pay a man such as me 100 a year. I have a great mind to throw up the whole thing but my spirit is broken by poverty. I hardly know what to do and they say a half a loaf is better than no bread.

Pugin believed he was being exploited, but he continued to respond to Barry's requests, sending design upon design to Barry who approved and transmitted them to be manufactured. After a meeting in London in late December 1850, Pugin wrote to Crace:[35]

1. I have been with Mr. Barry to the houses and I think we can now settle the ceiling for the conference room if you will send me back by return the full size of the panel.
2. Mr. Barry has asked me about the *leather chair* you were to make and I did not know what to say. Pray let me know if you have got it ready for he will put the order now for a *whole lot* if he is satisfied.
3. I have got 6 patterns of papers settled and I send them up to you full size tomorrow [cp. Pls. 86, 87]. Mind I have got the authority for you to cut the blocks.
So I think I have done some good.

At the onset of Pugin's fatal illness Barry was unaware of the dire distress which had overtaken his collaborator. On 23 February 1852, a matter of hours before Pugin's final collapse, Barry wrote asking for assistance in the design of the clock tower.[36] Pugin had been ill before and recovered, and Barry must have understood the vagaries of his temperament and the waves of depression he experienced when the hopes and ideas to which he was pledged were thwarted. Barry was not insensitive; he must have found it impossible to believe that a man so much younger than he, so vigorous, creative and close to him was to die suddenly. But this time Pugin did not recover, and in September 1852 he died.

VIII

Barry's Last Years: The New Palace in the 1850s

ENERGIES in the 1840s had naturally been concentrated on getting the building to the point of occupation. The 1850s, a period of rising prices, were marked by less willingness to spend on public objects in general; and once the new Houses were in use, by criticism of the 'bedizening' of the New Palace and its mounting cost—for the worst fears of the critics were being realised.

The first tremors of these ground movements had been experienced in 1848, at a time of 'great mercantile and industrial depression', when the ministry's financial proposals had met such fierce objections that a Commons' committee had been appointed to investigate public expenditure, and the budget had been remodelled three times. To keep down taxes at the same time as providing additional armaments to meet a supposed French threat, the vote for the New Palace was limited to £100,000, compared with £150,000 the previous year. Lord Morpeth, First Commissioner of Woods, announced that all works of a merely ornamental character were to be postponed.[1] Barry, already committed far in advance of parliamentary votes, failed to reduce the scale of his operations accordingly. When the Commons required alterations in ancillary accommodation to meet the great increase in parliamentary business over the past decade, he could only provide for them by stopping 'other works equally important to the fulfilment of the expectations which have been held out as to an early occupation of the building.' The Treasury refused to cover a deficit, saying that it was for the Treasury to lay down how much should be spent annually on the works, and the actual allocation of that sum was for the New Palace Commission to determine. This characteristic but short-sighted decision compelled the contractors to discharge picked craftsmen.[2]

The Royal Commission for the completion of the New Palace was a body set up in March 1848 at the behest of the House of Commons. With the Lords completed in March 1847 and the new Commons chamber still far from ready, MPs became increasingly restive. Against a background of financial exigency and dissatisfaction with the Office of Woods and Works a series of debates about the New Palace took place in early 1848. Opinion in the House had become suspicious of the efficacy of a select committee in dealing with the building. Committees seemed only to lead to increased expenditure, and public opinion condemned their doings and called for a

89. The House of Commons as first completed, 1850. Members objected to the poor acoustics, and complained of inadequate division lobbies (cp. Pls 90 and 91).

III. (left) The Houses of Parliament: The Central Lobby. The Gothic dome became a theme in Revival architecture. Barry's great octagon has been altered in detail since his death: the dark stained glass removed, the roof brightened with Salviati mosaics (1868–9), and four large mosaic panels installed (1870, 1898, and 1923–4). Hardman's great chandelier, however, was installed in 1855.

IV. (above) The Houses of Parliament: the Chapel of St Mary Undercroft, looking east. Begun in 1292, the Lower Chapel in the Chapel of St Stephen was completed in the early fourteenth century. Its lierne vault is the earliest ever built. The stonework was heavily restored by Sir Charles Barry in 1858–9. The decoration carried out by his son Edward in the 1860s makes the chapel a masterpiece of High Victorian Gothic. The decorative painting is by Crace, the metalwork and windows by Hardman.

controlling authority. So the weak Whig government tried to shuffle off responsibility by appointing a commission charged with the completion of the Palace.[3] Lord de Grey, president of the Institute of British Architects and himself an enthusiastic amateur architect, agreed to serve with the former Commons' Chairman of Committees, Thomas Greene, MP, under the chairmanship of Sir John Fox Burgoyne, Inspector-General of Fortifications. Subject to the Treasury's financial control, they were to determine the designs for and extent of decorations, fittings and furnishings. Thus the chain of command starting with the co-ordinate powers of Parliament and the Treasury descended through the Works Department and now the Commission to the architect and thence to the contractors. But precise definition was not a characteristic of this system of government. The Commission found its position equivocal. On one hand they had Barry to deal with, on the other the House of Commons; nor did they supersede the Office of Works: in truth the Commission was a buckler for government rather than a two-edged axe to hew a speedy path through the thickets of waste and profusion and the tangles of local disputes and rivalries. 'Had such a commission been appointed 10 years sooner', de Grey wrote in his 'Memoirs', 'I have no doubt that more than a million of money would have been saved; but now, though nothing was completed, everything was begun; and so far advanced that all attempts to diminish the expense or control the architect were perfectly futile.' Feeling 'powerless and useless', the Commission recommended its own extinction in December 1851, by which time the main working parts of the Palace had been completed.[4]

Of these the latest and most controversial was the new House of Commons. Ready for experimental sittings in May 1850, it had a family resemblance to the House of Lords, but was somewhat squarer (a decision of the select committee of 1835). Though intended to be less gorgeous in its decoration, it had a handsome wooden ceiling formed into compartments, and large windows containing heraldic stained glass (Pl. 89). The mood of members, used to their comfortable if somewhat bare temporary chamber, was critical after years of vexation, and they did not give the new House a fair trial. Barry had planned seats for 462 MPs on the floor of the House and in galleries, with 32 seats in a reporters' gallery at the back of the Speaker's chair, 96 in the Strangers' Gallery, and 52 in the Speaker's and Peers' Gallery. One behind the Speaker designed for 120 members was disliked and consequently removed; a wit wished to know whether that substituted was intended as a gallery or as a shelf for *Hansard*.[5] A. J. Beresford Hope later recalled that he had never known scenes

less creditable to the sense and seriousness of the House. It was a hot summer, and the sittings in the new House were on a few Wednesdays. There was a lull in politics just then, and no serious or grave questions . . . were then before it. The consequence was that Members almost got up debates for the sake of trying the House. To use a vulgar phrase, they regarded the thing as 'a lark'.[6]

At the first sitting, on 30 May 1850, one Member complained that he could not hear from the gallery opposite the Speaker, but another coyly asked how one on his legs could possibly be heard when a hundred on their 'head's antipodes' were also talking. The upshot was the appointment of yet another select committee, which failed to agree on a final report.[7] Barry's suggestion of lengthening the House was rejected, however, as likely to make hearing more difficult. But evidence from experts in acoustics was inconclusive. A boarded roof was tried as an experiment:

90. House of Commons: Division lobby. Members complained that the lobbies as originally constructed were too small, and Barry had to throw out oriels. Note Faraday's gas lights.

THE NEW HOUSE OF COMMONS, FROM THE BAR.

91. House of Commons as altered, February 1852. A lower ceiling was installed, cutting the height of the windows in half. The stained glass, representing the arms of the boroughs, was illuminated externally by gas. The fronts of the widened galleries were ornamented with a brass cresting. The ladies' gallery, at the Speaker's end of the House, was concealed by a grille; immediately above the Speaker's Chair was the reporters' gallery. The gas pendants were replaced by Reid's lights (Pl. 151) in April, 1852.

opinion was divided whether it improved hearing. A strong critic of the expense of the New Palace, Sir Benjamin Hall, put forward his own plan for the House, which was printed with Barry's modifications. This provided two rows of seats (instead of one) in side galleries to take 150 Members, with only a Reporters' Gallery behind the Speaker, and a Strangers' Gallery with five rows of seats opposite. Thus ample seating was provided for as many MPs as were thought 'likely generally to attend'. The division lobbies on either side of the House were also enlarged by throwing out oriels (Pl. 90). It was on this basis that Barry altered the Commons in 1850–1, with one other drastic alteration on which the committee had been divided— the replacing of the original ceiling by one 'which shall rise from some point not higher than the transoms of the windows, and which, instead of being a flat surface, shall rise from the sides toward the centre' (Pl. 91), a deformity imitated in the post-war House. Decorative heraldic painting was stopped by the Chancellor of the Exchequer. Barry refused to acknowledge the monstrosity that was foisted on him and, it is said, never entered the chamber again.[8] These alterations occupied the whole of 1851.

This point marks the nadir of Barry's fortunes. 'Mr Barry had found it convenient to get committees appointed, to recommend alterations, and to be answerable for them, he receiving a percentage on the cost', was the sort of allegation that MPs bandied about. 'The money they had expended', declared Hume, '. . . was enough to have provided golden seats'; they were now called upon to waste more public money on a 'man who had shown himself utterly incapable of adapting the building to the purpose for which it was intended.' A Tory agreed that 'the principal room was a complete, decided, and undeniable failure.' The chairman of the last committee remarked that 'Mr Barry had had the uncontrolled expenditure of the largest sum of money that any one architect had ever had before' and he ought to consider himself 'morally responsible' for the result. Disraeli suggested that if the government were to hang the architect it would put a stop to such blunders in the future.[9] The government, however, preferred to knight the architect, an act performed by the Queen a few days after the state opening of the session of 1852, when for the first time both new Houses were in use.[10]

*　　　*　　　*

At this same period the Commons were trying to obtain an idea of the total cost. The drawing up of a balance sheet was a prolonged undertaking which when at last published showed an increase of nearly £1,200,000 over the original estimate of some £700,000.[11] There were many items which had not formed part of the original estimate, such as purchase of additional land (£82,000), Reid's ventilation scheme (£120,000), fireproofing (£80,000), furniture (£500,000), and the architect's fee (put down at £75,000). The original could not, it was argued, 'be considered as having comprehended much more than the mere shell', though the Members who had approved it thought it represented the whole cost.[12] There were also items such as extra foundations (£35,000), the probability of which ought to have been foreseen and provided for in 'contingencies'. Another element was rising labour and material costs (£68,000), but on the other hand many customs and excise duties had been repealed since 1837. Some expense was due to Members' own second thoughts, such as the demand in 1848 for a smoking room (Pl. 92). However explicable, the total was frightening to economy-obsessed ministers and MPs. The New Palace Commissioners invited Barry to consider possible savings, and he responded with proposals to cut out the middle-man's profits. For greater efficiency and convenience in conducting the works and for ascertaining at any time the liabilities, he suggested

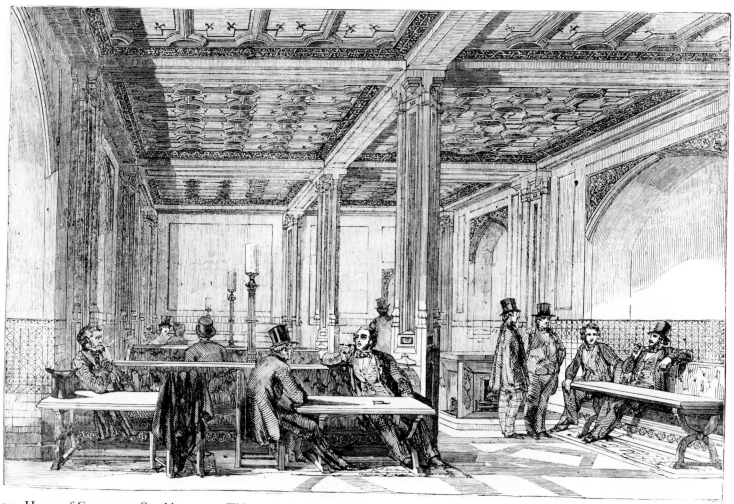

92. House of Commons: Smoking room. This opened onto the Terrace. It was designed with tiled floor and partly-tiled walls, so that the odour of tobacco would not be retained by furnishings. Rugs under the tables protected members' feet from the cold floor. The stove had open grates on three sides.

that no sub-contracting be allowed; that all stone-carving be placed entirely under the control of the superintendent, Thomas, the wages being paid weekly by the Government (as for the wood-carvers); that the salaries of Thomas and Pugin should each be cut by £100; that lump sum contracts should be made wherever practicable; that all outstanding balances due should be at once ascertained, a sufficient number of measurers being employed to make up the accounts; and that in future measuring and making up accounts should keep pace with the works. The Commissioners replied that, advantageous as this would be, it depended on the immediate measurement of all the work completed.[13] Payments on account without the work being measured as executed (as hitherto) were 'in every respect very objectionable'; the longer measurement was delayed, the more difficult a final settlement would be. Barry calculated that if he employed ten measurers at a cost of £1,800 he could clear off the arrears in twelve months: this shows the size of the problem.

It might seem that nonetheless it was a straightforward matter and that measurers could forthwith be set to work. The truth was quite otherwise: their employment impinged on the vexed question of the architect's fee. Past experience had confirmed the Office of Works in its view that paying an architect by a commission on expenditure was a thoroughly bad principle. As the historian of the building industry has remarked, 'the architect is in the position of a commission salesman whose interest is to get as big a value of turnover as possible. . . . It is a curious position in which a client pays his disinterested agent a commission for advising him to spend more.'[14] In 1838 the Treasury had agreed with the Woods and Works' proposal to pay Barry a fixed sum, and the figure of £25,000 had been based on the Office of Works' practice between 1815 and 1832: official architects had been paid a retainer fee of £500 p.a. and received three per cent on outlay, the measuring and making up accounts being done by the Office. Barry's fee was accordingly calculated as three per cent on his estimate, plus £500 p.a. for the six years he had stated the job would require. This decision was carelessly not communicated to him until 1839, when he was too heavily engaged to withdraw. He contented himself with protests, warning that he would raise the subject again when the work was sufficiently forward to justify his claim. In 1841 Barry asked the government to pay for measuring, which it refused to do on the ground that his remuneration was intended to cover all such expenses; again he acquiesced.[15] As the river front was a lump-sum contract, there should not have been much measuring necessary, anyway. Up to January 1848 Barry had been paid £24,735. In 1850 Sir Charles Wood as Chancellor of the Exchequer conceded his right to some addition to the original sum, and he received a further £10,000 in 1850–2. But the government was not prepared to discuss the principle on which it acted.[16]

Barry's proposals for additional measurers thus put the fat in the fire. A protracted dispute developed, to become another factor retarding completion. The new issue was not one of cash but of responsibility. Lord Seymour, Morpeth's successor as First Commissioner, wanted as measurer an independent person 'selected by and to be held exclusively accountable' to his Office.[17] Barry attacked the inference that the public interest lacked protection:

The architect himself is the paid servant of the Public, and the protection of its interests as well in the important departments of the accounts as in those of design and construction, constitutes his especial duty; a duty in these respects more likely to be well and efficiently performed by him, than by any person in a lower grade of the profession paid by a percentage on the outlay and having no such motive as an architect's character must have, in keeping down the cost of the work . . . The appointment by an employer of one professional person expressly to check or control the proceedings of another of much higher grade to whom the employer had for a long period entrusted the sole care of his interests, could not be submitted to by any member of standing and character in either of the liberal professions.

Only the architect, with his knowledge of circumstances, of orders given as to the mode of executing works, could superintend making up of accounts or successfully 'resist extravagant claims on the part of the contractors.' Not only was Seymour's proposal impracticable; it was derogatory, Barry held, 'to my own character and position, subversive of my proper authority in conducting the works of the new Palace in future, and detrimental to the public service'.[18]

Seymour giving way, Barry engaged the services of H. A. Hunt and four additional measurers.[19] But Seymour's intention was not only to clear off arrears before the 1852 session of Parliament, but also that the architect should cease to employ as measurers certain clerks of works paid by the public. Barry retorted that Seymour misunderstood the relationship. Though paid by the employer, the clerk of works was the servant of the architect: 'He is appointed by him, acts exclusively under his orders, and is subject to dismissal from him alone.' It was therefore the undoubted

93. New Palace Yard, 1851–2, showing masons' sheds and temporary committee rooms next Westminster Hall. Note the incomplete west face of the lower stages of the Clock Tower (where Barry hoped to build a range of offices) and the absence of external scaffolding.

right of the architect to employ him in any way conducive to his employer's interests. 'Who', he asked, '. . . having the requisite qualifications, can be so competent to measure work, and bring it to account as the person whose duty it is, not only to see that it is properly performed, but also, to take notes and diagrams of the manner in which it is constructed, and to keep a vigilant eye upon the amount of day work incurred in the execution of it?' This time however the Office was firm, and Barry yielded, retaining Quilter and Strudwick as measurers but ceasing to employ them as clerks of works paid by the government.[20]

Throughout this dispute Barry's insistence on a strict professional hierarchy with the architect at the summit is noteworthy. He was a leader of the architectural profession's struggle for respectability and for power.[21] He continued to fight for his own fees, too, urging the traditional principle of the architect's remuneration, a commission of five per cent on outlay. While conceding this principle in new public works, the government steadfastly rejected it for the Houses of Parliament.[22] By 1854 Barry had received £40,000 commission. When he applied for a further £5,000, the Treasury reviewed the situation. Considering the great increase in expenditure, the governing circumstances, and that advice other than Barry's had been obtained and paid for, 'My Lords' thought that 'a fair and even liberal remuneration' would be '*3 per cent* upon the cost of the works . . . performed under [Barry's] supervision including the fittings etc. of the building: but subject to a deduction of the amounts . . . paid for the assistance rendered by Mr Pugin.' However, as public architects previously paid three per cent had been relieved of the

94. Old Palace Yard, *c.*1852. Travelling cranes can be seen on the scaffolding, and the chimneys of steam engines overtop the hoarding. A wagon laden with large stones for the new front is arriving.

cost of measuring, Barry also 'should be held free from any charge on that account'. Barry replied that the fee was too small; parliamentary interference had obliged him to make extensive alterations, and 'ever varying directions from Chiefs of Departments' had involved re-designing some parts as many as four times. As for Pugin—nearly two years in his grave—'that gentleman was employed not for the purpose of making designs or of assisting him in doing so, but in superintending the execution of designs made by Sir Charles Barry.'[23]

After negotiations, the Treasury made an improved offer in May 1855: three per cent on outlay plus, for measuring, another one per cent, up to 2 October 1853; thereafter, three per cent on outlay plus one per cent on all measured works. Barry rejected this proposal too. But reviewed by the Treasury in January 1856 it was promulgated as a final decision: no further payments of commission were to be made until 'a final settlement of the past and an agreement as to the future are concluded.'[24] Barry riposted by publishing his argument in *The Times* (18 February 1856), complaining that the Treasury had 'constituted themselves the judges in their own case.' While paying 'at the least five per cent to all architects and engineers of independent practice for works of the plainest and most simple, though most expensive, character, they make the New Palace at Westminster, which undoubtedly is the most elaborate and complicated edifice in modern times in this country, the sole exception.' He urged that the differences between him and the government should be submitted to arbitration (as had been done not long before in Reid's case). Making no progress in that direction, he then challenged the basis of the government's calculations, alleging that the original £25,000 represented four per cent upon his original estimate of £626,500; so he should receive *four* per cent on outlay, plus one per cent for measuring. Thus provoked, the Treasury carefully reconsidered the whole correspondence: 'My Lords find that they were . . . under misapprehension on some points of detail respecting Sir Charles Barry's case.' The original estimate was not, as they had assumed, for merely the shell of the Palace, but for everything save certain fittings. Barry had in 1839 accepted a lump sum as his remuneration for the 'superintendence, direction and completion of the intended edifice', and it was therefore too late for him now to raise questions as to the principle on which the original recommendation was based.

On reconsidering the whole circumstances, the only doubt which My Lords entertain, is whether they have not taken too liberal a view of the considerations by which the Board of Woods, &c, were influenced when they recommended the payment of a fixed sum of £25,000; and whether, especially, in admitting Sir Charles Barry's claim to the payment of the expense of measuring, they have not gone beyond the intentions of the arrangement of 1839.

Nevertheless, they were still willing to give effect to their proposals of January 1856.[25]

In face of this clear warning, Barry (like Scott on the Foreign Office some three years later) surrendered.

No individual in my position [he wrote] could with the least chance of success contend with the government . . . I have no course left, but to yield to necessity, and accept the terms dictated to me . . . nothing would induce me to continue my services upon the reduced rate of commission proposed but the strong and natural desire I have to complete a work, which, by the devotion of so many years of labour and anxiety I have endeavoured to render not unworthy of the Country.[26]

Nor did his disappointment end there: he found his claims reduced by the Office of Works without explanation: 'I am utterly at a loss to draw the line as to what is, and what is not, due to me, according to the equivocal terms of the minute.' His situation was 'wholly unprecedented in the experience of the [architectural] profession.'[27] However much one may sympathise with Barry's attempt to secure the 'rate for the job', it must be recognised that the situation was one in which he had landed himself by his characteristic pliability and by his subsequent and equally characteristic slipperiness. His continued protests made no impression in the government's resistance to the principle of a universal five per cent. Hunt, once Barry's quantity surveyor whom First Commissioner Hall had deftly appointed surveyor to the Office of Works, supplied counter-arguments. For the new government offices much skill and personal attention on the architect's part would be needed to adapt the design to departmental requirements; but the expenditure would not be greater than for 'substantial buildings with plain internal finishings'. At the Houses of Parliament, on the other hand, with its 1180 rooms, 126 staircases and more than two miles of corridors, there must have been 'repetition of the same mode of finishing and the extent to which one design or one set of details was applicable'; while all the work was of an expensive character. 'Brass and gold abound; many of the windows are filled with stained glass; heraldic and other costly

95. (right) St Stephen's Hall (on the site of St Stephen's Chapel), looking towards the Central Lobby.

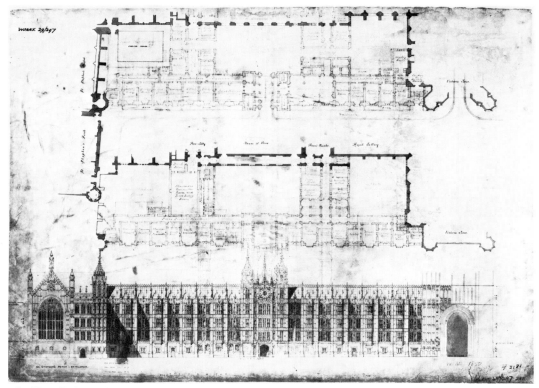

96. New Palace of Westminster: Old Palace Yard front. Proposed elevation, drawn on paper watermarked 1850 (not as executed), with floor plans.

decorations meet the eye at every turn . . . [These] add vastly to the cost of the buildings and immensely to the remuneration of the architect without demanding of him a proportionate amount of additional labour.' Furthermore, the price increases of the 1850s benefited the architect without any effort on his part. Had cheaper materials been employed, his labour and responsibility would still have been as great. Though he might have been put to some trouble by the different orders he had received at various times, had he been erecting fifty mansions (which might have cost about the same) his trouble would have been much more.[28]

This controversy illuminates the still uncertain standing of architects at that time. Against professional claims for authority and independence, the government set up the public interest, and appointed its own salaried technical officers to check professional pretensions. Its history has taken us to the late 1850s; we must now return to another recommendation that Barry made in response to the request for economies in 1850.

Barry's proposal to make lump-sum contracts where practicable should have been advantageous, for prices had fallen in the 1840s. By the time action was taken, it was too late to secure the full benefit—but Parliament's mood was economical. When Barry recommended that Grissell should proceed with the Commons' private entrance and the restoration of St Stephen's Cloister on the same terms as contract number 5, Lord Seymour had the prices investigated and found them unfavourable to the public. He gave Grissell notice to terminate his contract in December 1851. Grissell felt this blow to his pride, for he had hoped to carry the work to completion. He pointed out that costs and charges had been very thoroughly examined when the finishings contract, number 8, had been made, and that prices had risen since then. Nevertheless, though his experience in 'this most unusual and elaborate work, and in consequence of the extraordinary quality of the workmanship' showed his prices now to be 'but barely remunerative', he was willing they should be reviewed.[29] But official opinion was convinced that the work could be done more cheaply: tenders were obtained from ten contractors, three others declining and Grissell himself ignoring an invitation. John Jay won, contractor for King's Cross Station, the Metropolitan Railway (Euston Square to Farringdon Street) and fortifications including those at Portland. This changeover of course much delayed progress in 1852.

In this competition the range of tenders had not been wide, indicating the efficiency achieved in the preparation of quantities and their pricing. Jay's at £152,333 was about four per cent lower than the next (Myers) and one-third lower than the highest (Lee & Son). The contract concluded in June 1852, number 11, was for prices, not in gross, to run for four years, and offered a saving of more than thirty per cent on Grissell's. Within three months Jay was seeking a revision on the ground of a 'very great advance' in costs of labour and materials.[30] However, when in May 1856 the tenders for contract number 12 were opened, Jay was again the lowest at £94,929. This marked an increase of forty-four per cent over his previous prices—greatest in painter's work (seventy-nine per cent), plasterer's (sixty-six per cent), and carpenter's and joiner's (sixty-four per cent); while that in mason's (twenty-four per cent) and bricklayer's (twenty-seven per cent) was comparatively modest. Barry's rule that no work should be measured until it was fixed put him now at a disadvantage, as Jay claimed the higher prices on work prepared but not fixed under the old contract. Only four other tenders were received in 1856. Barry thought that builders believed they had little chance of beating Jay with his knowledge of the work.[31]

Jay therefore remained the principal contractor for the New Palace until after Sir Charles Barry's death. It was he who was responsible for the upper parts of the three great towers above 162 ft and the House of Lords offices fronting on Old Palace Yard,[32] with their bays of almost continuous glazing undulating in a manner recalling the porch of Cirencester parish church, and looking forward to modern non-structural glass walling.[33] Though this was executed after Pugin's death, the relevant drawings being dated between 1852 and 1855 (Pl. 96), he may have had a hand in the design. It is clear from the letters printed by Edward Pugin that Barry was taking A. W. Pugin's 'advice and assistance' for external decorations as well as internal.[34] Barry declared on 23 February 1852: 'I am much pressed respecting the Clock Tower and the new front in Old Palace Yard, as the building is at a stand in respect of those portions of it, for working drawings. I cannot bear that you should be bothered upon the subject, particularly as several new thoughts have occurred to me respecting it'—which sounds as if they had discussed it previously, and is surely an implicit request for further assistance. But Pugin was almost at that very time committed to a mental hospital, and never returned to work. Within eight months he was dead.

Barry's letter also raises the question of the remarkable design for the Clock Tower, with its overhanging clock stage which immediately became a favourite theme in Victorian architecture. Edward Barry's assertion that his father was referring to the clock tower in the Old Palace Yard front is not entirely implausible, but Barry distinguished 'the Clock Tower' from 'the new front'. There are sketches of the Old Palace Yard tower dated 16 March 1852, but the working drawings were not made

Elevation of the Clock Dial and upper part of the Tower

97. (left) New Palace of Westminster: Roofs of Clock Tower. Proposed design (not as executed, cp. Pl. 103).

98. (right) Sir William Molesworth, Bt, MP (1810–55), First Commissioner of Works, 1852–5. An energetic Radical, who thought to obtain firm estimates for the completion of the New Palace.

until June 1855. On the other hand, the great Clock Tower stood then some 150 ft high, or about half its final height. Drawings of changes in the traceried panelling of the Tower are dated May 1852. The Barrys' story of the designing of the upper part of the Clock Tower, the lucubrations resulting in one precedent at last remembered and adopted, goes only to support the ascription to A. W. Pugin: the 'precedent' was surely Pugin's own tower at Scarisbrick Hall. But when this was first thought of is another problem: a reference to Barry's 1844 Academy drawing of the Palace describes the Clock Tower as strongly resembling 'an old-fashioned upright clock case', which suggests that the overhang may have already been tried out, though there are no drawings to support this possibility. The iron roofs or spire of the tower (Pls 97, 103) are doubtless Barry's.[35]

*   *   *

After the failure of the New Palace Commission to realise the hopes held of it, the duty of controlling the architect was thrown back on the Office of Works, which was re-organized in October 1851, shedding its 'Woods' and responsibility for Crown Lands and becoming purely a department of public works presided over by a minister unfettered by permanent colleagues.[36] The personality of the minister thus became a more considerable factor in our story.

We have seen something of Lord Seymour's intervention. His successor, the energetic Sir William Molesworth (Pl. 98), an aristocratic radical, was not unsympathetic to Barry, though determined to settle matters on a firm footing. When in 1853 a Member accused the government of knowing 'nothing whatever of the expenditure that was being incurred', the charge rang too true for comfort. Parliament year by year voted for the New Palace a sum that the Chancellor of the Exchequer had decided the country could afford, based on Barry's estimate of what he could spend. Not until measuring arrears had been eliminated could what was due be

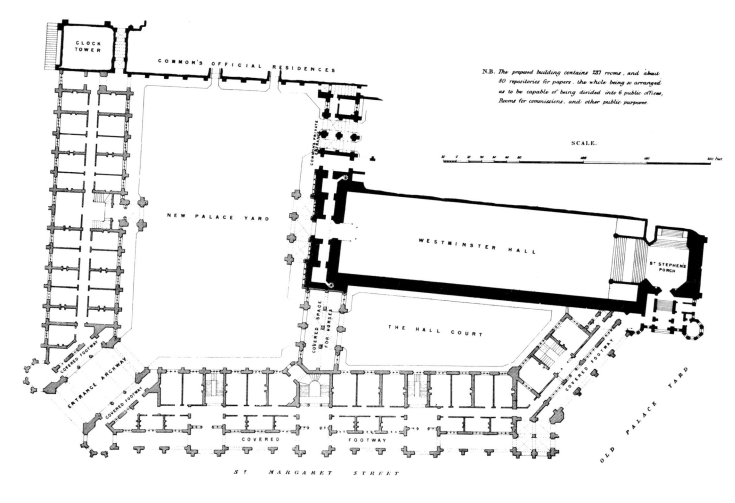

N.B. The proposed building contains 257 rooms, and about 80 repositories for papers, the whole being so arranged as to be capable of being divided into 6 public offices, Rooms for commissions, and other public purposes.

SCALE.

CLOCK TOWER

COMMON'S OFFICIAL RESIDENCES

NEW PALACE YARD

WESTMINSTER HALL

ST STEPHENS PORCH

THE HALL COURT

COVERED SPACE FOR HORSES

ENTRANCE ARCHWAY

COVERED FOOTWAY

COVERED FOOTWAY

COVERED FOOTWAY

COVERED FOOTWAY

OLD PALACE YARD

COVERED   FOOTWAY

ST. MARGARET STREET

99. Sir Charles Barry: Proposed plan for enclosing New Palace Yard with offices, 1854.

known and votes satisfactorily related to estimates for specific works. Beyond that, however, an estimate was still required for the completion of the Palace, or as one Member put it, 'to carry out [Barry's] fancies in connexion with the Houses of Parliament', a sum which might then be allotted over a given period. Otherwise, Members could see no end to expenditure. Hume in 1853 recalled that five years previously he had warned that as long as Barry lived the Houses of Parliament would never be completed, and complained of alterations constantly made 'to please some middle-aged taste. Why the very locks and bolts on the doors appeared as if they belonged to the age of Tubal Cain.' John Bright, a man who was listened to, accused the architect of 'destroying their credit as guardians of the national finances.'[37] Molesworth worked with 'zeal and determination' in co-operation with the Treasury Secretary, James Wilson, to solve this problem.

To satisfy the Treasury's insistence that funds should henceforth be applied strictly to the service of the year for which they were voted, and should not be exceeded, Molesworth proposed that accounts for Jay's contract should be rendered every two months, and the other accounts every quarter. As a further security, Barry's annual requisitions were to be accompanied by a plan coloured to show the portions of the building to which the vote was intended to apply. Beyond this, however, he was unable to suggest 'any check that could with any practical utility be imposed upon the architect of a building so exceptional in all its circumstances as that of the New Palace at Westminster.'[38]

Happy in the belief that annual expenditures were now firmly under control, Molesworth next tackled the question of the total sum required for the completion

160

PRESENT BUILDING.   PROPOSED   NEW BUILDING.   PRESENT BUILDING.

VIEW OF PROPOSED NEW BUILDING FROM PARLIAMENT STREET.

100. Sir Charles Barry: Proposed offices enclosing New Palace Yard and Westminster Hall, 1854. Lithograph of elevation.

of the building. In June 1854 Barry submitted an estimate of some £280,000 for works already sanctioned, of which the bulk was for residences and apartments (Speaker (Pls 108, 109), Black Rod, Lord Great Chamberlain and various officers)— nine officers having residences of twenty or more rooms, and a total of 281 being allotted residentially.[39] He had, however, in the previous December proposed extensive additions which he deemed 'necessary for completing this great national work in a fitting and proper manner'. His long-matured plan, known from 1843, proposed the removal of the Law Courts from the west side of Westminster Hall, and enclosing New Palace Yard on its north and west sides, so as to convert it into an interior court (Pl. 99). At the north-west corner, looking up Parliament Street, would be a towered gateway forming the principal public entrance (Pl. 100). 'By means of these additional buildings', Barry argued, 'the irregular, disjointed, and incongruous character of the present building on the land side would be removed, and a degree of unity would be given to the New Palace on that side in harmony with that already obtained on the river side, and the principal entrance to the Palace would then be a marked and important feature of the building.' These additions he estimated at £278,285. Add the cost of raising the roof of the Hall, and his gross estimate for 'completing, fitting, furnishing, decorating, and rendering fit for occupation', including all incidental charges, came to £583,557. On this basis, he calculated the total cost of the New Palace at not more than £2,166,846. The whole, he thought, might be completed in four and a half years from July 1854.[40]

No government with the Crimean War on its hands could be expected to welcome such an estimate; but there were strong practical arguments in favour of Barry's

161

proposals. This was the age of the select committee, of railway bills and the like. Despite the large number of committee rooms already provided, yet more were in demand. It was generally admitted, too, that the Law Courts were unsatisfactory, and that they could not with advantage be rebuilt adjacent to Westminster Hall. Many of the government offices had outgrown their accommodation, much of which was merely ill-adapted old houses, needing constant repair: new offices would one day have to be built. Royal commissions also frequently if intermittently and at short notice required accommodation. As a result of their inquiries into the public offices, Northcote and Trevelyan had just recommended that new government offices should be built.[41] Barry's proposals were not therefore rejected out of hand, but no decision was taken upon them.

* * *

In a reconstruction of Palmerston's administration in July 1855 Molesworth was succeeded at the Office of Works by Sir Benjamin Hall (Pl. 101), an adept and experienced politician, 'who had the power of saying no, and could shut his ears to the blandishments of Mr Barry.' Hall at once summoned the architect and told him that 'he wished to bring the works of the New Palace at Westminster to a close as soon as possible', instructing him to undertake nothing which had not already been sanctioned by Parliament without special authorization. For new government offices Hall had his own schemes.[42] Unfortunately First Commissioner and architect viewed matters from totally different standpoints. Not unreasonably, Hall thought that the architect's estimates for the completion of the building should, after all this time, be detailed and accurate: 'You should', the Office of Works told Barry, 'be able to inform him [Hall] whether any particular item is contained in any of them, and in which.' Increased expenditure beyond the estimate should have been immediately reported and sanction obtained for it. Similarly, new contracts should not be made until they were authorized. Hall was determined, he told a sympathetic House, 'to the utmost of his power, to confine Sir Charles Barry to the works which had received the sanction of Parliament'.[43] But Barry held different opinions. His concern was to carry through to completion the greatest building of the age, if not of all time, his own cherished offspring. Used as he was to following the bent of his own mind without interference from government departments other than some limitation perhaps of the money voted in a given year, he considered that he possessed as architect a general authority to carry out everything needful for the completion of the approved plan—indeed, he appears even to have made preparations for the unapproved additions that he had recommended in December 1853. Hall's orders not to undertake any works not sanctioned by Parliament save with the especial authority of the Office of Works he had understood to refer to those proposals, and not at all to the great building already under way. He made new contracts, but they were only means to ensure the economical execution of what had already been approved. Works actually in hand could hardly be supposed to fall under the First Commissioner's interdict, and 'from the peculiar nature and diversity of these works, and the extent of them' being out of Barry's control, it was impossible for him, he claimed, to estimate their cost with any degree of accuracy.[44]

Parliament voted in 1854–57 some £245,000 for the New Palace; the estimate for 1857/8 was £68,000, making an excess of nearly £36,000 over Barry's estimates of June 1854. But a general increase in prices of materials and labour which characterized the period caused him to add another £50,000 to the gross total.[45] 'The difficulty of restraining an architect', remarked Hall sadly, 'must have been practically felt by any

101. Sir Benjamin Hall, Bart., MP (1802–67), First Commissioner of Works, 1855–8. He sought to control Barry's works.

gentleman who ever employed one.' He charged Barry with carelessness, failure to spell out estimates in sufficient detail. Barry retorted that in 1854 he had not been able to allow either for fluctuations in prices or for extras that might be ordered. It had been impossible to prepare detailed specifications and drawings because of 'the uncertainty as to the nature & extent of the requirements which prevailed.' Hall did not challenge the architect's remarkable statement, but pressed for detailed estimates of works as yet unexecuted, so that he might decide 'whether any or all of the ornamental works shall be proceeded with, postponed, or abandoned.' 'Cunning literary fence' was the *Building News'* summing-up of this correspondence. At this point Barry's argument became 'so oily and saponacious that no one could grasp it' (as Lord Westbury said of Bishop Wilberforce). He could not (he said) supply the information required until he had resolved outstanding disputed claims for executed ornamental works and had completed his detailed estimates; he had not previously mentioned the probable excess on decorative works because a statement (6 March 1857) of additional charges had referred only to 'works of construction', so that 'any mention of ornamental works . . . would have been irrelevant, particularly as allowances for such works, with any excess upon them due to advance of prices, had been included in another portion of the estimate for the financial year 1856–57.'[46] Yet when Hall asked what these ornamental works were, Barry replied: 'The ornamental are so much a part of the constructive works of the New Palace at Westminster, and are so essential to the realization of the design, that no separation was attempted to be made of them in the allowance of my estimate for the vote of the year 1856–57.'[47] Such tergiversation (of which this is merely one example) may be described as a justifiable endeavour by the architect—already suffering from the government's refusal to pay him his customary five per cent commission and wearied by his long struggle with the Ventilator—to accomplish the realization of his masterpiece and prevent its frustration by bureaucratic philistinism. It may be, too, that Barry was irritated by Hunt (whom he had so often himself employed) querying, as government surveyor, the rate of pay, for instance, allowed for Crace's painters.[48] Even so, his conduct can hardly be considered to accord with the standards imposed by the concept of a professional relationship of architect and client. The tone of the professional press, so ready to plunge into the fray in defence of architects' claims, was somewhat muted, directing attention to the 'evils of our administrative system . . . divided authority, lax and indefinite powers, and uncertain responsibility.' And critics in Parliament could be bitter-tongued: 'It was very difficult at any time to control an architect', remarked Lord Claud Hamilton; 'but those who had watched Sir Charles Barry's career for the last eighteen years must have observed that he exceeded in his ingenuity in devising extra charges, every other member of his profession.'[49] After their experiences it cannot be wondered at that the Office of Works should, as in Ayrton's First Commissionership, treat with scepticism and even with contempt the claims of architects to stand upon clear and certain professional principles that should be accepted by Government. On the contrary, official efforts to bind architects and hold them to their responsibilities to the public whose service they had (albeit temporarily) entered, become comprehensible and indeed praiseworthy.

Barry followed up his bewildering manoeuvres with a refusal to analyze his estimate for additional works 'inasmuch as the amounts of such of the items . . . as relate to the advance in prices, are merely assumed, to the best of my judgment, and upon very rough and uncertain data, I do not pledge myself to their accuracy, and therefore I think it right to withhold any statement of them in detail, which might possibly lead only to error and misconception.'[50] Perhaps Barry took this stance in order to cover himself against Hunt's investigations. Hall expressed his 'surprise' at Barry's reply, but held on his earlier tack, firing another shot: why had Barry not given earlier warning of the likelihood of increases in works 'of an ornamental character not comprised in Mr Jay's contract?' Barry's contemptuous, almost insolent reply was that estimates, drawn up to meet the First Commissioner's wishes, were an attempt 'to define what is really undefinable.' As for the work being of an ornamental character, 'the proportion of pure ornamentation, unconnected with the constructive works and fittings of the building, is extremely small.' The minister's surprise he could attribute only to 'the want of a due appreciation of the difficulties, amounting indeed to impossibility, in affording it [the estimate] with any degree of accuracy'— this despite his declaration of 7 July that 'I see no difficulty in forming a positive estimate' for completing the Palace.[51] Barry's arguments recall those with which Nash in 1828–31 justified his inability to control mounting expenditure at Buckingham Palace: the work was unprecedented in character; it was impossible to price it; market prices were fluctuating; and any way it was impossible to separate the works into distinct accounts. Hunt now advised the First Commissioner to suspend all the works so that accounts might be rendered, and what had still to be done let in lump-sum contracts. Though he would not take such drastic action, Hall made it clear that he had had enough:[52]

Under these circumstances, the First Commissioner desires me to inform you that he will not apply to Parliament for any further grant towards defraying the cost of the works for the completion of the New Palace at Westminster until you shall have rendered to him—
    1. Accounts for works already executed.
    2. A statement of the works for which orders have already been given to the contractors or other parties, but which are not yet completed, together with the probable cost of such works.
    3. Drawings and specifications of all the works remaining to be done for the completion

of the building, and which are not yet ordered or commenced, in order that estimates in gross may be prepared before the works are proceeded with.

The First Commissioner will then be able to give some definite and positive assurance to Parliament as to the ultimate cost of the building, which at present it is quite impossible for him to do.

I am therefore to request that you will give no further orders for any works at the Palace to be proceeded with, the cost of which cannot be defrayed out of the balance of the vote of the current year . . .

Barry however had still a shot or two in his locker. For ten weeks he did not reply, the victim of a 'sudden and serious illness . . . which entirely incapacitated him for all business whatever.' Then he delivered a mere general abstract of works required to complete the Palace, with a general estimate of some £69,000 beyond the sums already voted, remarking: 'As all works necessary for the completion of the entire building are already ordered and in hand, no further designs and specifications are necessary.' This bland smile was accompanied by a paralysing punch:[53]

With reference to the request . . . that I would give no further orders for works . . . the cost of which cannot be defrayed out of the balance of the vote of the current year, I have to acquaint you, that previously to the receipt of your letter I had given orders for the completion of the works of the whole building; but it is right to state that the cost of the works so ordered exceed the amount of the balance of the vote for the current year, and that it is out of my power to countermand any portion of such works without a breach of covenant with the contractors.

Such flagrant disobedience of the minister's orders could not be excused on the ground that, as Barry claimed, it had been customary and indeed 'absolutely necessary' to 'order from time to time a considerable scope of work, which often requires more than a twelvemonth to execute, so as to avoid periodical stoppages.'[54] Since 1854 he had known that he was not to exceed the annual vote; and for seven months Hall had been expecting to receive his drawings and specifications for the works required to complete the Palace, works that Barry had been told not to order. By a masterly process of misunderstanding, bland assurance and equivocation Barry quite outplayed the Office of Works. His timing was impeccable: his last letter was dated 18 February 1858; on 20 February the ministry resigned. Hall's Tory successor, Lord John Manners, did not feel the animus against Barry that had clearly been aroused in Hall. He pressed, nonetheless, for the drawings and specifications of the final works, to be told that there were only the working drawings that were already in use—a sample was enclosed with a request for its speedy return! Adequate specifications were also sent at long last.[55] But the effort to obtain lump-sum contracts was thwarted by Jay's refusal to tender, on the ground that it was too difficult to estimate with any degree of accuracy for the works required. Jay was however willing to give up his subsisting contract if properly compensated. Convalescent at Brighton, Barry found the energy to pursue his feud with the late minister, who had left a memorandum (which he had printed as a Parliamentary Paper)[56] summarizing his case against the architect. Barry denied the charge that he had withheld information, and attacked Hall: 'Any difficulty . . . that the late First Commissioner may have experienced, the Architect can only attribute to his having failed to avail himself of his assistance in a frank and cordial manner, by which much needless and futile correspondence has been the consequence, and a great deal of misapprehension has been created.'[57]

When Palmerston returned to power as a result of the 1859 general election, he

102. New Palace
of Westminster:
The Victoria
Tower and façade
to Old Palace Yard.

103. New Palace
of Westminster:
The Clock Tower,
upper stage and
roofs.

104. New Palace of Westminster. Decaying stonework, *c.* 1926. A vent has entirely bisected this pinnacle on the Central Tower. It also shows surface decay, ascribed to inaccurate bedding. The finial (bottom right) has been split by the corrosion of the iron dowel that secured it on the pinnacle.

chose as First Commissioner Henry Fitzroy (1807–1859), who assured the House that no new works had been undertaken or were contemplated. An early death on 22 December spared him the disillusion inherent in a First Commissioner's lot.

*   *   *

Commissioners, contractors and costs by no means exhaust the list of Barry's problems in the last years of his life. Not every controversial issue can be examined here—whether, for instance, ladies in their gallery should be visible in the House of Commons as in the Lords, or whether they should there remain concealed behind a heavy brass grille, in 'something between a birdcage and a tea-caddy'.[58] An important anxiety was the condition of the stonework of the Palace. As early as 1848 comments had been made on signs of deterioration. A number of indurating compositions had been tried to prevent decay, of which the most successful seemed to be N. C. Szerelmey's secret formula. But one Member objected that this use of 'architectural cosmetics' was making the building look like Joseph's coat. More important, Edward Barry (who succeeded his father in the great work in 1860) was not satisfied with any of them; the increasing decomposition of the stone led to the appointment of a committee in 1861. After hearing scientific witnesses and masons, it concluded that decay was chiefly to be ascribed to London's pernicious atmosphere.[59] Later experience however was to show that the variable quality of the stone itself (not inspected at the quarry) and the misplacing of the horizontal natural bed of the stone in a vertical position were the basic causes, and the use of iron cramps to fix stonework a major contributory factor (Pl. 104).[60]

The difficulties of ventilating and lighting the House were not solved by the final dismissal of Reid in 1852, and are considered below. Another problem that caught public attention may be outlined here as presenting Barry with one of his worst headaches.[61] For fierce controversy raged about the clock to adorn the great Clock Tower (Pl. 103), and the protagonist was one of the rudest of Victorian controversialists, Edmund Beckett Denison (1816–1905, created Lord Grimthorpe 1886) (Pl. 106).

This story begins in March 1844 when Barry asked Benjamin Lewis Vulliamy (1780–1854), the royal clockmaker (father of one of Barry's early pupils), about the terms on which he would prepare a specification for the Westminster clock, required for completing the design for the Clock Tower. In November 1845 Edward John Dent (1790–1853), a manufacturer of marine chronometers who had lately made a turret clock for the new Royal Exchange, applied to be admitted to the competition for the Westminster clock, producing a testimonial from the Astronomer Royal, G. B. Airy. The following summer, the then First Commissioner, Lord Canning, consulted Airy on how to obtain 'the very best [clock] which the science and skill of the country can supply.' Airy prescribed general conditions only, recommending Dent as executant, with Vulliamy or Whitehurst of Derby as alternatives. Barry's idea of a common specification was abandoned, and scope offered to the clockmakers' inventive powers. Vulliamy regarded a competition as *infra dig.*, rejected Airy's specification, but sent in his own which Airy damned as 'a village clock of very superior character'. By September 1846 the government also had Dent's and Whitehurst's tenders. At £1,600 Dent—making a bid to secure the turret clock trade—was asking only about half his competitors' prices. In July 1847 he successfully demanded to be allowed to compete also for the clocks for the interior of the Palace, which Barry had been ordering from Vulliamy.

E. B. Denison entered the lists in May 1848 with a letter to the First Commissioner recommending Dent as the best man for the job. Denison, author of the *Encyclopaedia Britannica* article on clocks, was to publish *A Rudimentary Treatise on Clock and Watch Making* in 1850, and to be appointed chairman of the horological jury at the 1851 Exhibition. By profession he was a barrister, by disposition a bully. Seymour, when he settled into office, consulted Airy again, who asked that Denison be associated with him in designing the clock, which they recommended Dent should make. His tender of £1,800 was accepted. But then it was found that the space available was too small. Barry was blamed, but it was arrogance typical of Denison not to have ascertained the dimensions before designing the clock—which had to be modified at a cost of £100. Then Dent died, leaving his business in the hands of his stepson, Frederick Ripon (later Dent), and vultures hovering to snatch back the prize. The Office of Works looked to the Law Officers, who in October 1853 advised that the contract was void, but six months later recommended that Frederick (Ripon) Dent should be allowed to finish the clock. He made good progress, incorporating in his apparatus Denison's recently-invented three-legged gravity escapement. By March 1856, when a rumour was circulating that the clock was 'like Farmer Flamborough's

V. (far right) The Houses of Parliament: The Prince's Chamber. Much of the detail here is by Pugin, including the remarkable octagonal tables. The bronze bas-reliefs are by Theed. The paintings of the House of Tudor were executed in the late 1850s by pupils of the Government School of Art, South Kensington. Gibson's statue of Queen Victoria (originally flanked by figures of Justice and Mercy) dates from 1854.

105. (right) Edmund Beckett Denison (1816–1905), cr. Lord Grimthorpe, 1886, by 'Spy', 1889. A gifted and irascible amateur horologist and campanologist.

106. (below) Arrival of the Great Bell ('Big Ben') at Westminster, 28 May 1858. This bell, cast by Warners, cracked, and was re-cast at Mears' Whitechapel foundry.

picture . . . too large for his room', it was complete and waiting only for the bells that were to hang above it in the as yet uncompleted roof.

For the bells, Barry had recommended a limited competition on a specification to be drawn up by Denison, the casting to be supervised and certified by Denison and the Reverend Dr W. Taylor. With his specification Denison advocated the new method of casting patented by Warner of the Cripplegate Foundry, devised with the assistance of the proposed referees. The addition of the First Commissioner to their number kindled Denison's ire: 'I will be no party to any such absurdity as that of subjecting the bell founder to the control and the competent referees to the interference of an incompetent one, who is, moreover, pretty sure to act under the advice of somebody else behind the scenes.' A change of minister enabled Denison to resume direction of the business and entrust the casting to Warners. In August 1856 the great bell was cast at Warner's Norton Foundry, then transported by rail to West Hartlepool and after some misadventures by schooner to London, arriving on 21 October: the pull over Westminster Bridge required sixteen horses (cp. Pl. 108). So 'Big Ben' arrived—first so called by the foundrymen, doubtless observing the First Commissioner's name, Sir Benjamin Hall, inscribed on the bell and naturally adopting the familiar and appropriate nickname of a champion boxer.[62] It was hung on a temporary frame at the foot of the tower while the quarter-bells were cast at Warner's Crescent Foundry in London.—Denison had one re-cast. Then in October 1857 Big Ben cracked. Warners blamed the heavy clapper on which Denison had insisted, Denison blamed the excessive weight of the bell. Another blamed Denison's recipe for bell-metal, with a higher proportion of tin than was normal. Warner's tender for recasting was rejected as too high, but Mears (who previously had refused to compete because of Denison's bias) proved willing to do it. The new bell, cast at Whitechapel on 10 April 1858, delivered to Westminster on 28 May, was raised to the top of the Clock Tower in October 1858 (Pl. 139), and Denison tolled it in November. More problems appeared: first the framework proved weak, then the bell was found to be bolted too rigidly. By the summer of 1859 Big Ben was deafening MPs and could be heard as far away as Richmond Park. But the minute hands stopped: they were too heavy.[63] Barry at once declared that they had been prepared under Denison's direction. Denison retorted with a letter to *The Times*, commenting that on all the alterations at Westminster Barry had been getting 'the pleasant little solatium which architects do, on all his extravagancies and miscarriages at Westminster, while other people have got the blame', and continuing in a vein of calumnious aspersion and denunciation of Barry's 'carelessness and blundering'.[64] But the answer to a bullying barrister was the cracking of his bell. Holes were found in it which, like bad teeth, had been plugged with cement. Denison promptly blamed bad casting, concealed by deceitful filling and colour-washing. Mears instituted libel proceedings, and *The Times* refused to print any more of Denison's letters 'so long as he continues in his present frame of mind, pouring out peals of jarring abuse': he was 'in the position of his own bell', something requiring to be 'taken down . . . as speedily and silently as possible.'[65] Denison believed the bell to be useless. The 'inquiries of scientific gentlemen' proved inconclusive.[66] First Commissioner Cowper, who complained that the bell's 'loud and dismal' tones drowned ministers' voices, proposed that the largest of the quarter-bells should be used instead for striking the hour; and Earl Grey too hoped Big Ben would remain mute.[67] But turned slightly so that the hammer fell in a different place it was found to be quite effective. It rings there to this day.

IX

The Completion of the New Palace, 1860–70

WHEN Sir Charles Barry died in May 1860, the New Palace at Westminster appeared substantially complete. The two Chambers were in use, with their ancillary services of committee rooms (Pl. 73), libraries (Pl. 107), refreshment and smoking rooms (Pls 92, 120), and residences for great officers or essential staff. The Speaker had moved into his palatial house (Pls 108, 109) a few months earlier. In the Prince's Chamber (Pl. V) a series of life-size portraits of the Tudors had recently been completed, and in the other state rooms the frescoists were making good progress. Certain works of small extent remained to be finished, notably the iron work of the roof and the glazed lantern of the Victoria Tower (Pl. 102); the parquet flooring, wall-framing and fireplace of the Queen's Robing Room (Pl. 122); the stone frieze and borders for the Royal Gallery (Pl. VI) and Stairs (Pl. 110); and the crypt of St Stephen's Chapel (Pls IV, 114, 115). But no one expected these to take more than a matter of months.[1]

To superintend their completion, William Cowper (Pl. 111), the new First Commissioner of Works, turned to Edward Middleton Barry (1830–80) (Pl. 112), the late architect's second son, who had served his father for nearly ten years and to whom Sir Charles had bequeathed his architectural drawings. Edward Barry had already earned an independent reputation as architect of the new Covent Garden Theatre and adjoining Floral Hall (1857–8) and the Endell Street Schools (1859).[2] In order to complete his father's great work, Edward Barry accepted the invitation to supervise the items already sanctioned for which funds had been voted, although it carried only the reduced rate of commission, four per cent, that had been paid to his father. In a typically Barry-like letter he delivered himself of a protesting non-protest at this departure from professional custom and (he claimed) governmental usage.[3] 'It might also be observed', he wrote, 'that if any arguments could heretofore have been deduced from the exceptional character of the works at the New Palace, as regards either largeness of outlay or private agreement, they have now necessarily ceased to be applicable to present circumstances.' Nevertheless, 'from the peculiar feelings with which I approach the work . . . I do not wish in any way to introduce pecuniary considera-

107. (above) House of Commons' Library, completed 1848. Furniture and some desk furniture designed by A. W. Pugin.

108. (left) Speaker's House, completed 1859: Entrance hall and state staircase. The residences, of which the Speaker's is the largest and finest, form an important element in the Palace of Westminster.

109. (above) Speaker's House: The State Dining Room. The decoration, though of a Puginesque character, post-dates Pugin's death, having been completed in 1858 (see also Pl. 121).

110. (right) Palace of Westminster: The Royal Stair. The unbroken ascent, with its 5-in. rise and 16-in. tread for easy mounting, was designed by Charles Barry in the early 1840s; the marble and mosaic ornaments were applied by E. M. Barry in 1868–9, but his proposals for further enrichment were rejected by the Commons.

111. William Cowper, MP (1811–88) (afterwards Cowper-Temple), First Commissioner of Works, 1860–6. Cowper, Palmerston's step-son and heir, was an art-lover who used his position to encourage the fine arts.

112. Edward Middleton Barry, RA (1830–80), Architect at the Houses of Parliament, 1860–70.

tions.' But instead of the very limited undertaking that he had expected, he was to become involved in the continuing saga of the New Palace. For ten years, until his unceremonious dismissal by a ruthless First Commissioner of Works, Acton Ayrton, Edward Barry was called upon to advise on projects for improving conditions in the building, as well as the 'general architectural care and superintendence', executing works totalling some £130,000, 'requiring considerable artistic skill' and 'involving responsibilities and demands on my time and attention out of all proportion to my fee'. That fee, however, he did persuade Cowper should from 1862 be charged at the customary five per cent.[4]

Like his father, Edward Barry was no convinced Goth. As Professor of Architecture at the Royal Academy he not only recommended classical styles for secular buildings, but also suggested that not all churches need be in Gothic. Himself an Associate of the Institution of Civil Engineers, he told the Academy's students that it was not wise for the architect to leave new inventions to the engineer; and 'more, perhaps, than most architects, he studied principles of construction, and applications of mechanical contrivance.'[5] In his most obvious work at Westminster, the arcade along the east side of New Palace Yard (Pl. 113), he was to modify the character of his father's work, as contemporaries did not fail to notice.[6]

'From little into more' might have been his motto for this duty. Almost immediately in 1861 a further vote of £21,000 was taken. A great part of this was for clearing off Jay's contract on a schedule of prices, and some £7,000 was nearly equally divided between three lump-sum contracts with Field (mason), Hardman (metal work) and Crace (decorative painting). Barry protested that he had had to measure Jay's

176

works and to take out the quantities for the other contracts: 'it is not usual for architects to undertake either of these services, even when they receive their full commission of 5 per cent.' As more work came his way, he put forward a hopeful non-claim, pointing out that to accept a lower rate than the usual

might be construed as implying a professional inferiority which I am unwilling to admit . . . If, therefore I were disposed to put any claim before the Government, it would probably be for an allowance of 5 instead of 4 per cent on the sum of £20,895.3s. voted by Parliament in the Session of 1861. I wish, however, to repeat that I leave the whole question to the First Commissioner to be dealt with or not as he may think right.

Edward Barry was fortunate on this occasion in having to deal with the liberally-minded William Cowper as First Commissioner, 'a man who was quite without

113. Houses of Parliament: West Front overlooking New Palace Yard. Arcade designed by E. M. Barry, 1864, with statues by H. H. Armstead. Unlike the rest of the building, the arcade was built of Portland stone.

official airs . . . considerate and accessible.' Although Cowper recommended that for new works Barry should be paid at the usual rate, this left the question of measuring unsettled for a further controversy in 1866–7. When Lord John Manners then insisted that measuring must be included in his five per cent Barry acquiesced although it was contrary to the rules of the Royal Institute of British Architects.[7]

The most important of Edward Barry's works at Westminster were the completion of New Palace Yard and the decoration of some conspicuous parts of the interior. It was not until 1864 that the elder Barry's idea of forming New Palace Yard into a quadrangle with office blocks to the north and west (Pls 99, 100) was definitely abandoned. Cowper told Parliament that the magnificent view of the Abbey obtained by leaving a large open space between Westminster Bridge and Victoria Street made it inexpedient to cumber the ground with buildings, a late triumph of the picturesque over the utilitarian.[8] In the hope of completing his larger scheme, Sir Charles Barry had left the lower part of the west side of the Clock Tower unfaced (Pl. 93); Edward Barry had now to complete the Clock Tower and design a layout for New Palace Yard. In place of the houses between the Yard and Bridge Street, he proposed an ornamental iron railing and gates (executed by Hardman), supported at intervals by stone piers. To adapt the East front of the Palace overlooking the Yard from an inner quadrangle façade to an external one, he designed a covered arcade linking the Commons' entrance with a proposed public subway under Bridge Street—already the most 'dangerous crossing in all London'. Lump sum contracts for completing the Tower and enclosing the Yard (£24,917), and for the arcade (£7,700) were concluded with William Field in 1865 and 1866. In 1865 £15,000 was voted for these works, and another £28,000 the following year, when Cowper explained that his aim was to make the spot 'the chief feature of London', 'surrounded by noble architecture', a purpose the more readily achieved as the other side of Bridge Street was also Crown property. The railing around the Yard was to be 'of a light character, so as not to intercept the view. The lamps, at intervals, would naturally contribute to the decorations; and niches would be provided in which statues of statesmen might hereafter be placed.' The arcade was not merely to be useful, but was also 'to give more dignity and massiveness' to the base of the Clock Tower; it was to be of Portland stone, which 'experience has shown was the most capable of resisting the London atmosphere'— and 'would greatly improve the architecture of the lower block of building which was rather bare'; an interesting indication of changing taste. When the character of the new arcade (Pl. 113) became evident by the summer of 1867, protests that it was inharmonious and out of proportion with the existing façade included one from Pugin's son Edward. These works were completed with the construction of the subway by Field & Co. in 1869 at a cost of £4,250.[9]

The restoration of the 'crypt' of St Stephen's, regarded by contemporaries as 'one of the best specimens of thirteenth-century architecture', was, we are told, the work in which Edward Barry took the greatest delight (Pls IV, 114, 115). Carried out with the 'warm support' of Cowper, it had to be done, 'rather quietly' because of the 'rigid economic utilitarianism and anti-ecclesiastical prejudice in the House of Commons.' In the early part of the nineteenth century this crypt—more properly, the chapel of St Mary Undercroft—had formed the Speaker's State Dining Room. Protected by its stone vault against the fire, it had subsequently fallen into use as a lumber store. However, because the stonework had been much calcined in the fire, it had to be entirely renewed. This was begun in the mid-1850s, included in the contract for the building at large, so that the precise cost could not be stated to Parliament.

114. Chapel of St Mary Undercroft (St Stephen's Crypt): view looking west. The calcined stonework of the fourteenth-century chapel was renewed with great skill by Sir Charles Barry in 1858–9. Here the masons are seen working on the roof by the light of gas jets.

115. Chapel of St Mary Undercroft: Detail of roof, showing original angel boss. The painting by Crace was executed under Edward Barry in the 1860s. E. Barry also designed the metalwork, executed by Hardman.

Edward Barry's estimate for the stone renewal was £2,200, and his own works, including altar, reredos, altar-rail and pulpit, fitting-up the baptistry, and gas-lighting, were completed by 1869 at a cost of £6,568 though contemporary rumour put the whole at £30,000. What Ayrton contemptuously termed 'bedizening with gold' cost only £830. Edward Barry had designed the decoration to 'bear reference to [the chapel's] former character and to its possible use at some future day as the private chapel of the New Palace at Westminster'; but prejudice prevented the room's use for ecclesiastical purposes. Ayrton condemned such 'a spectacle of the most absolute waste of public money'; but the Radical MP Mundella called up against him a sentiment that echoed Hume's in his struggle for the free Sunday opening of art galleries and museums:[10]

He [Mundella] was a strict economist; but that was not economy but scandalous parsimony which grudged what was necessary to support our national monuments, or to restore such a structure as that below the House to as splendid a condition as it was in the power of this great nation to do. He wished hon. gentlemen who grudged the expenditure could witness the enjoyment that the crypt afforded to the thousands of working men that walked through it.

Even more controversial than the crypt was the decoration of the Central Hall (Pl. III). Successive First Commissioners had implemented the elaborate programme of the Fine Arts Commission for the decoration of the New Palace, as described in Chapter XII. When Austen Henry Layard (Pl. 116) took that office on Gladstone's coming to power in 1868, he found the Queen's Robing Room (Pl. 122) and Royal Gallery (Pl. VI) completed, but the Central Hall a gloomy place, its unfinished walls covered with decaying paper and a brown encaustic composition used by Charles Barry to 'secure uniformity of colour and to prevent dirt from being too obvious.' To let in more light Barry suggested opening the lantern, as well as taking out some of the dark stained glass, as had already been done in the Royal Gallery under Lord John Manners. For the painted stone columns Barry wished to substitute banded marble; and for the decoration of the walls he proposed mosaic rather than the unsatisfactory fresco painting which the Fine Arts Commissioners had advocated. This met a ready response from Layard, who had in 1866 assisted in raising capital for the Italian Salviati, reviver of working in enamel mosaic. Barry accordingly, acting as he was wont, on his own authority, made a contract with Salviati's son for mosaic designs for the panels of the roof, incorporating national symbols, so that the work could be completed in the parliamentary summer recess. In addition to this background, there were to be mosaic pictures, and Layard invited designs from Albert Moore and Edward Poynter, young men whose work he had admired at the Academy Exhibition, as well as Val Prinsep. That these works had been commissioned without prior parliamentary approval annoyed some Members, and there were others who disapproved of their taste. When the relevant vote was brought forward it met with a hostile reception, and Gladstone himself had to intervene. He attempted to define the principle on which the government acted here: money on account should only be applied for established services. It was customary to make contracts for such services before the funds had been voted. The decoration of the Palace fell into this class; structural alterations did not, and those that had been mentioned would not be executed. The consequent reduction of some £3,000 in the vote was an annoyance to Barry, who complained that he would have made a much finer job if allowed to alter the glass and columns; nevertheless he thought he had achieved a 'general cheerfulness and lightness':[11]

116. Austen Henry Layard, MP (1817–94), First Commissioner of Works, 1868–9. Layard saw his role as that of 'Minister for the Fine Arts'.

117. Acton Smee Ayrton, MP (1816–86), First Commissioner of Works, 1869–73. He conceived it his duty to prune expenditure.

In decoration I have gone on the principle of doing thoroughly as much as I could, leaving the obvious incompleteness of the work to tell its own tale and possibly be removed at some future time when England possesses funds enough to finish its public buildings. The roof is quite finished [he informed Layard] and the mosaics are very fine . . . All the brown is gone from the stone work, which is now of its natural colour. Of course the want of vertical lines to connect the floor and roof is felt, with the result of some apparent diminution of height. I grieve over the refusal of the marble columns, which when banded together with colour would have been superb and would have completed the design.

Layard had seen his role as that of a Minister for the Fine Arts, and he found the chill climate of ministerial and parliamentary economy uncongenial. In a reshuffle Gladstone gave him the Madrid Embassy, replacing him by Acton Smee Ayrton (1816–86) (Pl. 117), whose rigid application of economical principles as Secretary of the Treasury had proved too much even for his departmental colleagues. 'With a lukewarm zeal for art, but with very strong instincts for economy and a very decided distrust of the artistic race', Ayrton was just the man to kill any notions of lavish spending by the Office of Works.[12]

The mosaics soon fell under his axe. Poynter's *St George* had been completed, but was by no means universally approved of: one of the duty policemen thought the dragon looked like a pig, Salviati was not satisfied with the execution, and Poynter wanted some parts re-worked. Ayrton took the opportunity to appoint a committee of painters (including Poynter) who not surprisingly recommended that mosaic decoration should be suspended until a number of professional problems had been resolved and that it was premature to abandon fresco painting as the failures might yet be traced to specific causes. But one MP's reaction was that with Blucher nearly obliterated and the Duke of Wellington's nose dropping off, (in Maclise's *Waterloo*) the money might as well be thrown into the Thames as spent on more fresco painting. Ayrton, however, argued that very strong views had been expressed that the embellishment of the Houses of Parliament ought to be the means of 'encouraging original work of art of the highest order'; that mosaics were merely 'mechanical copies of the works of others'—though expensive copies, for the cartoon cost £150 and the execution of the mosaic upwards of £500. 'I hear he is trying hard to avoid having any more mosaics from Salviati', wrote Edward Barry of Ayrton, 'and is making all sorts of strange proposals'. When the Commons appeared doubtful about further trials of fresco, Ayrton, prompted by Henry Cole, urged the merits of Colin Minton Campbell's 'new method of producing durable mural paintings by fictile vitrification.' Cowper Temple (as William Cowper was now known) urged that mosaic 'being in its infancy was capable of much improvement, and was admirably suited to large buildings.' In the upshot nothing more was done (no doubt Ayrton's intention), and it was half a century before the decoration of the Central Hall was brought to its completion. *St David* was installed to Poynter's design in 1898 at a cost of £927, and the benefactions of Sir William Raeburn MP and Mr Patrick Ford MP enabled Miss Gertrude Martin to carry out the *St Andrew* and *St Patrick* designs of Anning Bell in 1922–4.[13]

Edward Barry was also much employed planning alterations in the New Palace, though very little that he proposed was ever executed. These proposals were principally a consequence of the prolonged and fierce debates on parliamentary reform in 1866 and 1867. In the general run of business, Barry's House of Commons was found large enough. But when a major political controversy developed, with the great men speaking and Members whipped for a series of divisions, there would be more than 500 MPs in a House that seated only 300 in the area and 120 in the gallery.[14] Even after Disraeli's success in steering the passage of a controversial Reform Bill, high attendances were maintained as Gladstone opened his assault on the Irish Church and then, after winning the general election, proceeded to disestablish it. Members of course attempted to make sure of getting a seat. Standing Orders forbade the reserving of places, but after Prayers it was permissible to mark one's seat by leaving one's hat there, an indication of a purely temporary absence. Naturally this was abused. It was said that before a busy evening the House looked 'like a great hatter's shop. Hundreds of hats were to be seen from end to end of the Benches.' Some MPs were alleged to have two hats, and even to send a servant down to the House with one of them. One Member, said to be in the habit of leaving his hat in his place 'at an early hour of the day and going away into the passages and lobbies of the House, . . . provided against the risk of catching cold by going about the Committee Rooms in an ornamental smoking-cap.'[15]

When some members behaved like this, there were naturally demands for improvements in the House from those for whom high office or seniority did not ensure a customary seat. Gladstone as Prime Minister admitted that he had not experienced the inconvenience apparently suffered to a considerable extent by others. Sir Charles Dilke wrote in 1886, 'The greatest nuisance about being out [of office] is that I shall have to go down in the mornings to get my place, and sit in the library all day.'[16] It was private members such as Thomas Headlam (1813–75) who made the running. The actual accommodation in the Chamber was not the only object of complaint. Back-benchers asserted that they could not hear properly—again a difficulty not

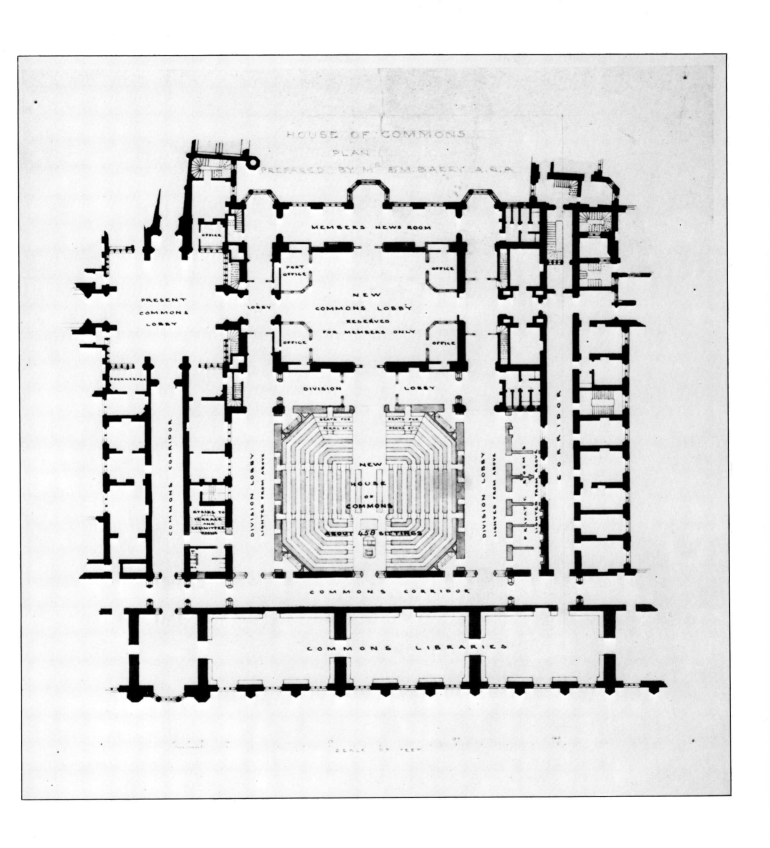

HOUSE OF COMMONS

PLAN

PREPARED BY MR E.M. BARRY A.R.A

MEMBERS NEWS ROOM

OFFICE

POST
OFFICE

PRESENT
COMMONS
LOBBY

LOBBY

NEW
COMMONS LOBBY

OFFICE

RESERVED
FOR MEMBERS ONLY

OFFICE

DOORKEEPER

DIVISION   LOBBY

COMMONS CORRIDOR

CORRIDOR

SEATS FOR
PEERS &C

SEATS FOR
PEERS &C

DIVISION LOBBY
LIGHTED FROM ABOVE

NEW
HOUSE
OF
COMMONS

DIVISION LOBBY
LIGHTED FROM ABOVE

PRIVATE
ROOMS
LIGHTED FROM ABOVE

STAIRS TO
TERRACE
AND
COMMITTEE
ROOMS

ABOUT 458 SITTINGS

COMMONS   CORRIDOR

COMMONS   LIBRARIES

SCALE OF FEET

118. E. M. Barry: Plan for New House of Commons, 1869. The existing Chamber was to be converted into a Members' Lobby.
Crowded debates on contentious issues in the late 1860s had led to demands for a larger Chamber.

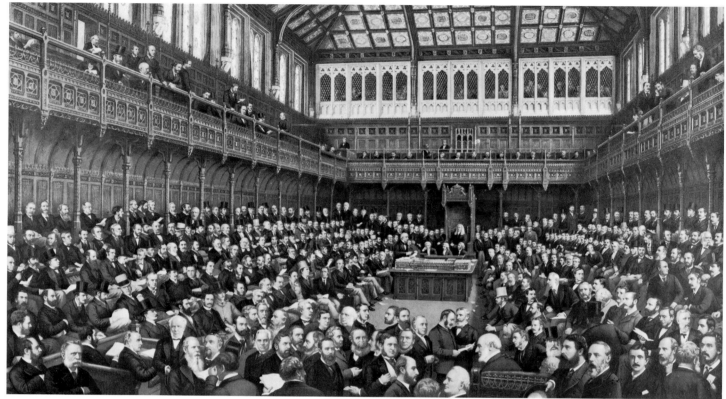

119. New Houses of Parliament: The House of Commons in session. Gladstone introducing the Irish Land Bill, 7 Apr. 1881, by F. Sargent, 1882.

experienced by the Treasury Bench, because members either spoke across to that bench or towards the Speaker, near at hand. Too often, front bench speakers used a conversational tone which could not be heard by those on the back benches. Of ancillary arrangements, too, there was considerable criticism. Cowper Temple thought that 'the grandeur of the central hall and corridors uniting the two Houses had been obtained by the sacrifice of convenience in the parts adjacent to the House', a view shared by his predecessor, Lord John Manners: 'nearly every one of the subsidiary offices connected with the House was inconvenient.' Division lobbies, dining rooms, newspaper room, vote office, post office and Members' lobby—all were too small. Beresford Hope, a rich aristocrat, thought that the House of Commons 'ought to be the best club in the world. Now it was the worst news room.' To visitors it gave the 'most scanty and grudging accommodation' of any popular representative assembly in the world. Vernon Harcourt, a practising barrister, remarked that 'of all places for the transaction of Public business in his experience the most uncomfortable was the House of Commons.' Another Member declared that 'the Libraries were too large, the Dining Rooms too small; the Committee Rooms were the most uncomfortable rooms for business that were ever invented.'[17]

All these complaints were a reflection of the House's having been designed for an essentially aristocratic body playing a somewhat limited albeit essential role in an aristocratically-dominated form of government. Complaints about the dining room (Pl. 120) of the House were an indication of its slowly-changing social composition: members drawn from the aristocracy, enjoying town houses, had earlier in the century

184

120. New Houses of Parliament: Commons' Dining Room. By 1853 some two or three hundred members dined here daily.

not been in the habit of dining in the House, and this was still true of the Lords. 'One reason given, indeed, for the longer life of the Lords was that they so seldom dined in the House.' In 1835 the competitors' instructions had required a members' dining room for thirty and a strangers' dining room of the same size. Now, however, thirty years later, there were many MPs who did not have their own establishments in London, and who did not, apparently, dine at the clubs which in some measure supplied that lack. In the 1867 session up to May, 6,412 dinners were served to members, upwards of 200 dining on several evenings and many being turned away.[18]

On Headlam's motion, a select committee was appointed in June 1867 to 'consider whether any alteration can be made . . . so as to enable a greater number of Members to hear and take part in the Proceedings.' This committee was subsequently charged with considering the arrangement of rooms and offices attached to the House, with a view to members' greater convenience in the discharge of their duties, and also with considering the provision of accommodation for transacting ministerial business during the sittings of the House. Not only social change, but the growing participation of Parliament in the whole life of the nation was here making its impact upon the New Palace. The Secretary to the Treasury, G. Ward Hunt, said that at least eight ministerial rooms were needed, as well as one for the Opposition chief whip, who had to make do with 'only a sort of cupboard'. Among the inconveniences of which members complained was that to go from the House to the library or the vote office 'one always had to run the gauntlet of all the persons who are in attendance in the lobby'. The complaint serves as a reminder that MPs were not the only users of the

New Palace. In the Commons Chamber it was necessary to provide for peers, officers of the House, government officials there to advise ministers, and reporters, not to mention members of the public. The number of places allotted for all the various categories of non-Members was 263, a figure which could not be conveniently reduced. Edward Barry proposed an alteration of the existing seating in order to provide more for Members, and accordingly less for non-Members. Two other schemes he drafted involved lengthening the House and re-arranging the seats to give a maximum of 852. A fourth, the solution he recommended as better and cheaper than the others, was for building a new House in the adjoining court (Pl. 118). He rejected as impracticable a suggestion by a member of the committee for opening upper lobbies above the division lobbies, or reconstructing the House by building up the outer walls of the division lobbies—which were not strong enough to bear the additional weight.[19]

Headlam's committee did not complete its deliberations before the end of the session, and during the recess plans were sought of other Parliament Houses: Paris, Washington, Ottawa (Pl. 202), Berlin, Vienna, Florence and Brussels.[20] In the following session the committee decided against lengthening the House because it would have exacerbated the acoustical problem. They agreed that any lateral extension would require a move into a temporary House while the work was being carried out. No rearrangement within the existing walls would provide the necessary number of seats. The committee therefore recommended as the best solution the building of a new House of Commons in the Commons' Court.[21] Barry's plan was for a chamber $63 \times 63 \times 69$ ft to accommodate 419 MPs on the floor and 150 in the gallery, together with 330 'strangers'. With a solid wooden floor, the proposed chamber would have been ventilated by air from below introduced through double-framed seat backs. A sloping wooden roof with a flat glazed central compartment, lighted from above by gas (as in some Parisian theatres and the *Corps législatif*, and similar to the old temporary House of Commons), was suggested by Barry, a mode objected to by the committee as both hot and expensive: they preferred small burners as both simple and effective. Lighting apart, foreign legislatures had little to contribute to this plan: most of them were more or less makeshift, the Italian Chamber of Deputies, for instance, sitting in the Palazzo Vecchio, Florence. Further-more, they were nearly all arranged on a principle fundamentally different from the British: that of the assembly being addressed from a tribune. Were the House of Commons to adopt this pattern, 'the difficult question of acoustics would be much more easily solved, and a very much larger building recommended without fear of inconvenience'; but so radical a departure from custom the committee thought to be 'open to serious objection' and not in conformity with the wishes of the House. If Barry's proposal were adopted, the existing House might be restored to its original condition and made to serve various purposes.

There was however a fatal objection to the committee's recommendation: Barry's estimate of £120,000. Members had learned to be highly suspicious of architect's estimates; this, as Viscount Bury pointed out, might grow into a total expenditure of £400,000 or even £600,000.[22] One comment was that an 'economical' parliament should not vote indefinite expenditure for its own comfort. When MPs heard Layard declare that the new House would be 'one of the finest things in Europe', Hunt's warning of an hour before must have recurred to them, about the 'fascination a coloured plan exercised over the minds of hon. Gentlemen of artistic taste; it was impossible to resist the desire to see it carried into effect.' Gladstone effectively ditched the whole conception. Although he remarked that ministers, who did not suffer the inconveniences experienced by other Members, looked to the House for guidance, he warned that they must have a care as to expense. After 1832, he recalled, the initial crowding had died away; and he would prefer delay now before embarking on some large scheme of reconstruction.[23]

Nevertheless, Headlam was a man of some pertinacity of purpose; in the following session he raised the matter once more, suggesting then that a new dining room should be constructed during the summer recess, after which the larger question of a new House might be considered further.[24] Edward Barry submitted an estimate of £24,500 for converting the Conference Room and adjoining committee rooms into a common dining room for Lords and Commons, forming a new Conference Room on the site of messengers' rooms on the east side of the Peers' Inner Court, and on the site of the existing Lords' refreshment room a tea room, library and committee room, with kitchen below. But Ayrton took over the Office of Works shortly after, and determined on changes in the plans, proposing to have the work executed under the professional staff of his department, 'competent to perform the function of architects . . . much better than it had hitherto been performed'. He had the justification that the committee had regarded Barry's estimate as extremely high. Ayrton even claimed for himself the merit of originating some years before the idea of using the Conference Room as a new refreshment room. The persistence of the Lords in maintaining a separate kitchen service, however, left the Commons to make their own improvements, though not before Barry had protested at the Works' officers' appropriation of his plans.[25]

Edward Barry had been called in to advise the House of Lords also, where the problem was in general the converse of that facing the Commons. 'Their Lordships' House was fitted up for great pageants and State ceremonials, and not for the transaction of ordinary business.' For that a smaller chamber was desirable. Much of its ordinary business was hearing of appeals in legal cases. The great lawyer Lord Cairns, who had frequently addressed the House as counsel from outside the Bar, remarked that 'there never was a chamber of the same size in which it was more difficult to make the voice of a speaker heard for any length of time.' The Liberal leader Lord Granville, however, had a better opinion of the Chamber, and blamed their lordships. He admitted that he was among the mumblers; but 'when we speak out and the House chooses to listen, the room performs its function perfectly.' Barry suggested that one solution would be to leave the Chamber untouched, for use on state occasions, and to enlarge the Peers' Robing Room (used not for its nominal function but for the Lords' Standing Orders Committee)—now called the 'Moses' Room—at a cost of £40,000 for the ordinary business of the Upper House. This failed to find favour with a select committee, which preferred arrangements both procedural and structural for maintaining better order, but peers were too evenly divided between the two schools of thought for any action to be agreed upon.[26]

The Barry family's connexion with the New Palace at Westminster was now to be rudely severed by the new First Commissioner, Ayrton, '*par excellence*, the economical Minister', 'totally devoid of aesthetic ideas, and with the wish only to save money.'[27] On 22 January 1870 the Assistant Secretary of the Office of Works, George Russell, informed Edward Barry that from the end of the financial year, 31 March next,[28]

in consequence of various arrangements now being made for the conduct of the works under this office, the New Palace at Westminster will . . . be placed entirely in the charge of the officers of this Department . . . The First Commissioner will be obliged to you to have all the

121. New Palace at Westminster: Queen's Robing Room Chimney-piece, 1864–6. The greater elaboration and richness that characterizes the younger Barry's work is clearly seen here. Field's marble chimney-piece cost £250; Hardman's grate, £120 (the firedogs are similar to those in Pl. 109). The figures were added in 1870.

contract plans and drawings of the Houses of Parliament, and all other papers necessary for affording a complete knowledge of the building, and of the works carried on in connection therewith, arranged together and deposited in the office of the clerk of the works in order that they may, when required, be at once handed over to this Department.

This missive was described in the Commons as 'a letter which no gentleman would send to his butler.'[29] Barry's immediate reaction was to consult the Chancellor of the Exchequer, who assured him that it was not intended that a newly-appointed Works' officer, the Director of Public Works and Buildings, should act as an architect. In a rather pathetic reply to Russell, Barry recalled his own long connexion with the Palace and his 'ardent desire', unmindful of pecuniary considerations, to 'maintain and supplement' his father's work 'and to remove any partial or accidental inconveniences which may obscure those great architectural merits'. Not only would his dismissal be an undeserved injury to his reputation, but the proposed arrangement, calculated to lead to neither efficiency nor economy, might result in the serious disfigurement of the architecture or injury to the construction of a building which '(whatever may be said against it) is at least one of the most remarkable architectural achievements of the 19th century.'[30]

A month later Russell reminded Barry that he had as yet taken no steps to place the plans and drawings in the clerk of the works' office. 'The First Commissioner', his letter continued, 'desires me to add that he has not thought it necessary to enter into any discussion of the topics raised in your letter . . . based upon assumptions which he does not recognise, and he requests that you will be good enough to comply with the directions contained in my letter to you . . .'. Barry inquired further as to Ayrton's intentions: it was unfair to a professional man that others should be entrusted with the completion of his half-finished work. As to the plans: there were those prepared in the last ten years; but there were also those made in Sir Charles Barry's lifetime, specifically bequeathed, as previously mentioned, to Edward. 'Many of these are invaluable to me, being by his own hand, and they constituted his only bequest to me at his death; I therefore value them accordingly, and regard them as a sacred deposit.' Russell's reply invited Barry to put aside those drawings that he regarded as a 'sacred deposit' for the First Commissioner's consideration; but 'working plans and sections, and specifications, &c, used for the construction of the building and foundations, embankments and sewers, do not come within the class of documents which you desire to retain.' Further, 'The First Commissioner declines entering into any question relating to your future employment under this Office until you have complied . . .'.[31]

While Ayrton and Barry engaged in legal wrangles about ownership of the drawings,[32] questions were asked in Parliament and Lord Devon moved for a copy of the correspondence between the two.[33] Cowper Temple defended his own appointment of Edward Barry and called attention to the way he had been 'harshly and severely treated', concluding with an attack on Ayrton's narrow views of economy. Where former First Commissioners had 'sought to foster and improve art', developing friendly relations with artists, Ayrton 'appeared to think it his duty to discourage art . . . He looked upon artists as a set of persons who were always trying to put their hands in the public purse.' But there was more to the wealth of a nation than money: it consisted also in 'intellectual development, in elevated sentiment, and in patriotism'. Paris and Germany were examples to follow. Applying such general considerations to his immediate theme, he stressed the importance of employing architects to design Britain's public buildings and hoped they would always be treated with the consideration 'due to gentlemen who followed a liberal profession'. This argument was pursued by other speakers, one of whom declared: 'The profession of architect is a high one, and the higher we can keep it the better for the country.'[34]

Two other important issues were raised by Ayrton's action: that of the ownership of architects' drawings, and that of true economy as against reduction of immediate expense. The latter gave a splendid opportunity for a ding-dong battle between Barry's defenders and detractors. Ayrton, '"Stiff in opinions", if not "always in the wrong"',[35] was often his own worst enemy. The manner of his correspondence with Barry offended many; but his arguments in debate read cogently. He was not the only critic of Barry's alleged propensity to extravagance. Osborne, always hostile to father and son, demanded that the taxpayer be freed from the 'family architect': Barry had been 'round the neck of the public a great deal too long'. Another MP claimed that Barry was 'ever devising new schemes . . . to further swell the enormous outlay.' Lord John Manners, on the other hand, pointed to the state of the Central Hall as proof of the need for an architect to advise the minister.

The debate was carried onto fresh ground however by Ayrton himself, by Lowe (Chancellor of the Exchequer) and by Gladstone, the ministers insisting that the real issue was that of responsibility: throughout the century the bane of public works.

VI. (above) The Houses of Parliament: The Royal Gallery. Barry preferred Halls of State to Grand Stairs or Corridors. This grand processional hall between the Robing Room and the Parliament Chamber was to have been frescoed throughout, but Maclise was exhausted by the difficulties of painting the two 45 ft long frescoes of *The Meeting of Wellington and Blucher on the Field of Waterloo* and *The Death of Nelson at Trafalgar* (Pls 183–4). The gilded statues of sovereigns by Birnie Philips replaced in 1868–9 others by different sculptors that proved too large.

122. (left) Queen's Robing Room. The frescoes, 1848–64, are by Dyce, who, working in *buon fresco* on wet plaster and painting only in the summer, died before he had completed his commission. The panels in the frieze were therefore decorated by Crace, as was the ceiling. The bas-reliefs in oak are by Armstead, 1867–70. The Throne was designed by E. M. Barry and supplied by Crace.

Barry's dismissal was, in their view, a necessary part of the process of establishing a proper system of responsibility for all public works, a system from which the Houses of Parliament had too long been exempt: a governmental department headed by a Parliamentary minister. With the *res* thus firmly established, the *modus* became relatively insignificant, and the government easily outvoted Ayrton's critics. The disapproval of Ayrton's behaviour voiced by cultivated society could safely be ignored.[36]

Having failed to mine Ayrton's position, Barry was compelled to return to hand-to-hand combat. He inquired whether he was to supervise the completion of the subsisting contracts for decorating the Royal Robing Room and Stair, only to be told that there was 'never any question as to [his] duty to see the contracts . . . duly completed.' To this he retorted: 'No such question has been raised by me. If any doubts have arisen on the subject, they have been wholly caused by your letters to me'. In reporting these works completed, Barry remarked:

It is with no ordinary feelings that I find my present official connection with the Palace abruptly terminated, and the completion of my work entrusted to others. As Architect to the building since my father's death . . . and accustomed from boyhood to give it the foremost place in my thoughts, and to visit it almost daily, I cannot however fail to retain a lively interest in all that relates to it.

Accordingly he commented on his exclusion from the council of artists that was considering the decoration of the Central Hall. The official reply was that 'no public advantage would result' from associating Barry with inquiries with which 'you have no concern.'[37]

Meanwhile the Law Officers of the Crown had advised Ayrton that 'contract plans and elevations of the New Houses of Parliament and all other papers necessary for affording a complete knowledge of the buildings are the property of the Crown.' Barry protested at the stating of an *ex parte* case, and Ayrton eventually agreed to his proposal to submit a joint case to a retired judge. But the joint case was never drawn up: a bench of three judges in the Court of Exchequer decided that architect's drawings of a building belonged to the employer of the architect. Barry at once gave way. Although he thought there were exceptional circumstances in his case, and although the absence of copyright exposed an architect to the risk of his drawings being used 'to the detriment of his reputation', now that the law was stated, 'I hasten at once to comply with it.' Rather than select what he thought he might fairly retain, he would prefer the First Commissioner to take whatever he might think proper, excepting only drawings made by his father and himself specifically with a view to publication: and these he was willing to sell, an offer Ayrton declined. All the others were transferred to a committee room, where one of the department's surveyors inventoried them and selected 1,648; the remaining 2,072 were returned to Barry in March 1871.[38]

Ayrton still, however, continued his vendetta against Barry, who naturally enough had now sent in a bill for his services to the various select committees.[39] When the annual vote for the Houses of Parliament was moved in June 1871, Ayrton hit back vigorously at his critics, asserting that Barry's services had been 'by no means disinterested' and that 'What had been written to Mr Barry had been written advisedly . . . When anyone desired to get a statement of reasons from a Minister for any course he might pursue, it was not desirable to fall into his trap.' A few days later Beresford Hope retorted, protesting 'against the Treasury bench being made the arena from which private feelings of liking and disliking should be vented in regard to any public servants whose position rendered them so incapable of meeting the taunts which were thrown out'. Imputations against Barry might harm his professional reputation. Ayrton retorted that in consequence of Barry's departure there were no more suggestions for a large expenditure: whether the architect made the suggestion and the First Commissioner took it up or *vice versa*, the result had been the same.[40]

Though Ayrton's manner was boorish and his behaviour high-handed, there is nevertheless a strong case for his policy. The Office of Works had indeed in the past shuffled its responsibility off onto the architect.[41] For this there may have been valid reasons, more particularly for the New Houses of Parliament. But government was flexing its muscles and beginning to assert its authority again. The New Palace at Westminster could not be allowed to continue its singular course. Edward Barry was a victim of the characteristically Victorian tension in government between the call for governmental action and the laissez-faire hostility to interference. National pride mounted high: England must be seen to shine in the Arts as a reflection of her imperial glory—but preferably not at the expense of the taxpayer. Occasional outbursts of spendthrift indulgence were succeeded by troughs of retrenchment which undermined grandiose plans. By means of architectural competitions the nation would obtain the finest designs: but the unfortunate winner would be vexed to death by disappointment, frustration and contention. Edward Barry, winner in truth of the competitions of 1866–7 for both new Law Courts and a new National Gallery, was disappointed of the opportunity to build either.[42] After that, his ejection from the Houses of Parliament must have been a crushing blow. A commission for additional rooms at the National Gallery was poor compensation, and he died a disappointed man in 1880. One cannot but sympathize with him, however reasonable Ayrton's policy.

The dismissal of Edward Barry really marks the end of the building of the New Palace at Westminster. Ayrton set his own mark on the Clock Tower: an electric light as a signal to the distant Member that the House was sitting.[43] In face of his opposition and that of Gladstone no enlargement of the House could be accomplished, and the agitation died of despair, though it was said that MPs' attendance continued to be greater than before 1866.[44] In 1894 upon a select committee's recommendations new kitchens were built and Ayrton's modifications of Edward Barry's dining arrangements of 1871 improved; but by 1901 things were as bad as ever, and alterations in the dining and smoking rooms were required to cope with the great numbers of witnesses at public committees (sometimes 1,800 a day), as well as the 235 reporters of the Press Gallery, a large staff of telegraph operators, and an increasing number of lady typists—a development since 1871, when a Member who referred to the need for a room where 'Members with clerks' could write had been told by Sir James Elphinstone:[45] 'It was new . . . to hear of an hon. Gentleman coming to the House with a private secretary, and he would just as soon think of keeping a pipe in the House. What was required . . . was to recur to the custom of their forefathers, and have some place where they could keep a gridiron, and eat a good beefsteak, and drink half-a-pint of good port wine.'

It may be appropriate to conclude this story of the building with a brief comment upon the success of the New Palace at Westminster—ventilation apart—as a 'machine for Parliamenting in'. Ayrton once complained of the inaccessibility of the upper floor, a plaint that may be echoed by the Member today waiting for his electric lift: but that lift reminds us that Charles Barry's masterpiece has proved enormously adaptable. Since Sir Gilbert Scott's rebuilding of the Commons' Chamber after its destruction by Nazi bombs, considerable additions have been made, partly in the courts, but more by building on the roof. High in the centre of the building is a telephone exchange; in another eyrie MPs have private rooms. The tendencies discernible in the 1870s have now fully developed: Parliament has been democratized; MPs have to have the means at Westminster to discharge their vastly-increased constituency functions. With remarkable ingenuity the official architects have provided for the ever-extending requirements of a modern legislature, a process that can hardly be taken further within the bounds of the building that Charles Barry conceived and brought into such vigorous life.

X

The Techniques of the Building

To engineers as well as to architects the reconstruction of Parliamentary buildings after the fire presented a tremendous challenge. Before the successful competitor could start his building, extensive site preparations required the skills of the civil engineer. In a surviving building it is relatively easy to describe *what* was done as, apart from archival material, the building itself, however modified, is a source of evidence. It is more difficult, but just as important, to attempt to reconstruct *how* the work was carried out. The scale of the building at Westminster made careful organization essential. Problems of access and handling of materials had to be solved. The growth of railways was making unprecedented demands on the construction industry and Barry's building was certainly to demand ingenuity from its builders. Its early stages were contemporary with the invention of photography, but were completed before the process became sufficiently mobile to record scenes on site. We have therefore to rely on artists for graphic evidence, and although there are fine engravings of the completed buildings the Houses of Parliament lacked an observer like J. C. Bourne, whose railway drawings provide interesting details of contractor's equipment and methods.

The decision to increase the site by reclamation from the Thames necessitated a major work of civil engineering. A new river wall was proposed some 80 to 100 ft out from the old wharf wall. As early as June 1835, the Office of Woods and Works commissioned a report on the possible effects of such a wall on the river. Sir John Rennie (1794–1874) and James Walker (1781–1862), two of the most eminent civil engineers of the day, were asked to comment, and if necessary to suggest a modified line for the wall. Rennie thought the wall would project 'rather too far' into the river, but Walker claimed that it would 'not be injurious to the navigation'.[1] To build the new wall in the dry it was necessary first to construct a cofferdam. During 1837 Walker made test borings in the river bed in the line of the proposed wall (Pl. 123).[2] The huge cofferdam, although only a temporary structure, was itself a major engineering feat (Pl. 124). It was placed under the joint direction of the civil engineering partnership of Walker & Burges and the architect, who 'divided equally between them the customary remuneration of 5 per cent for their services.'[3] Messrs J. and H. Lee of Lambeth won the contract, at £24,195 excluding engines and pumps, with £7,000 to be deducted for the cofferdam timber when removed.[4]

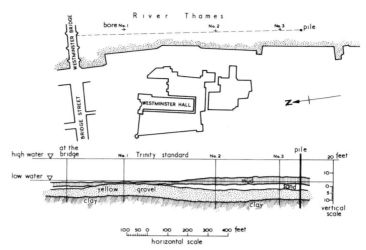

123. New Houses of Parliament: Terrace and river wall. Test borings in the bed of the Thames, 1838. Plan and section.

124. New Houses of Parliament: Terrace and River Front. Section looking north through cofferdam and concrete raft; and plan.

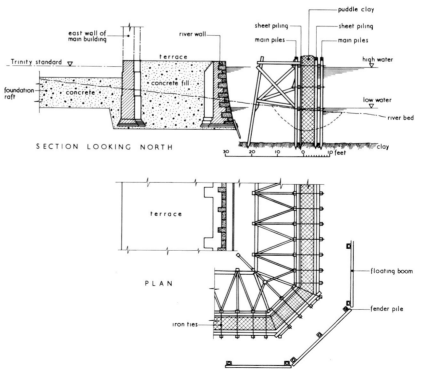

A trench 27 ft wide and 8 ft deep was dredged in the river bed in the line of the dam, which was 920 ft long and returned into the old wharf wall at the north and south ends to form a watertight box. The walls were composed of two rows of timber guide piles 10 ft apart, each pile 12 in square and 36 ft long, driven at 6 ft intervals into the clay substratum (Pl. 124). They were shod with wrought iron and left projecting 4 ft 6 in above Trinity High Water level. Waling pieces, horizontal timbers 12 in square, were bolted in three rows on the inside of both lines of piles. Inside these again were two rows of close-driven sheet piling, the outer row 12 in thick, the inner 6 in thick, sawn square on all sides to ensure close joints. The space between was then dug out down to the clay substratum and filled with puddle clay which, if kept moist, is an effective water barrier. The first pile was driven on 1 September 1837, and the huge dam took nearly sixteen months to build by traditional methods, for Nasmyth's pile-driver came just too late.[5] A 10-horsepower steam engine pumped out the water, however, and to keep the works dry ran constantly, driving two 18 in diameter pumps working fourteen 3 ft strokes per minute. The hitherto-unequalled dam was said to stand 'remarkably firm, and . . . tolerably free from leakage.'[6] It stood for twelve years and with the terrace provided space for the contractors' workshops.[7]

In the shelter of the dam, excavation for the river wall and terrace began on 1 January 1839. Excavation was muscle-powered, using pick and shovel to dig out 50 ft lengths. The detritus had to be 'carted or barged away' by the contractor; all 'coins or other articles of antiquity' were to be delivered to the architect.[8] Carried down 25 ft below Trinity High Water, the excavation was levelled to receive the footing courses. These were laid on a bed of concrete varying in thickness from 1 ft at the north end to 'between 5 and 6 feet in the centre and south corner, where the substratum was loose and spongy.'[9] Two layers of York stone landings each 6 in thick and 11 ft wide below two layers of Bramley-fall stone each 1 ft 3 in thick comprised the footing. Above this rose the granite river face, built to a curve of 100 ft radius and backed with brickwork making a thickness of 7 ft 6 in at the bottom and 5 ft at the top. Counterforts strengthen the wall at 20 ft intervals. The foundation stone of the wall was laid early in March 1839, and in May it was reported: 'Nearly the whole length of the wall is founded. At the north end, nearest Westminster bridge, several heights of fine-wrought Scotch granite has been laid.'[10] By the end of the year the wall, 876 ft 6 in long, was described by a professional periodical as an outstanding hydraulic work.[11] Behind it at a distance of 28 ft 9 in are the footings for the east wall of the main build-ing, constructed like that for the river wall. The space between was cleared and filled with 26,000 cu yd of concrete, composed of 'ten measures of gravel and sand, to one of unslacked lime, washed in with water, and levelled in regular and thin courses.'[12] This formed the solid base of the terrace (Pl. 124).

Excavation for the foundations of the main building could then be undertaken. The superstructure is carried on a mass-concrete oversite raft still called 'the Barry raft' by the resident engineering staff. This varied in thickness to suit local loading and ground conditions (Pl. 125). The use of concrete for foundations, on a large scale, had been introduced into London a few years earlier by Sir Robert Smirke at the Millbank Penitentiary and the British Museum. His specifications stipulated the sources of materials, their mixing and placing. To compact the concrete, Smirke required it to be throw into the pit from a height of at least six feet.[13] Barry's specifica-tion at the Houses of Parliament required that: 'The concrete forming the founda-tions is to consist of 6 measures of gravel and sand to one of ground stone lime mixed dry and then well worked together with water and in this state teemed and thrown into the trench from a height of at least 10 ft from the present surface of the ground, the

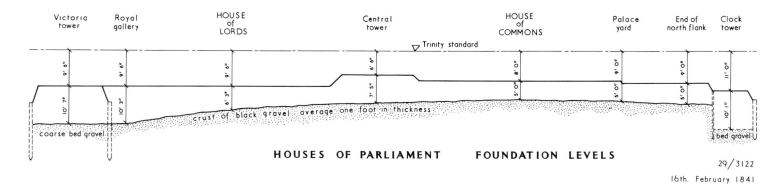

▽ Trinity standard

crust of black gravel average one foot in thickness

coarse bed gravel

bed gravel

HOUSES OF PARLIAMENT   FOUNDATION LEVELS

29/3122

16th. February 1841

125. New Houses of Parliament: Foundations. Section through concrete raft, south to north.

top to be levelled.'[14] This poor technique had its contemporary critics; one textbook, recommending compaction in the modern mode, remarked: 'Another practice, which we cannot too strongly condemn, but which has the sanction of many professional men of high standing, is that of throwing the concrete into the foundation-pits from a raised stage, with a view to consolidate it. Our own experience confirms us in the opinion that the contrary effect is produced.'[15] Nevertheless, the terrace and oversite raft, requiring some 70,000 cu yd of concrete, have proved an effective foundation.

It is not surprising on a seven-acre site, without advanced soil-investigation techniques, that nineteenth-century builders were faced with unexpected problems. Barry's son remarked that 'Few buildings have been more unfortunately placed than the new Palace at Westminster. A site full of quicksands and below low-water mark is seldom an agreeable incident in an architect's practice.'[16] Excavations for the foundations of the Victoria Tower, for instance, early in 1841, revealed quicksands. A double row of sheet piles had to be driven around the perimeter to form a permanent cofferdam, the enclosure excavated and concrete 'thrown in' to a depth of 10 ft 7 in. Two 6 in courses of York stone landings were laid as footings to the main walls of the palace. The basement was formed with brick walls and piers terminating in groined vaults with a rubble fill to support the flagged floor above.[17]

In the superstructure, the principal materials used were the traditional brick and stone, together with iron, both cast and wrought; timber was used only for finishing, to achieve as fireproof a structure as possible, consistent with its character. Cast iron had begun to be used on a large scale in the later eighteenth century, notably in the bridge over the Severn at Ironbridge, completed in 1779. In buildings it was used in mills, first for columns and later for beams, in order to reduce the fire risk. The typical mill or warehouse structure of the early nineteenth century employed single-storey cast-iron columns with the materials in compression only. The fireproof floors would have cast-iron beams spanning the columns, with the perimeter beams bearing on the external walls. Shallow jack-arches of brick would be struck from the bottom flange of the inverted 'T' beams with a rubble fill to form the level floor above. Barry used all these techniques in the Houses of Parliament. The structure is principally of load-bearing masonry bonded with iron cramps, with little structural innovation generally, though the scale of the building was unprecedented. Other contemporary buildings in London made extensive structural use of iron, notably Buckingham Palace, the British Museum, and the Public Record Office (begun in 1851) with its particular need for fireproofing.[18] Where Barry introduced structural

198

ironwork it was to satisfy the requirements of fireproofing, heating and ventilation, except in the Victoria Tower where it was used to reduce the deadweight of the floors. He also used iron cramps to secure the ashlar to the brickwork backing and to plug together the masonry of the pinnacles and turrets (Pl. 104). But his brick and masonry walls were load-bearing as well as space-enclosing and weather-excluding.

The principal floor of the Houses of Parliament is 20 ft above Trinity Standard level. The floors of the main corridor and House lobbies are of the masonry and iron construction previously described, but those of the two Chambers are supported on cast-iron columns with a grid of cast-iron beams and floor plates. The present Commons chamber was rebuilt after the second world war, but the Lords is still largely original with its cast-iron floor and roof, a double cube 90 ft long and 45 ft 2 in wide (Pl. II). Plate 126 shows the layout of its floor beams. The floor loading is transferred from the beams, binders, and joists partly on to the ten cast-iron columns (S) which carry the load down to the brick vaults of the basement, and partly on to the walls of the chamber. All these beams were proof tested (Table 1). Hollow cast-iron floor plates 3 ft by 2 ft were laid on the grid of horizontal beams. The tiered seating is carried on raking binders (D), spanning from beam C to the masonry wall. The span of none of these beams was comparable with those used at the British Museum.

The roofs of the two Chambers were the greatest span required; and the needs of fire resistance and ventilation made their design one of the most interesting features of the whole structure. The cast-iron trusses span the clear width of the chamber at 7 ft 3 in intervals, the truss shoes bearing on the masonry walls. The compression members are cruciform in section, the tension members either rectangular or of I-section, and all slot into cast-iron sockets at their junctions. At eaves level an open-mesh metal grid floor allows passage through the roof-space (Pl. 127), and at certain points the chamber below may be glimpsed through the suspended ceiling. The roof-space is divided horizontally, midway between eaves and ridge, by a tile jack-arch

126. House of Lords: Plan of iron flooring beams (see Table 1).

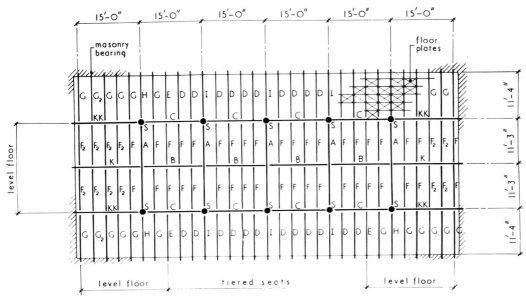

PLAN of FLOOR

127. (above) House of Lords: Photograph of the roof space, showing the complex structure of iron beams.

128. (right) New Palace of Westminster: St Stephen's Porch. Photograph of battlements and roof, showing the cast-iron roofing plates and dormers.

floor designed to contain any fire. But undoubtedly the most interesting feature of the roof is the external cladding: the interlocking cast-iron plates, with their cast dormer windows, which one sees from the street. These were adopted throughout the building to meet 'the requirements of the ventilation scheme which provided smoke flues stretching along the roof in all directions, and which being necessarily heated to a considerable temperature required a fire-proof covering not likely to be injured by heat'.[19]

The cast iron plates, being cast of sufficient size to span the distance between each adjoining pair of principals, dispense with the necessity for any kind of boarding whatever . . . The corners of each plate being firmly secured by screws and snugs to the rafters on which they lie, a greater degree of lateral strength and stiffness is attained than can be had with any other kind of covering; in fact, the whole roof, principals, and covering become one piece of framework, well knit and secured together at all points by metal connections.[20]

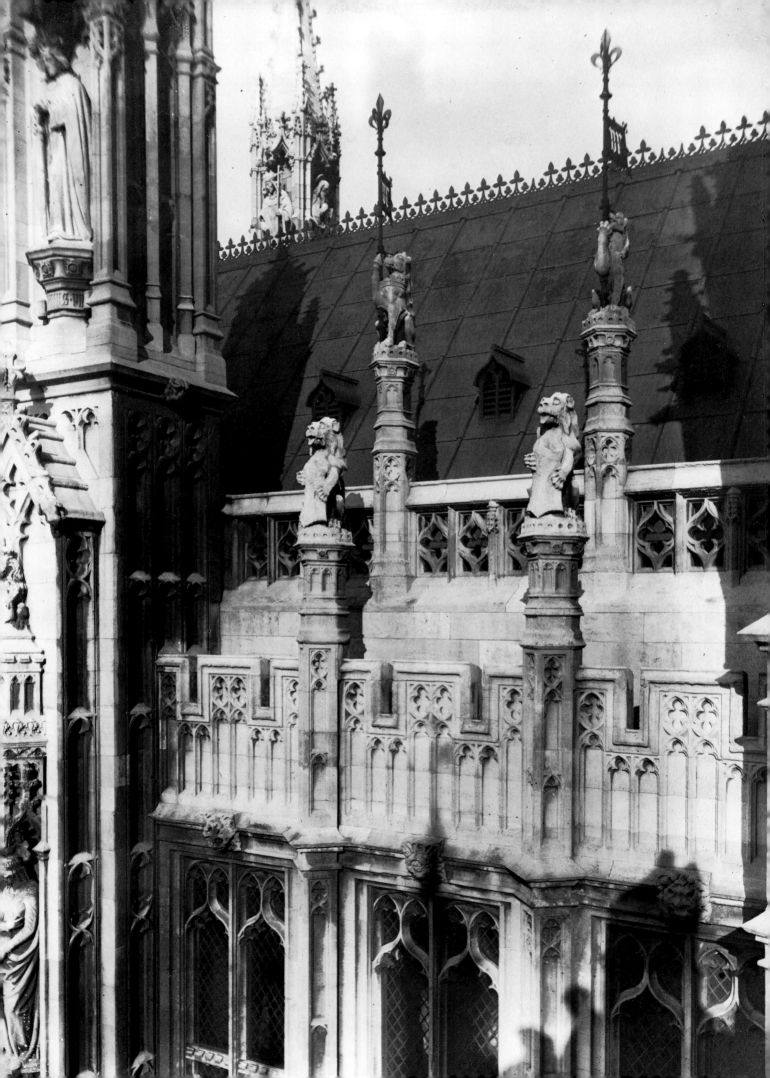

The plates were three-sixteenths of an inch thick. They were cast 'with extreme accuracy as to thickness and flatness' by Messrs Bramah & Cochrane in Birmingham, with decorative rolls as an architectural feature, and interlocking joints completely impervious to the weather (Pl. 128). Iron plates needed protection from corrosion: the first method tried was to cover them with zinc 'defending' plates, a method not tried to any extent in England before 1844.[21] Barry cited examples in Paris, notably the Opera House. Nevertheless Edward Barry later admitted:[22]

Experience has shown that, however well it may serve elsewhere, galvanised iron will not long resist the injurious effect of a London climate and atmosphere; and the means of protecting the iron roofs at the new Palace have occupied much of my father's attention. At last, after a great many trials of different paints and other compositions, one by Mr Szerelmy, a Hungarian gentleman, has appeared to him to promise great success.

Szerelmy's secret process, used also for the stone, was used for a number of years subsequently.

A particularly interesting example of iron roof construction occurs over the Commons' lobby. Measuring 44 ft 6 in inside the walls, it is intersected by two corridors each having a pitched roof; that of the north–south corridor has a greater span than that of the east–west corridor, but they have a common ridge height and

Table 1. House of Lords: Ironwork to floor of Chamber.

Description	Mark	No.	Span ft in	Proof load tons	cwt	Deflection inches
Main beams	A	5	22.6	12	5[1]	0·05
Main binders flanches both ends	B	4	15.0	9	12	0·3
Main binders with flanch and seat	K	2	15.0	9	12	0·3
Main binders flanches both ends	C	8	15.0	9	12	0·3
Main binders with seat at one end	KK	4	15.0	9	12	0·3
Raking binders or joists for seats	D	24	11.4	2	0	0·05
Raking binders for ends of seats	E	4	11.4	2	0	0·05
Raking binders with flanch at one end	I	6	11.4	2	0	0·05
Joists with dovetail at each end	F[2]	52	11.3	2	0	0·05
Joists with dovetail and seat	G[3]	24	11.4	2	0	0·05
Joists with flanch and seat	H	4	11.4	2	0	0·05

Notes: 1. This proof is between the seats on the columns
2. Those marked F_2 to be $\frac{7}{8}$ in thick.
3. Those marked G_2 to be $\frac{7}{8}$ in thick.

consist of cast-iron truss principals with interlocking roof and gutter plates. Over the lobby the larger trusses are carried on two cast-iron girders 3 ft deep, of open web construction, which span the lobby walls. At each corner is an area of flat roof with a slight fall to the gutters, formed of iron plates carried on cranked beams with pinned supports on the masonry. A suspended ceiling screens all this construction. The roofs intersecting over St Stephen's Porch provide another characteristic example (Pl. 129).

The three great towers of the Palace are major examples of nineteenth-century structural engineering. The Victoria Tower (Pl. 102), originally 'the largest and highest square tower in the world',[23] was designed as royal entrance and record repository; subsequently it was used also for ventilation. The masonry walls of the lowest stage, forming the Sovereign's Entrance, rise to groined vaulting some 60 ft above ground. In the crown of the vault is an access hole 6 ft 6 in in diameter, through which were hoisted the 3-ton girders used in the structural reconstruction of the tower in 1958–61. The access hole is closed by a sliding trap door consisting of a hollow octagonal cylinder mounted on a platform running on bridge rails, and operated by a rack and pinion device from the floor above. There were to be nine floors, 51 ft 6 in square, together with two others in the roof-space (Pl. 130).[24] The tower floors were of fire-proof construction—stone slabs, brick jack-arches, and cast-iron beams—delivering their load partly onto the 6 ft thick perimeter walls and partly onto

129. New Palace of Westminster: St Stephen's porch. Drawing of iron roof framing, dated 5 May 1847.

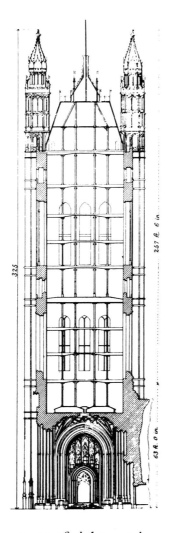

130 (left) New Palace of Westminster: Victoria Tower. Section showing structural ironwork.

131 (right) New Palace of Westminster: Clock Tower. Section, showing manner of construction without external scaffolding.

132. (far right) New Palace of Westminster: Clock Tower. Plan, section and details of the wrought iron bell frame and cast-iron standards. Pen, ink and wash drawing on tracing paper, dated 20 Feb. 1857, and signed 'Charles Barry 24 March 1857'.

groups of eight cast-iron columns collecting the floor load in the central area of the tower. Of 8 in diameter on the top floor, the columns increased in size down through the tower until they were of 14 in diameter when finally delivering their load onto four large cast-iron girders just above the vault of the Sovereign's Entrance. These girders, set at 45 degrees to the external walls, were 4 ft deep with a bottom 2 ft flange and an upper of 1 ft, both 3 in thick; each weighed about 12 tons. They delivered the total column load onto the external walls, leaving the vault to carry only its own weight in the true gothic manner. Investigations in 1958–61 showed that these girders and several other parts of the structure had been overstressed 'even before the tower was completed'.[25] It was then calculated that the compressive stress in the masonry of the great arch piers at the bottom of the tower was approximately 19 tons per square foot (average on brick and stone). When four floors were removed and seven new ones inserted in 1958–61, the 276-ton roof load was transferred to a new steel framework, leaving the original iron girders to carry only half their former load.

Access to the tower from the main building was gained at first floor level, 68 ft 6 in above ground. The remaining eight floors, each divided into eight rooms, had iron doors and frames with rubber seals. Access to the upper floors was by a dramatic spiral staircase, 'one of the earliest and most remarkable instances of the cast-iron stair worker's art ever to be built.'[26] It was 3 ft wide, having 416 cast-iron lattice steps leading to the roof, some 190 ft above, with a central well-hole of 6 ft diameter. The treads were supported from ring plates at the floor levels by tension rods. Now only the lowest 80 ft of the stair remain.

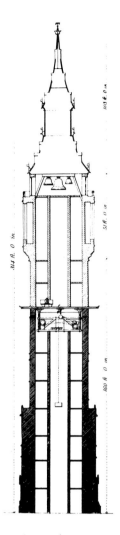

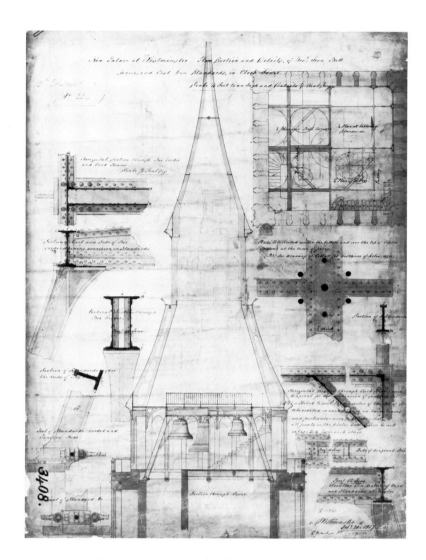

At each corner of the Victoria Tower an octagonal stone turret, 14 ft 6 in across the flats, contains a central shaft of 8 ft diameter. The caps are surmounted by octagonal crowns 'partly of iron and partly of copper',[27] the tops of which are 331 ft from the ground. These turrets were not merely decorative: the south-west and north-east ones were used for ventilation, and the others contained spiral staircases. A guardsman used to be placed in the north-west turret for signalling visually to Buckingham Palace at State Openings of Parliament. The pyramidal roof, 34 ft 6 in high, is again of cast-iron framing, clad with interlocking iron roof plates and weighing 276 tons. Surmounting the roof is a 120 ft high wrought iron flagmast, 2 ft in diameter at its base and tapering to 9 in at the top where it carries a 3 ft 6 in diameter iron crown, 395 ft above ground.[28] The flagmast, carried in a socket supported on diagonal riveted wrought-iron girders, is stayed by a system of decorative cast-iron flying buttresses. The roof ironwork is marked with the contractor's name in relief cast letters: 'J.Jay City Road Basin Foundry 1860', a reminder that the tower took nearly twenty years to complete. The quantities of building materials for the tower were given as about '117,000 cubic feet of stone, 428,000 cubic feet of brickwork, and 1,300 tons of iron; and the weight of the whole is nearly 30,000 tons which gives a pressure of about 8 tons per foot superficial on the foundations'—very high for London soil conditions.[29]

Professor H. R. Hitchcock has suggested that 'several essential ingredients' of the skyscraper were present in the structure of the Victoria Tower. This is true as far as it relates to the iron skeleton of the upper portion. But the essential structural feature that makes the sky-scraper possible is the separation of the load-bearing and space-enclosing functions. In the Victoria Tower the perimeter walls discharged both functions, but it is noteworthy that the tower was taller than the first American skyscrapers.[30]

The Clock Tower (Pl. 103) has become a symbol of London throughout the world. Its foundation was constructed like that of the Victoria Tower, on a concrete raft 10 ft 1 in thick with York stone landings from which the brick walls rose to form the basement-level vaults. The tower is 28 ft square inside, and 310 ft high to the top of the finial. The loads on this structure are transmitted down through the brick walls vertically to the foundations. Iron is used only for beams in fireproof floors, the bell frame, roof structure, and horizontal wrought-iron ties in the walls. The external walls of brick faced with stone are 3 ft 6 in thick. Below the clock room is a central masonry core enclosing a shaft for the weights and lines which drive the clock, and this has a considerable stiffening effect on the tower. On the west side a vertical air shaft included for ventilation purposes was intended as an air intake for the main buildings (Pl. 131). A stone staircase in the south-west corner gives access to all eleven storeys. The lowest were intended as prison rooms for offenders committed by the Houses. All floors in the tower are of iron beam, brick and stone construction, the beams spanning from the masonry core to the perimeter walls. Thirty feet above the clock room of the overhanging storey, itself some 195 ft above ground, is the belfry. The five bells weighing over 21 tons hang in a frame of riveted wrought-iron girders; the great bell, 'Big Ben', hangs in the centre from two girders parallel to the walls whilst the quarter bells hang from girders spanning the corner angles (Pl. 132). The belfry is enclosed by a pyramidal iron roof comprising cast inclined rafters spanned by iron purlins and clad with iron roof plates. Seven unglazed dormers in each sloping face help to disperse the sound, but make the belfry a draughty platform. The inclined rafters are marked, in the way in which ironwork is so often its own memorial, with the maker's name, 'Jabez James Engineer 28A Broadwall Lambeth 1856'.

The Central Tower was added specifically for ventilation, 'the first occasion when mechanical services had a real influence on architectural design.'[31] To contrast with the other towers it was treated architecturally as a spire, but structurally it has affinities with the dome of St Paul's. It comprises three distinct elements: a huge frustum of a cone in brick and masonry (Pl. 133) on which is mounted a lantern and finally a spire, the top of its finial cross about 261 ft above the floor of the Central Hall. The foundation was based on the concrete raft, thickened to 7 ft 5 in, with its top 6 ft 6 in below Trinity standard. On this were laid York stone landings, and the 5 ft 6 in thick walls of brick with corbelled footings were carried up to form the octagonal hall, 60 ft across the flats.[32] At each of the angles there is an external turret.

The masonry vaulting of the Central Hall obstructs any view up into the lantern from the floor. Just above the central oculus of the vault, however, a platform offers dramatic views down into the Hall and up into the huge cone, 57 ft 2 in in diameter at its base and 28 ft 4$\frac{1}{2}$ in at the top, 40 ft above (Pls 133, 134).[33] At the cone's base the horizontal forces tending to burst it are contained by wrought-iron tie-rods anchored in eight cast-iron cotter plates at the angles of the octagon and held down on the masonry by 2 in diameter rods (Pl. 135). These cotter plates also serve as skew-backs or abutments for the horizontal brick arches which take the bursting forces in

133. (right) New Palace of Westminster: Central Tower. Internal view of the inner cone and lantern. The oval vents for vitiated air from Reid's ventilating system may be clearly seen.

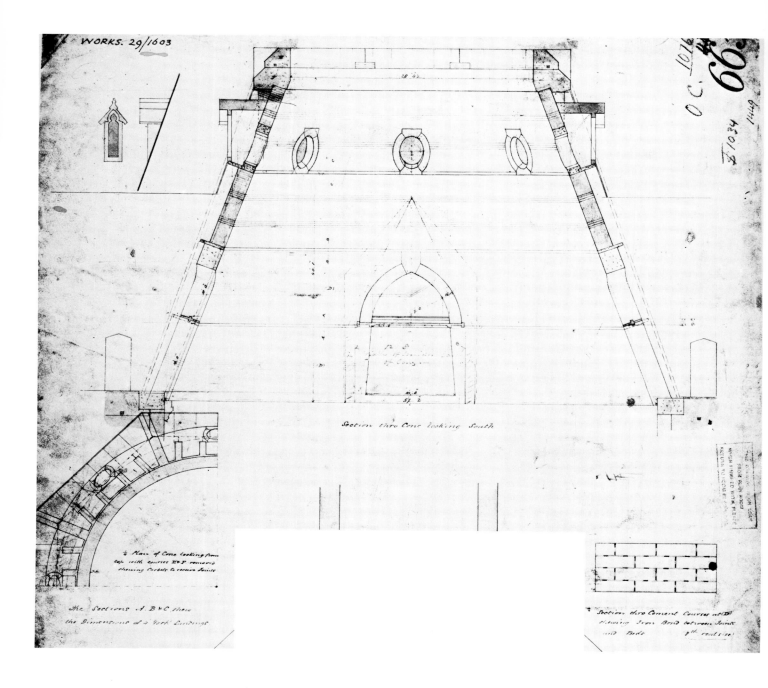

Section thro Cone looking South

The Sections A. B & C show
the Dimensions of 4 York Landings

Section thro Cement Courses at D
showing Iron Bond between Joint
and Beds   full real size

compression and transfer them, through the cotter plates, into the tie-rods acting in tension. There is a second iron course 10 ft above the cone's base and a third at the top. The thickness of the cone wall varies in three stages: 2 ft 4 in in the lower half, reducing to 2 ft and finally to 1 ft 6 in. The four large openings in the lower part and the eight elliptical holes above, screened by external stone dormers, were intended, like those in the lantern and spire above, for the exit of vitiated air from the whole palace (Pl. 134).[34]

Not only the design but the construction of these towers called for skill and ingenuity. Throughout the building the lifting and placing of massive quantities of facing stone, some blocks weighing 4 or 5 tons, some carved, 'the result of three months labour in the workshops', was an important technical problem.[35] The traditional scaffolding of poles and ropes had begun to be superseded at this time by a braced, bolted framework or 'whole timber' scaffold which could support a travelling crane. This had been used on Barry's Birmingham Grammar School in 1833, by Grissell and Peto at Barry's Reform Club in 1838, and by the same contractors for

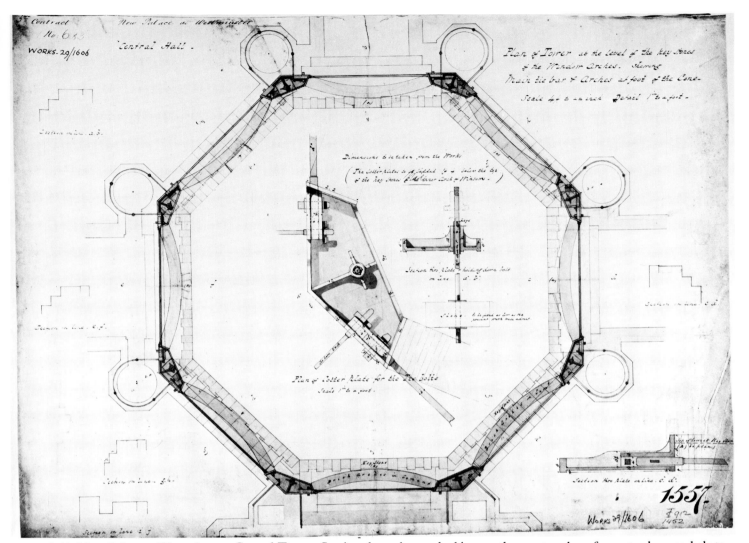

134. (left) New Palace at Westminster: Central Tower. Section through cone looking south, quarter plan of cone to show corbels to receive joints, and section through cement courses at (D) showing iron bond between joints and beds.

135. (above) New Palace at Westminster: Central Tower. Plan at level of key stones of window arches, showing main tie bar and arches at the foot of the cone.

erecting Nelson's Column in Trafalgar Square, begun in 1840. A view of the Houses of Parliament in 1842 (Pl. 77) shows the diagonally braced scaffolding and even the travelling cranes on top. Grissell's foreman, Allen, is said to have devised improvements in the application of these cranes, as well as in the system of scaffolding itself.[36]

Apart from this embracing timber frame, special methods were devised to build the three towers. The Central Tower, the first completed, required internal scaffolding for its lower stages, built in the middle of the Palace. The temporary works comprised three main elements—an inner rotating scaffold, timber centering for the ceiling vault, and an external timber tower (Pl. 94). No drawing survived of the vault centering, even in 1857 when Barry's son recalled 'several novel and peculiar arrangements'.[37] The revolving scaffold spanned the Central Hall (Pl. 136); 40 ft high, it could be rotated by two men turning winch handles to drive gear wheels meshing with a rack on the circular base curb. A lifting crab winch traversed the 80 ft gantry. The brick and stone cone above the ceiling was built without centering, the

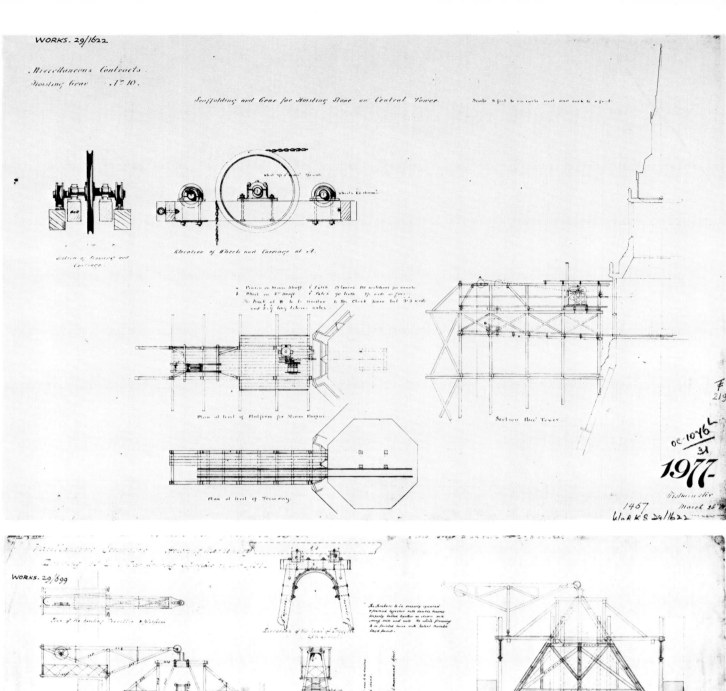

Miscellaneous Contracts.
Hoisting Gear. No 10.

Scaffolding and Gear for Hoisting Stone on Central Tower.

Section of Bearing and Carriage.

Elevation of Wheels and Carriage at A.

Plan at level of Platform for Main Engine.

Section thro' Tower.

Plan at level of Tramway.

219

1977

1467
WORKS 29/1622

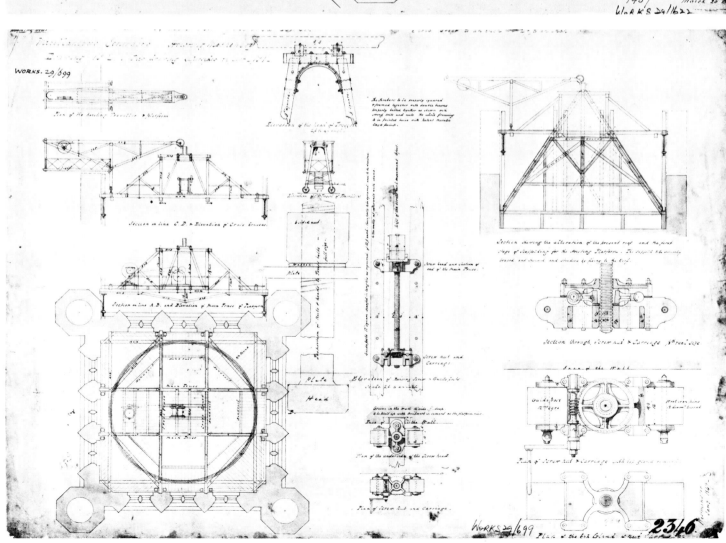

WORKS 29/699

234

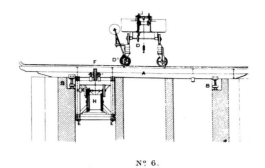

N.º 6.

SECTION THRO' CLOCK TOWER.

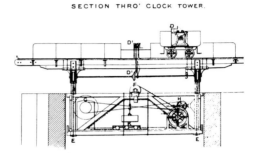

136. (left) New Palace at Westminster:
Central Tower. Scaffolding and gear for
hoisting stone. Drawing dated 26 Mar. 1847.
Much ingenuity was shown in devising means
of constructing the towers.

137. (below left) New Palace at Westminster:
Victoria Tower. Plan, section and details of
hoisting machinery, dated 'Jany 1847'.

138. (right) New Palace at Westminster:
Clock Tower. Two sectional drawings (at right
angles) of hoisting gear.

placing of material being controlled by a revolving striker.[38] Materials were lifted
to the upper stages in the external tower by means of a portable engine, said to have
cost 'under £100'—and the scaffold 'about £500 more'.

For the Victoria Tower a massive climbing scaffold was designed, which often
carried 40 tons of material in addition to its own weight, also 40 tons. Enormous
perimeter beams 14 in square and 51 ft long carried the platform (Pl. 137, 'A'), and
diagonal members ('Z') of the same section braced the corners. The decking was of
$2\frac{1}{2}$ in thick planks, with an octagonal well-hole trimmed with a handrail. The whole
apparatus could be lifted in 6 ft stages, by eight $3\frac{1}{2}$ in diameter screws ('H') mounted
at the ends of four deep stiffening trusses spanning the mullions. Eight men working
at the cranks ('K') provided the necessary power. Three trussed timber gantries,
pivoted at the centre, could rotate on a circular cast-iron track fixed to the decking.
Powered by a steam engine, boiler and winch mounted on the platform, one gantry
lifted materials outside the tower (the vaulting of the Royal Porch closing the interior)
whilst the other two placed the masonry. The 6 h.p. engine ('Gough's Patent')
and tackling cost about £1,800. It generally worked about five hours a day, burning
three hundredweights of coal in that time, and making ten lifts an hour, the transit
from the ground to a height of 250 ft averaging $3\frac{1}{2}$ minutes. Its safe load was four tons
and the $\frac{5}{8}$ in diameter chain was proved to six tons. The steam engine was not used
during the first 85 ft of construction. The scaffold's effectiveness was amply demonstrated by constant use over nine years in which no accident occurred.

A climbing scaffold was also used on the Clock Tower: as the material was lifted
up the inside without external scaffolding, 'the tower seemed to grow . . . by some
inherent vital power' (Pl. 138). Main timber beams ('A'), 2 ft 3 in deep and 14 in wide,
spanned the external walls from east to west. Iron rails on top of these enabled a
travelling crane to move in an east–west direction on which a crab traversed to place

the stone. A platform slung below the main beams fitted into Reid's vertical air shaft and carried a $2\frac{1}{2}$ horsepower steam engine and winch. The whole scaffold weighing about 16 tons 'had frequently to carry 30 tons of material', and could be raised by six screws ('B') through lifts of 3 ft 6 in. The cost of scaffold, engine and machinery was about £700. It raised some 30,000 cubic feet of stone, 300 rods of brickwork, and many tons of iron. It also lifted the ironwork of the belfry and roof, but not the bells themselves. So efficient was it that 'forty men were constantly preparing stone at the bottom' for each setter aloft, whereas with the ordinary framed scaffold and traveller one stone-setter required only twenty-five masons.

Any description of nineteenth-century building techniques reflects the dearth of source material, but the Palace was much in the public eye, and fortunately several technical journals were founded just in time to record the evidence. With temporary works the problem is obvious: 'The scaffolding is cleared away with jealous care, as though to *prevent* any record of it remaining, while the structure stands to attest its claims to admiration for truth and beauty in future times'.[39]

In addition to the travelling cranes on the scaffolding, other hoists were used to lift hods of bricks, buckets of water, and other materials. They comprised an endless chain driven by a winch on the ground and were of a type described by Pierre Journet, similar to Spurgin's patented hoist. They dispensed with mortar-carriers or 'hod-men', a class 'exclusively composed of emigrants from the sister island (another grievance for Ireland)'.[40]

Although temporary works would normally be the contractors' responsibility, Barry's son Charles lamented: 'The architect was not paid extra for designing the scaffolding. He found himself expected to render that service as part of the work to which his fixed commission was applicable, although the builders would not have undertaken at the ordinary contract prices the handling and moving of such elaborately carved stonework, at the unusual altitudes required.'[41] But Barry must share the credit with his engineer, Alfred Meeson, the principal clerk of works, Thomas Quarm, and Grissell & Peto's foreman, Allen. However, these temporary works showed, claimed Charles Barry jr, that 'architects are equal, when called upon, to devise and carry out works of construction requiring *originality* and *daring* as successfully as the members of the kindred profession of engineers.' The younger Barrys were always reluctant to acknowledge that their father was the coordinator of a team.

Another task of daring at Westminster was that of lifting the bells some 200 ft into the belfry (Table 2). The four small bells were raised in September 1858 in $16\frac{1}{2}$ hours. The large bell, the re-cast 'Big Ben', presented a greater challenge. Fears of vibration ruled out the use of steam-power; instead, a hand-driven crab winch was modified to provide a treble-purchase. A special chain, of $\frac{7}{8}$ in diameter, 1,500 ft long, was made by Hawks Crawshay & Co. in Newcastle, and proved link by link under the superintendence of Quarm and Jabez James, contractor for the belfry ironwork. As the central shaft of the tower measured only 8 ft 6 in by 11 ft 1 in and the bell was 9 ft in diameter at the sound bow, it was necessary to lift it on its side, in a strong timber cradle (Pl. 139). The centre of gravity was found by means of short lifts and adjusting the clip and shackle. Friction rollers on the cradle bore on timber guides bolted to the masonry the full height of the shaft. The lift began at 6 a.m. on 13 October 1858 and proceeded uninterruptedly until noon the following day, rising 201 ft $3\frac{1}{4}$ ins. Executed by James's assistant, Henry Hart, the operation was supervised personally by Quarm.[42]

The vast quantities of materials required for this huge building with its massive towers were chiefly brought to Westminster by water and landed at the adjoining

139. New Palace of Westminster: Clock Tower. Lifting the great bell, 13–14 Oct. 1858. A specially forged and tested chain was used to hoist the bell, which on account of its size had to be raised cradled on its side.

wharves. From early 1843, for instance, Caen stone for the interior was trans-shipped downstream into lighters. Other supplies could be brought by canal barge—the Yorkshire Anston stone, iron roofing plates from Birmingham, bricks and iron girders from Westbrook's at Heston and the Regent's Canal Ironworks, nearer at hand.[43] The organising of a constant flow of materials called for considerable resources on the part of the main contractors. Messrs Grissell & Peto, one of the earliest large-scale contractors, were employing more than a thousand men on their Houses of Parliament work by early 1845. They not only embraced all the building trades, but also offered a degree of vertical integration, leasing quarries for Cornish granite and at Anston for the external facing stone.[44] The quarrying, however, was let in the traditional way 'to half-a-dozen gangs, at so much a foot.' By the summer of 1843 about three hundred men were working at Anston, and Grissell provided additional tackle and horses to ensure a constant supply of stone.[45] Even so, two years later there were delays because not enough was reaching the works. The stone was roughly shaped at the quarry according to dimensions taken out by Grissell's foreman, Allen. The clerk of the works recalled that:[46]

213

Such parts as the projection of the buttresses &c, &c, always came scabbled to the shape, and the ashlar also; it was the usual practice throughout Mr Grissell's contract not to saw any stone . . . they were usually split with plug chisels till the stones separated . . . I believe that if economy had been studied in Mr Grissell's time, he would have sawn all the stone, but he thought perhaps that the carriage of the waste to London, and paying so much a ton for it, would counteract any profits that might arise from the stone being sawn in London.

Unfortunately that stone was not inspected before despatch, or even marked to show its natural bed. In consequence, much was incorrectly laid in the building, adversely affecting its durability (Pl. 104).

Allen, the foreman of masons, used to go to the quarry about once a fortnight: he claimed a decisive role in its working; but one Clark was foreman there, and John Barker assisted him at Westminster. The precise structure of management is not clear: Richard J. Wardle, who 'had the management of the quarries previous to the stone coming to the Houses of Parliament', claimed also to have been general manager at Westminster under Grissell, but in 1841 he was described as 'pay clerk' there. He clearly had no authority over Allen, who himself called him the 'principal clerk'. One incident from the late 1840s is doubtless characteristic: Wardle recollected that when he asked about a workman who was applying some mixture to the stonework, Allen retorted that 'he had got his instructions, and that it was no business of mine.' And that was that. Allen was sufficiently valuable to his employers for them to sit out the strike aimed against him. *The Times* credited him with 'the introduction of

Table 2. The Clock Tower: Lifting of Bells 1858. Total lift 201 ft 3¼ in.

Bell	Date Delivered	Date Lifted	Weight Tons Cwt Qr lb	Time Taken
First Quarter (Warner & Co. Crescent Foundry London)	18 June	23 September	1. 1. 0. 23.	3 hours
Second Quarter (Warner & Co. Crescent Foundry London)	18 June	24 September	1. 5. 1. 2.	3½ hours
Third Quarter (Warner & Co. Crescent Foundry London)	10 September	26 September	1. 13. 2. 13.	4 hours
Fourth Quarter (Warner & Co. Crescent Foundry London)	18 June	30 September	3. 17. 2. 13.	6 hours
'Big Ben' (Whitechapel Bell Foundry)	28 May	13–14 October	13. 10. 3. 15.	18 hours

140. Westminster: Wharf and store yards for the New Palace, *c*.1855. 'Sketched on the spot' by J. W. Carmichael. The bulk of the building materials was delivered by water.

zinc plates or moulds in lieu of the old wooden templets', as well as the improvements in scaffolding mentioned above.[47]

Despite using the cofferdam and terrace, the contractors did not have adequate space; in August 1843 Grissell required a further area of New Palace Yard for 'additional sheds for workmen and . . . for the storage of stone.'[48] When Barry negotiated a 'finishings' contract with Grissell in December 1844, he determined to concentrate the preparation of joinery in off-site workshops. Thomas Cubitt had lately done this in Pimlico, where his steam-powered shops broke down the traditional insulation of building processes, 'so that the fullest possible mechanization could be employed'.[49] Barry, too, taking premises formerly used by Cubitt next the great open culvert of the King's Scholars' Pond Sewer at Thames Bank (Pl. 141), investigated the opportunities machinery offered to economize both time and cost—but he was concerned only with woodworking. Samuel Pratt's patent carving machine, in use since 1843, bosted an outline, leaving the greater part of a carving still to be done by hand. Messrs Taylor, Williams & Jordan designed a more efficient version, producing up to eight copies of a carving simultaneously. This would give an average saving of 60 per cent compared with Pratt's 44 per cent. Five machines at £100 p.a. each were therefore hired from Taylor & Co., each fitted with three cutters, with means of adding a further three. But Barry's expectations were not fully answered. Grissell complained in May 1846 that the joiner's work was 'of a much more expensive and elaborate nature than was contemplated . . . and that a considerable amount of work has been executed by hand labour, which was . . . contemplated to be done by machinery.' Nevertheless, Taylor and Jordan's machines were still at Thames Bank in 1859.[50]

215

141. Thames Bank Workshops. The carvers' shop is the last surviving portion of the government workshops where much of the material for the Houses of Parliament was prepared.

Table 3. Graph to show numbers of workmen employed 1840–52.

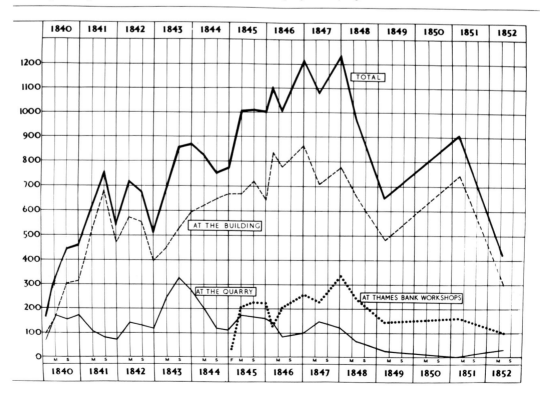

Brought into use in February 1845, the original workshops soon proved inadequate. Barry went ahead with a £7,000 extension (authorised in November) after complaining of the 'great inconvenience' and even 'risk' incurred for want of space. Otherwise, men would have been discharged to make room for storing carving for seasoning 'before it is made up'.[51]

The Thames Bank workshops were organized in two divisions, carvers' and contractor's. Housed in a four-storey block, 340 ft long, the carvers, superintended by Richard Bayne, were employed directly by Government; payment for wages up to June 1851 totalled over £40,000. As well as Jordan's machines, powered by a 10 h.p. condensing steam-engine and boiler, an inventory of 1859 mentions twenty-five carpenter's benches and 260 ft of carvers' benches, and two more benches in the modelling room.[52] Presumably it was here that John Mabey (foreman, 1842–58) conducted the modelling department: of all its work there are now two examples in the New Palace: models of the Central and Victoria Towers.[53] The contractor's department was in a similar four-storey block next Bessborough Place. In 1859 it contained twenty-five carpenter's benches in the basement, thirty-three on the ground floor, fifty-three on the first, and sixty on the second floor. There too was a steam-engine for the woodworking machinery—a morticing machine, a tenoning machine, an iron circular saw bench, a wooden circular saw bench and two iron saw benches. Often more than 200 men were working at Thames Bank in 1845–8, and during late 1847 well over 300 (Table 3). These government workshops were on a scale comparable with those of the largest and most advanced private contractors.[54]

In addition to stone and wood, the New Palace also contains a vast quantity of iron, both cast and wrought. Thomas Grissell sub-contracted much of this to his nephew Henry of the Regent's Canal Ironworks, who in 1847 claimed to have constructed 'a very large proportion of the iron floors and roofs'. For his castings he used hot iron blast, old iron, and Blaenavon Welsh iron in equal quantities; claiming that, thanks to mixing in scrap iron, London castings were at least fifteen per cent stronger than country ones,[55] an assertion perhaps borne out by the exclusive choice of London founders for the structural work. Robinson & Son (late Bramah) of Pimlico supplied the floor of the Commons, John Jay of the City Road Basin the ironwork of the upper stages of the Victoria Tower, and Jabez James of Lambeth the iron belfry and roof of the Clock Tower. Since it was virtually impossible to tell whether a cast-iron structural member contained internal honeycomb flaws, each beam had to be 'proved', and the specification required the contractor to do this at his own cost after each was 'delivered on the works'. There were three methods: by suspending a dead-load at mid-span; by a lever mechanism; or by the hydraulic press—the method preferred by Grissell, surely reflecting his pupilage with Bramah. If under proof a girder should break, or exceed the specified deflection, it was to be replaced at the contractor's expense. Manufacture of wall-spanning ironwork proceeded in step with the building, as the general contractor had 'at his own cost to cause to be taken from the building all the requisite measurements and dimensions to fit all moulds and templates and to be answerable for the correctness and accuracy of his work';[56] and a frequent note on drawings of ironwork required 'All dimensions to be proved on the works.' As protection against corrosion, all castings before leaving the foundry were to be 'heated to a high temperature, in which state they are to be covered with linseed oil, which is to be well rubbed in', and when delivered to the works 'to be further secured from rust by one coat of lithic paint.' Such notes encapsulate the problem of new materials and new methods so frequently occurring in the New Palace at Westminster.

XI

The Building Services

A building as large and complex as the Houses of Parliament requires a whole range of services to meet the basic needs and maintain the comfort of its occupants. These include water supply, drainage, artificial lighting, and those which control what we now call its 'micro-climate'. Air has to be supplied, filtered, heated, cooled, moistened or dried, and eventually extracted. All these aspects, now termed air-conditioning, were considered during the construction of the New Palace, and most were the subject of experiments there.

The ventilation of mines has a long history,[1] but only in the early part of the nineteenth century did that of public buildings begin to attract the attention of scientists. Thomas Tredgold (1788–1829) said in 1825: 'I do not know of anything more grateful to the senses, or more essential to health, than pure and wholesome air; nor any subject on which less care and less science has been bestowed.' Even twenty years later, Charles Hood (1805–99) could write: 'we have much cause to regret the small degree of attention which has generally been devoted to the subject by scientific men.'[2] Domestic buildings relied largely on opening windows which, with the draught produced by open fires, was considered adequate if often uncomfortable. It was generally considered 'very difficult to lay down a plan for the ventilation of public buildings particularly as the sites and users present so much variety.'[3] Both the method and the amount of ventilation were the subject of discussion and investigation. Basically, two methods were available—either the 'upcast-shaft' system with a draught induced by a furnace and chimney, or mechanical means using a forced draught produced by bellows or a fan driven by muscle-power, water-power, or the only prime-mover available, the steam engine. In the eighteenth century Dr John Desaguliers (1683–1744) had installed a hand-driven fan to ventilate the House of Commons. Reid used the thermal method successfully in the temporary Commons. Dr Andrew Ure (1778–1857) calculated that '38 times more fuel is expended in producing the same effect by chimney draughts than by mechanical power',[4] so there was ample incentive to develop mechanical methods.

Opinions varied about the volume of air considered necessary: Tredgold recommended not 'less than four cubic feet of air removed per minute by ventilation for each individual in a room'. Reid decided experimentally that in general 8 to 10 cu ft

142. Dr David Boswell Reid (1805–63), 'Ventilator' of the Houses of Parliament. His megalomania brought him into conflict with Barry, and he was finally superseded in 1852.

per minute per person ought to be changed; but Hood thought this 'unnecessarily large'. In St George's Hall, Liverpool, opened in 1854, Reid provided '7 to 10 cubic feet of air per minute to each person occupying the building'.[5] Theatres, hospitals and prisons were beginning to be scientifically heated and ventilated: but there was no model of scale and complexity comparable with the New Houses of Parliament. Two contemporary London buildings, however, are of technical interest: Barry's Reform Club (1837), and Pentonville Prison (1842).[6]

A series of select committees reviewed the problems, and the evidence presented tells a fascinating if complicated story. The first merely resolved, in June 1835, that 'special provision be made for the due ventilation of all the rooms in the new House'.[7] During August another committee explored the best methods of 'Ventilating, and Warming the New Houses . . . and of rendering the same favourable to the Transmission of sound', calling in George Birkbeck, John Sylvester, William Brande, Sir Robert Smirke, Michael Faraday and David Boswell Reid (Pl. 142), all men of 'high scientific reputation'.[8] In view of Reid's subsequent role, it is significant that during the 1834 Summer Meeting in Edinburgh of the British Association for the Advancement of Science, a group including Members of both Houses paid a visit to his lecture rooms.[9] They saw the unique experimental heating, ventilating and acoustic arrangements designed by Reid. Within a few months the Houses of Parliament were burned. It was therefore not surprising that Reid's experiments should be called to mind when Members considered the new buildings.

Reid emerges as the one witness self-confident and convincing on a topic otherwise full of conjecture; he probably dazzled Members with his technical detail. Drawings illustrated his proposal for an upcast shaft thermal ventilation for the temporary House of Commons (Pl. 143). At one end of the Chamber would be an air inlet turret, at the other an exit chimney and furnace. Air was to be admitted from beneath the Chamber floor and 'heated or cooled to the required temperature by hot or cold

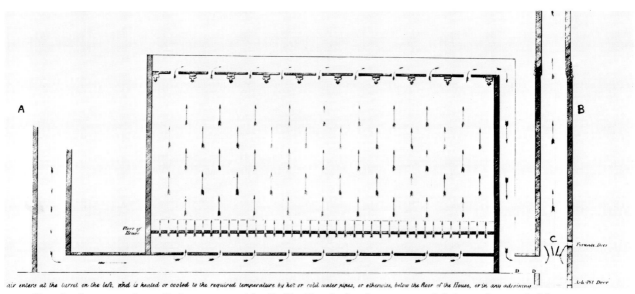

air enters at the turret on the left, and is heated or cooled to the required temperature by hot or cold water pipes, or otherwise, below the floor of the House, or in any adjoining

143. Sketch of system of ventilation proposed by Reid. Air admitted at a turret A is heated or cooled by apparatus below the floor of the House. Numerous small apertures permit the air to rise into the House without causing draughts. As it becomes impure, the air rises and passing through apertures in the ceiling is led into the chimney B. Doors DD acting with a small furnace C control the velocity of the current from and into the House.

water pipes, or otherwise.' His system had elements of monitoring and control: doors between the furnace and the House would govern the air flow; 'delicate but large thermometers, placed within the House, and also in the main ventilating pipes, as they enter and leave it, guide the attendants, and are, at the same time a complete check upon the regularity with which every part of the operation is carried on'. The committee, impressed with his ideas, resolved that some if not all of his proposals should be 'subjected to the test of actual experiment during the ensuing recess' in order to test the accuracy of his principles. In relation to the new buildings, the committee's only positive recommendation was that the 'whole space immediately below the two Houses . . . as well as between the ceiling and Roof should be prepared and altogether reserved for such arrangements as may be necessary.'[10]

Reid's upcast shaft system was introduced in the temporary Commons Chamber. An illustration of the site in 1842 (Pl. 77) shows his 'great round chimney', which was '120 ft high, by 11 ft wide at the bottom, and 8 ft wide at the top, with a fire grate near the bottom, having 25 sq ft of bars or surface, and therefore big enough for a steam engine of 25 horses power.' This apparatus consumed 'about two chaldrons [of coke] per day'.[11] Under Reid's supervision, it worked with some success, so when in 1839 Barry asked for technical assistance, Reid was a natural choice. His position was subordinate to the architect only in respect of the solidity or architectural character of the building.[12] Unfortunately, differences developed between the two men in ensuing years, causing considerable delay. Reid explained his philosophy to a select committee in 1841:[13]

In ventilation generally, I have always considered it an object to derive the plenum movement, where it was possible from the natural current of air, so that the current itself should be the power by which the air was forced inwards, and that the rarefaction of the air when it

220

meets with heat in various apartments, should also be the power by which it was forced outwards; so that if we imagine an apartment with two shafts, one turned to the wind, and leading air inwards, and another turned from the wind, and carrying off the air after it is once used, we have ventilation in its simplest form; but if the apartments are to be crowded, so that a vast movement is required within a certain space . . . . then it is necessary to have a mechanical power to make up the deficiency.

His experiments at Westminster found the air often 'exceedingly impure' so that 'it would be desirable . . . to take in air from a very considerable altitude, more particularly by the two towers.' He also proposed that 'some central shaft be erected' as a single exit for all the foul air. Having two inlets for fresh air would prevent contamination from the central exit, whichever way the wind blew. For general space-heating Reid proposed warming the incoming air to the two Chambers, but for the smaller rooms preferred 'the appearance of a cheerful fire-place', burning coke or 'a material that would give no soot'. Smoky chimneys were a common fault in contemporary buildings: the single exit for vitiated air was essential to Reid's scheme, and he suggested joining 'every chimney flue connected with every one of the 400 rooms that may be constructed into this central shaft, so that at no time will there be any possibility of a return of smoke.'[14] In September 1841 Barry summarized the new requirements for ventilation:[15]

A tower above the octagon hall in the centre of the building, for the discharge of vitiated air; flues under all the floors, roof, &c.; vertical air shafts in connexion with them; vaulting of the basement storey, and various miscellaneous works, the entire cost of which would be about £32,320; and if that part of the system of Dr Reid which relates to the prevention of smoke and down-draughts from the chimneys should be adopted, a further expense will be incurred of about £20,680.

The committee, doubtful about the proposed single vent, nevertheless recommended strengthening the foundation of the Central Hall so as 'to admit of the erection of the tower'.[16] In 1842 a further committee, still doubtful, approved the tower but recommended 'a double provision of flues . . . so as to leave the ultimate arrangement open for future consideration, after an experiment shall have been made.'[17]

By early 1846 the differences between Reid and Barry were acknowledged, and the delays they imposed so serious that committees of both Houses investigated.[18] The upshot was that Barry was charged with ventilating the Lords, Reid the Commons. Reid was lucky to preserve so much. *The Times* had denounced his management of the temporary Commons, where he had 'rendered rheumatism a parliamentary complaint'. 'Like the unclaimed bodies of paupers', the temporary Houses were resigned 'to all the vicissitudes of scientific experiment'; while the New Palace and the Members were regarded as 'instruments for advancing the great cause of ventilating philosophy' (cp. Pl. 144).[19]

From the start of the 1852 session when the Commons moved into their new home there were endless complaints about the ventilation, heating, lighting and drainage. Bernal Osborne spoke for many of his fellow-members:[20]

It was said by the late Sidney Smith, with reference to the practice of locking up passengers in railway trains, that no attention would be given to that subject until some great dignitary of the Church was roasted in a railway carriage. I am of opinion that until some of the more robust Members who now occupy the Treasury benches are ventilated into another place . . . we shall have no remedy for the crying evils to which we are now subject.

DR. REID'S PROCESS.

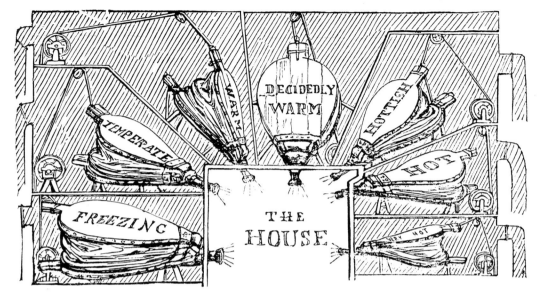

144. Reid's process seen through hostile eyes: 'the single air which is wanting is the air of practicability'.

In March Lord Robert Grosvenor asked whether the Commissioner of Works 'was able to hold out any hopes of relief to the sufferings of the Members from the present state of the ventilation of the House'. Not in all England was there 'to be found another public edifice in so wretched a condition with regard to ventilation'; some Members 'were conscious of a burning sensation of the most painful description around the head; others said that they felt a swelling in the temples; others that they experienced a kind of nervous fever; and some complained of a terrible sensation, resembling that which distinguishes a fit of apoplexy . . . It was a question of life and death.'[21]

All this criticism induced the House first to examine Reid, who 'believed he could make everything clear on the subject in the space of ten minutes';[22] and then to appoint the committee which was to make 1852 a landmark in the ventilation of the Palace.[23] Reid still controlled the Commons Chamber, 'with its division and gallery corridors, the House Lobby, and the Speaker's and Cabinet rooms'; all the rest was under Barry's supervision. The two systems were separated by screening round from floor to ceiling the ring of iron columns in the basement immediately below the Central Hall.

Barry described his own scheme for the committee:[24] 'Steam and hot water constitute the heating powers employed, and the motive power for the supply and discharge of air, independent of gravity caused by differences in temperature, consist of a powerful fan worked by a steam-engine, local rarefactions, and steam jets'. Barry used a turret of the Victoria Tower for his fresh air supply, drawing it down the shaft 'at the base of which the air is purified by water, and then passes through a main channel in the basement of the building, aided, when necessary, by the tractive power of the fan which forces it into a chamber under the Central Hall' (Pl. 145). Here in the 'tempering chamber' the air was warmed by passing it through a range of vertical steam pipes close to the fan, and thence distributed southwards to the Lords' Chamber and Royal Gallery, eastwards to the river front, westwards to St Stephen's

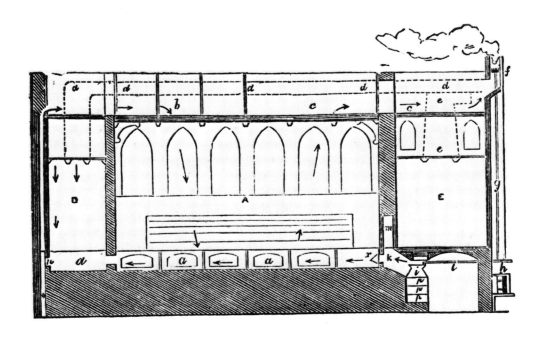

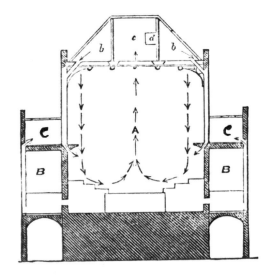

145. House of Lords: Barry's system of
ventilation. In 1847 Barry was given control of
ventilation for the Lords, and replaced Reid's
'upcast' system by a 'downcast'.
A House of Lords.   B Lower Corridors.
C Upper corridors.   D Prince's Chamber.
E Lords' Lobby.
Admitted at ground level, fresh air passes
through heating apparatus, i, into diffusing
chambers, aa, and up flues, n, into chambers bb
in the roof. Thence it descends into the Lords, at
a rate of upwards of 7000 cu ft per minute. The
impure air rises through the ceiling to other
chambers, cc, and so to the discharge shaft, g,
where a steam-jet, f, moves the air. Other foul
air tubes, dd and ee, remove air from the Royal
Gallery and the Lords' Lobby.

Hall and Porch and Westminster Hall, and vertically to the Central Hall. Valves in
each of the main distribution channels gave control in detail over any part of the
system. Each section of the building had additional heating apparatus in the basement
for use in very cold weather, and the windows on the river front had radiating pipes
below them. Tempered fresh air was supplied to each room through vertical flues in
the walls, connected with the main air channels in the basement and entered partly
through the ceiling, skirting and wall-framing—the supply to each room controlled
by valves and 'delivered in such abundance as to create a plenum, by which all in-
setting drafts consequent upon the opening of the doors are avoided.'

The vitiated air from each chamber is discharged through a portion of the ceiling, . . . and in . . . the House of Peers partially through the floor, into main foul air flues in the roofs of the building, from whence it is conveyed into exit shafts in the Royal Court, and Speaker's Court, the central tower, a tower used for the smoke flue of the boilers west of the central tower, a tower west of the public lobby of the House of Peers, and a tower at the north end of the House of Commons, wherein rarefying apparatus and steam jets are employed to ensure a constant current of sufficient velocity.

The total air-intake area was about 100 sq ft, that of discharge about 230 sq ft, and the space warmed and ventilated by Barry about 3,644,000 cu ft.

Reid characteristically complained that he had had 'to act under disadvantages, and amidst incessant alterations, of which he had often no notice till he saw them in process of execution on the works.'[25] He used the Clock Tower as his principal source of fresh air, with other intakes at ground level near the Central Hall, on either side of the Chamber, at roof level in the centre of the river front and on the west side opposite the Abbey—eleven openings totalling $911\frac{1}{3}$ sq ft, the largest that in the Clock Tower ($219\frac{1}{3}$ sq ft). Reid's scheme involved the removal of soot and dust from this incoming air, but until satisfactory arrangements had been made for the supply of water, this could 'only be effected by temporary measures'. Heating was by hot-water plant worked normally at a temperature of 90 degrees during sittings, together with steam coils under the cold windows of corridors, and open fires in division lobbies and Cabinet rooms. Cool air was obtained in summer by drawing it from the 'greatest possible altitude', and by using cold water in the heating apparatus. The air was moistened and dried as necessary for controlling the humidity of the Chamber. It was moved principally by the furnace in the extract shaft but also by fans driven by a steam engine later 'replaced by manual labour'. Distribution was mainly upwards through the perforated floor of the Chamber which could 'be considered completely porous, though from the state of the paint it has hitherto been only partially brought into use.' This arrangement was strongly criticised by some Members who thought it made the air dirty. A great number of the holes were closed about 1870 by Ayrton, who was 'very susceptible to draughts'. Part of the floor was also used for radiant heating by circulating hot water through hollow cast-iron floor plates (Pl. 146). Air was extracted through the suspended ceiling of the Chamber, through openings totalling nearly 270 sq ft.

Reid was finally dismissed in September 1852, when the ventilation of both Houses was put for a limited period in the hands of Barry's engineer, Alfred Meeson, under the Office of Works.[26] By May 1853 Meeson had already effected many alterations:[27]

Covering with lead that portion of the perforated floor which is usually walked upon, to prevent dust being carried upwards, and to obviate also the inconvenience felt from currents of air; in substituting openings for free admission of air in all available positions in the risers of steps and gangways; in cleansing, raising, and putting in good order the air channels of the vaults, &c.; in fixing screens for purifying and moistening the air; in laying on water, and making arrangements for washing, moistening, and cooling the channels and chambers; in examining and cleansing the drains; in improving and putting in order the steam-boilers, and the apparatus connected therewith; and in making provision for a certain supply of air from the ceiling.

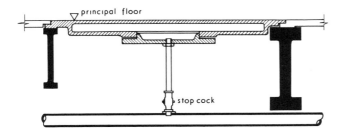

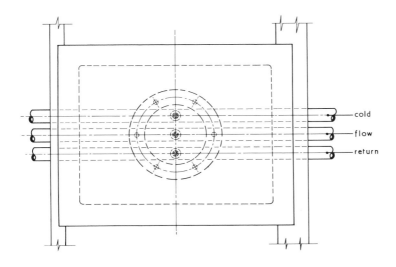

cold

flow

return

146. (above) House of Commons: Hot water floor plates. Special provision was made for the Speaker and the Front Benches.

147. (right) Goldsworthy Gurney (1793–1875), knighted 1863. As well as arranging lighting for the temporary House of Commons in 1839, Gurney superintended the heating and ventilation of the Houses of Parliament, 1854–63.

As the principal rival expert, Goldsworthy Gurney (1793–1875) (Pl. 147) was in March 1852 asked to investigate Reid's system. He had given evidence in the inquiry of 1846, arguing that Reid's upcast shaft method must fail as being 'too limited in its range of power'; he preferred the 'vis-a-tergo' arising from the escape of high-pressure steam as more manageable. The committee had then pointed out that 'no evidence of the application of his system to any public building has been adduced in its favor'; and *The Times* warned against replacing one deluded fanatic by another.[28] Now he seized his opportunity, and within a month submitted the first of three reports, pledging himself 'to remove all the material evils that at present exist, at a very trifling expense'.[29] He undertook extensive temperature and hygrometric measurements. Questioned about draughts, he pointed out that: 'It is a very difficult thing to manage a feather balance of the atmosphere by artificial means; . . . You may manage a railway train, a heavy weight, but you cannot manage a train of subtle, light, and practically imponderable air, without much difficulty.'[30]

In 1854 a Lords' committee entrusted Gurney with the ventilation of their House.[31] As already stated, the Lords' air supply was taken from the Victoria Tower and passed along the main air duct in the basement. Gurney's experiments were similar to earlier trials by Reid:[32]

I had the air in it, as it passed along, charged with gunpowder smoke in sufficient quantities to render it visible . . . by flashing small portions in rapid succession . . . I watched the first appearance of the smoke in various parts, its apparent quantity, and noted the time it took in coming in and going out . . . upwards of 60 lbs. of gunpowder and composition were burnt. The volume of smoke . . . would be sufficient to render the whole of the incoming air visible.

During 1854 Gurney completely reversed the air supply system, converting both the Victoria and Clock Towers into upcast shafts. The air, drawn in at ground level at various places, was expelled at the tower-tops. Gurney did not give a reason for this change; at first thought an improvement, it soon proved a disaster.[33] Despite frequent modifications, complaints continued. The Thames, having become the general sewer of the metropolis, 'stank unbearably in hot weather'. About 1857, bone-boilers in Lambeth began to work at night, so that the stench was wafted over to the sitting Houses. The following year, Disraeli (having been driven out of committee by 'the pestilential odour') introduced a bill for the main drainage of London, which eventually deodorized the river.[34] Meanwhile, palliatives were tried, not always with much success: when the House was very warm, complained A. S. Ayrton,[35]

Cold air was pumped in at the foot of the Hon. Members, the effect of which was to drive the blood to their heads, and to produce those injurious effects which were so constantly complained of and which had often compelled him and others to leave the House. Then, recently, the most abominable odours had been pumped in through the House and slits at their feet. The smell of the chloride of lime which was used was pleasant enough; but at other times the uncorrected atmosphere of the Thames was wafted through the floor, and then the effect was dreadful indeed.

Sir Harry Verney 'kept a pair of worsted stockings and gaiters for wear in the House, in order to protect his feet from the cold air.' William Tite commented that 'so far as he had observed all artificial systems of ventilation were a failure. Whether you had to ventilate a large room or a House of Parliament, the best way was to open a window. There was, however, a difficulty in opening the windows in the neighbourhood of the Thames', and as a remedy '100 tons of lime were now poured every day' into the

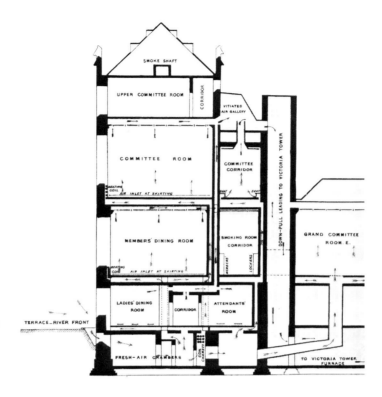

148. The Houses of Parliament: Ventilation of committee rooms and ancillary accommodation in the 1860s. The ventilation of the two Chambers was not regarded as entirely satisfactory, but that of other parts of the palace was much criticised. This diagram shows the complexity of the task.

river. Even these drastic measures failed; in 1865 it was said that 'between the hours of four and six in the afternoon many Members were in a state of semi-asphyxia.'[36]

Accordingly, in October 1865 the Commissioners of Works invited Dr John Percy, F.R.S. (1817–89) to report on the ventilation, warming and lighting of the Palace. He reported in March 1866 that 'Much . . . yet remains to be done', but it should not require 'any considerable outlay' as the appliances for effective ventilation already existed at the site, though many details were 'defective and need completion.'[37] The art and science of ventilation had progressed since Reid's original scheme was prepared: 'The volume of fresh air, which only a few years ago was considered sufficient for perfect health, would now be regarded as wholly inadequate.' The minimum was 20 cu ft a minute, but the 'best authorities' agreed that 33 cu ft a minute was desirable. Numerous measurements had been made in the previous session to determine the quantity of air flowing: on the night of 12 February 1866, when the House was full to discuss the Whig Reform Bill, about 1,500,000 cu ft of air passed through the Commons every hour.

Of the existing system Percy observed: 'The plan of mechanical propulsion by fans has long since been abandoned, and the air is now exclusively put in motion by means of heat, precisely on the same principles as in most of our collieries' (Pls 148, 149). The existing upcast shafts would be more than adequate 'if suitable communications existed between them and all the rooms and passages'. Noting sources of contamination of the air supply at ground level, he stressed the need to keep the courtyards clean: 'If horse-dung happen to fall near any of the inlets the air entering will instantly be thereby more or less infected'; if a smoker crossed the Commons Court, 'in a few seconds a distinct odour of tobacco-smoke will be perceived, especially near the Speaker's chair'. To avoid this unpleasantness, about 1869 air intakes were constructed on the Terrace.[38]

What emerges most strikingly from Percy's report is the chaos resulting from the lack of drawings of the building services.

There are many hundreds of air-courses under as well as above ground, beneath floors, in walls, over ceilings, and in roofs; . . . there are enormous smoke-flues running horizontally within and immediately under the roofs, with hundreds of chimneys in communication; there are, it is asserted, steam pipes of which the aggregate length is about 15 miles, and about 1,200 stopcocks and valves connected with these pipes; and there is a multitude of holes and crannies as intricate and tortuous as the windings of a rabbit warren. It is not possible that any man should accurately remember these details, even if he had seen every stone and brick laid; and in the absence of plans occasional blundering will be inevitable.

As a result, an architectural draughtsman spent several months with 'two of the most experienced men of the staff' producing the necessary drawings. Much was discovered, and erroneous ideas corrected.

Another aspect of Percy's investigation concerned the fire risk in the Commons' roof due to the high temperature produced by the lighting and ventilation, so that the wooden fittings were, as Edward Barry put it, 'in a state highly favourable for ignition.'[39] Alterations carried out by Imray in the roofs of both Houses enabled Percy to improve aspects of the ventilation. Under his management air was supplied uniformly at 64 degrees. Percy tidied up many details of the palimpsest system, and it was 1884 before another major revision was undertaken.[40] In all essentials Percy's arrangements lasted into the twentieth century.

The air conditioning apparatus as it functioned under Percy was described by Joly in 1869:[41]

The fresh air is admitted on the side of the river through louvres A, the opening of which may be regulated in a chamber B. In this chamber, according to the seasons and requirements of the moment the air passes between jets of cold water thrown out as spray from a tube C. If it is desired to increase the moisture of the air without cooling it, a divided jet is let fall from the pipe E, which jet is vaporized by the steam-pipe D placed beneath. In the next chamber, F, are the heating apparatus proper. These are Gurney steam-batteries, formed of plates of metal 1 ft. in diameter, arranged around a steam-pipe at a distance of $\frac{3}{4}$ in. apart. Their number, that is, the extent of surface, is calculated according to the volume of air to be heated. From thence the air is passed through a gauze veil, to intercept the dust and soot from the atmosphere. From the large chamber H it ascends through circular ducts I, and is distributed over the assembly chamber, into which it is admitted through gratings in the floor covered with matting.

Eventually the lighting, heating and ventilation of public buildings was to be revolutionized by electric power—electric batteries were already in use in 1852 to produce the simultaneous ringing of division bells, and also to establish telegraphic communication between the Speaker and the ventilator.[42] Now there is a sophisticated control room with closed-circuit television monitoring of the proceedings in the Houses. One steam-engine remains in use below the Central Hall. It is a two-cylinder horizontal engine driving an air compressor connected with the ejector system on the main drainage.

Several difficulties, then, recur. The lack of established fundamental principles was an obstacle to obtaining sound advice. Michael Faraday described ventilation as 'an excessively difficult subject'. Robert Stephenson commented: 'Several men of great accomplishments have varied so much in their views, and upon points so essential, that I have been a good deal surprised.' Furthermore the problem at

Westminster was peculiarly complex—the labyrinth of rooms, and the widely fluctuating numbers in the House. Many architects had ventilated large buildings successfully, but 'here . . . everyone seems to have failed'.[43] Another factor was that all contemporary systems of artificial lighting required combustion to take place within the building, so affecting ventilation and heating. Of this problem we can make only brief mention.

Goldsworthy Gurney had in 1826 invented 'limelight' or the 'Drummond' light. In 1839 he invented the 'Bude' light, heralding 'a new era in the science of illumination'. This supplied a jet of pure oxygen to the flame of either an oil or a gas lamp, so considerably increasing the light. The House of Commons, previously lighted by wax candles, was in May 1839 'fully lighted for the first time with Gurney's Bude light': each lamp was said to equal thirty candles.[44] After further experiments, pendant lighting was tried; gas replaced oil, and a jet of air the pure oxygen. Gurney's was referred to in 1842 as 'a cheap, beautiful, and effective system of lighting, which may be applied to the future Houses of Parliament.' He was later grudgingly paid £1,600 for his services from 1839 to the end of his contract in 1843.[45]

The Bude light was not applied to the new Houses. Barry and Reid, as well as Gurney, each tried out their different ideas. In April 1844 Reid was appointed to light the new buildings, but his scope was curtailed in 1846. Barry lit the Lords by gas, on Faraday's principle (Pl. 150), as part of his overall scheme of heating and ventilation; and the first scheme used in the new Commons was his, employing massive

149. The Houses of Parliament: Ventilating Department. Furnace to promote current of air. By opening or closing adjoining doors the flow of air could be controlled.

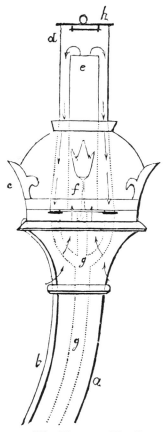

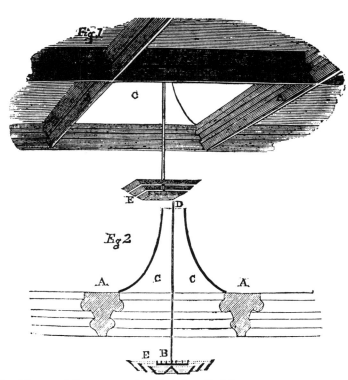

150. The Houses of Parliament: Gas lighting. This was installed in 1847 on Faraday's principle. Gas passed along the pipe, b, into the perforated ornamental coronal, c. 'Consumed air' passed from the gas-light, f, through an inner glass chimney, e, to an outer glass chimney, d, whence it was drawn through four small tubes into a large waste tube, gg.

151. The House of Commons: Gas lighting. Reid's system, installed in April 1852, after complaints that Faraday's lights produced too much heat. Panels were removed from the ceiling, the aperture, G, painted white, and gas burners introduced at B, with shades E.

gasoliers. In April 1852, on the recommendation of a select committee, these were supplanted by a method of Reid's which entailed removing panels in the flat part of the ceiling. Above the holes thus formed were fitted pyramidal boxes (painted white inside), from which was suspended a gas pipe with a ring of jets (Pl. 151). Some thought the interior of the House 'completely spoiled by this arrangement'. More light was obtained, in addition, by gas lights placed outside the windows, in which some of the stained glass was replaced by plain.[46] Locke and Stephenson, MPs as well as eminent engineers, were appointed a standing committee to consult with the First Commissioner of Works on the lighting. Within a year, Gurney's system was substituted for Reid's.[47] But dissatisfaction remained general. In 1854 another committee consulted John Leslie, who had effected great economies in lighting the General Post Office in London. He thought the Lords Chamber was not lit in a 'proper manner', and declared that the gas was used 'not in gas burners, but in gas furnaces', with adverse effects on ventilation. Committees of both Houses recommended Gurney's appointment to superintend the lighting, heating and ventilation, which he did till his retirement in 1863.[48] Dr Percy did not recommend specific changes in the lighting in 1866, but did provide some interesting statistics. The gas supplied by the Chartered Gas Company through a special main from their Horseferry Road works was mainly of a 'quality known as 20-candle gas'; it cost six shillings per thousand cubic feet. There were no fewer than 38 meters in the Palace, and in one year £3,505 was spent on gas for lighting and cooking.[49]

Perhaps the most important theme of this story of the building services lies in the division of authority between architect and technical adviser. Edward Barry called it 'an administrative blunder of the highest order'.[50] The 1852 committee recognized that it was 'vain to expect good service or economy' until the whole ventilation was 'confided to one competent person' under the control of the Office of Works (Second Report). Reid, an example of Babbage's *genus irritabile* 'among the lower ranks of science ... disposed to argue that every criticism is personal', had a consistently bad press compared with Barry, who was said to produce 'airs from heaven' as against Reid's 'blasts from hell'.[51] His failures, as at the Law Courts, made better news than his apparent successes (as at St George's Hall, Liverpool). Yet even in 1852 he received strong support in the Commons. Perhaps his personality obscured problems insurmountable at the time.[52] Spon's *Dictionary of Engineering* (1871) summed it up: 'Every existing system was examined, every authority consulted, numerous experiments were made, and no expense was spared, to obtain a perfect plan of ventilation. We may therefore regard the one finally adopted as the embodiment of all that was at that time known concerning the subject.' The story of the building services in the New Palace at Westminster, and the unprecedented way in which they dictated to the architect, make it our most important building in this aspect of nineteenth-century technology.[53]

XII

The Palace of History and Art

1. Introduction

THE New Palace at Westminster was pre-eminently Victorian in one notable aspect: its didactic function. It was to be more than an attractive feature in the townscape assimilated to its ancient neighbours; more even than a comely and well-functioning palace of the legislature. Barry from the outset saw it as a 'sculptured memorial of our national history'. The luminaries of the day believing in a relationship between art and society seized the opportunity not only to instruct the people in their history but also to elevate their taste and to raise the arts and craftsmanship of England to new heights. Our very legislators were to be improved by working surrounded by the noblest productions of art.

Such high hopes were not altogether fulfilled. The results of the public encouragement of sculpture and painting were disappointing, though the *Art Journal* could claim at the time of Barry's death in 1860 that the New Palace had 'given an impetus to the three sister arts of painting, sculpture, and architecture, they in all probability would never have [otherwise] received.' The impact on the public was not as powerful as Ewart, Hawes and their friends had hoped; and some of the legislators disliked their surroundings. But in the field of what Eastlake called 'Art Manufacture' the Houses of Parliament made a significant contribution, due largely to the opportunity given to Pugin to exercise his genius in the design of furniture and woodcarving, metalwork, stained glass, encaustic tiles and decorative painting, and establish new principles of interior decoration. Barry provided him with the means to train that school of craftsmen the lack of which he had earlier found such a handicap to the realization of his designs; craftsmen whose skills were employed in churches and houses throughout the country and even overseas.

2. The Architectural Sculpture

Barry's 'great idea' was to make the New Palace at Westminster a monumental history of England. 'Sculpture without, sculpture, painting and stained glass within,

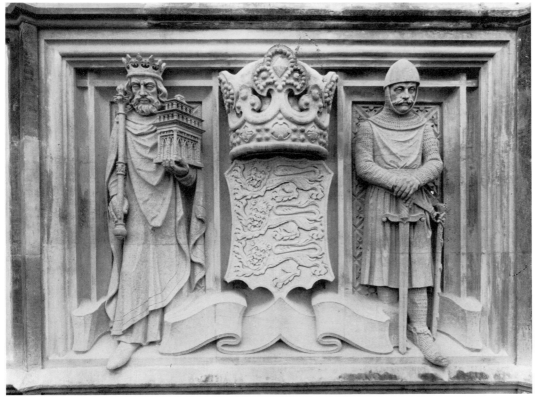

152. New Palace at Westminster: External sculpture. Royal Arms from the River Front.

were to preserve the memorials of the past, and declare the date and object of the building.'[1]

From an early stage of the work there was drawn a distinction between architectural and free-standing or 'insulated' sculpture, a distinction which clearly lies behind the division of responsibility for sculpture between Barry and the Fine Arts Commission. In February 1843 the architect declared: 'With respect to any further encouragement of the Fine Arts in the exterior of the building, I am not aware of any opportunities that offer, as arrangements have already been made for all the architectonic or conventional sculpture that will be required to adorn the several elevations.'[2] Barry's firmness thus confined the Fine Arts Commission's encouragement of sculpture largely to the insulated monuments; though part of Barry's programme they did not materially affect the architecture, so are not considered here. For two exceptions responsibility was shared: the figures for the Lords' Chamber and for the Royal Gallery. Both sets are intrinsic to the architectural scheme, yet both were sufficiently autonomous for individual sculptors to be employed: but divided responsibility gave rise to problems. For the Lords' Chamber, the subjects were selected by a committee under the Fine Arts Commission, and the sculptors by the Commissioners. Barry however had his own ideas which the sculptors had to accept: 'Mr Barry will not allow us room for them' was the sculptor's reply to a complaint about the narrow shoulders of his figures.[3] A committee under the Commission reported on the position, size and material of the figures for the Royal Gallery; various sculptors then executed the statues, which proved too large. Edward Barry then removed them to Westminster Hall, and replaced them by a series by Birnie Philip.[4]

233

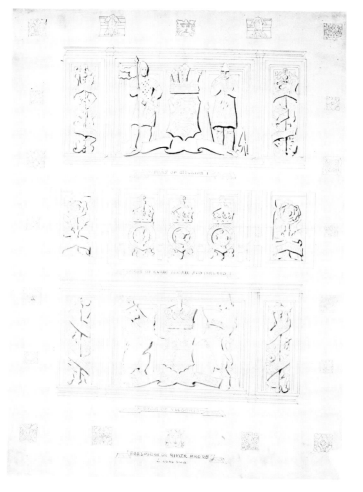

153. (left) New Palace at Westminster: External sculpture. Tracing of drawing for sculpture of River Front, Arms of William the Conqueror and Victoria, and national badges.

154. (above) New Palace at Westminster: External sculpture. John Thomas, drawing for royal arms, River Front.

155. (right) New Palace at Westminster: External sculpture on the South Return, seen from Black Rod's Garden. Some of the Saxon kings are seen in the two lower tiers, with royal badges in the panelled transom above.

Within the architectural section there was a further distinction of sculpture by type, between representational and more purely decorative work. The former relates to Barry's 'great idea', and consists of figures, heraldry, symbols and lettering. The more purely decorative foliage, crocketing and tracery (both window and blind) was equally essential however to the overall architectural effect. Both types relate closely to each other and to the architecture, as an examination of the building shows.

The main sculptural feature of the River Front is the series of royal coats-of-arms above the windows of the principal floor, beginning at the south end with William the Conqueror (Pl. 153). Each sovereign's name and dates are inscribed in a band of Gothic lettering below the windows. The shields have their appropriate supporters (Pl. 154); but as conventional supporters were not used before Richard II's time, the earlier shields are held by human figures relating to important contemporary events (Pl. 152): the observation of heraldic accuracy is punctilious. Flanking panels contain sceptres, labels, appropriate badges and inscriptions. In the parapet of each bay is a niche containing an angel bearing a shield. On the six oriel windows along the front, carved panels contain the arms of Queen Victoria, signifying that the building was erected during her reign.

At either end of the River Front the Wing Towers have identical sculptural programmes. A square buttress divides the north and south faces of each, ornamented with six canopied niches occupied by statues of the patron saints of the united kingdoms and Saints Peter and Paul representing London's two principal churches.

On the east face, above the parapet, canopied niches contain statues of Queen Victoria; while on the west, looking towards his Abbey, are figures of Edward the Confessor, first to build a palace at Westminster. Below and beside the tower windows are areas of carving: the arms of Queen Victoria, the royal cypher, the mottoes of the three kingdoms, crowns over shields bearing crosses and the emblematic flowers of the kingdoms, and panels containing a sword and sceptre adorned with mottoed ribands and entwined foliage and flowers (Pl. 153).

The North and South Fronts (Pl. 155), overlooking Speaker's Green and Black Rod's Garden respectively, have similar programmes. The two pairs of windows in each bay are separated by niches containing statues of the kings and queens of England from the Heptarchy to the Conquest, in historically appropriate costume. The North Front has thirty-two figures in four stages of eight, the South Front forty-four in four stages of eleven. As on the River Front, there are bands of appropriate coats-of-arms and inscriptions, but simpler, lacking the flanking panels.

On the Clock Tower (Pl. 103), the decorative panelling becomes more ornamental towards the top, displaying symbolic devices and foliation. The upper stages of the Victoria Tower are similar, though the density of ornament is still heavier (Pl. 156). The lower stage has figures in niches on its west and south faces: on the west, Queen Victoria with her parents and uncles, and Saints Peter and Paul; on the south she is flanked by her grandparents, an uncle, five aunts and, again, the local saints.

Between the two great towers, the fronts overlooking New Palace Yard have three

235

tiers of niches with figures of the kings and reigning queens of England from William I to Victoria, appropriately costumed. The arcade along the west side added by Edward Barry in 1866–9 has six figures set in niches against buttresses, representing Kings Alfred, William I, Henry II, John, Henry VII and James II; these, by H. H. Armstead, are supplementary to the original programme. In Old Palace Yard there is a group round the window of St Stephen's Porch, with Queen Victoria at the apex; then, descending on the left, Edward III (who completed St Stephen's Chapel) and Queen Philippa, St George and St Andrew; on the right, Henry VII and Elizabeth of York (looking towards their monumental chapel), St Patrick and St Stephen. The west front of Old Palace Yard (Pl. 96), the last to be completed (1852–60), bears no figures, but their absence focuses attention on the more purely decorative carving present there as on all the external fronts of the Palace. Its main constituents are window tracery, blind panelling tracery, devices like shields and bosses disposed about the wall surfaces, and crocketed pinnacles punctuating the main elevations. The basic vocabulary of both types of tracery is simple, consisting of a panel topped by single or double cusping, according to width. A single wide panel may have an ogee head dividing the panel above it, itself topped out by a quatrefoil or even two side by side. The elevation at Speaker's Green, for instance, has panelled battlements; the merlons contain a quatrefoil above a single cusped blind arch; the area below the embrasures contains two blind arches of this type (Pl. 64). The buttress panelling starts at the bottom with an ogee arch with two cusps per quadrant; this is repeated, with a moulding rising from the point of the arch dividing the next section into two parts, each of which finishes in a single cusped arch, sometimes beneath a common Tudor arch. The upper panels on the buttresses start in this way, but the centre moulding continues and the panel is topped by two quatrefoils with elongated vertical foils (cp. Pls 63, 64). The window tracery uses the same elements with variations in their disposition. Each light of the windows of the second floor has a lower aperture headed by a two–cusp–per–quadrant element; the upper opening ends in an ogee, again with two cusps per quadrant; the centre moulding continues to the top of the opening with a tilted quatrefoil on either side (Pl. 64).

This type of composition, subject to minor modifications, is standard throughout the building. On the Clock Tower, for instance, there are larger panels consisting of a rectangular unit with central lozenge usually bearing some device such as a portcullis or a rose. Vertical mouldings above and below the lozenge further subdivide the panel, and the two upper units end in a simple single–cusp arch (Pl. 103). Further variations can be found on, for example, the gables of St Stephen's Porch. The only major variant within this type is found on the west front of Old Palace Yard, where, as already mentioned, there are no figures or large armorials. The panelling of the battlements here and that between the windows (though not that of the buttresses) is much more intricate (Pl. 96). While this effect may have been intended to match the patterning of Henry VII's Chapel opposite, Edward Barry stated that the design was modified to get more light and shade.[5] On the exterior surfaces of the walls of the inner courts (Pl. 69) there is almost no sculpture (claimed as a merit of the original design), except for tracery in the windows and occasional bosses set in the string courses.

This relationship between the presence of sculptural decoration above a certain degree and its public visibility emphasizes the part sculpture had to play in Barry's 'great idea'. Inside the building, too, its use is selective according to the same principle, with the further operational consideration that sculpture was no longer the only practicable decorative medium. The Royal Approach, the main public access and the Lords' Chamber are all display areas with a high degree of decoration, whereas the

156. New Palace at Westminster: The Victoria Tower. Detail of the arcading, showing the luxuriance of ornament.

purely business areas and service premises are more simply fitted up, with little carved stonework. The original Commons' Chamber (Pl. 89), however, was treated rather as a business than as a display area, Barry stating that the nature of the design and the extent of fittings for the accommodation required would not admit of the aid of either painting or sculpture.[6]

In the Royal Approach, the fairly elaborate ribbed vault of the Royal Porch under the Victoria Tower has carved bosses of foliage or badges; inside the large boss-studded archway leading to the Royal Court are two superimposed compartments, the upper containing in five niches the patron saints of the three kingdoms flanked by angels with shields bearing the royal arms, the lower containing the arms of Great Britain with the badge and motto of the Prince of Wales on either side (Pl. 157).[7] The elevation of the Royal Entrance on the north side of the Porch is similar. In the niches of the upper compartment stands Queen Victoria supported by emblematic figures of Justice and Mercy, 'the two best prerogatives of the British Crown', flanked, again, by angels bearing inscribed scrolls.[8]

The Royal Stair (Pl. 110) leads up to the Norman Porch, where it was originally proposed to place statues of the Norman sovereigns, but only the pedestals are there.[9] Off the Norman Porch opens the Royal Gallery (Pl. VI), where in niches either side of the doorways and of the bay window are gilded figures of sovereigns. Ornamental stonework here includes the canopies and niches (Pls 83, 158);[10] there are also carved panels dividing the mural paintings. This exemplifies the integration of the stonework with other parts of the decorative scheme. Similarly in the Lords' Chamber (Pl. II), the stonework blends in well with the dominant woodwork. There, bronze statues represent the barons and prelates who witnessed Magna Carta, a subject chosen by a committee under the Fine Arts Commission. The artists however found themselves working, as already noted, within limits imposed by the architect to ensure the architectonic harmony of the whole.

The remaining major internal decorative scheme involving sculpture covers the Public Approach: in a series of niches bordering the archways at either end of St Stephen's Hall (Pl. 95) and in the Central Hall (Pl. III) are statues of the kings and queens of England from the Conquest; friezes of angels project above the four main doors of the Central Hall; in the vaulting are bosses sculpted with coats-of-arms, heraldic devices and foliage. Some of those in St Stephen's Hall are historiated. In addition to these schemes there are in certain areas throughout the building examples of blind tracery panelling, tracery in the spandrels of doorways, decorative devices, bosses—that is, the more purely decorative sculpture. The composition of the tracery again depends on a certain basic vocabulary from which variations are constructed, and it resembles that of the exterior.

Precise dating for the various parts of the sculptural programme is not easy. Specific contemporary references to the sculpture are rare and often incidental. Nevertheless, an outline chronology can be constructed. As far as the North, South and River Fronts are concerned, Barry's progress reports for March 1842 and April 1843 mention large quantities of masonry and carving as prepared for setting.[11] By February 1843 Barry had already made arrangements for external architectonic sculpture. John Thomas exhibited his 'View of the Workshops at the New Houses of Parliament' at the Royal Academy in 1843. *The Book of Art* (1846) illustrates 'The Statuary Room, New Houses of Parliament, in January 1844', in which the figures may be identified as belonging to the series of Saxon kings on the North and South Fronts (Pl. 159). In the Victoria Tower, the vaulting in the Royal Porch was complete, except for the carvings, by Christmas 1846; the carving of the stone groin was com-

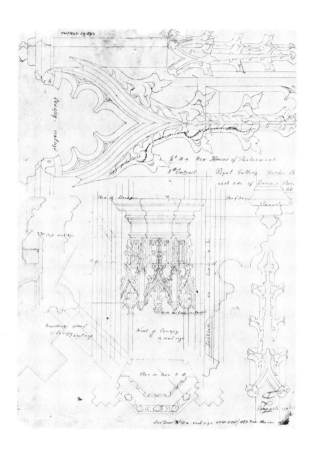

157. (above) New Palace at Westminster: Victoria Tower. Tracing of drawing for the Royal Arms over the carriage gateway in the Royal Porch.

158. (right) New Palace at Westminster: Royal Gallery. Tracing of drawing (?by John Thomas) for canopy to niches each side of doorway.

pleted by 30 June 1847. Ryde's *Illustrations* of 1849 shows the Queen Victoria flanked by Justice and Mercy, and writes of the sculpture of the Porch as if it were *in situ*. With regard to the figures on the exterior, Ryde stated that no arrangements had yet been made except for the raised central niche intended for a statue of the queen. In an illustration of the State Opening of Parliament in 1852 the figures are shown in position.[12] The bosses in the vault of the Central Hall were being carved at Christmas 1847; the *Illustrated London News* for 18 March 1848 shows men actually at work on them. By November 1852 bosses, niches, and canopies were all there, but no figures. Most of the statues had arrived in the Central Hall by September 1853; the others were nearly completed. The entire series of figures in the Central and St Stephen's Halls appeared in the *Illustrated London News* during 1854 and 1855.[13] Sculptors were selected in 1847 to execute models of bronze statues for the Lords' Chamber, the models were completed between 1848 and 1851, the first statue was cast in 1850 and the series reported complete in 1858.[14] In the Royal Gallery the carved panels dividing the murals were nearly complete at 31 March 1858, the first, unsatisfactory statues installed in 1868; these were replaced by Birnie Philip's and the work finished by 24 November 1869.

The implementation of this extensive and complex programme was not easy for Barry, because of the state of architectural sculpture in England when the work at Westminster began. In architecture the Gothic Revival flourished alongside other styles, but the position of architectural sculpture within the movement was less satisfactory. The more purely decorative carved work (such as crockets) being an essential part of the style was carried out and flourished, but there was no equivalent revival in Gothic figure sculpture for a number of reasons. Finance was one: figure

239

159. (left) The Statuary Room, Westminster: Sculptors at work on the Saxon Kings, 1844.

160. (below left) New Palace at Westminster: Central Hall. Workmen sculpturing the bosses on the groined roof, 1848.

161. (right) John Thomas (1813–62), superintendent of stone-carving at the Houses of Parliament.

sculpture was expensive and easily dispensable without detriment to whatever Gothic effect might be aimed at. There were strong Protestant reservations based on the Second Commandment, while the Roman Catholic church had Italianate leanings and usually little money. There was a shortage of models on which to base concepts or even to work from, thanks to the depredations of previous ages. Moreover, neo-classicism predominated in contemporary sculpture so that even a man of Eastlake's breadth of artistic outlook seemed capable of thinking of sculpture only in essentially classical and occasionally Italian Renaissance terms.[16]

This was the situation Barry faced concerning the essential figure work; and to a certain extent in the decorative work also, for the scale was exceptional. His solution was to engage John Thomas (1813–62) (Pl. 161) to supervise the stone-carving throughout the Palace. Thomas's background clearly helped make him the appropriate man. Born in Gloucestershire, his earliest employment locally, restoring the lettering and sometimes the sculptural decoration of gravestones gave him experience of an important area of Perpendicular churches. A visit to Oxford focused his attention more specifically on drawing architectural details correctly and developing skill and knowledge as a carver. Then at Birmingham, where his brother was an architect, he worked on a number of large buildings including Barry's King Edward VI Grammar School, and it was as a result of his competence in Gothic detailing that he came to Barry's notice.[17] There is no evidence to support E. W. Pugin's allegation that Thomas's practical education was due to his working from A. W. Pugin's drawings and under his instruction at Birmingham Grammar School.[18] Thomas was employed largely on the exterior stone-work decoration, Pugin at a later stage on internal fittings.

Thomas was not officially appointed Superintendent of stone-carving at Westminster until 1846.[19] But Barry probably engaged him soon after the completion of the Birmingham school, and on 13 May 1841 the Office of Woods approved Barry's arrangement with Thomas for the stone carving.[20] Barry, in the context of his own

percentage, later claimed that this was done 'under the immediate direction and control of the architect', and in 1856 defined Thomas's position as an 'artist workman' employed as 'carver in chief . . . essentially an executant and not as superintendent. His office is to prepare full sized working drawings, and models, and set out the work, under my own control and personal direction.'[21] He was clearly an important member of the Barry team. In consequence of his 'great talent and ability' in executing 'the sculptural effigies and other decorations confided to his directions', his salary was increased from £200 *p.a.* to £300 for 1846 and £400 in 1847–50. The total cost of the work in his department up to 1850 was estimated by Barry at £32,000.[22]

There is some evidence relating to the execution of the sculpture. Thomas P. Garland, an architectural modeller who worked at the Houses of Parliament, described how the heraldic devices were produced:[23]

My work was principally to prepare the full size models for the carvers to work from . . . there was generally a small drawing made in Mr Barry's office showing the general design, which was enlarged by Mr Thomas and others, and the models were then made in the shops full size, Mr Barry invariably giving his personal attention to them before they were carved.

Thomas superintended modelling and carving, both the important stages, that is, in the execution of the sculpture. Garland's account is confirmed by other evidence. There are working drawings at various scales which indicate the positioning of representational sculpture in the architectural scheme, with the formal detail either sketchy or absent.[24] There are separate drawings for the actual form of this type of

162. (above left) St Stephen's Cloister. The ruins after the fire of 1834, showing stone tracery and panelling.

163. (above) John Thomas: Pencil drawing for statue of King Edgar.

164. (above right) John Thomas: Pencil and wash drawing for statue of Queen Victoria.

165. (above, far right) John Thomas: Drawings for bosses.

166. (right) John Thomas: Models of Saxon kings for the South Return, Houses of Parliament, as exhibited at the Crystal Palace, Sydenham, and destroyed in the fire of 1936.

sculpture (Pls 163–5).[25] The models made from the drawings no longer survive, but photographs exist of some of the models for the kings and queens, on display at the Crystal Palace where they were destroyed in the fire of 1936 (Pl. 166).[26]

With the purely decorative carved stonework the procedure was somewhat different. In the smaller-scale elevation drawings, details such as cusping and crocketing are rather sketchy, though the overall composition is indicated.[27] As the scale increases, a distinction in treatment seems to arise. The delineation of the tracery becomes precise,[28] but the crocketing is still delineated in a fluid style (Pl. 83).[29] For the execution of such details the workmen may have relied on the presence of exemplars rather than working entirely from drawings—one (Pl. 158) is inscribed 'For Groin see model',[30] and casts may well have been used for this purpose, similar to those collected by Pugin for the work under his supervision.[31]

The actual location of the stonecarving workshops is not always certain. By the time the 'Thames Bank Workshops' had been acquired about the end of 1844, some of the carving had been completed and subsequent references to work there do not mention stonecarving.[32] For most of the carving one must assume a close association with the building operations: the Central Hall bosses and the ornamentation of the later arcade in New Palace Yard were both executed *in situ*; stone in other parts was carved before being lifted into position.[33] One workshop was in Grissell's yard in New Palace Yard; another, 'where Labour toiled and Art planned', was by the Lords' Front in Old Palace Yard. The modellers' shop was at first located on the river terrace.[34]

Barry's own contribution to the design of the sculptural programme cannot be in much doubt. He would undoubtedly have drawn up the overall plan, subsequently delegating certain specific areas to qualified specialists. Details such as tracery, though, came from his office, as the drawings referred to earlier indicate. To argue that the scheme as executed from 1840 depends on Pugin's contribution alone to the 1836–7 specification and estimate drawings would be a little far-fetched, and would go against the testimony of some of those involved. Pugin was not unique at this date in his ability to produce Gothic ornamental detail. Quite apart from an architect such as Rickman who could in the 1820s produce church designs that if they do not dispose their Gothic ornament in an archaeologically satisfactory way at any rate seem to have the form of the ornament reasonably correct,[35] there was in Barry's office from at least as early as 1832 someone who could turn out competent crockets (Pl. 44)— some three years, that is, before the first association of Pugin with Barry.[36] It is always possible that this person was Barry himself. He might not be able to recall instantaneously relevant examples of Gothic architecture, but as an architect using Gothic he could without Pugin's help turn out the requisite formal details, as a friend in fact testified.[37] He might not be able to reproduce the authentic Gothic 'spirit' as Pugin could; but one of the main features of the Gothicness of the New Houses of Parliament is its correctness in the forms of Gothic detail used rather than in its overall spirit—and all this notwithstanding Barry's constant calling on Pugin's assistance for details of fittings after 1844. The detailed design of the representational sculpture can be largely ascribed to Thomas. Many of the surviving drawings relating to this are given to him, and some contemporary accounts attribute the entire design of such work to him.[38] The historically accurate royal coats-of-arms on the River Front, however, were ascribed at the time to Thomas Willement.[39]

To find specific stylistic sources for the Westminster work is not easy. The lack of mediaeval models for the figures may explain a certain stylistic indeterminacy; the heraldry lacks a specific stylistic character and the decorative ornamental work adheres to a general tradition. The relation of sculpture to edifice may be connected with the town halls of Belgium which Barry visited and which he sent Thomas to inspect before he started work;[40] and the fifteenth-century royal chapels offer patterns for the use of royal badges, but these are general, not specific points of reference. Only with the tracery can a particular source be identified: certain elements of the basic Houses of Parliament pattern, involving cusping, ogees, spandrel composition and panel joins existed in the original St Stephen's Cloister (Pl. 162),[41] specific features connecting the present building with an original if late Gothic structure associated with the history of Parliament.

The influence of the architectural sculpture at the Houses of Parliament was necessarily limited. There was no subsequent building of equivalent scale or significance to justify such a programme except possibly Street's Law Courts, where expenditure was pared to a minimum. Barry's son claimed some influence on later architectural sculpture,[42] but it is hard to substantiate; this type of sculpture was as flourishing in parallel styles of building, particularly the neo-classical, and even supposing the work at Westminster distinctive, the differentiation of styles diminished as the century progressed. Moreover the extent of sculptural adornment depended on architects' wishes as well as on the amount people were willing to spend—Manchester's expensive Town Hall has very little. Among sculptors known to have worked at Westminster were Henry Hugh Armstead (1828–1905), John Lawlor (1820–1901), Alexander Munro (1825–71), John Birnie Philip (1824–75) and Alexander Handyside Ritchie (1804–70), but apart from Armstead's New Palace Yard arcade, the insulated statues in the Lords' Chamber and those by Birnie Philip in the Royal Gallery, it is impossible to make out individual contributions to the architectural sculpture. Only Robert Jackson (fl. 1840–78) can be identified specifically as Thomas's chief assistant.[43] John Thomas himself clearly benefited from his experiences at Westminster, building up in consequence a thriving career as sculptor and architect.[44]

3. Stained Glass

Barry discusses stained glass in the Report on Internal Decorations which he drew up early in 1843 and it is clear that, from the beginning, he saw it as a major element in the furnishing of the Palace. His aim was to create a sense of extreme richness without doing violence to the main lines of the building. This he sought to achieve by 'a general spread of minute ornament, a kind of diapering of the whole . . . His feeling always was that ornamentation, if right in kind, could not be overdone.'[1] In this, moreover, he had the wholehearted support of Pugin. He too had a passion for lavish and intricate surface detail.

Stained glass lent itself to their aim, 'if right in kind'. This in practice meant an emphasis on heraldry. In his Report Barry proposed windows 'bearing arms and other insignia in their proper colours . . . the ground . . . covered with a running foliage or diaper, and occasionally relieved with legends in black letter.'[2] There were to be only two important figured schemes, of which one, in the Lords' Chamber, was almost as formal as heraldry, with rows of figures under canopies, while the other, in the Crypt Chapel, was a late addition and not typical. Almost all the other glass was heraldic, presenting an endless series of repeating patterns, rich in detail, bright in colour, abstract in design. Indeed, so uniform did the glass become that windows designed for one position were frequently adapted for another.

It is not surprising that neither Barry nor Pugin liked the currently fashionable Munich glass, which sought to overcome the traditional conventions of the medium and emulate paintings. This had been much recommended during the deliberations of the Select Committee on the Fine Arts in 1841. Instead they sought inspiration in earlier sources. Samples of stained glass were among the numerous specimens of medieval art they collected as models for the workmen at Westminster.[3] Barry urged Pugin to introduce 'a sufficient amount of white glass to produce the jewelled effect he admired in many ancient windows', especially in churches at Nuremberg.[4] Pugin's own knowledge of the subject was encyclopaedic. For years he had studied and copied stained glass during his extensive travels. He was familiar with the windows at York, Chartres, Strasbourg and Cologne as well as Nuremberg, and one of the delights of his visit to Florence in 1847 was the glass in Santa Croce.[5]

Barry's first attempt to put his ideas into practice failed. It underlined the fundamental weakness in the methods of the Fine Arts Commission. The Commissioners approved his Report and printed it; and at their request he submitted recommendations for the decoration of the House of Lords. These in turn the Commissioners approved. In June 1843 decorative artists, including those working in stained glass, were invited to compete for commissions,[6] and in February 1845 Barry was invited to report on 'the mode in which the artists selected . . . might be employed'. The Commissioners, having approved his 'design in detail' for the stained glass, thereupon commissioned one of the successful competitors, Messrs Ballantine and Allan, to carry out the work 'in accordance with the principles of that design', at an estimate of £2,400. In May 1845 they themselves drew up a list of the monarchs of England and Scotland who were to form the subject of the windows of the Lords' Chamber;[7] and a month later they recommended Barry's plans for the decoration of the Lords to the Treasury.

The only part Ballantine and Allan were to play in the design was to prepare the final cartoons; and it was a condition of the contract that Barry should supply these too if theirs failed to satisfy him. Yet when the cartoons were ready and Barry found them 'not such as he could approve', the Commissioners let him down. The cost of furnishing the Lords had already risen to over £21,000 and Barry's proposal to have the cartoons re-drawn by a 'first rate artist' of his own choosing involved an additional expense of £84 a window. More important, however, the Commissioners felt that Barry was assuming too much responsibility for the decoration. On 6 June 1846 they complained to the Treasury that he had ignored the results of the competition and employed workmen on his own initiative; and that even in the field of stained glass (which they admitted was an exception) 'the artist recommended by the Commission has been instructed by the architect to adopt his designs instead of following his own conceptions'.[8] Barry was naturally indignant. The system of competitions, while it might be suitable for frescoes and free-standing sculpture, was totally impracticable for minor decorative work. And in any case the Commissioners' attitude was unfair, considering their own part in the proceedings. Barry pointed out (23 June) that they had approved his plans at every stage; that they had specifically empowered him to use his discretion in employing workmen so long as the estimates were not exceeded; and that as for Ballantine and Allan, it had been fully understood as one of the conditions of their contract that he was to refuse their cartoons if these failed to come up to standard.[9] Nor was this the end of the matter. When Ballantine and Allen rendered their account four years later, they claimed compensation. Barry upheld their claim. The Treasury then consulted the Commissioners, who replied that in their view the claim was quite unjustified.[10] What the outcome was is not clear, but Barry's attitude to the whole episode may be guessed. He had long regretted his own exclusion from the Commission on the grounds that, as a member, he could have helped to prevent exactly this kind of bureaucratic muddle.

Ballantine and Allan, the winners of the competition, were an Edinburgh firm. James Ballantine, the senior partner, was born in 1808, the son of a brewer. In 1830 he set up as a house-painter, but after learning drawing at the Trustees' Academy he turned to stained-glass, and executed a large number of windows throughout the country until his death in 1877.[11] He worked hard to secure the Westminster commission. Firms had been asked to submit only one (or at most two) coloured designs for an entire window together with a specimen of glass representing part of the same design. Ballantine apparently submitted with his entry a series of watercolour sketches for all twelve windows in the Chamber with elaborate notes on the proposed inconography pasted on the back of each drawing, as well as a printed letter and 'explanation' of his scheme (Pls IX, 167).[12]

Yet more evidence suggesting that Ballantine, like many self-made men, had a well developed sense of self-promotion, is his *Treatise on Painted Glass* (1845). His firm had only been one of several whose work was 'noticed' when the results of the competition were announced in May 1844,[13] and it may well have been the *Treatise* which tipped the balance in his favour when the actual commission was given. It abounds in ideas likely to recommend it to official taste. Nature, Raphael, and 'Secondary Pointed' are all commended in turn. The Fine Arts Commissioners—'these distinguished and enlightened promoters of Art'—are praised for their decision to decorate the Lords with stained glass, which 'coincides with the views attempted to be defined in this little Treatise, and may be considered as no unimportant evidence of their accuracy'.[14] Even Eastlake receives a pat on the back, for an opinion on stained glass in a note in his translation of Goethe's *Theory of Colours*. Comparison of the texts also suggests that Ballantine was consciously echoing Barry's 1843 Report on the decoration of the Palace.

Yet from Ballantine's sketch designs it is not difficult to see why his cartoons were rejected. The general plan of figures under gothic canopies set against alternate red and blue grounds must have been laid down in Barry's detailed design, and was to be retained in the windows as eventually executed. But the figures are Ballantine's and there is something ludicrous about them. Gauche in gesture and unsure in pose, they are made still more absurd by the pretentious iconography, explained so laboriously in the accompanying text. The Commissioners had stipulated that competitors should treat 'either figures or heraldic devices relating to the Royal Families of England . . . [which] may be accompanied by borders, diapered grounds, legends, and similar enrichments.' But they can hardly have bargained for an image of Henry II carrying a bleeding heart 'to denote that he died of a broken heart, caused by the undutiful behaviour of his children', or 'mottoes' from the 'recorded expressions' of such relatively obscure figures as Queen Matilda or Fitz-Osbern, Earl of Hereford.

In the event, then, Ballantine did no more than make the glass for the Lords. The Commissioners wisely laid down their own scheme of iconography, and Barry turned to his 'first rate artist' for new cartoons. This, of course, was Pugin. In 1844, officially appointed Superintendent of the Woodcarving, Pugin had undertaken to supply Barry with designs for the House of Lords. Now the glass, first in the Lords but soon throughout the building, was to be his responsibility too.

He was ably supported, however, by his friend and collaborator John Hardman of Birmingham, already engaged on metalwork in the House of Lords. In 1845 at Pugin's suggestion he began to make stained glass. Pugin had previously employed

VII. The Houses of Parliament: Tiles on the floor of
the Lords' Lobby. Pugin's designs for encaustic tiles,
executed by Minton, are an important feature of the
New Palace. His skill in using medieval forms as a
point of departure is clearly evidenced here.

IX. The Houses of Parliament:
House of Lords. Cartoon for stained
glass by James Ballantine, 1845.
The Royal Fine Arts Commissioners
recommended Ballantine for the
Lords' Chamber windows as a
result of their 1845 competition.
But the general feebleness of
Ballantine's figures led Barry to
stipulate that though he should be
employed to make the windows,
Pugin should design them.

VIII. A. W. Pugin: Cartoon for wall paper for the
Houses of Parliament. The designs for wall paper are a
further example of Pugin's superlative skill in providing
appropriate designs for Barry's requirements.

X. (above) The Houses of Parliament: Queen's Robing Room. W. Dyce, *Sir Galahad, or The Spirit of Religion*, 1851–2. Dyce was a leader in the movement for reviving fresco-painting in England. This owed much to the example of the German Nazarenes, and was encouraged by Prince Albert. Dyce's Arthurian frescoes in the Queen's Robing Room come closest of the Westminster wall-paintings to the Nazarene ideal.

XI. (left) J. M. W. Turner, *The Burning of the Houses of Parliament*, 16 Oct. 1834. Detail. Turner was among the thousands who, like Pugin and Barry, turned out to see the great fire. His vividly immediate painting also shows the way that old Westminster Bridge dominated the site.

167. (left) James Ballantine:
Cartoon for stained glass, House
of Lords, 1845: Stephen and
Henry II with their queens.
These windows were to depict
English and Scots sovereigns
from the Conquest.
Ballantine was recommended by
the Royal Fine Arts Commissioners, but in view of his poor
figure drawing, Barry insisted
that Pugin should design the
windows, though he allowed
Ballantine to execute them after
Hardman had made a model.

168. (right) A. W. Pugin:
Rough sketch for stained glass,
House of Lords. Pencil and pen
on light blue paper; inscribed
'James II' [of Scots] and 'Mary
of Guelders', with other notes—
'shield', 'ermine', etc.

169. (far right) A. W. Pugin and
J. H. Powell: Study for House
of Lords glass. Pencil and
mauve wash. The pencil work is
Pugin's.

three other firms: William Warrington (who had entered the Houses of Parliament competition and, like Ballantine, was commended by the judging Committee), Thomas Willement, and William Wailes of Newcastle. Each, however, had been discarded in turn. They charged too much or insisted on having a hand in the designs; and Pugin's own standards were rising. To achieve these standards he turned to Hardman. With the exception of the windows in the Lords' Chamber, Hardman was to carry out all the glass in the New Palace.

Hardman had also supplied Pugin with his chief assistant in the arduous work of designing the glass. His young nephew John Hardman Powell arrived at Ramsgate as Pugin's first pupil in November 1844. He had been warned that Pugin would prove an exacting master.[15] But he soon established himself as a trusted collaborator and many of the surviving drawings are from his hand. They are generally recognizable, for his style tends to be harder and coarser than Pugin's, though in his sketches he adopts the flickering touch which is so characteristic of Pugin himself.

Indeed, as the work progressed, Pugin found himself master of a busy workshop. He himself would first rough out a scheme in a slight, evocative sketch (Pl. 168). Powell would give this greater definition (Pl. 169), and finally, from their drawings, a team of draughtsmen would prepare the cartoons, working in a room specially built for the purpose. These included Francis Oliphant, who came regularly from London and drew the cartoons for the House of Lords; Casolani, a former pupil of Overbeck;

and Frederick Hill, Edwin Hendren and John Early, three young men also sent from Birmingham by Hardman. Pugin himself watched constantly over their progress. Several of the cartoons, of which many exist in the City Art Gallery at Birmingham, are inscribed with pencil notes in his hand.[16]

The glass in the Lords' Chamber, to which Pugin and his team addressed themselves first, was the most ambitious project in the whole building. As we have seen, it consisted of twelve lofty windows, each divided into lights arranged in two tiers, filled with figures of kings and queens standing under elaborate gothic canopies. Nothing of it survives, and the cartoons have also disappeared. There is, however, a hint of what it looked like in a design of four monarchs, one standing under a canopy, in the Moulton-Barrett volume of drawings from Barry's office.[17] We also have a slight sketch by Pugin himself for two of the figures (Pl. 168),[18] and a long series of more elaborate studies (Pl. 169), mainly by Powell.[19] Four of these, all at Birmingham, are especially interesting, for they reveal something of the sources used. Two, of Anne Boleyn and Jane Seymour, are inscribed 'Print of Hollar'. As Professor Stanton has shown,[20] Hollar exercised a general influence on Pugin as a draughtsman, and he owned many of his etchings, including those used for the Lords' glass.[21] Another study, of Anne Neville, wife of Richard III, is inscribed 'Shaw' and 'Trace carefully a cord Stothard'; and a fourth, of Catherine of Aragon, 'Shaw's Queen Margaret'. These are almost certainly references to C. A. Stothard's *Monumental Effigies of Great Britain* of 1817 and Henry Shaw's *Dresses and Decorations of the Middle Ages* published by William Pickering in 1843.[22] Both are reference books of exactly the kind we should expect to find in daily use in Pugin's studio, as no doubt they were used by many artists of the day.[23] Certainly Shaw was familiar to the Pre-Raphaelites ten or more years later.[24]

Not content with having Pugin re-draw the cartoons for the Lords, Barry had Hardman make a specimen window.[25] He was clearly taking no chances. The Fine Arts Commissioners had virtually forced him to employ Ballantine: he would at least make sure the work was carried out as he wanted. By this time, moreover, Hardman was employed on the glass in other parts of the building, so there was also a question of homogeneity; and, since the Lords was to be occupied in February 1847, time was short. In the first week of November 1846 Pugin sent him 'a cartoon which is to be a standard for the lower compartments' of the window. On 29 December Barry, 'painfully anxious' to know how the work was going, demanded a 'full report' by return of post. The window was placed experimentally before 3 February, when Barry wrote to say that, in order to forestall criticism that the glass made the chamber too dark, he had 'determined to have the canopies and inscriptions of the whole of the lights removed and others upon clear glass without either stippling or shadowing substituted.' By 26 February, when the window was on its way back to Birmingham for alteration, he had changed his mind again, and wanted the canopies 'partially stippled and relieved with yellow', an effect he had indicated on the glass itself. He also wrote elaborate instructions about what he called the 'backgrounds' of the canopies, probably the recessed areas in shadow. These were to be of a 'grey stone colour' of 'the tone of the greyish patch which you will find upon a piece of clear glass which is sent with the lights.' Although he hoped to lighten the glass generally, Barry was anxious to avoid too strong a contrast between the canopies and the grounds of deep ruby and blue behind the figures. Hence the careful gradations in the tone of the painted stonework, and also his suggestion that while the ruby and blue should be left alone under the canopies, these colours should be 'considerably lighter' where they appeared above them. So anxious was Barry to achieve the results he wanted that he volunteered to 'run down to Birmingham by the express train to witness the effect.' The work was put in hand immediately,[26] and the window was installed again by 17 April when it was noticed in *the Builder*. The writer assumed that Hardman was to carry out the other windows as well, but this was corrected in a footnote the following week, stating that Ballantine and Allan were to do them using the Hardman one as a model 'as to colours and general treatment'.[27] According to an early guidebook the window in question was the first on the west or right-hand side, showing William the Conqueror, William Rufus, Henry I and Stephen, with their respective consorts.[28] This in fact is the window for which a drawing survives in the Record Office of the House of Lords.[29]

The glass in the Lords' Chamber was still not finished by April 1848,[30] but it must have been complete by September 1850 when Ballantine rendered his account.[31] Barry regarded the windows as 'well executed'.[32] When the State Opening of the Palace took place on 3 February 1852, they made a dramatic effect, the gas lights blazing outside converting them into vast transparencies.[33] In fact a considerable amount of glass was in place by this time. The internal lights which survive in the region of the Lords' Library were there.[34] So were four other major schemes—the great window in the remodelled south end of Westminster Hall, the Commons Chamber, the Peers' Lobby, and the Victoria Hall (now the Prince's Chamber). The Peers' Lobby windows, displaying the arms of the peerage and costing £55 each, and the much simpler glass in the Victoria Hall, were in place as early as spring 1847.[35] The Commons, showing the arms of the cities and boroughs,[36] was evidently a more difficult job. The final solution seems to have been reached by a process of trial and error. Specimen lights went backwards and forwards between Birmingham and London all through the summer of 1849 and were then displayed in the Commons itself. Further delay must have been caused by the decision to lower the ceiling to improve the acoustics, thereby cutting the windows in half. All was finished, however, by 26 July 1851 when the *Builder* described the glass as 'good in colour and effect, but unsatisfactory in design and drawing'. The Westminster Hall window, with Royal arms, was installed at the same time.[37]

Before he died in 1852 Pugin had turned his thoughts to further schemes. He was contemplating figured glass for windows in the Central Lobby and St Stephen's Hall, as well as a series illustrating the life of the Black Prince on the Commons' public ('polygonal') stair (Pl. 170).[38] In fact, however, the Central Lobby was to be filled with heraldry about 1856: some of the lights made redundant by the lowering of the Commons' ceiling seem to have been utilized here. St Stephen's Hall was also filled with heraldic glass (some at least from the Commons) two years later; and at the same time a similar scheme was installed in the Royal Gallery. Cartoons for both series survive at Birmingham.

After Pugin's death in 1852 J. H. Powell supplied his place, designing the attractive grisaille glass in the Norman Porch, shattered in the 1939–45 war but now restored to its original state,[39] and other later schemes such as the series in the Queen's Robing Room, an heraldic history of the Queens of England which was still in progress in 1870. Powell's chief work at Westminster, however, is the set of windows still in St Stephen's Crypt, installed about 1865 as part of the restoration of the Chapel by E. M. Barry. Seven four-light windows tell the story of St Stephen, the scenes being arranged in central medallions with scroll patterns above and below. The drawing, highly conventionalised, is unequal: the Saint distributing alms on the north side is one of the better groups.[40] But the firm overall design and subdued colouring (too subdued in places, owing to poor external light) makes this glass an unspectacular

170. (left) A. W. Pugin: Pencil sketch for window in St Stephen's Hall. The programme here alternated historical figures and heraldry.

171. (right) John Hardman Powell: Two small heraldic lights with Royal Arms. Pencil, pen and wash. Not identified, but very characteristic of Powell's more finished studies for glass at the New Palace.

success. It takes its place perfectly in the general scheme of rich polychromy (Pl. IV).

The Crypt windows are the only original scheme of any importance that still exists. The process of removal and destruction from which so much of the glass has suffered began even before the whole programme was complete. As early as 1841 W. J. Bankes, giving evidence before the Select Committee on the Fine Arts, had suggested that 'the light in London is so imperfect . . . that there are few positions where painted windows could be applied without interfering with the utility of the building.'[41] His fears were soon realised. In August 1853 George Bowyer complained that the windows 'might be handsome enough as specimens of medieval art; but no one would pretend that, with those beasts daubed over them, they admitted light; and they certainly did not admit air, because they did not open.' Would members, he asked, 'be guilty of any breach of the rules if they broke the windows, and destroyed the extraordinary beasts which disfigured them and astonished naturalists?'[42] His comments reflected a widespread concern among members, and as a result much of the glass was removed during the next few years.[43] The Lords' and Commons' Corridors were treated in this way in 1863: so was the Central Lobby a few years later.[44]

Further glass was nearly lost at this stage for another reason. The Select Committee on the Fine Arts had also considered in 1841 the question of whether or not stained glass would conflict with the frescoes. When consulted, the leading German painter Cornelius gave it as his opinion that they were not necessarily incompatible.[45] The evidence of C. H. Wilson, Director of the Government School of Design, pointed to the same conclusion. Indeed Wilson went so far as to argue that the exclusion of white light would improve the visibility of any painted surfaces.[46] In practice, however, the question proved more complex. Daniel Maclise, who had already declined to paint murals in St Stephen's Hall in 1857 on the grounds that it was too dark to work in, ran into further trouble when he started to paint *The Meeting of Wellington*

255

and Blücher in the Royal Gallery two years later. 'When the sun did *not* shine', he wrote to Eastlake, 'I could barely see, and when [it did] the heraldic devices . . . griffins, dragons, and all—in gules, and gold, and azure, were emblazoned in form and colour over the forty-six feet of compartment, shaming and falsifying, in their dazzling passage over them, my poor earthy, lime-burnt tinges.'[47] Maclise's complaints were communicated to Prince Albert who decided that the glass must be removed. But he died before his orders could be carried out.

The glass suffered again about thirty years later. On 24 January 1885 a Fenian bomb exploded in Westminster Hall, shattering the south window and damaging the glass in the Commons, the Division Lobbies, St Stephen's Hall and the Crypt Chapel. At this date Hardmans were still able to carry out repairs from the old cartoons.[48] But when the next blow fell during the 1939–45 war the damage was irreparable. A few windows were removed, but the great majority were either destroyed or severely damaged in the air-raids that ravaged the building between 1940 and 1944. Nor was much restoration possible. The task was again undertaken by Hardmans. But there were no records of the original schemes, and though many of the cartoons survived, these were found to be dilapidated, often wrongly named, or specimen designs never used. Only one major scheme, that in the Crypt Chapel, was restored to its original state, together with the glass in the Norman Porch and a number of small internal lights at various points in the corridors adjoining the Library of the House of Lords. In St Stephen's Hall, the Royal Gallery and the Peers' Lobby, Hardmans produced new sets of windows, based only in general arrangement on the old designs. Elsewhere there was no attempt to keep to the original schemes. The large south window in Westminster Hall was re-designed by Sir Ninian Comper as a memorial to members killed in the war. The House of Commons had been destroyed, and the new design required only leaded lights of plain glass. For the Lords' Chamber a new series was commissioned, the original figured glass being replaced by heraldic windows. Designed by Carl Edwards, the work was carried out by Powells of Whitefriars, as were the new Commons windows and those of simple quarry glass now in the Central Lobby.[49]

Today it is almost impossible to picture the glass in its original state. However, from surviving drawings and documentary evidence, we can at least see it in the context of the Victorian stained glass revival. In many ways it was advanced for its time. Pugin's remarkable ability to re-create the medieval idiom convincingly made him more 'modern' than Ballantine, for it was towards greater historical accuracy that the tide of revival was moving. Pugin's and Barry's strong preference for leaded windows as against large panes of painted glass reflected a general reaction against the German ideal. We know, too, how assiduously Pugin and Hardman tried to recapture the richness of early glass, seeking material of unusual thickness and experimenting with broken colours. Their efforts anticipated by a few years Charles Winston's better-known search for the secrets of medieval glass, and there were soon others working in the same field.[50] Moreover, as Ballantine had predicted in his *Treatise*, the Westminster competitions themselves stimulated craftsmanship. Hardmans are the obvious example. Soon they had built up a large stained glass practice. Street and Butterfield were among those who employed them extensively, and the lessons they had learnt at Westminster they put to good account elsewhere.

Theory, however, tended to outstrip practice. It is significant that the glass which indicates most clearly how Hardmans' work would develop,[51] that in the Crypt Chapel, was never characteristic of the Westminster scheme as a whole, and was designed after Barry and Pugin were dead. *Their* work had been the great heraldic schemes, which were chosen partly for decorative purposes, partly to further Barry's vision of the Palace as 'a monumental history of England'.[52] These schemes may be seen as the culmination of an older tradition, best represented, perhaps, by Thomas Willement, an expert on heraldry who executed a large number of heraldic windows for country houses, colleges and livery halls in the 1830s and '40s.[53] They belong to a world in which men played unashamedly at being medieval knights, the world of Young England, of the Eglinton Tournament, of a Tennyson d'Eyncourt. By the time the programme was complete, a new, subtler approach to the Middle Ages had emerged, and the spirit in which it was conceived was already long out of date.

4. Metalwork

Barry gave Pugin his greatest opportunity to produce rich metalwork on a large scale at the Palace of Westminster. The palace still contains more examples of brass and ironwork designed by Pugin than any other building in the country. But the qualified enthusiasm with which he began designing in 1844–5 was succeeded by bouts of exasperation, fury and despair at Barry's frequent modifications of his work. As he drew and re-drew, and arranged for new models and trial pieces to be produced for Barry's inspection, Pugin's rage became tempered by a desperate humour which shows itself in the surviving letters to his friend and manufacturer, John Hardman of Birmingham.

Pugin's resourcefulness as a designer in the decorative arts is as apparent in the variety of his patterns for door furniture (Pl. 172) as in the details of the huge brass candelabra standing at the foot of the throne in the House of Lords (Pl. II). The furnishings of the Palace were still uncompleted at the time of his death in 1852, but by then he had been responsible for most of the metalwork on the principal floors,

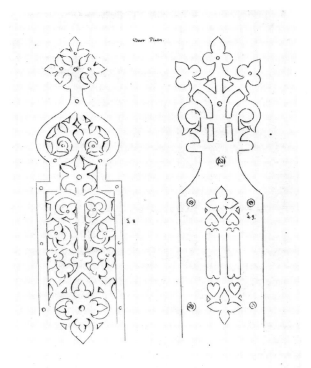

172. A. W. Pugin: Two designs for
door-plates for the Houses of Parliament.

grates for waiting halls No 1

the drawings to be all sent to Birmingham with the model.

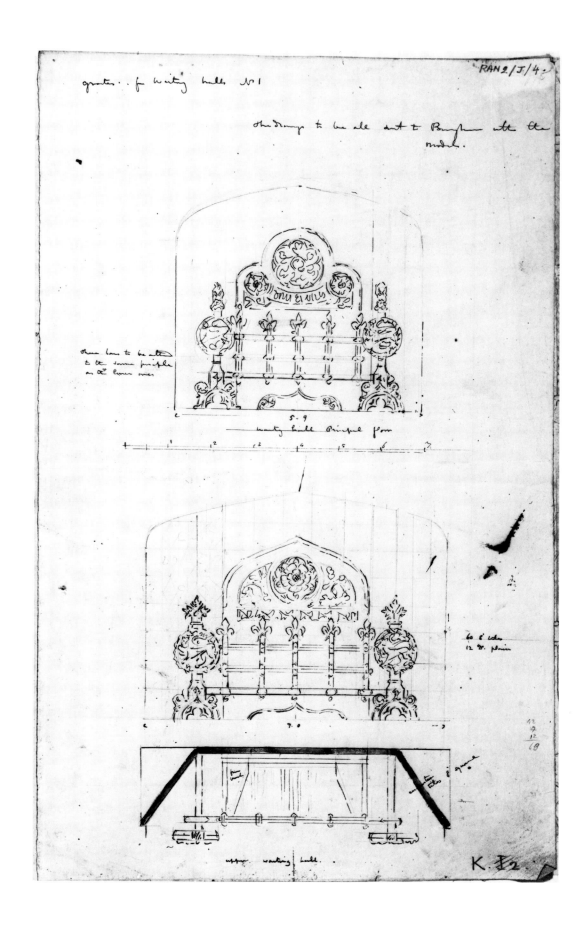

these bars to be set to the same principle as the lower ones

5·9

waiting halls Principal floor

to 6 inches
12 in. plain

7·0

upper waiting hall

K. ½

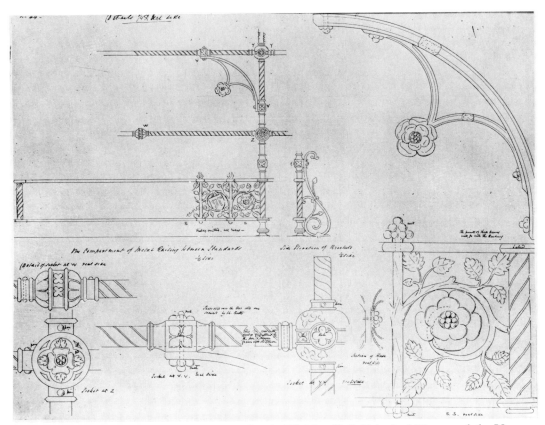

173. (left) A. W. Pugin: Designs for grates for the Waiting Hall, Principal Floor, and the Upper Waiting Hall, Houses of Parliament. Annotated by Pugin, 'The drawings to be all sent to Birmingham [Hardman's] with the models'.

174. (above) A. W. Pugin: Working drawings for brass rail to gallery, House of Lords. Annotated by Pugin, 'shields omitted, all roses', as Barry had required.

including the refreshment rooms, the libraries on the River Front, the conference room between them, and for the committee rooms above them. Still abundant enough to impress its character on the Palace, much of Pugin's metalwork has disappeared, jettisoned in the cause of modernization. The Peers' lobby and the Commons' lobby long ago lost his tall gasoliers,[1] prototypes of many lighting standards designed for use in cathedrals and churches by later architects of the Victorian Gothic Revival.[2] Unhappily, although gas pendants, unlike gasoliers, were more easily converted into electric lamps, Pugin's own designs had largely been replaced before the need arose.

It was Pugin's familiarity with historic precedent that enabled him to produce a seemingly endless series of designs for locks, hinges, escutcheons, handles, grates and fire-dogs (Pl. 173) for the palace. He worked so easily in the gothic idiom that he was able to apply the same principles of design to a wide variety of post-medieval, utilitarian innovations, making drawings for angle plates and complex hinges for swing doors,[3] finger-plates (Pl. 172),[4] name card holders,[5] bell pulls,[6] thermometer cases,[7] calendar cards[8] and letter boxes.[9] That his sources were invariably ecclesiastical accorded well with Pugin's view of the indivisibility of gothic as the only fit style for all forms of architecture and design in a Christian country.

Most of Pugin's ideas about metalwork are enunciated in his *True Principles* of 1841. He disliked modern cast iron, not because it was cast, but because it was either produced with a lack of depth and insufficient variety of surface or as a sham, painted to simulate wood or stone. He demonstrated what could be done with the material by illustrating an antique cast iron andiron of heraldic character, and it was specimens such as this which provided the inspiration for his own fire-dogs at Westminster, including those in the Peers' lobby (Pl. 173). Another 'splendid example of ancient ironwork', the late fifteenth-century grille belonging to the monument of Edward IV in St George's Chapel, Windsor, is cited in his book, the text making it plain that he was fascinated by the craftsmanship of late medieval ironsmiths. He was knowledgeable about their techniques, describing the construction of elaborate screens of wrought tracery mounted on a carcase, the components of which were often filed and jointed, entailing the use of 'beautiful studs and busy enrichments'.[10] The great studded brass gates leading from the Peers' lobby to the Chamber are Pugin's equivalent of these medieval works (Pl. 79). Characteristically, his own gates are less ornate than some of the ancient originals he admired, their showiness being to some extent pictorial. Depth and shade are imparted by the superimposition of brass on iron.

Pugin's fondness for brass ran counter to his theory that all craftsmanship should be firmly rooted in the past, both as to material and design. To use brass as he did on the Peers' doors, and indeed elsewhere in the Palace, has no recognizable medieval precedent. What he was doing was to translate the idiom of wrought ironwork into brass. Although this was unarchaeological, he chose to ignore this divergence from his professed beliefs, as he often did when his practice failed to conform to his high antiquarian ideals. He was a proselytizer both public and private, and could afford no confession of weakness.

Everywhere Pugin went, he filled notebooks with sketches of architectural details and artifacts,[11] and, partly in the interests of educating Hardman's workmen, he often acquired antique specimens of metalwork for which Hardman was required to meet the bill.[12] The craftsmen were also directed to St Marie's College, Oscott,[13] the Roman Catholic seminary near Birmingham where Pugin, as Professor of Ecclesiastical Antiquities, had assiduously added to the college treasury. He was anxious to encourage Hardman's employees to appreciate the reasons why he required them to master old techniques—forging iron where appropriate instead of invariably casting it, or saw-piercing brass instead of stamping it out by machine. In his view, the quality and workmanship of the old pieces were a powerful vindication of his arguments.

Pugin himself kept a tight hold on the design of Hardman's manufacturers, and although he employed assistants, they were made to conform to his style. It was not difficult to acquire the rudiments of Pugin's manner. His forms are archaeological, in the sense that their derivation is usually obvious, but his repertory of ornament consists of a few favourite motifs. The fleur-de-lis, the trefoil and the quatrefoil, separately or in combination, appear in nearly all his work. It was nevertheless almost impossible for his assistants to emulate his mastery as an ornamentist.

Pugin's collaborator John Hardman (1811–67), a fellow Roman Catholic, was a button manufacturer by trade, a member of the prominent Birmingham firm of Hardman & Iliffe. Pugin persuaded him to launch a new venture in 1838, making metalwork in the gothic style from Pugin's designs. Starting in a very small way, the business expanded in the early 1840s, attracting commissions for both ecclesiastical and domestic work from Roman Catholics and Anglicans alike. Several members of

Hardman's family entered into the concern, and one of these, his nephew John Hardman Powell (1827–95), went to Pugin's house in Ramsgate as a pupil in 1844. Pugin disliked Powell's background, for he had worked in the design department of Elkington, Mason & Company of Birmingham, the patentees of electroplating. Hardman had in fact enjoyed close relations with Elkington's since 1837.[14] Although he now had a business which overtly rejected current commercial practices, Hardman nevertheless drew on the expertise of the larger firm, and this Pugin was prepared implicitly to overlook. Hardmans frequently used electroplated nickel silver for their goods, compensating for its lack of medieval authority by lavishing as much craftsmanship upon it as if it had been sterling silver.

Progress by trial and error became the standard procedure for the Palace metalwork, a system established during Hardman's first commission, the making of a set of vanes of varying sizes in copper-gilt.[15] The scale of the building was so large that Barry found it impossible to judge the effect of some of the metalwork until a trial piece had been made and put into position. Moreover, Pugin's ecclesiastical experience had encouraged a propensity for rich detail which Barry had to control.

The most drastic revisions of Pugin's designs were made to the brass railing of the gallery in the Lords' Chamber (Pl. 174). Ironically, this troublesome commission was the subject of the only tender by Hardman to be submitted by Barry to the Commissioners of Woods and Forests, thus gaining for the firm in July 1845 the official status of sub-contractors to the Palace of Westminster.[16] There must have been times when Hardman thought the distinction dearly bought. Pugin probably made the first design for the railing in February 1845; early in March, he discussed it with Barry, who decreed the use of solid components instead of the hollow tubes proposed. Pugin appreciated that solid brass, being stronger, might also be thinner, thus allowing for greater lightness of effect. He then produced 'an entirely new drawing', apparently after further consultations with Barry, who had insisted that Pugin simplify the frieze in the lower part of the railing by omitting the shields which he had interspersed with rose motifs. Pugin was allowed to retain the shields on the uprights only. The petals of the roses themselves were to be turned back to catch the light, as Barry found them too dark. The fleur-de-lis motifs in the spandrels were to be reduced in size, while the height of the lighting branches intended for attachment to the uprights was to be increased. All these changes were made as a result of Barry examining a trial compartment *in situ*, and carried through despite Pugin's protests about the waste of dies and patterns already prepared.[17]

Hardman had to set to work again and sent up another piece for Barry's inspection. Owing to the uncertainty about the means of lighting to be used he had to allow for 'the possibility of a small gas pipe passing up the centre of the stanchions' on the edge of the gallery floor and also to make screw attachments for the branches in case they were not needed. The revised version was approved in April, although Hardman's tender of 10 May shows that the size and shape of each panel had not yet been finally determined: he carefully priced only an individual compartment 'of one upright & standard for the light with three feet nine inches of lateral bars and scroll work' without indicating the total number.[18] In accepting the tender on 14 July, the Office of Woods chided Barry for sanctioning such calculated vagueness. Nevertheless Barry's contract of £2,310 for the complete railing is dated 22 November 1845,[19] indicating that only at this juncture were the measurements settled. The final cost of the railing, even with the extra bars and stays ordered by Barry early in 1847, and the expense of the installation by Hardman's shortly afterwards, was £300 less than the estimate. This was because the lighting fittings had by then been abandoned,

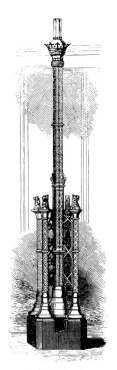

175. A. W. Pugin: Standard for gas light in the Peers' Lobby. This stood about 12 ft high, the plinth coloured like black marble and the standards gilded, relieved by gilt bronze.

although Hardman very properly included in his account all the wasted patterns.[20]

The obvious question raised by this story, largely pieced together from Pugin's letters to Hardman, is whether the design of the railing in its final form should be attributed to Barry rather than to Pugin. Certainly Pugin is unlikely to have minimized the true extent of Barry's alterations in his letters, for he was anxious to deny any responsibility for the extra burden of work which was inevitably laid upon his friend. But there is no indication that Barry added to Pugin's motifs; on the contrary, he pruned and re-ordered them; but he did not make his own designs. It was Pugin who was invariably required to incorporate Barry's changes in new drawings. In this sense, the railing can be construed as a collaborative effort.

Pugin used Hardman as a safety valve, although occasionally, when the news was particularly bad, he made strenuous efforts to reassure his friend that their work had not been in vain. It was difficult for Pugin to find any words of comfort late in 1846, when Hardman lost the whole order for gas branches for the Lords' Chamber after a lighting trial had been pronounced a technical failure. The recommendations of Michael Faraday led to the employment of apparatus devised and manufactured by his brother James, and the gallery of the Chamber was thus supplied with 'thirty-two branch lights, springing from the sides of the niches, burning gas on Faraday's ventilating principle' (Pl. 150).[21]

Barry was apologetic but firm and Pugin furious, for not only had Barry cast aside designs of which he was particularly proud, but he was immediately involved in new tasks as a result. Barry's final word was that while the gallery might be illuminated by gas, the floor of the Chamber was to have only candles. Pugin asked Hardman to send up immediately his 'drawing of the great candlesticks as I have to prepare branches', adding that he had to do the same for the standards he had designed for the bar end of the House.[22] The two huge candelabra standing before the throne (Pl. II) had been initially designed as gasoliers and were now to be converted, together with the bar standards.[23] New branches were essential; there was no time to make any major innovations in design, however, and Pugin, sending off his sketches to Hardman early in December, remarked that 'The old [drip] pans as drawn will do, with some cresting on top. They must be made so [as] to receive glasses if necessary & you must get a *candle* from Mr. Barry [or] Quarm for the size of the nozzles.' Pugin was unable to disguise the top-heavy appearance of the clustered branches, especially at the second stage, despite the generous use of foliation to distract the eye. Somehow Hardman managed to complete the candelabra and standards before the end of March 1847, although Pugin (admittedly ill), had written with gloomy relish in the New Year to tell his friend that he would 'never get half done even without the gas fittings'. At Pugin's instigation, Hardman again charged for all the alterations.[24]

There was some suggestion that Hardman's might make branches for their gasoliers in the Peers' lobby, but Pugin strongly advised against it. Barry's decision to have the gasoliers made of cast iron, gilt, offended against his principles. Though brass was eventually incorporated into the design, the finished versions, with marbled plinths, failed Pugin's test for ironwork. The gasoliers were nevertheless admired; their structure, consisting of a single shaft surmounted by a coronal for gas jets and surrounded by four detached columns springing from the base (Pl. 175), was essentially the same as that of the standing candelabra in the House of Lords, allowing both for differences of proportion and detailing and for the absence of clustered branches at the top.[26] Pugin reasserted his true principles eventually: his brass gasoliers for the Commons' lobby were very much more costly and splendid.[27]

The rest of the metalwork completed by Hardman's for the interior of the Chamber itself in time for the opening was of a comparatively minor nature. Barry ordered only a small railing for the throne; a larger one, consisting of 'Compartments & Gates of Twisted Bars & Uprights with Ornamented Fittings, Bosses, Roses etc.' was installed in 1848. Likewise, the tinned iron railings and gates to flank the bar were completed late in December 1847 and in January 1848.[28]

The preparation of the metal fittings for the throne and its surround was a task that appealed strongly to Pugin's antiquarian tastes. His fondness for heraldic devices is shown in the smallest details like the enamels he designed for the back of the throne, which was executed by the furniture dealer and antiquary John Webb.[29] The enamels and stones have survived intact; the enamels on the throne back display heraldic lions taken from the Royal Arms, while those surrounding the crystals on the arms are embellished with a running trefoil pattern, one of Pugin's most characteristic motifs.[30]

Two enamelled shields, both with the Royal Arms, and '8 Richly Gilt and Enamel painted Banners' similarly decorated, all made for the throne area, share a common source of inspiration with the boldly decorated brass plates set in the centre of the pavement in the Peers' lobby, forming a border to the Tudor rose made of Derbyshire marbles (Pl. VII). The plates, engraved with a running pattern of rose leaves and Tudor roses, were once inlaid with mastic or enamel paint.[31] The Hardman firm were already making memorial brasses in the medieval manner for churches and Pugin drew on this experience in designing engraved and coloured brasses for the Palace. He had already started work on the Palace brasses when he visited St George's Chapel, Windsor on 28 February 1845, and saw how much he could learn from the medieval stall plates there. After his visit, he told Hardman that he must cut his brasses deep and lay the enamel paint on an uneven surface, remarking that 'the effect is very fine, it will be worth trying.'[32]

Barry, for once, interfered very little with the engraved brasswork, but Pugin worried at the problem, sending Hardman a drawing 'on a different principle' for one of the shields surrounding the throne.[33] By mid-June, Hardman was coming nearer to what he wanted, but Pugin again asked him to increase the depth of the engraving before the brasswork was shown to Barry.[34] Thereafter, the story is obscure and it is possible that the shields and floor brasses were not finally approved until 1846. But Pugin's insistence upon bold and deep cutting has meant that the pattern of the brasswork on the floor of the Peers' lobby is still marvellously clear, although the colouring has been trodden away (Pl. 79).

Pugin's cast-iron grates for the Prince's Chamber (Pl. 176), apparently modelled at the Thames Bank workshops before the approved designs were executed by Hardman's, and his door furniture likewise probably escaped major changes by Barry. It is nevertheless worth noting that both categories were subjected to later embellishment. The grates were supplied only with brass-mounted andirons of heraldic design and with sets of fire-irons.[35] The whole of Pugin's door furniture in the Lords' area comprised hinges, saw-pierced finger-plates, escutcheons, locks and lock-plates, handles, knobs, and plates for swing doors, made of brass or tinned iron. There is no reference in the Hardman day books during Pugin's lifetime either to fenders for fireplaces or to the brass grilles which now decorate the doors of the Lords' Chamber, the Prince's Chamber, the Peers' lobby and elsewhere. They possibly belong to the early 1860s, when E. M. Barry secured a new contract for John Hardman & Company.

One of Pugin's great scenic triumphs in the Palace, the brass gates leading from the Peers' lobby to the Chamber (Pl. 79), must also be counted among the designs passed by Barry with few fundamental changes. Pugin was working on the sketches for the

gates when Barry made his drastic revisions of the gallery railing in the Chamber, and he begrudged the time spent on drawing the required alterations. But in May or June he sent Hardman his first general drawing of the gates. As Barry had asked for an estimate, Pugin suggested that the total cost, allowing for a full-size model to be made in wood 'here under my own eye', and 'wax models for the bosses, roses etc', as well as fitting up, might be £497. In the event, Hardman's had to charge more than £800 for the completed gates before installation.[36]

The wish expressed by Pugin to have the models made in Ramsgate and not at Thames Bank strongly suggests that J. H. Powell was actively concerned in the project. Powell was usually given the task of making detailed drawings in ink from his master's pencil sketches, but he much preferred modelling and if given the chance did nothing else. The wooden structure of the model gates was probably made by a local joiner, but the wax details, which required an experienced artist-craftsman, were well within Powell's capacity. If Powell was permitted to indulge his tastes, he did so under the close supervision of Pugin, who wrote to Hardman to enquire how far to allow 'for contraction in the patterns'.[37] The only modification in the design, which may have been the result of technical requirements rather than any aesthetic judgement made by Barry, is outlined in the Hardman day book for 1845-9. The entry concerned cites two additional strips of metal and a 'Plain Pinnacle to drawing etc.'; perhaps Pugin's first attempt at a pinnacle was not sufficiently effective in concealing the junction of the gates.[38]

The 'magnificent brass gates' were immediately popular, for Pugin had cunningly calculated the balance of his design, combining allusions to state and monarchy with the sheer visual splendour of his traceried brass panels. The gates were engraved for the *Builder* in 1847 in a view that was to become stereotyped.[39]

The prodigality of Pugin's invention is demonstrated by the design numbers noted in the Hardman day book entries relating to the Palace. It is difficult to compute precisely how many designs he made for Westminster. Between 1845 and 1851, when the volume of work for the Houses of Parliament tapered off, the Hardman day books enumerate nearly 1600 different patterns for metalwork produced from Pugin's designs. These include other secular commissions as well as ecclesiastical, although Westminster predominated. As Pugin progressed through the building with his designs, he repeated remarkably little, except for some door furnishings such as hinges and door knobs. Sometimes his variations were minimal: he would reverse the quatrefoil or trefoil motifs on his finger-plates, perhaps voiding them where previously they were set solid against a pierced ground. New design numbers were always allocated to the revised versions. It is possible that Thomas Quarm, Barry's Clerk of Works, influenced some of the work. Sets of door furniture for the River Front, marked for the 'Principal and 1 Pair Floor' (i.e., the second floor), entered in the day book on 16 October 1848, were all allocated design numbers, but some had an additional symbol, consisting of the letter Q followed by a Roman numeral. It is known that Quarm had frequently to deal with Hardman; their relations appear to have been cordial, sweetened, perhaps, by the occasional gift of a desk seal designed by Pugin, or a candelabrum on lion feet.[40]

It is clear that by 1847-8 Hardman's were also making handles and other fittings for furniture, as for the first time these are particularized in day book entries.

176. (left) New Palace of Westminster: Chimney-piece in the Prince's Chamber, 1847. Pugin's designs for grate and fire-irons were executed by Hardman; the fender is later. The Minton tiles are alternately red and blue, bearing the lions of England and the Royal monogram respectively. The bronze bas-relief above is by Theed.

comparatively few of these fittings are identifiable, partly because it is only occasionally that the day books give more than a general indication of location, and partly because so much furniture in the Palace has been moved from its original site. The rare exceptions include the original throne and the flanking chairs, and the great table for the clerks (Pl. 188), in the Lords' Chamber. Some of the other pieces remaining in place were made as fitments; among them, a set of panelled cupboards below bookcases lining the Lords' library are distinctively ornamented with traceried roundels of wrought iron, from which spring trefoils on stems. Pugin sent off drawings for the roundels and for a set of elaborate hinges for the cupboard doors late in 1847, adjuring Hardman to 'make the frame of the pierced work nice and sharp in the section and well flattened down for the trefoils';[41] the fittings were all completed by the end of January 1848.

Hardman's also supplied lavish metal furnishings for the Lord Great Chamberlain's rooms which have since been jettisoned, brass gas pendants for the Peers' library, kitchen and elsewhere which were speedily replaced, and cast-iron grates of different designs, those in the Lords' library being among the most expensive. Most of the grates have survived, their appearance betraying nothing of the disasters attending the installation of some of them, for they were made to the wrong measurements and had to be altered. A set of gas pendants designed for the corridors repeated the same story. Pugin's surviving letters to Hardman in 1849, the year of the gas pendant crisis, are far fewer than those of earlier years, and so it is difficult to determine his reactions. Probably he and Hardman had become inured to crises of this kind. Pugin's premature death at least spared him the realisation of how few of his light fittings would have more than an ephemeral existence. To cite one instance, Harrington's *Abbey and Palace of Westminster*, published in 1869, includes a view of the Lords' library in which a pendant lamp of classical inspiration looms large, clearly a replacement of Pugin's design.[42] As a final irony, his drawings for the great chandelier in the Octagon were never executed at all; the existing corona of lights (Pl. III), installed in 1855, is nearer to Pugin's ecclesiastical light fittings than he intended for the Palace and was probably put together by J. H. Powell under the supervision of Barry.[43]

Pugin's last contributions to the metal furnishings of the Palace were a series of designs for St Stephen's Hall and the Commons area, including a simple brass and iron railing for the Chamber itself, door furniture and gas lamps, although E. M. Barry judged the Palace to be in need of many more of the last when he took over his dead father's responsibilities in 1860. By this time, Pugin himself had been dead for eight years, and the responsibility for designing the remaining metalwork for the Palace had been assumed, as far as can be judged, by Edward Pugin and J. H. Powell. Powell had married Pugin's eldest daughter Anne in 1850 and succeeded his master as head of design at John Hardman & Company. Edward joined his brother-in-law in Birmingham when his father died. The two young men had both been moulded by Pugin but they lacked his fluency in design, tending to overload their work with obtrusive detail by way of compensation. The brass work for the Speaker's House, a painstakingly Puginian exercise (Pls 108, 109), post-dates the elder Pugin's death; this and other work such as the fireplace in the Queen's Robing Room (Pl. 121) display the tendency to overstatement that betrays the hand of his successors.

E. M. Barry's list of uncompleted works in the Palace in April 1860 includes the fireplace cited above, the candelabra at the Royal entrance, ironwork and gas apparatus in the Clock Tower, fireplaces, grates and gas fittings in the Peers' Robing Room, the fireplace in the Peers' Entrance, and the handrail of stairs leading to the Principal

177. New Palace Yard: Railings. E. M. Barry's design, executed by Hardman.

Floor. Ironwork in the Victoria Tower had still to be painted and gilded. Barry ended his survey of work outstanding with a composite entry for 'door furniture, gas standards, brackets and guard bars, chandeliers and gas supply generally.'[44] Hardman's, following Barry's recommendation in November 1861, were contracted to execute the outstanding metalwork and stained glass for the Palace.[45] Their task was largely completed by the end of 1863. To this period must belong the four large gasoliers in Westminster Hall, two of which are visible in Harrington's *Abbey and Palace of Westminster*.[46] The railings in New Palace Yard (Pl. 177) were also executed by Hardman's, while E. M. Barry himself designed some of the metalwork and altar furnishings in St Stephen's Crypt (Pl. IV).[47]

Most of the designs for these later furnishings, as has already been remarked, smacked strongly of filial piety. Both Pugin and Barry had powerful personalities and Pugin especially, with his insistent eagerness, had little difficulty in imposing his views on his son and son-in-law. Motif for motif, device for device, his spirit lives on in the Palace in the work of his successors. Their designs for the Speaker's House and elsewhere stand up well to comparison with the Peers' Chamber (Pl. II), still containing the richest and most striking ensemble of metalwork by Pugin himself, even if we disregard for the purpose of argument the Pugin/Barry railing and the loss of the standards on the bar. Despite the lack of originality, the thickening of profile and detail, and the lack of tension that characterises their work, their pastiche rarely descends to parody, a tribute to the effectiveness of their training. But the Peers' Chamber, with its adjacent lobbies, must always remain preeminent for their fittings, evidence of how two original and inventive minds, not always in accord, sparked each other off to produce some of the most splendid and influential metal work of the nineteenth century.

5. Painting

The conflagration that destroyed the old Palace of Westminster profoundly impressed the artists of the time. Turner, to whom the blazing scene had a powerful appeal, painted two versions of it in oils (Pl. XI).[1] Constable watched it with his two eldest sons from a hackney coach on Westminster Bridge and painted several watercolour sketches of it.[2] Benjamin Robert Haydon gazing on the 'sublime' spectacle from among the crowd where 'jokes and radicalism' were 'universal', comforted himself with the reflection that 'there is now a better prospect of painting a House of Lords.' He had long been advocating state patronage, pestering successive prime ministers with manifestos and interviews.[3] Now the new Houses of Parliament forced a measure of patronage on the state. Parliament had first evinced its interest in the arts by appointing in 1835 a Commons' committee under the chairmanship of William Ewart, the advocate of the cultural rights of the working classes. This committee had considered the relationship between the arts and manufactures and was responsible for the formation of the Normal School of Design in 1837, but during its sessions it had also considered the influence of the Royal Academy, the National Gallery and the British Museum on the arts of the country, and it ended its report with the aspiration that before long fresco painting, the highest branch of the visual arts, should be given official patronage and opportunity in England.[4]

There was a general opinion that British prestige required art to be patronized at its most sublime: further, if high art flourished, subordinate branches would receive 'nourishment and strength', so that it was 'the best policy, even in a narrow and merely commercial sense . . . to give the greatest possible encouragement to historical and poetical art.' Public patronage avoided the danger of individual ostentation, without depriving the country of 'the Beautiful and the Magnificent'; without it, why train artists in academies and schools, 'and store our galleries with the productions of the illustrious dead?' 'Is the artist whom we have taught to emulate the glory of a Raffaelle, to be compelled either to sink into utter despair, or to drivel away all his powers in labouring to become the fashionable portrait painter of the day?' Above all there was the profound if vague conviction that the Fine Arts were 'capable of eminently subserving the progress of morality'. There were absolute laws of art as of conduct, and to get near discovering one might well lead to discovering the other.[5] Moved by such precedents and considerations the President of the Board of Trade, Henry Labouchere, asked in 1841 for a grant for technical experiments in fresco painting; a month later a select committee was appointed to consider 'the promotion of the fine arts of this Country in connexion with the rebuilding of the Houses of Parliament.' This step inaugurated one of the most ambitious attempts at state patronage in this country, and resulted in a series of frescoes which, though neglected and now little admired, remain the most remarkable English attempt in that medium since the close of the Middle Ages.

The committee included Sir Robert Peel, Labouchere, Ewart and a group of *cognoscenti* prominent in matters of taste. There is something of a stage army about this governmental group of connoisseurs, but on the whole they were fairly representative of the art-historical knowledge of the time. Charles Barry was the first witness called and was at times hard put to it to cope with the display of learning presented. Sir Robert Inglis asked about the Campo Santo at Pisa; Mr Gally Knight about St Stephen's Chapel, Canterbury crypt, seventeenth-century paintings in houses in the City and San Vitale at Ravenna; Mr Pusey was interested in 'the large historical figures on the remains of Byzantine architecture.' With the second witness, Sir Martin Shee, PRA, the committee came to more practical matters. Shee thought that there was no question that fresco was the most durable method. This was also the view of William Dyce, Director of the new Government School of Design at Somerset House, whose opinion was much respected; he urged that fresco as opposed to oil was less dependent on light and placing, and that it could be easily cleaned with bread. He did not think that there were any artists in England with experience of working in it except J. Z. Bell, William Bell Scott and himself. Dyce spoke from an intimate knowledge of all the German experiments. He pointed out that preliminary attempts would be necessary before artists set to work in Westminster. He thought that £700 a year would certainly secure the best English painters of 'subjects', but not those who had a prosperous practice in portrait painting. Finally the committee recommended that a Commission should be set up to deal with the question of decorating the new Palace; they stated reassuringly that, 'independently of the beneficial and elevating influence of the fine arts upon a people, every pecuniary outlay, either for the purpose of forming or extending collections of Works of Art in this country, has been directly instrumental in creating new objects of industry and of enjoyment, and therefore in adding, at the same time, to the wealth of the country.'[6]

In autumn 1841 Peter von Cornelius (1783–1867) came to London. It is difficult to-day to realize the dominating position held by this dictator of the arts. He had played a great part in the renaissance of Munich under Ludwig of Bavaria; he was to play as great a part in Berlin. His vast, pretentious designs seem to-day cold and mechanical, but they had a quality of correctness which, coupled with his administrative powers, made him the schoolmaster of Europe in all matters of wall painting. Munich was looked to as an example not only of taste but of organization, of 'the employment of pupils upon the old German plan': 'I believe', Thomas Wyse had told the committee, 'that nowhere is the division of labour in art carried to a greater extent than it is in Munich',[7] and 'division of labour' was one of the magical phrases of the time. Sir Robert Peel wrote to Charles Eastlake, whose evidence had earlier much impressed the committee, asking him to obtain from Cornelius the fullest information on the mysteries of his art. On 10 November Peel asked Eastlake to be secretary of the new Commission of which Prince Albert was to be the President. As yet little was known of the latter. It was soon realised that not only had he considerable knowledge of the subject, but a Germanic thoroughness and much good sense in his conduct of affairs.[8]

The Commissioners made their first report in the following April: Eastlake's general survey of the situation, and notes of Cornelius' information; some papers on the technique of fresco painting; and the announcement of a competition for cartoon drawings 'executed in chalk or charcoal, not less than ten nor more than fifteen feet in their longest dimension; the figures to be not less than the size of life, illustrating subjects from British History, or from the works of Spenser, Shakespeare or Milton.' Entries were to be sent in by the first week of May 1843 and there were to be three premiums of £300, three of £200 and five of £100.[9]

The opening of the exhibition of the cartoons, 140 in all, in Westminster Hall in the summer of 1843, inaugurated by a visit of the Queen, caused the widest interest. 'It was a surprising scene, new to English art, and in its immense quantity and high excellence astonishing everyone . . . Instead of our being without historic art, in London, it was found to be plentiful and admirable.' So wrote William Bell Scott,[10] a little sarcastically, for he notes that, of the prize-winners, Selous had hitherto been 'an assistant painter of panoramas' and Townsend 'a surgeon now become artist.' The winners were in fact comparatively unknown men: the £300 premiums were assigned to Edward Armitage for his *Caesar's Invasion of Britain* (Pl. 178), G. F. Watts for *Caractacus Led in Triumph Through the Streets of Rome*, and C. W. Cope for *The First Trial by Jury*. £200 prizes were awarded to J. C. Horsley, J. Z. Bell (Archer Shee's pupil) and H. J. Townsend; £100 to W. E. Frost, E. T. Parris, H. C. Selous, John Bridges and Joseph Severn. Some of the senior artists, however, were included in an additional award of ten £100 prizes, paid out of the money taken in the first fortnight of the exhibition, when one shilling was charged for entrance. Haydon, who had sent in two cartoons, received no award.

The choice of subjects by the competitors occasioned some comment and is not without interest. Of the historical subjects only one was later than 1500 and the majority preceded the Norman Conquest: Milton (40), Shakespeare (12) and Spenser (11) provided themes for sixty-three of the cartoons. 'It would have been quite as well to have had a little more of history and less of fiction', commented *The Times* and noted that there was 'but one subject from Holy Writ'. This is hardly surprising as scriptural subjects, unless used by Milton, had not been specified as admissible.

Of the cartoons themselves few now remain. Drawn, according to the conditions laid down, 'in chalk or charcoal' on paper 'not less than 10 ft nor more than 15 ft in their longest dimension', they have mostly perished. Watts' cartoon after the Exhibition was sent with the other prize-winners on a provincial tour and then, while Watts was absent in Italy, was sold to an art dealer, Dickinson, who cut it up into various pieces. Three of these were later bought by the first Lord Northbourne,

178. Lithograph by W. Linnell of cartoon by E. Armitage (1817–96), *The Landing of Caesar*, awarded first prize by the Royal Fine Arts Commissioners, 1843.

and are now deposited on loan at the Victoria and Albert Museum along with a sketch of the whole composition. Watts thought he had ruined his cartoon by endeavouring to fix it by steaming, and had nearly given up the idea of submitting it. It has, even if in a fragmentary state, outlived most, if not all, of the other entries.[11]

Within ten days of the exhibition's opening Longman, Brown & Co. announced that they had purchased the copyright of the first eleven awards, and these were published in lithographs by J. J. and W. Linnell. Frank Howard published the additional ten awards, of which both his father and himself had been recipients, in a series of lithographs many of which were cut by himself. Thus rapidly these pictures were brought to the public by quantity-production techniques.

The Commissioners then proceeded in 1845 to a further competition for specimens of fresco painting, as a result of which it was announced that six arched spaces in the Lords' Chamber would be the first parts to be painted. After many delays and further discussions as to the most suitable medium, one subject, *The Baptism of Ethelbert* was definitely assigned to William Dyce (Pl. 179). In the following year Maclise was commissioned to paint *The Spirit of Chivalry*, Cope *The Black Prince Receiving the Garter*, and Horsley *Religion*. It was also announced that Cope, Horsley, Herbert,

271

179. (left) House of Lords: Central fresco above the Throne. *The Baptism of Ethlebert* by William Dyce (1806–64).

180. (right) C. W. Cope (1811–90): Sketch of Maclise fresco-painting in the House of Lords, *c.*1847.

Severn and Tenniel were to be entrusted with the frescoing of five smaller spaces in the Upper Waiting Hall. Cope and Horsley thus emerge as well established in the Commissioners' favour. Herbert had not received any award, but in the Academy of 1844 his *Sir Thomas More and his Daughter* and *The Acquittal of the Seven Bishops* had been much approved. He was a friend of Pugin and a convert to Roman Catholicism. Severn had been a prize-winner in the Exhibition of 1843. Tenniel for his cartoon of the *Allegory of Justice* had received an award in the 1845 Exhibition, where the other two successful candidates were Armitage and Noel Paton (both having *The Spirit of Religion* as their subject).[12]

On receiving his commission, Dyce (Pl. 185) went to the Continent to study certain frescoes in detail. His account, published in the Commission's Sixth Report (1846), gives a remarkable analysis of the reactions of various pigments used by the Italians, the effects of damp on the adhesion of the paint, the combination of tempera and true fresco, the particular problems associated with ultramarine, and ends with a comparison between the frescoes of the Sistine Chapel and of the Siena Library as examples of the results of candle smoke. Horsley and Cope had also been travelling abroad and had met Dyce in Florence. Cope went on to Munich, where he had long discussions with Hess on fresco technique.[13] On his return, he set to work on his fresco (Pl. 180), work that had to be carried on under considerable difficulties, for plasterers and masons were still busy, and there were many visitors. Dyce complained that it was flattering but off-putting to have one's tracing held up by the Prince Consort. By July 1847, however, his fresco was completed, and by April 1848 the other three frescoes were visible to the public. In 1847 Maclise had been commissioned to paint *The Spirit of Justice* (Pl. 181) as a companion to his *Chivalry*, and the series was completed with Cope's *Prince Henry acknowledging the authority of Justice Gascoigne*.

The subjects for the other rooms in the Houses of Parliament were now defined in

an elaborate programme of significant events of English History up to Cook's discovery of Australia and the emancipation of negro slaves. One is reminded of the *ragionamenti* of *cinquecento* Italy and Vasari's discussions about the decoration of the Palazzo Vecchio. Little came, however, of the schemes. There was some friction with Barry over the independent line that the Commissioners were taking in their decoration of the building; Parliament was becoming restive at the delays and expenditure and the personnel of the Commission was changing. In July 1850 Peel died, a great blow to its prestige and policy; the Prince Consort was becoming more and more involved in public affairs, not least in the plans for the Great Exhibition. Eastlake's growing reputation made him in increasing demand. His materials for *A History of Oil Painting* had appeared in 1847; originally designed as a communication to the Commissioners, it was published on the Prince's advice as a separate volume. In 1850 he succeeded Archer Shee as President of the Academy and five years later added to it the Directorship of the National Gallery. He remained however secretary of the Commission, and further works were now initiated. Dyce had in August 1848 been assigned the frescoes in the Queen's Robing Room, with a salary of £800 for six years. In July 1850 J. R. Herbert agreed to undertake the nine in the Peers' Robing Room (now the Moses Room) at £1,000 each. A year later E. M. Ward was commissioned to paint in oil eight pictures for the Commons' Corridor at £500 each. In 1853 a similar contract was made with Cope for the Peers' Corridor (Pl. 182). By then work was proceeding in the Upper Waiting Hall where Cope, on completing his fresco of the Garter, had painted (1849) a Chaucerian theme, *Griselda*. He also illustrated Byron's Lara; Watts was given Spenser, Horsley Milton, Tenniel Dryden, Armitage Pope and Scott, Herbert Shakespeare. 'The frescoes were painted on lime and plaster spread on a framework of laths, and there was a space at the back of some inches, to separate them from the outer wall of stone; and in this space the damp

181. (left) House of Lords: Left-hand fresco above the Strangers' Gallery. *The Spirit of Justice* by Maclise.

182. (right) Houses of Parliament: Peers' Corridor. *The Burial of Charles I* by C. W. Cope.

accumulated and had no exit or ventilation.'[14] There was soon also a deposit of London dirt, which Prince Albert tried to have removed, as Dyce had earlier advised, by rubbing with stale bread; the frescoes had previously been sponged over to test the fixity of the colour. Nothing, however, prevented the action of the damp; after four years the colours were blistering and peeling off. By 1861 there were many gibes in Parliament about their condition. Sir George Bowyer had heard 'they were coming off the walls and he thought it would be a good thing if they did.' There was some confusion about them. Mr Osborne apologized for having said that the face of Cordelia was decayed, it was the nose of Regan; Mr Cowper thought he had confused both ladies with the dragon in Mr Watts' *St George*.[15] Two years later it was reported to Parliament that the Commissioners had appointed a committee (Sir Coutts Lindsay, Mr Ruskin, Mr L'Estrange, Mr Gambier Parry) to examine the frescoes, but that the only conclusion so far reached was that all further work should be carried out in the waterglass method.[16] The Lords' Chamber frescoes had to be repaired at various times between 1862 and 1895. In 1868 Cope treated the Poet frescoes with a solution of paraffin wax, but nothing could stay their disintegration. In 1895, when Professor A. H. Church was called in to report on them, he decided that Tenniel's *St Cecilia*, a dull, insipid work, which could never pass for anything other than a Victorian masquerade, was the only one worth preserving.[17] With this one exception they were all covered over in 1895. Tenniel had painted thinly with very fluid washes, whereas Armitage and Watts had used opaque colour on a preliminary drawing in

274

terra-verte, following what they believed to be the prescriptions of Cennini.[18] Church hoped at first to save also Herbert's *Lear Disinheriting Cordelia*, but this proved impossible. Today none is visible. They are known only in poor engravings, preliminary sketches, or versions in oil.[19] Thin boards, papered with a diaper pattern, have since 1956 covered them, while mysteriously, carved on the stone sills beneath, the titles still recall the vanished scenes, 'Satan touched by Ithuriel's spear while whispering evil dreams into the ear of Eve,' 'Personification of the Thames and the English Rivers,' and so forth.

Ward began his work in the Commons' Corridor with *The Last Sleep of Argyll* and *The Execution of Montrose*. Being oil paintings they were exhibited at the Academy and were much admired, particularly the former.[20] Cope painted, also in oil, *The Pilgrim Fathers*. It was found, however, that 'the gloss of surface, necessarily characteristic of painting in oil, was detrimental to their effect'. It was decided that the paintings should be carried out in fresco and the payment was raised to £600 for each subject.[21] This was a medium with which Cope had already had some experience; to Ward it was a new field, and one on which he embarked 'with considerable reluctance'. He went to Paris and consulted 'Delaroche, Delacroix and other distinguished artists'. On his return he executed four of the paintings in fresco; with the fifth, *Charles II Landing at Dover*, he began to work in the waterglass process. Cope executed his four last frescoes, *The Defence of Basing House*, *The Expulsion of the Fellows of an Oxford College*, *The Train Bands*, and *Speaker Lenthall* in waterglass.

275

This was a German method and its introduction was due to the Prince Consort. The 'fresco' was painted in water-colour on the dry wall of mortar, lime and sand and then sprayed with liquid silica. It allowed of much more detailed and careful work, admitting, as Herbert pointed out in the discussions of 1864 over payments, 'of the utmost refinements of treatment and subtleties of art'. Maclise had been the first to try this new method in his fresco of Wellington and Blücher, and Cope eagerly watched the experiment. The corridor frescoes of Ward and Cope were painted not on the direct wall but on plaster laid on slate panels and fixed with an air space between them and the wall.

The Commissioners had in 1854 approached Maclise with a request that he would reproduce in fresco 'in the Painted Chamber, or Conference Hall' his *Marriage of Strongbow and Eva*, which, as an oil painting, was being immensely admired in the Academy of that year and was a subject already proposed by the Commissioners. It is clear from a letter of Eastlake that the intention was to entrust the frescoing of the whole Chamber to Maclise. The lighting was poor and, though the payment offered, £1,500, was not out of line with others made by the Commission, Maclise did not consider the remuneration adequate.[22] The Prince Consort, however, was eager that Maclise should be employed, and in 1857 Eastlake once more approached him, this time proposing frescoes in St Stephen's Hall. Maclise replied suggesting as an alternative the Royal Gallery, 'as containing subjects, on the whole, more interesting to me'. It was agreed that he should undertake the thirteen smaller compartments at £1,000 each and the two large compartments, each 45 ft 8 in in length, at £3,500 each. They proposed that a beginning should be made with one of the smaller compartments, but actually it was the Wellington and Blücher for which Maclise produced the cartoon which is now in the Royal Academy.[23] It was exhibited in 1859 and caused 'astonishment and admiration'. Forty-three of his fellow-artists 'in and out of the Academy' presented him with a gold porte-crayon 'not so much as a token of our esteem and admiration as of the honest pride which, as artists and fellow-countrymen, we feel in the success of the cartoon you have lately executed.' It was therefore a great blow when in August 1859 Maclise wrote to Eastlake resigning the commission, because of the insuperable difficulties he had found when trying to plan the work on the spot. Three days later he wrote specifying the difficulties: the elaborate nature of the uniforms which would mean that only small portions could be painted at a time and there would be the most intricate joinings; the lack of light alternating with splashes of colour from the painted glass; the ill success of experiments with waterglass; he concluded by asking if the works could not be undertaken in oil. At this point the Prince Consort intervened, writing typically to Eastlake:[24]

If Mr. Maclise feels disgusted at the dry and rigid materials for his production, and longs for oil, it is because he feels pain in the struggle to have cast away the peculiar means of producing effects in finishing up minute details in which he excels. But a grand historical work requires the sacrifice of these details; and fresco is a protection to Mr. Maclise against himself, and insures his rising by this work to a height as an artist which he cannot himself comprehend as yet.

The Prince promised that the stained glass would be taken out and drew an elaborate diagram of reflectors to diffuse light over the picture space. He then followed his letter by arriving from Osborne and personally interviewing Maclise; in the end he persuaded him to visit Berlin and to report back to the Commissioners on the methods in use there. This resulted in a paper by Maclise, printed as an appendix to the twelfth Report of the Commission in 1861, entitled 'Report on the "Waterglass" or "Stereochrome" method of painting'. As a result of long discussions with various German painters, in particular Kaulbach, Maclise became a complete convert to the method. It had for his two great paintings the immense advantage of working on a completed ground, instead of on small areas of plaster to which another had to be added daily.[25] *The Meeting of Wellington and Blücher* was completed in December 1861 and unveiled in March 1862.[26] It was at once followed by a brisk controversy in the journals whether the meeting on the battlefield had in fact ever taken place. The Commissioners became alarmed, and at Eastlake's request the Queen wrote to her daughter, the Crown Princess, who obtained confirmation from the aged General Nostitz, Blücher's aide-de-camp, that the subject of the painting was historically accurate.

In February 1863 the oil sketch for the *Death of Nelson* was approved by the Commissioners, and Maclise set to work on it. He had received £3,500 for the Wellington and was to receive a further similar sum for the Nelson (Pls 183, 184). The remainder of his contract for another sixteen smaller wall paintings for the Royal Gallery, for three of which highly finished designs had been prepared, was now cancelled, but the Commission's recommendation that the total sum paid should be raised to £10,000 was never acted upon, though an increased payment was made to J. R. Herbert who had been much more vociferous in his own interests than had been the reticent and dignified Maclise. There is no doubt that Maclise was hardly used; and these were unhappy circumstances for the completion of the Nelson.[27] It was, however, finished in 1865.

The cancellation of the contracts was the last act of the Commissioners.[28] In their twelfth Report (February 1861) they reviewed their work, referred once more to the difficulties with the architect and repudiated any responsibility for the purely decorative ornament, apologized for the delays, which they feared had 'occasioned great inconvenience to Your Majesty' in completing the Queen's Robing Room, while regretting that recent interruptions in Mr Dyce's work had arisen from illness.[29] 'In noticing the greater or lesser assiduity of the artists', they thought it their duty to mention the 'unremitting industry of Daniel Maclise, R.A.'.

The fate of the other frescoes ordered by the Commission can be quickly told. Dyce died early in 1864, having completed five of the seven wall compartments in the Queen's Robing Room (Pl. 122), where he had been working since 1848. He worked in *buon fresco* on wet plaster and claimed that this could in England only be practised during the summer months. He also complained that the Arthurian subjects involved 'a great quantity of chain mail', (Pl. X) which took long to paint.[30] Rising standards of antiquarianism were in fact making accuracy, or assumed accuracy, of detail as imperative in Avalon as at Waterloo or Trafalgar.

In the Peers' Robing Room Herbert was in 1861 still painting the *Moses and the Tables of the Law*. He had begun it in fresco in 1858, but had later, at the advice of the Prince Consort, cut out the work done and restarted it in the waterglass technique. It was completed in 1864. The designs for the *Judgment of Daniel*, *Daniel in the Lion's Den* and the *Judgment of Solomon* had been accepted. Herbert had throughout argued about the payment, which had been fixed at £9,000 for the whole room. Eventually he received £5,000 for Moses and the rest of the contract was cancelled, though later (1880) the *Judgment of Daniel* was painted in oil on canvas and hung in the same room. In the Peers' Corridor, Cope finished his work in 1869, Ward in 1874.

The results of all these debates and endeavours were not it must be admitted works of any great merit. They made it all too apparent that historical and allegorical painting had few roots in English art. Dyce's knowledge of contemporary continental

183. Houses of Parliament: Royal Gallery. *The death of Nelson at Trafalgar* by Maclise.

184. Detail of Maclise's *Trafalgar* fresco.

185. William Dyce, RA (1806–64). Dyce played a leading role in reintroducing fresco painting in England.

schools seems to have limited rather than stimulated him, and his Arthurian scenes, with curious Raphaelesque motifs, have little force behind them (Pl. X). Cope was an honest story teller (Pl. 182), and his works, with some retouching by his own hand in 1874–5, are well preserved. He could plan also a certain continuous rhythm along his corridor. Ward's technique has fared less well, and his discoloured faces weaken the impact of his scenes. Engraved they have enjoyed considerable popularity as illustrations for history books, but the scale required was too much for him. He belongs, with some competence and sense of colour, to the anecdotal tradition of Wilkie and Leslie, and was unable to move beyond it. The vigour which the Pre-Raphaelite movement had briefly injected into English art is not reflected in the Palace of Westminster. Even Dyce, who had some understanding of it, reverts here to his Germanic manner. The great experiment ended in a discouragement rather than an impetus to the grand manner in England. Maclise's frescoes have, however, a place apart. The long narrow space consigned to them was a most exacting commitment, but one that he brilliantly overcame. The frescoes can be both read in detail and seen as a spiralling design across the wall. Much faded, long blackened by unguarded radiators beneath them, now happily removed as has also been the accumulated deposit, they have lost the brilliance of colour that must once have held the design even more firmly together. In both, the central episode is set in an oval, Maclise's favourite formula of the vignette, but in the *Wellington* the lines lead upward, and in the *Nelson* sink to the dying hero (Pl. 183). There is much carnage but there is also compassion, in the man binding up the wounded guardsman's leg; in the group raising the body of 'young gallant Howard'; in the woman bathing the bleeding sailor's head and in the dazed, desperate look of the young powder-monkey. English art in the high, romantic vein has seldom reached such narrative power and found such force and range to set it out.

186. (left) Houses of Parliament: Commons' East Corridor. *Henry VIII and Catherine of Aragon before the Papal Legates at Blackfriars* by Frank O. Salisbury (b. 1874), 1910. Much richer in colour and more complex in design than the work of Cope and his contemporaries.

187. (right) Houses of Parliament: St Stephen's Hall. *King John assenting to Magna Carta* by Charles Sims (1873–1928), 1927. The wall paintings in St Stephen's Hall are in paler tones, but maintain the tradition of decorative history painting at Westminster.

There followed a long pause. In 1906 a select committee of Peers was appointed to consider remaining empty spaces, and interviewed amongst others Poynter, Alma-Tadema, Lethaby, Norman Shaw and Gilbert Scott. The committee recommended an annual grant of £4,000, but nothing came of it. Then in 1908 a group of artists, under the general supervision of Edwin Abbey, was commissioned to paint a series of Tudor scenes for the East Corridor, and in 1910 these were put in position. The artists, F. C. Cowper, F. O. Salisbury (Pl. 186), D. Eden, E. Board, H. A. Payne and Byam Shaw, represented an academic manner that was already becoming outdated, but their paintings have a richness not found elsewhere in the building.[31] Fresco was abandoned, and a system known as Maroflage, wooden panels covered with canvas, was adopted. Meanwhile in 1909 the Royal Academy had presented Andrew Gow's *Holles and Valentine Holding the Speaker in his Chair* to be hung in St Stephen's Hall, followed by a similar gift from Sir Alfred Bird of *The Flight of the Five Members, 1642* by Seymour Lucas. Both pictures have now been moved to a Committee Room. Presentation by individuals, a curious revival of aristocratic patronage, was now common practice, and each painting in the East Corridor had been financed in this way. When in 1927 St Stephen's Hall at last received its mural decoration, a similar procedure was followed. The theme selected was 'The Building of Britain', and a new generation of artists now had their opportunity, V. Forbes, A. K. Lawrence, W. Rothenstein, W. T. Monnington, G. Clausen, C. Sims (Pl. 187), G. Philpot and C. Gill. The first impression is of a new range of lighter colours, and of a subordination of the forms to a decorative pattern. Little in fashion of late, they have merits which will bring them back into favour. Here again many of the artists were attempting work for which they had no previous experience, and the success achieved

280

is very variable, but they have a panache and a gaiety which their predecessors could not have aimed at.

There was to be one further controversy. The Royal Gallery with Maclise's frescoes had never received any further decoration. In 1924 Lord Iveagh agreed to pay the expense of filling the empty panels, and Frank Brangwyn, who had much repute in America and on the continent as a mural painter, was selected as the artist. The original plan was to continue Maclise's theme with a new series of wars and victories, but eventually this was changed into a celebration of the products of Empire, a subject more congenial to the artist and well suited to his gifts of colour and over-all pattern. In 1930 five of these panels were placed in position in the Royal Gallery and the Royal Fine Arts Commission was asked to report on them. Their opinion was that they were not suitable for the proposed position, and this was endorsed by a debate in the House of Lords. Lord Iveagh had died in 1927, but his son and successor encouraged Brangwyn to continue the work, and the completed series was exhibited in the Ideal Home Exhibition of 1933. In autumn of that year a setting was found for them in the new Guildhall at Swansea, where they remain, remarkable examples of decorative ingenuity, now more in favour than they have been in the intervening period since their commission.[32] The glow of colour they would have added to the Gallery would have been strikingly effective and their at times almost abstract design would not have competed with *Nelson* and *Wellington*. It is hard not to feel that a great opportunity was missed.

XIII
Furniture

FURNITURE has tended to be neglected in any discussion of the interiors of the New Palace of Westminster; fixed decorations such as stained glass, tiles and sculpture have received far more attention from historians of architecture and design. The variety, quality and quantity of the surviving furniture was not realised until a survey of that in the House of Lords was undertaken in 1971–2. A number of pieces, some typical and some unique, were illustrated in a published precis of this survey.[1] It established that in the House of Lords over eleven hundred pieces of original furniture survive which represent over three hundred distinct functional types. A similar survey of the House of Commons will shortly be undertaken but until this is completed no clear idea of the amount of furniture surviving there can be arrived at.

Thousands of documents in the Public Record Office relate to the furnishing of the New Palace; these contain a wealth of material including descriptions of much of the furniture supplied. The records of the cabinet-making firms involved sometimes survive and include further material and in some cases drawings of pieces supplied. There are, in the House of Lords Record Office, the RIBA Drawings Collection and the Victoria and Albert Museum, a considerable number of Pugin and Barry drawings of furniture for the building. Engravings, early photographs and guide books provide further illustrations and descriptions. When all this material has been carefully analysed and the information concerning the furniture extracted, we shall have very complete information on the pieces of furniture provided to furnish each of the hundreds of rooms.

Unfortunately unlike the metalwork, tiles and architectural woodwork, a piece of furniture, if it survives, has often been moved from its original place in the room for which it was designed to another part of the building. It is therefore impossible to tell whether a surviving piece—even if it is identical in appearance and description to one supplied for a known location at a known date—is the *actual* piece supplied or merely a much later piece of the same design. The complications extend even further, since several firms were supplying furniture for the building. Separate contracts were awarded for the furnishing of each stage of the building, sometimes one firm being given one contract and another firm the next. The furnishing of several different parts of the building was often going on simultaneously, with different firms supplying identical pieces of furniture. Though stamped by different firms their identical appearance was ensured by the exact specifications laid down in the contracts and by the existence of detailed contract drawings.

The important factors as far as the history of furniture design is concerned are: who designed the piece, for which location, for which function, and the date when the first piece of each type was supplied. Which firm supplied the subsequent pieces, the date of their manufacture, and the size and value of the contract are of course all of specific historical interest. These facts would naturally be fully dealt with in an exhaustive treatise on the furniture of the New Palace of Westminster but will only be given here when of especial relevance.

Pugin's role in the design and manufacture of the furniture and internal wood-work is quite clear. He designed almost everything—as with the metalwork, tiles and glass—and provided the craftsmen with models in the form of plaster casts. He submitted all his designs for approval by Barry and in some cases had pattern pieces made up for Barry to see after the original design had been approved.[2] It would seem from Pugin's letters and drawings that he took an especial interest and care in the construction and the design of the New Palace furniture. It must be remembered that he had had a distinct career as a furniture designer before he became an architect.[3] When he became involved with the New Palace competition his formative years as a practical designer had been spent designing furniture. His intense interest in ancient furniture and woodwork found expression at this time in two published books: *Details of Antient Timber Houses of the 15th & 16th Centuries* (1837) and *Gothic Furniture of the 15th Century* (1835).

Some account of the main firms involved is certainly needed. The firm of Gillow submitted in May 1851 a tender for about £20,000 for the furniture for the House of Commons, including Libraries, Dining Rooms and Offices. This was accepted on 16 May[4] but in November 1856 their tender for £3,139.15s for furnishing the new offices for the House of Lords was rejected and that of Holland and Sons for £2,959.3s. accepted.[5] Gillow were a well known and long established firm and their stamp appears on a considerable number of surviving pieces of furniture. Those Gillow records which survive illustrate and list only about thirty pieces of mainly bedroom furniture supplied between March 1852 and January 1855.[6]

Holland and Sons, the largest and most important nineteenth-century cabinet-making firm, supplied furniture to a wide range of government offices. Their records survive[7] and prove their involvement with the Old Palace in the early 1830s. After 1834 they were continuously involved in the maintenance and supply of furniture and furnishings to the temporary Chambers and the temporary Speaker's House. This continued throughout the 1830s and 1840s during which time they supplied a considerable amount of the internal woodwork for the new building. They played a more significant role than Gillow with whom they seem to have co-existed in the building during the Gillow contract of 1851–6. A large number of pieces of furniture stamped by them survives.

The most important pieces of furniture in the Lords were supplied in the late 1840s by John Webb of Bond Street. In 1851 along with Gillow, Holland and Sons and others he was asked to submit a tender, but after he failed to do so,[8] his involve-ment seems to cease. Though he is not well known today, he was not only a very important antique dealer but also ran a cabinet-making business as well. His work-shop produced the highest quality furniture; for example between 1853 and 1855 it made a copy of the famous 'Artois Jewel Cabinet' for Lord Hertford at a cost of £2,500.[9] In 1849 he was awarded a Society of Arts Silver Medal for 'Carving in wood a Cellaret' which had been designed by John Bell and made by Webb for Summerly's Art Manufactures.[10] Pugin, who certainly knew him by 16 February 1837 ('All day in London. Called on Bury, Webb and Hull.'),[11] possibly met him through Hull, an antique dealer, who was one of Pugin's close friends. Webb was to produce other important furniture to Pugin's designs even after Pugin's death: from July 1852 Webb not only supplied the furniture but also carried out the interior decoration of Horsted Place, Sussex,[12] a table from which is now in the Victoria & Albert Museum.

The role of the firm of Crace in the supply of furniture is somewhat obscure. They certainly carried out most of the internal painted decoration of the building and supplied some of the carpets, wallpapers and curtains. Since neither Webb or Crace stamped their furniture, the comparatively small number of surviving pieces not stamped by Gillow or Holland could have been made by Webb or Crace. The letters from Pugin to Crace for 1844–52 fortunately survive in the RIBA Drawings Collection. The first definite mention of furniture for the New Palace was on 11 November 1850: 'Mr Barry wants 4 octagon tables and 2 large do. for the House lobbies, they are to be as simple as possible, oak tops and oak framing, let me have an estimate by return . . . Mr Barry also wants a lot of plain useful chairs . . . we must have some very simple chairs which will not come very expensive or the board of works will be putting in modern things.'[13] It seems likely that 'During the period 1849–51 Pugin came to some sort of agreement with Crace which gave him some responsibility for supplying some of the furniture . . . it seems probable that this arrangement which may have been for chairs and tables only did not survive Pugin's death'.[14] Some of the furniture mentioned in the letters in 1849 may have been for the New Palace but the first specific mention was that given above. There is as yet no positive evidence that Crace supplied any cabinet furniture: the number of chairs and tables he supplied is also unknown.

One very important method of dating and determining the suppliers of furniture is the series of entries in the Hardman day books.[15] These entries range from chair nails to lock plates, clock faces and hinges. It is interesting that some of this metal-work was obviously attached to the furniture at the Thames Bank Workshops. Hardman sent some of the metalwork direct to 'Mr. Barry' and some of the furniture was sent by the cabinet-makers to Westminster without metalwork. The Holland records show however that pieces were occasionally fitted with their metalwork before they left their workshops.

Another aspect of the manufacture of furniture relates to machine carving. The statement that much of the woodwork in the New Palace is 'machine-carved' is often made, for instance: The Lords Throne and Canopy 'is of an inexhaustible wealth of invention. One reads so much about the dead and mechanical work of the Victorian craftsman. It is to these pieces of Pugin's design that we ought to look to appreciate what craftsmen in the 1840s were capable of, if spurred by a fanatic mind. Yet the repeating details were made by Jordan's patent machinery.'[16] On 7 April 1845 the agreement to use Thomas B. Jordan's wood-carving machinery was made by the Office of Woods.[17] When in February 1847 Jordan described his machine to the Society of Arts (for which soon after he was given their 'Gold Isis Medal' by Prince Albert) he admitted that 'neither can it produce that smoothness of surface and delicacy of finish requisite in good works . . . and there is a point in approaching towards the finish of a piece of carving at which the machine becomes more expensive than hand labour and therefore it is a matter of commercial calculation how far it is desirable to finish on the machine and when to deliver it into the hands of a workman.'[18] The *Builder* said in 1847 of the carvings in the Lords' Chamber: 'The carvings were all first bosted by Jordan's machine (a most important invention) and then finished by hand.'[19] It will therefore be seen that the final carving was done by hand, all the machine did was to rough out the details from the solid wood. Its great importance to the internal woodwork of the building is obvious, although to what extent it was used to carve furniture details is not yet known. Some of the furniture could well have been machine-carved after it arrived at Thames Bank, and there was at one point a suggestion that furniture be made on site.

The date when the first piece of furniture was supplied to the New Palace has not yet been established. It would however seem likely that no part of the building was in a sufficiently finished state to receive furniture before the autumn of 1846. On 14 August that year Barry, appearing before a Lords' committee, was asked, 'Is it necessary that you should have further communications with the Board of Works, or any other Public Office, in order to ensure the furnishing and the fittings before the Meeting of Parliament other than you have already made?' He answered, 'It is necessary that I should be in communication with the Office of Works with reference especially to the furniture, but not the fittings which are generally agreed to and are now being fixed ... I have no doubt that you will be able to have the House completed as to be conveniently occupied by your Lordships next session.'[20] By 27 February 1849 it was still being stated that 'with respect to the remaining portion related to the Fitting-up, the Furniture &c, &c, we have found it impossible to enter into a detailed examination of such large and indefinite items of expense until the works shall be more advanced.'[21] Until the official documents relating to the early supply of furniture are fully analysed a number of questions relating to the period 1846–50 will remain unanswered. Unfortunately the records of John Webb's firm are not known to survive but from the sources mentioned above it is possible to establish the basic facts.

First the royal throne for the Lords' Chamber (Pl. II); Hardman's sent Webb on 8 January 1847 '22 Gilt Enamels of Lions with studs, 22 oval crystals in gilt mountings with studs' and on 24 February '2 Richly Gilt Enamels, with crystals set in etc, for the Arms of Throne'. The *Builder* of 3 April carried a description of the throne from the *Observer*: 'It is of Mahogany standing about seven feet in height the whole is richly gilt and is surmounted by an open gothic crown ... The cushioned back is composed of regal velvet of the finest pile bordered with the arms of England. Surrounding the Royal Arms are enamel ornaments in the Byzantine style, alternating with crystals of the purest water.'[22] Although the throne was not in place when the *Builder*'s reporter made his visit at the end of March, by 17 April the Chamber was complete. 'The centre of the southern end of the House is occupied by the golden throne ... The fittings of the House, save a few minor points were finished by Tuesday evening; and by Wednesday the superb edifice was prepared for the inspection of Her Majesty.'[23] The throne was closely based upon the Coronation Chair in Westminster Abbey. An appropriate prototype, it was one of the few documented pieces of mediaeval furniture known in Pugin's day. It was also the only Coronation Chair to survive in this country from the Middle Ages. Pugin would have known not only the Chair but the best contemporary description also, 'composed of oak ... along each side of the pediment ... decorations presumed to be armorial bearings enamelled or emblazoned on small plates of metal of different sizes ... The whole Chair has been completely covered with gilding and ornamental work ... the thickness of the whiting ground laid on to receive the leaf gold may be seen in almost every part.'[24] Pugin's throne has an openwork base with three quatrefoils at the front below the seat, similar to those which originally adorned the front of the Coronation Chair. They had disappeared long before Pugin's day but he would have known John Carter's engraving of the Chair in its original form.[25] These quatrefoils originally formed an openwork screen through which the 'Stone of Scone' could be seen. Pugin copied this feature even though it was meaningless for his throne. The lions *couchant*, the gabled back, the gilding and the enamels feature in both; it is sad that Pugin could not persuade Webb to use oak rather than mahogany for the Lords throne. The final piece of documentation is a manuscript label under the webbing of the seat which states that it was upholstered in Webb's workshop in 1847.

Two X-frame chairs flank the throne; one was 'Prince Albert's Chair' and the other 'The Prince of Wales's Chair'. Both were made in Webb's workshop. They are very richly carved and gilded and are based upon the grand upholstered X-frame chairs of the later sixteenth and early seventeenth century. Prince Albert therefore sat some little distance from the Queen during the State Opening of Parliament. In 1901 Edward VII had a second throne made for his Queen, which is still in use today. This second throne was made by Holland and Sons and the watercolour from which it was made, now in the Victoria & Albert Museum, is inscribed and signed by Edward VII: 'This represents the King's Throne in the H of L. The Queen's will be *exactly the same* except for some minor details and a *little smaller*. Feb 8th 1901.' Queen Victoria had died on 22 January!

The royal throne acts as a focus during the State Opening of Parliament, but in the every day proceedings of the House of Lords the Clerk's Table plays a more important part (Pl. 188). This splendid piece of furniture was described thus in a contemporary guide-book:[26]

Eight feet long, seven feet wide, and two feet ten inches high. It is of wainscot, [oak] with a panelled top standing on decorated carved legs which divide it into compartments each capable of accommodating one person . . . The legs are fashioned like small octagonal clustered pillars, decorated with leaf ornament, having moulded bases and capitals. They are connected with each other by a deeply moulded bar, and bars stretch across from foot to foot having sunken panels between them, so as to convey in plan the general character of a portcullis—intended to represent the ancient arms of Westminster . . . On the surface of the table the wood is inlaid in lattice fashion and is very highly polished. This table was made by Mr. Webb.

The explanation of the source for its curious design, though strange, is probably the correct one. It was in place by the queen's visit mentioned above and is shown in an engraving published on 17 April 1847.[27] It seems likely that the metalwork sent by Hardman to Webb on 6 March 1847 was for this table: '12 Iron Tinned Handles and Rose plates and pins, 6 small Drawer Locks, 2 keys, engraved escutcheons'. The table has six drawers with locks and escutcheons, twelve handles and rose plates all in tinned iron. A tracing of Pugin's original drawing for the table exists in the House of Lords Record Office.

The Prince's Chamber was, in 1847, known as the 'Victoria Lobby' and like the Peers' Chamber itself was furnished by the time of the queen's visit in April 1847. The furniture was described thus:[28]

The furniture in the Victoria Lobby is of truly artistic design and character and shows how much is gained in effect and style, by having the artists master mind to direct the upholsterers skill . . . the chairs and tables . . . In point of workmanship they are of exquisite finish and add to the repute of Mr. Webb of Bond Street in whose establishment they were made. The chairs are of oak, they have straight backs with lions heads at the top, Russia leather of a red colour is strained tightly over the backs and secured by brass nails of a gothic pattern and form, tudor roses are stamped on the leather and gilded . . . there are sixteen chairs in all . . . two tables are in the Lobby of octagonal form . . . ogee arches span from leg to leg, each ornamented with elaborate paterae in sunken panels and on the sides boldly carved enrichments . . . The tops of the tables are pargetted or formed of small pieces of wood inlaid in a lattice fashion and very highly polished. The general character of these tables is great strength blended with richness of decoration. On brackets over each fireplace are clocks in oak cases beautifully carved. The cases have gables with crockets and finials and at the corners are small buttresses with pinnacles, they are made by Webb. The works of the clocks are by Vulliamy, the dials are exquisitely enamelled in blue and gold.

All this furniture survives in its original setting. In the House of Lords Record Office are tracings of Pugin's designs for the chairs and the tables (Pls 190 and 191). The sixteen chairs could either stand against the walls or one could be drawn up to each of the sixteen sides of the two octagonal tables. Hardman supplied to Webb

188. House of Lords: The Clerk's Table, made by John Webb in 1847.

on 8 January 1847 'A Brass Rose Die to stamp leather', and between 12 and 19 January seven gross (1,008) 'Richly Gilt chair nails, New Pattern'. Each chair has sixty nails in its upholstery, sixteen chairs need 960 nails. The Hardman day books show Webb as the purchaser of chair nails for Pugin chairs since 1844. He wrote to them in November 1845: 'I shall require about $3\frac{1}{2}$ gross of large brass headed chair nails the same as you sent me last year for Mr. Pugin'. The phrase 'New Pattern' first occurs as quoted above and these nails like the 'Rose Die' must surely have been for the Prince's Chamber chairs. These nails were subsequently used on all the New Palace chairs (Pls 190, 191, 193, 194 and 199). The Speaker's Library was subsequently supplied with chairs, identical to those in the Prince's Chamber (Pl. 191), which still survive in the Speaker's Cloister but are unmarked and their maker has not been established.

The octagonal tables (Pl. 189) are the most important and elaborate to be designed by Pugin for any of his buildings. He was particularly fond of the octagonal form and a number of important examples still survive. The device of inserting a network of quadrant braces behind the carved ogival arched braces to form a very elaborately structured system of supports is particularly exciting. These tables had polished oak tops of similar construction to the top of the Clerk's Table but they, like the Clerk's Table, were covered with leather early in this century. It is obvious from the Hardman day books that Webb was supplying other chairs and desks—of what description is unknown—during 1848 and 1849. But Holland and Sons were also supplying furniture and fittings at the same time. They noted in their records for August 1847, 'Fitting up New Committee Rooms, Cabinet-Makers $69\frac{1}{2}$ days, Upholsterers $14\frac{1}{2}$ days, Polishers $6\frac{1}{4}$ days, Porters 38 days, Joiners $19\frac{1}{2}$ days, Women 3 days.' None of the pieces supplied by them at this time has yet been identified.

The Hardman day books show that a considerable amount of the metalwork for furniture was sent direct to Barry at Westminster. This was probably attached to the pieces of Holland furniture on the site. As we have seen, Webb had some at least of his metalwork sent direct to his Bond Street premises. It is possible that he sent some of his furniture to the Thames Bank Workshops without its metalwork. There are a number of unstamped pieces which are far more likely to be by Webb than Crace but their metalwork was sent direct to Barry. No metalwork was sent direct to Crace and as we have seen there is no mention of carcass furniture in the letters from Pugin to Crace. Webb was the likely supplier of the House of Lords Refreshment Room Sideboard, but Hardman sent the metalwork direct to Barry. The tracing of Pugin's drawing of it and the novel corner shelf units which went with it survives in the House of Lords Record Office (Pl. 192).

The very fine Librarian's Desks for the Lords' Library and the Speaker's Library (Pl. 191) were probably made by Webb. It is obvious from the Hardman day books that those in the Lords' Library and the splendid large tables for the centre of the Library were supplied in early 1849. A detail of the leg of the large library tables is seen in Pl. 192. One of these large tables which were a simpler version of the Clerk's Table is shown in place in an illustration of the Lords' Library in 1849.[29] The Libraries of both Houses are still amongst the most splendidly furnished rooms in the building. The impression which they gave when completed and to a great extent still retain was described thus in 1855:[30]

189. (left) The Prince's Chamber: one of a pair of octagonal tables made by John Webb in 1847.

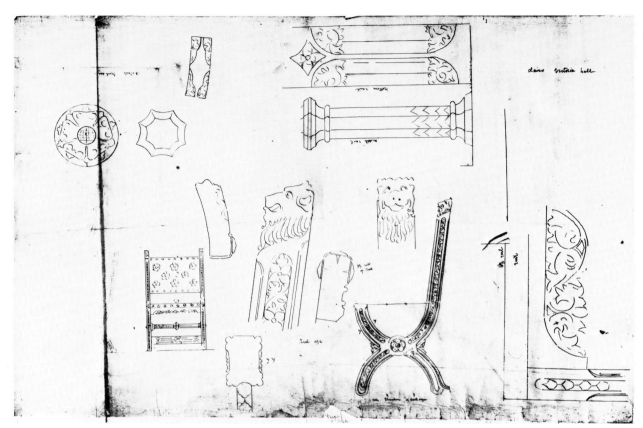

190. The Prince's Chamber: Chair. Tracing of Pugin's design.

The Peers Libraries . . . Every portion is complete and harmonious and every article of furniture in the rooms has been designed and manufactured in accordance with the architecture, indeed we could fancy ourselves in one of those artistic and Lordly apartments of olden time, once to be found in old mansions of Henry's and Elizabeth's time such as Nash and Cattermole delight to paint but few of which now remain . . . Commons Libraries . . . the perfume of Russia leather pervades the atmosphere . . . the minute and beautiful carved woodwork . . . the shining fire-dogs . . . the carpets . . . comfortable chairs and thick hangings at the windows [Pl. 193].

On 3 February 1852 the Commons' Chamber was ready for use. The May 1851 Gillow Contract mentioned above had included furniture for 'The New House of Commons, Division Lobbies, Refreshment Rooms, Committee Rooms, Libraries . . .' and a sum of £2,020 for 'House of Commons, Benches complete, The Speakers Chair, The Door Keepers Chairs, The House Table, Chairs for the Clerks of The House . . .' All this furniture was of course destroyed with the Chamber in the last war. The Speaker's Chair and the elaborately carved Clerk's Table were especially sad losses: 'The Chair of The Speaker of the House of Commons [is] placed at the north end of the House, and elevated on a dais of three steps. In design and execution the Chair is a splendid example of wood-carving, the details being most elaborately finished. The whole is oak. The arms are fitted with every convenience, including desks for writing; and the seat is covered with green morocco leather.'[31]

One of the most important surviving pieces of furniture in the House of Commons is the cabinet shown in the photograph (Pl. 194) of the Prime Minister's Room

191. The Speaker's Library in 1903.

192. New Palace at Westminster: Tracing of Pugin's designs for dining room and library furniture.

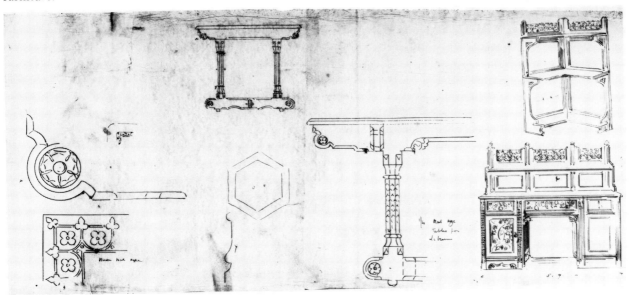

taken in about 1903.[32] A drawing of this piece (Pl. 195) was executed in January or
February 1852 by Richard Norman Shaw. Both Shaw and his friend William Eden
Nesfield had obtained special permission from Charles Barry to visit the New Palace
to draw architectural details and objects. Their drawings and watercolours done at
this time provide a fascinating record of what they as aspiring architects found
fascinating and inspiring in the building. It is perhaps worth noting that the cabinet
is shown by Shaw without its lock plate and hinges; did he perhaps sketch it at the
Thames Bank Workshops before the metalwork had been fixed to it?[33]

The supply of furniture and the completion of the interiors continued throughout
the 1850s and 1860s. After 1856 this is fully documented in the Holland records.
One of the last important pieces of furniture to be supplied was the throne in the
Queen's Robing Room. In March 1869 E. M. Barry mentioned in a letter Crace's
bill of £260 for final work on this throne. Crace certainly gilded several parts of it,
but whether he made the whole thing is not yet known. It was very probably designed
by E. M. Barry and is quite unlike any of Pugin's surviving throne or chair designs.[34]

The various residences, such as those of the Speaker, the Lord Chancellor, the
Clerk of the Parliaments and the Serjeant at Arms, were all fully furnished with
pieces designed by Pugin. Almost none of their interiors survive unaltered, the
Speaker's State Dining Room being the least mutilated. During the 1840s and 1850s
the Speaker had divided his time between his private residence in Eaton Square
and his official residence in Carlton House Terrace. He finally moved in to The
Speaker's House in the New Palace early in 1859, and the Holland records give full
details of the furnishing of the House. 'June 18 1858. State Bedroom, to be furnished

193. (above left) The House of Commons Library in 1868.

194. (above) New Palace at Westminster: The Prime Minister's Room in 1903. Note the characteristically Puginian wall paper, as well as the furniture.

195. (right) New Palace at Westminster: The Prime Minister's Cabinet. Drawing by R. Norman Shaw, *c*. 1852.

in the Mediaeval style, silk damask curtains for bay window . . . a walnut and gilt Arabian bedstead 7′6″ by 6′6″ with ornamental carved decorations, Drawing No. 3 . . . silk curtains . . . to enclose bedstead.'[35] This splendid bed (Pl. 196) would have been one of the most important nineteenth-century beds if it had survived.

A large number of pieces of furniture of a whole range of different types have not been mentioned. Details of those in the House of Lords can be found elsewhere,[36] but three characteristic pieces are illustrated here. Pl. 197 shows one of the most important small writing tables; simplified versions of this exist in considerable numbers. The most splendid office bookcase is shown in Pl. 198; neither its date nor its maker is known. Many pieces were designed to perform very specific functions, e.g. the interlocking horseshoe shaped tables designed for the committee rooms (Pl. 199).

Much more research needs to be done on the furniture and interiors of this

196. (left) Speaker's House: The State Bed in 1903, made by Holland & Sons in 1858.

197. (below) New Palace at Westminster: The most important writing table, probably made by John Webb, *c.* 1850.

fascinating building. Certainly as far as both the study of Pugin and the history of Victorian furniture and interiors are concerned the Palace of Westminster is of crucial importance. Some modern commentators have taken the attitude that 'the furniture—chairs, arm-chairs and tables—is Pugin's and it is heavy, with stop-chamfered legs and stretchers, and by no means attractive.'[37] I feel that the statement made by Crace in 1858 sums up the real historical importance of the furniture and interior decoration of the New Palace:[38]

That great benefit had been derived by the application in the Houses of Parliament of the true principles of decoration in metalwork, especially in gas fittings in the general lighting of the building, in ornamental ironwork, carpets, paper-hangings, furniture and every branch of mediaeval ornament. The theories on which this system of decoration were based came into definite practice when the great building was in progress and it was there shown that the principles were sound and capable of being carried out more ornamentally and beautifully than the false principles previously in vogue.

198. New Palace at Westminster: The most important and elaborated bookcase, c. 1850.

199. New Palace at Westminster: A Committee Room, as originally furnished, c. 1903.

XIV

Mother of Parliaments? Architectural Influences from the New Palace of Westminster

By the time the New Palace of Westminster was completed in 1860 it was out of fashion. The Gothic Revival had moved back in time from the 'late' styles approved in the 1830s to the thirteenth-century models approved in the 1850s. Yet, even if Ruskin called the new legislative palace 'empty filigree', that down-to-earth historian James Fergusson thought it 'perhaps the most successful attempt to apply Medieval Architecture to modern civic purposes which has yet been carried out.'[1]

'Modern civic purposes': that was the point. Whatever the shifts in English taste, here was a new treatment of a then rare building-type, the parliament house, of increasing interest to new varieties of political consciousness then emerging in the world.[2] There were other models, such as the classical Chambre des Deputés in Paris and the Capitol in Washington, both conceived in the eighteenth century, the former with its half-moon chamber, a shape copied for the two original chambers in Washington, where at first a low dome was intended to rise between them. Nearer in nature to Westminster was the Northern European town hall, steep-roofed with a single central tower, that at Brussels being one of the grandest examples. Enlargement of the Hôtel de Ville in Paris, from 1837, carefully maintained the old town hall tradition.

During the building period at Westminster, most European governments were dealing with violent civil unrest, and no emerging colonial legislature could afford to house itself on the Westminster scale before that model was eclipsed by more fashionable Gothic forms. After publication of the principal entries for two major mid-century English competitions—for the Government Offices in 1857 and for the Law Courts in 1867—no one was likely to copy Barry and Pugin complete and direct again.[3] Yet, during the fifty years after building first began at Westminster, certain elements of that design did filter through, mostly into designs that were never executed including some of the aforesaid competition entries, until it suited Hungarian romanticism to fuse the plan of the New Palace with an unbuilt Law Courts design by Barry's son Edward. The filtering process went something like this.

In the late 1850s British colonial legislative assemblies were expanding. Around 1859–61, Canada, New South Wales, and Victoria announced building programmes for parliament houses and the chosen designs were published: a classical one eventually carried out at Melbourne, designed by a local firm influenced by Leeds Town

200. Sydney, New South Wales: W. H. Lynn's accepted design for Houses of Parliament and Government Offices, 1869.

Hall,[4] and two Gothic, the one for Ottawa built as designed and the one for Sydney never executed.

The Sydney design (Pl. 200) of 1861 by William Henry Lynn of Belfast, is the earlier in spirit, for it seems to have been the only post-Westminster parliamentary scheme to place two big dissimilar towers at the ends of a composition in the Westminster manner. But the ground plan was different, partly because of the shape of the site and possibly influenced by the Ottawa design; and the scheme included government offices. A certain Venetian Gothic flavour suggests that Lynn studied engravings of Woodward's entry for the Foreign Office in 1857. Although said to be 'now in course of erection' in 1869, Lynn's project 'was ultimately relinquished' and the legislators of New South Wales continued to sit in the converted 'Rum Hospital' on Macquarie Street.[5] The ornament on which the Sydney design depended for much of its character was expensive and out of date. And, as time went on, federation under one Australian constitution was in prospect. After the Commonwealth Constitution Act of 1900 provided for a new capital city and the site was chosen in 1909, an international competition for the design of Canberra was won in 1912 by Walter Burley Griffin of Chicago: the classical Parliament House opened in 1927 was basically his design.[6] The only element taken from Westminster was the traditionally English rectangular seating arrangement. Until 1927 the seat of federal government was the classical Melbourne Parliament House; in its Legislative Council Chamber a curvilinear cross-bench linked the parallel front benches.

At Ottawa the first Gothic parliament house on a large scale, after Westminster, was actually carried out (Pls 201–2). Since the union of Upper and Lower Canada in 1840, there had been a succession of capitals before selection of Ottawa in 1858; and earlier designs for legislative assembly houses seem to have been modest or abortive.

201. Thomas Fuller and H. C. Jones: Dominion Parliament Buildings, Ottawa, Canada, 1859–67.

The winning design for Ottawa was published in the *Builder* in 1859 and construction went on during 1861–6 (destroyed by fire 1916, except for the Library, and rebuilt). The chief architect was Thomas Fuller, a native of Somerset settled in Toronto, with a partner Chilion Jones; winners of the second premium were F. W. Stent and Augustus Laver (runners-up in the Sydney competition) who were then commissioned to design the government offices next door; subsequently Fuller and Laver became partners in the design of civic buildings for Albany and San Francisco.[7] The style Fuller & Jones employed in 1859 was the combination made fashionable by the Whitehall offices competition two years before, Italian Gothic with French roofs, although their tower with a carriageway run through its base was not new: various country-house architects had exploited this Picturesque device, and so had certain entrants in the Westminster competition.[8] The *tour de force* here was the round Library of Parliament 'on the plan of the British Museum' (that is, Sydney Smirke's classical Reading Room of 1857), but vaulted with semicircular ribs in the manner of the Abbot's Kitchen at Durham 'after a plan in Carter's *Ancient Architecture*'[9]—but undoubtedly inspired by the little abbot's kitchen of a laboratory

300

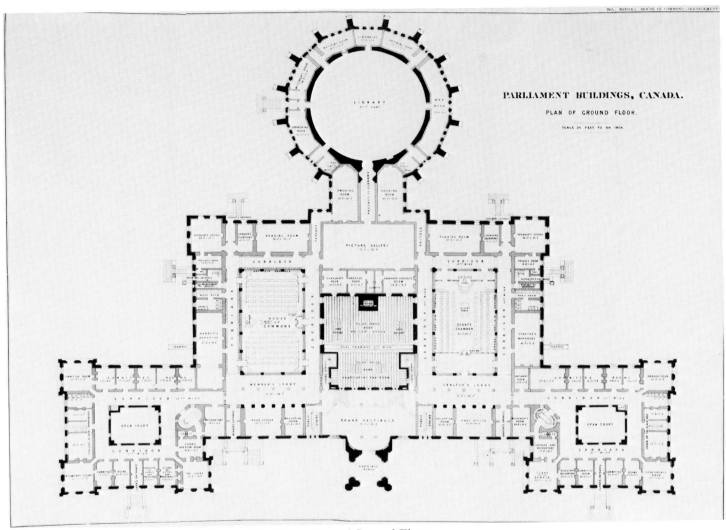

PARLIAMENT BUILDINGS, CANADA.

PLAN OF GROUND FLOOR.

SCALE 20 FEET TO AN INCH.

202. Ottawa, Canada: Dominion Parliament Buildings, Plan of Ground Floor.

recently placed beside the newsworthy Oxford Museum.[10] So, at Ottawa the library's bristling lantern-roof and the main tower's bunchy spire (with more eclectic borrowings behind them than there is room to hint at) combined with the crested pavilion roofs to produce a Mid-Victorian version of the pinnacled skyline at Westminster. The centrality of the Ottawa tower probably comes from Gilbert Scott's first Foreign Office design, which had apparently taken that feature from the Oxford Museum, with some Continental town hall precedent too.[11] Commanding though the tower at Ottawa was on its lofty site, it offered none of the violent contrast in size that exists at the Lords' end of the Palace of Westminster. As for proportions on the ground, in contrast to the long narrow site at Westminster between ancient hall and river, the sites at Ottawa and Sydney were much deeper in comparison to length. The two chambers at Ottawa, therefore, lay perpendicular to the main front; but they contained the traditional Westminster seating arrangement (Pl. 201).[12] For an Empire exhibition in 1911, a much reduced version of the Canadian Houses of Parliament was installed in the gardens of the Crystal Palace at Sydenham.[13]

Gothic as a style for government buildings waned in the Empire, as elsewhere.

203. Sir George Gilbert Scott and J. O. Scott, Premiated design for Imperial German Reichstag, 1872.

When Edwin Lutyens was asked to design New Delhi early in the present century, there was no question of adding Indian overtones to anything but a basically classical building—in contrast to a taste in the 1880s that had produced, for example, the Victoria Railway Station at Bombay.[14] When Lutyens in some of his preparatory sketches played with ideas for towers, these were of slender minaret proportions, as on the nearby Taj Mahal; for him, inspiration from Westminster was absolutely dead. Herbert Baker's circular legislative building at New Delhi was as far from Westminster as one could go, while Lutyens's overall layout owed something, perhaps, to Hawksmoor's conception for Greenwich. Yet, in the same years, there was the independence of Charles Voysey, employing his own simplified version of Gothic in unsuccessful competition drawings for government buildings at Ottawa, and later suggesting for the Devonshire House site on Piccadilly three tower-blocks of flats 'of the size and majesty of Pugin's Victoria Tower at Westminster.'[15]

Meanwhile, to retrace our steps to Europe, one emerging nation looked to Westminster for architectural direction during the troubles of 1848. The King of Prussia having conceded a parliament, his government sent a request to London for Barry's plans.[16] Although attempts 'to merge Prussia in Germany' failed, there came the eventual formation of a North German Confederation in 1866, and both legislative chambers in Berlin were then installed in existing buildings not made for the purpose. It was only in January 1872, a year after the formation of the German Empire in the ashes of the Franco-Prussian War, that an international competition for a parliament building was held. A classical design by a German, Bohnstedt, was selected, but there were site difficulties and the matter hung fire for several years. One of the five premiated designs was by the newly-knighted Sir George Gilbert Scott (assisted by John Oldrid Scott). Unwilling that his design should waste away unappreciated (or thinking still to influence events), Scott had it published in several resounding double-spread plates in *The Builder* and *Building News* in August 1875 (Pl. 203).[17]

No mean conception, Scott's Berlin design offered the new empire a building with the presence of the domed Capitol in Washington and a new brand of Gothic too, as if in secular rivalry with the unfinished cathedral at Cologne. Scott drew slightly on Westminster and more on various unbuilt designs, including Gottfried Semper's for St Nicholas, Hamburg, ousted by Scott's own design for that church thirty years before. The central feature was to be a great dome over a vast octagonal vestibule leading to the single rectangular legislative chamber containing semicircular rows of seats. The domed space was to be approached by a churchlike entrance hall flanked by courtyards fronted by cloisters; and there were to be towers with cupolas, towers with spires, and much small-scale Gothic detail. Scott blandly explained that he had worked up a type of Gothic that had never developed in Germany but which *would* have done so but for influences from France: 'founded on really Germanic elements', 'trained into' a thirteenth-century style as if France had never been. To this he added one 'modern' feature, the dome, accommodating 'this glorious form to the details and sentiment of Old German architecture'. *The Builder*'s one comment after giving Scott's description was: 'It is reported that another competition, *confined to German architects*, is to be invited.'[18] For Bismarck's *kulturkampf* Scott's Germanic elements were not enough. Yet Scott's colleagues will have noted with interest that his idea for a dome over a central octagon grew partly from his own Law Courts design, developed from the domed Central Hall (Pl. III) at Westminster and doubtless reinforced by E. M. Barry's more prominently domed Law Courts design; and that the entrance hall had been worked up from the St Stephen's approach to the Westminster octagon; while arcades fronting courtyards came out of Scott's War Office design. Scott was an expert in the recycling of old material.

An adaptation of his Germanic dome soon turned up in Connecticut. Richard M. Upjohn published his design for the State Capitol at Hartford in 1875, after apparently taking a good look at those engravings for Berlin in the building journals.[19] If nothing of Westminster filtered through to Hartford, an initial impetus came from there. In Berlin, however, Paul Wallot's thoroughly neo-Baroque Reichstag design of 1882, built 1884–90, used a plan similar to Scott's and nothing that could possibly be said to come from Westminster.[20] The Gothic style could not suit a German Empire declared at Versailles. And the most notable legislative building of the mid-century, with the world's first secular dome on a huge scale, had been completed in Washington and was not Gothic.

Mid-Victorian English architectural circles, however, clearly liked the notion of a Gothic dome. Fergusson in 1873 still found Barry's dome-cone-lantern-spire structure at Westminster 'the most successful attempt yet made to build a Gothic dome', comparing it to various medieval towered lanterns above central octagons, to Wren's inner cone at St Paul's, and to Wyatt's giant structure at Fonthill.[21] Among members of the architectural profession and its more knowledgeable critics, indeed, this structural arrangement at Westminster though little understood by the general public was one of the seminal parts of the building, and there had been a wave of interest in secular domes during the 1850s and 1860s. A vast unrealized bubble was proposed in 1851 for the Royal Panopticon of Science and Art in Leicester Square, inspired

204. E. M. Barry: Premiated design for New Law Courts, 1867.

partly by Paxton's great glasshouse in Hyde Park, partly by the domes of Islam. Barry suggested a set of domes for the Crystal Palace at Sydenham, and then for the new offices in Whitehall. Sydney Smirke's domed Reading Room at the British Museum, effective mainly from inside, was much admired. And as Thomas Walter's great iron-boned dome rose in Washington, in 1862 Fergusson assured his readers that the crossing at Westminster 'ought beyond all question to have been the principal feature' of Barry's design. In 1868 the *Builder* published a tall furrowed dome designed by the Austrian architect F. von Schmidt for a House of Lords in Vienna (though the eventual Parliament House there was wholly classical).[22]

Impelled by this continuing interest, Edward Barry, an eclectic like his father, carried the Westminster crossing structure further in his entry for the Law Courts competition of 1866–7.[23] Here he submitted his own idea for a full-fledged Gothic dome (Pl. 204) as centrepiece of a building too much like his father's in style to win (and then prepared a classical version for the National Gallery). It was the Gothic rendering that appealed to the only nation ready actually to build a Gothic-domed parliament building in the late nineteenth century: Hungary.

In Budapest, second capital of the Austro-Hungarian Empire, a riverside site was selected and money voted for a new parliament building in 1880. The ensuing competition was won by Emmerich (Imre) Steindl, a professor at the Polytechnic and architect of the Early Renaissance-style Rathaus (1869–75). Construction went on from 1884 until 1902 (Pl. 205).[24] Steindl's plan is basically the long-strung-out plan of Westminster, domed octagon and two chambers on one axis linked by corridors, with an overall length of about 850 ft. The great central dome has the vertical emphasis of Edward Barry's Law Courts dome, quite attenuated compared to Scott's 'mongrel affair' for Berlin. The legislative chambers, polygonal half-moons internally, are distinguished externally by their own tall roofs and spires,

304

205. Imre Steindl: Hungarian Parliament Buildings, Budapest, 1883–1902.

taking care of a contemporary criticism of Westminster that one could not tell from outside where Lords and Commons sat. The river front at Budapest has a tower-flanked central range as proposed for young Barry's Strand frontage; yet these towers, as well as seemingly infinite cloisters and window-arcades, could also come from Scott's Law Courts design. Volumes of the *Builder* and *Building News* must have stood on the library shelves at the Polytechnic in Budapest. Numerous spires and pinnacles, as on the younger Barry's design, and ornamental exterior stonework embellished with 'rich tracery' (*Building News*) and '90 statues' (Baedeker) in a small-scale repetitious regular way are quite reminiscent of Westminster. There is no large tower at the side, all is symmetrical—and yet it is romantic, picturesque, suited to river mists and reflections on and from the water. Doubtless Steindl had other sources, too, nearer home—some say Schmidt's just-finished Vienna Rathaus was one.[25] However, the New Palace at Westminster has long been recognized as a principal source, though no one seems to have noticed the equal relevance of its offspring designed for the Strand.

One of the two outlying towers at Westminster suffered a series of separate rein-carnations. The device of the projecting clock-stage crowned with an elongated lantern-stage become a symbol: the macrocephalic or long-headed tower-form known the world over, both for its shape and for its housing of Big Ben and the Westminster chimes, sounds and form making one symbol (Pl. 103). While it undoubtedly initiated the idea of the large Gothic clock tower in this country, later variations were not copies. When Scott applied this feature to several of his buildings, Westminster's waisted lantern-stage between two pyramids became a pinched needle's-eye spire and the clock-stage was flattened and gabled.[26] The clarity of separate parts of the earlier lantern-stage was much too simple for a Mid-Victorian: Scott's lanterns took after Fergusson's engraving of the Ypres Cloth Hall. His gables thrust up from

305

206. Sir George Gilbert Scott: St Pancras Station Hotel, London, 1867.

207. Alfred Waterhouse: Clock Tower, Eaton Hall, Cheshire, c. 1880.

below (also used prominently by Waterhouse on his Manchester Assize Courts design of 1859) were probably Italian Gothic in origin.[27] Scott's clock towers were 'versions of the "Big Ben" idea' only in their position at one end of a building (Pl. 206). A nearer version of that idea is the noble tower by Waterhouse at Eaton Hall, Cheshire, where building went on from 1870: its clock-stage, articulated in the Big Ben manner above the original medley of irregular roofs (Pl.207) had the true macrocephalic outline, though with a busier Mid-Victorian superstructure.[28] That contour formed many clock towers in France, the United States and elsewhere during the second half of the nineteenth century. And isolated clock towers were prominent features of street intersections in many Victorian cities: for example, the Haymarket Memorial

Clock Tower at Leicester (1868, by Joseph Goddard) and a little 'Big Ben' (Pl. 208) that from 1892 until 1964 embellished a traffic island *cum* public convenience at the junction of Vauxhall Bridge Road with Victoria Street in London, timing the tides of railway commuters.[29]

The special character of the Victoria Tower, aside from its end-position, is of course what Fergusson called its Brobdingnagian size. This trait is sometimes vaguely supposed to have exerted influence on the 'Collegiate Gothic' towers of the United States, products of a new attitude towards Gothic for university wear that began in the 1890s and lasted into the 1930s, a return to English medieval buildings as if the Victorians had never been—'a notable Gothic Renaissance amongst our colleges', Ralph Adams Cram called it in 1912.[30] Of his own firm's first quadrangle at Princeton, with the Cleveland Tower at one corner of it, Cram remarked: 'At present the placing of the great tower seems a little too like that of the Victoria Tower at Westminster to be wholly satisfactory, but in some distant future a second quadrangle will be constructed . . . which will restore the tower itself to the centre of the composition.' So much for influence from Westminster. Even the well known Gothic displays at Yale, Duke, Wellesley, Pittsburgh and elsewhere were not patterned on Barry's mode. With New York at hand, neither the new American Gothicists nor the new American Georgianists of the early twentieth century needed to try on the Early Victorians for size.

One more competition might be mentioned, that of 1926 for the League of Nations at Geneva.[31] The problems of a world parliament building are not quite those of one nation's parliament (a world legislature is, in a sense, one large cross-bench) and for Geneva the main requirements were for a secretariat (or government offices), an assembly hall for use only twice a year by 2600 people, and committee rooms etc. The sad tale of Le Corbusier's entry is not relevant here. Many of the designs submitted had towers, some purely symbolic and some for use. None of the published designs bore the remotest resemblance to Westminster in plan or elevation, and why should they? The last influences of that sort had died with the nineteenth century.[32]

208. (right) 'Little Big Ben'. Clock tower at junction of Vauxhall Bridge Road with Victoria Street, London (demolished).

Appendix I

List of Known Competitors in Competition for New Houses of Parliament, 1835, with Competition Mottoes or Devices where Known

THIS list has been compiled from the *Catalogue* of designs exhibited in the Royal Academy (7th.edn.1836), which also lists one unascribed competition motto, 'Auspicio Regis et Senatus'. Ninety-seven sets of designs in all were submitted. Francis Goodwin (1784–1835) died before completing his entry. Edward Blore (1787–1879) also sketched designs (now BM Add.MS 42028, ff.51–4) which probably date from 1833.

Fifteen competitors did not choose to exhibit or publish their designs.

Alderson, M. A. 'Pro patria'
Angell, Samuel (1800–66)
Ashton, [? Henry]
Baddock, H.
Bardwell, William 'The Building rose/In ancient English grandeur . . .'
Barry, Charles (1795–1860) 'Portcullis'
Baud, Benjamin (b.*c.* 1807) 'Spero'
Beaumont, Alfred
Benham, S. H.
Blore, John
Brees, Samuel Charles, *and* Griffiths, Joseph. 'ΔΩΜΑ ΕΛΕΥΘΕΡΟΝ'
Bryce, J.
Buckland, William (an amateur)
Buckler, John Chessell (1793–1894) 'Buckle with R'
Bunning, James Bunstone (1802–63)
Burrell, J. *and* Lugar, Robert (*c.* 1773–1855)
Burton, C.
Clark, John (d. 1857)
Cockerell, Charles Robert (1788–1863) 'Stet capitolium fulgens'
Cottingham, Lewis Nockalls (1787–1847)
Cumberlege, Charles Nathaniel (b.*c.* 1807)
Davis, J. *and* Catherwood, Frederick (1799–1854)
Desvignes, Peter Hubert (b.*c.* 1804)
Donaldson, Thomas Leverton (1795–1885)
Dowson, J.
Fairbank, John Tertius
Ferrey, Benjamin (1810–80) 'Quod potui perfeci'
Forster [i.e., Foster], [James ?], *and* Okely, William Ignatius
French, George Russell 'Spero meliora'
Frith, J.
Gillespie Graham, James (*c.* 1777–1855) 'H.R. with a rose and coronet between'
Goodridge, Henry Edmund (*c.* 1800–63)
Gwilt, Joseph (1784–1863)
Hakewill, Edward Charles (1812–72)
Hakewill, James (1778–1843)
Hamilton, David (1768–1843) 'King, Lords and Commons'
Harper, John (1809–42) 'Si non possis id quod velis, posse id quod possis'
Harrison, George
Hopper, Thomas (1776–1856)
Inman, William Southcote (1798–1879) 'Floreat'
Jearrard, Robert William
Kendall, Henry Edward (1805–85) *and* Hopkins, J. Douglas (d. 1869) 'Dum spiro, spero'
Kilpin, J.
Knowles, James T. (1806–84)
Lamb, Edward Buckton (1806–69)
Lapidge, Edward (1793–1860)
Lee, Adam (*c.* 1772–1843)

Mocatta, David (1806–82)
M'Gregor, A.
Morgan, J. D.
Mott, I. H. R.
Pain, R. *and* W.
Payne, Robert
Pennethorne, James (1801–71)
Pocock, William Willmer
Poynter, Ambrose (1796–1886)
Railton, William (*c.* 1801–77) 'Winged orb'
Repton, John Adey (1775–1860)
Rhind, David 'Pro Patria Semper'
Rickman, Thomas (1776–1841) 'Pro patria'
Robinson, Peter Frederick (1776–1858) 'Dum Spiro, Spero'
Russell, W.
Salvin, Anthony (1799–1881)
Sambell, Philip
Scott, Stevens *and* Gale
Savage, James (1779–1852) 'Denique sit quidvis

simplex duntaxat et unum'
Taylor, A.
Thompson, Peter [Designs not exhibited, but published]
Thorold, J. 'suo marte'
Trotter, J.
Thrupp, J. *and* Burchell, Stephen (b. 1806)
Turner, T.
Tyerman, Thomas 'En avant, si je puis'
Walker, S.
Wallace, Robert (b.*c.* 1790) 'Nec rege, nec populo, sed utroque'
Watson, [John Burges] (1803–81) 'Operam dedi'
Wetten, R. G. 'Justitia'
White, John (d. 1850)
Wilkins, William (1778–1839) 'ΦΙΛ ΑΡΧΙΜΗΔΗΣ'
Wyatt, Lewis (*c.* 1778–1853)
Willson, T.
Wood, Frederick 'Dum spiro spero'

Appendix II

Specifications of Accommodation to be Provided in the New Houses of Parliament, 1835

THE select committees of the two Houses drew up lists of the accommodation to be provided in the New Houses. The principal requirements are here summarized from *PP* 1835 (HL 73) and 1835 (262) xviii.

House of Lords:
That the House should be capable of containing 300 peers, allowing 2 ft for each, and the breadth should allow of one more row of benches on each side than in the old House. That the same space be allowed below the Bar and for the Throne. That a Lobby of not less than about 40 × 30 ft be provided next the House, and a Hall outside the Lobby; and a passage around the House. Separate galleries for MPs (100), strangers (150), and two others (40 and 24 persons), and retiring rooms for each.
Rooms: Royal Robing Room and Peers' Robing Room (each 36 × 24 ft); 6 committee rooms and 6 waiting rooms; cloak room; peers' servants' room; coffee room and dining room (each 24 × 24 ft); kitchen and conveniences; library (two 60 × 30 ft and one 30 × 30 ft); vote office; four rooms for lawyers and witnesses; marshalmen's room; conference room (48 × 25 ft); 2 interview rooms; Lord Chancellor, 5 rooms; Earl Marshal's room; 3 rooms for bishops and archbishops; 13 rooms for other officers of the House; doorkeepers' room; 19 rooms for Parliament Office (Journals and Papers); stationery room; residences for Black Rod, Resident Doorkeeper, Librarian, and Housekeeper; Lord Great Chamberlain, 4 rooms. A detached Guard house for 3 officers and 100 men.

House of Commons:
That the length of the New House ought not greatly to differ from the breadth; that sitting room be provided for from 420 to 460 members in the body of the House and adequate accommodation for all the rest in the galleries, not exceeding 1,200 ft of sitting-room in all; with a lobby adjoining either end (one of 1,800 sq ft, the other of 1,100) and a passage around the House; and an outer lobby for strangers. Galleries at the lower end of the House for 200 strangers, with retiring rooms; and accommodation within the House for 100 peers and distinguished strangers. Special provision for ventilation of all rooms.
Rooms: 30 committee rooms (ten 40 × 30 ft, ten 35 × 25 ft, ten 30 × 20 ft); library (3 rooms 60 ft long); two dining rooms each for 30 persons, with kitchen etc; Chief Clerk, 4 rooms; Clerks-Assistant, 2 rooms; 2 prison rooms; Clerk of Fees, 4 office-rooms; Clerk of Journals, 4 office-rooms; other departments, 13 offices; store-rooms for Journals and papers; Speaker's retiring room; Speaker's secretary, 3 rooms; chaplain's room; residences for librarian and deputy-housekeeper; official residence for the Speaker; post-office; watchmen; servants, messengers, doorkeepers; 2 waiting or cloak rooms for members.

Appendix III

List of Reports of Commissions and Select Committees of either House relating to the New Houses of Parliament, 1831–70

Reports of the Royal Fine Arts Commission are listed on p. 335, n.9. Reports relating to the temporary Houses are not included here.

'Lords', before the subject, indicates that the committee was a House of Lords committee. Its report, however, may well have been printed in House of Commons papers as well as House of Lords.

A name in brackets, after the subject, is that of the committee's chairman.

Session		Subject		Sessional number	Volume
1831		House of Commons buildings (Trench)		308	iv
		—reprinted in	1833,	17	xii
1833		House of Commons buildings (Hume)		269	xii
1835		Ventilation, warming, and sound (Hawes)		583	xviii
		Ladies' Gallery		437	xviii
		Plan for permanent accommodation		262	xviii
	Lords	Plan for permanent accommodation	HL	73	
1836		Plan for permanent accommodation		245	xxi
	Lords	Plan for permanent accommodation	HL	67	
		Commissioners for selection of designs		66	xxxvi
		Arts and Manufactures		568	ix
1839		Commissioners to inquire into qualities of stone		574	xxx
1841		Promotion of the Fine Arts (Hawes)		423	vi
1841, Sess.2		Plan for ventilation and warming, and rendering fireproof		51	i
1842		Plan for ventilation, etc., and accommodating the Clerk of the Commons with a residence		536	xiv
1843	Lords	Progress of the building	HL	40	
		—reprinted in	1844,	448	vi
1844	Lords	Progress of the building, 1st report		269	vi
		2nd report		629	vi
		Present state of the building (Lincoln)		448	vi
1846	Lords	Progress of the building (1st, 2nd and 3rd reports)		719	vi
		Present state of Westminster Bridge and the New Palace (Inglis) 1st report		177	xv
		2nd report		349	xv
		3rd report		574	xv

Notes

Chapter I. Introduction

1. 'Rambler', *Architect*, i (1869), 186–7.
2. *3 Parl. Deb.* cxi, 346–7.
3. PRO Works 11/1/2, ff.68–9.
4. *Fraser's Mag.* Aug. 1850, pp. 160 ff.
5. *3 Parl. Deb.* xcvii, 139; cp. cxi, 339–40.
6. *B*, i (1843), 275.
7. Statement by First Commissioner of Works, 1854 (*3 Parl. Deb.* cxxxiii, 1282).
8. PRO Works 11/1/2, ff.61–9, 6 Feb. 1849.
9. *Ibid.*
10. W. J. Reader, *Professional Men* (1966), 202.
11. *Architect*, iv (1870), 341–2.

Chapter II. The Old Houses of Parliament

1. *PP* 1833 (269) xii, q.929.
2. *Ibid.* q.928. For the ancient palace see H. M. Colvin (ed.) 'Views of the Old Palace of Westminster', *Architectural History*, ix (1966); M. Hastings, *Parliament House* (1950); E. W. Brayley and John Britton, *The History of the Ancient Palace and Late Houses of Parliament at Westminster* (hereafter cited as *Houses of Parliament*).
3. See Hastings, *Parliament House*, 82.
4. *Wren Society*, viii (1931), 16, 18–19, Pls I, VI; xviii (1941), 84–5; Brayley and Britton, *Houses of Parliament*, 395; *PP* 1833 (269) xii, 86; PRO Works 29/3358. For an account of the circumstances and of Kent's designs, see H. M. Colvin (ed.), *King's Works*, v (1976), 416–25.
5. *The House of Commons 1714–1754*, ed. R. Sedgwick (1970), i, 1; *C J* xliv (1788–9), 548–9, quoted in *King's Works*, vi, 512, 525.
6. J. Soane, *A Statement of Facts Respecting the Designs of a New House of Lords* (1799); J. Soane, *Three Designs for the Two Houses of Parliament* (1835); *Lords Jnls.* xl (1794–6), 253.
7. J. Topham, *Some Account of the Collegiate Chapel of St Stephen* (plans, elevations, etc. drawn by J. Carter, description of additional plates by Sir H. C. Englefield) 1795 [–1811].
8. *G M*, 1800, ii, 839.
9. *PP* 1825 (496) v.
10. For further details of Soane's work, see *King's Works*, vi, 520–4, 528–9.
11. See Sedgwick, *The House of Commons 1714–1754*, i, 1 and references there cited; *Pembroke Papers (1780–1794)*, ed. Lord Herbert (1950), 300, 381.
12. *PP* 1831 (308) iv, 655. The largest number of MPs recorded as taking part in a division before 1831 was 539 in 1819. The first reading of the Reform Bill was carried in a House of 607, and thereafter divisions in which more than 600 voted were not uncommon—D. E. D. Beales, 'Parliamentary Parties and the "Independent" Member, 1810–1860', *Ideas and Institutions of Victorian Britain*, ed. R. Robson (1967), 17.
13. *The Thames Quay, with Hints for some Further Improvements in the Metropolis* (1827).
14. *PP* 1833 (269) xii, q.13.
15. *Ibid.* qq.442, 448, 15–17.
16. For Toddington, see C. Hussey, *English Country Houses: Late Georgian 1800–1840* (1958), 161–7; J. Britton, *Historical Account of Toddington* (1841).
17. *PP* 1833 (269) xii, pl. 22.
18. *Ibid.* qq.575, 709–11, 714–19, 869–83, 957–60, 1045–6.
19. Topham, *op. cit.*
20. *G M*, 1810, ii, 301.
21. See M. H. Port, *Six Hundred New Churches* (1961).
22. *PP* 1833 (269) xii, q. 932.

23. *Ibid.* qq.1071, 933–6, 142, 586–9, 974–6, 1048.
24. *Ibid.* qq. 74–7, 356, 639, 779, 1098.
25. *Ibid.* q.604.
26. *Edinburgh Review* xlviii (1828), 165; *PP* 1833 (269) xii, q.461.
27. PRO Works 12/49/5, ff. 1–2 (7 July 1834). For the details of the following account, see 'Report of the Lords of the Council respecting the destruction by fire of the two Houses of Parliament', *PP* 1835 (1) xxxvii.
28. Spelled 'Weobley' in the Report.
29. Brayley and Britton, *Houses of Parliament*, 408–9.
30. *Ibid.* 411; *Creevey Papers* (1903), ed. Sir H. Maxwell, ii, 288. For other contemporary accounts of the fire, see *The Times*, 17 and 18 Oct. 1834, and *G M*, 1834, ii, 477–83.
31. *PP* 1835 (1) xxxvii, 10.

Chapter III. The Houses of Parliament Competition

1. Lord Broughton, *Recollections of a Long Life*, ed. Lady Dorchester, v (1911), 22–3; PRO T.1/4068, f.20177/34, Treasury minute, 21 Oct. 1834.
2. *PP* 1831 (329) iv.
3. *3 Parl. Deb.* xxxi, 234 ff; xliii, 695 ff. See also *The Times*, 18, 27 Oct., 5 Nov. 1834; *Spectator*, 1834, p. 1013 (25 Oct.); 1836, p. 250 (12 Mar.—strongly for old site); 'A.J.K.', *GM*, 1834, ii, 480 (for Gothic style on old site); *Architectural Mag.*, iii (1836), 101 (for new site).
4. *3 Parl. Deb.* xliii, 698 ff.; cliv, 1341; *Morn. Post*, 10 Feb. 1836 (report of Peel's speech of 9 Feb.).
5. *King's Works*, vi, 573; *Morn. Chronicle*, 18 Feb. 1835. The 'temporary' buildings had a long life. The Painted Chamber was used as a gallery of communication after the Lords moved into their new Chamber, until it and the old Lords' Chamber were cleared away for the final phase of building operations in 1851, together with the southernmost buildings by Soane that had survived the fire. Thus it was in the Temporary House that, e.g., the great debates on the repeal of the Corn Laws were conducted.
6. PRO Works 11/10/2, f.3.
7. *Ibid.* 2/1, p. 188; T.1/4068, f.20177/34.
8. PRO Works 11/1/1, ff.61–2. Smirke was employed by Peel on his private building works, see J. M. Crook, 'Sir Robert Peel: Patron of the Arts', *History Today*, 1966, pp. 3–11.
9. RIBA Drawings, J.11/37/1–5. See also Lord G. Somerset's statement, 25 Mar. 1835, 3 *Parl. Deb.* xxvi, 489.
10. *Morn. Herald*, 4 Feb., 28 Mar. 1835; *Mirror of Parl.*, 1835, i, 146–7 (2 Mar.).
11. *Morn. Herald*, 23 Jan. ('This vile system of jobbing must and will be' put a stop to.), 7 Feb. 1835; *Spectator*, 1835, pp. 156 (14 Feb.), 302 (28 Mar.).

12. [A. Alison], 'The British School of Architecture', *Blackwood's Edinburgh Mag.*, xl (1836), 238. *Blackwood's* was the most widely-read periodical of the day.
13. *Ibid.*
14. Archilochus, *What Style? The Royal or Baronial? The Priestly or Monastic? or the Squirely? for the New House of Parliament* (1837).
15. Charles Fowler, *The New Houses of Parliament* (1836), 2. Brougham made a very similar remark in a review of Hamilton's *Letters to the Earl of Elgin*, *Edinburgh Review*, lxv (1837), 174–5.
16. W. R. Hamilton, *Second Letter to the Earl of Elgin on the propriety of adopting the Greek style of architecture in the construction of the New Houses of Parliament* (1836), 49.
17. *The Times*, 18 Oct. 1834; *Spectator*, 25 Oct. 1834, p. 1013. See also Colburn's *New Monthly Mag.*, xlii (1834), 356.
18. *Westminster Review*, xxii (1835), 163–72. G. H. Weitzman, 'The Utilitarians and the Houses of Parliament', *Jnl of the Soc. of Architectural Historians*, xx (1961), 99–107, has suggested that the Utilitarians (with Hume as principal exponent) 'followed a developed and consistent position' in the debates on the New Houses, based on a functionalist approach. But their arguments were not 'developed and consistent', nor their views exclusively functionalist. 'Functional' criteria were part of the staple diet of contemporary architectural criticism, but were largely subjective. Cp. Hume's speech, *3 Parl. Deb.* xxxi, 236 (cited by Weitzman, 103–4).
19. *Morn. Herald*, 23 Jan., 7 Feb. 1835.
20. E. Cust, *A Letter to the Right Hon. Sir Robert Peel, Bart., M.P., on the expedience of a better system of control over buildings erected at the public expense; on the subject of rebuilding the Houses of Parliament*, 31 Jan. 1835.
21. *PP* 1835 (262) xviii, report of Rebuilding Committee. See also letter from Cust, *Morn. Herald*, 16 Mar. 1835; *Morn. Herald*, 28 Mar. 1835. Peel warned Cust that the Commons would not be indifferent (BM Add. MS. 40413, f.134, Peel to Cust, 8 Feb. 1835, quoted *King's Works*, vi, 575, n.11).
22. *PP* 1831 (272) iv.
23. See App. II below. For full list of the requirements for both Houses see *PP* 1835 (262) xviii and HL 1835 (73), reports of Rebuilding Committees. The resolutions of the Commons' committee were reported to the House by Lord G. Somerset on 3 June 1835, and are given in most parliamentary reports for that date.
24. *PP* 1836 (568) ix, q.2232 (Cockerell stressed that 'it gave with great precision the necessities, and it gave you the evidence upon which those necessities were founded … and at the same time it was not absolutely limited so as to be destructive of a good result'); *Morn. Chronicle*, 2 Feb. 1836. Cp. also B. Ferrey, *Recollections of A. W. N. Pugin* (1861), 241. In Britain in 1801 some 26,000 taxpayers received over £500 p.a.;

by 1867 there were 49,500 taxpayers receiving over £1,000 p.a. (H. Perkin, *The Origins of Modern English Society 1780–1880* (1967), 135–6.

25. C. Hussey, *English Country Houses: Late Georgian* (1958), 163.

26. *Ibid.*; *Morn. Chronicle*, 13 June 1835. See J. Britton, *History of Toddington* (1841), 26.

27. He had executed minor works on his father's estate, and subsequently was responsible for the north front of Ravensworth Castle (see *King's Works*, vi, 576, n.6 and references there cited). He also had recently built Beckett House, Shrivenham, Berks. for his brother-in-law, Lord Barrington (Lord De Grey, MS 'History of the rebuilding of Wrest House', Beds. C.R.O.)

28. J. Britton, *Autobiography* (1850), i, 235; J. Britton, *Toddington*, xiv; F. Boase, *Mod. English Biography.*

29. PRO Works 11/1/1, ff.14, 16, 17.

30. Cp. 'Architectus', *Architectural Mag.*, 1835 (ii), 283–4.

31. PRO MPE 1285; Works 11/1/1, ff.32–3; T. Hopper, *Hopper versus Cust, on the subject of Rebuilding the Houses of Parliament* (1837), 10.

32. *Athenaeum*, 1836, p.359; *Quarterly Review*, liii (1835), 338–71. Cp. *Wellesley Index*, ed. W. Houghton, i (1966) for authorship of articles.

33. PRO Works 11/1/1, 1 Dec. 1835; cp. *Athenaeum* 1836, p. 110.

34. *PP* 1836 (245) xxi, report of Rebuilding Committee, q.14 (A. Barry, *Life*, 155, carelessly attributes this statement to Cust).

35. *Spectator*, 12 Sept. 1835, p. 875; Brayley and Britton, *Houses of Parliament*, pt. viii, wrapper (reviewed in *Architectural Mag.* ii (1835), 504–6). See p. 53 below.

36. *3 Parl. Deb.* xxx, 621.

37. *Morn. Chronicle*, 2 Sept. 1835.

38. PRO Works 11/1/1, ff.30–1, 58; *Catalogue of the Designs for New Houses of Parliament* (1836, 7th edn.) 59; A. Barry, *Life*, 147; *PP* 1836 (568) ix, q.2232. See also p. 78 below.

39. M. McCarthy, *The Stones of Florence* (1972 Penguin edn.), 102; P. Collins, *Architectural Judgement* (1971), 148–9; *Architectural Mag.*, iii (1836), 539–41, and ii (1835), 12.

40. See e.g. *The Times*, 6 June 1836; *PP* 1828 (446) i, p. 84; E. W. Brayley, *Surrey*, v, 417; F. Beckwith, *Thomas Taylor, Regency Architect, Leeds* (Thoresby Soc. monograph 1, 1949), 68–70; T. W. Hutton, *King Edward's School Birmingham 1552–1952* (1952), 118 and lithographed paper bound up with the volume of contract drawings of the school; M. H. Port, *Six Hundred New Churches* (1961).

41. *Parl. Deb.* n.s. xl, 234 and 1437; *King's Works*, vi 432.

42. Barrington Kaye, *The Development of the Architectural Profession in Britain* (1960), 106 *et seq.*

43. *Architectural Mag.*, ii (1835), 13, 180, 381; iii (1836), 104. Cp. G. Foggo's declaration to select committee on Arts and Manufactures that competition was 'absolutely essential' to art, *PP* 1835 (598) v, qq.724–5.

44. For a discussion of competition and professionalism in general in the early nineteenth century, see H. Perkin, *Origins of Modern English Society, 1780–1880* Chap. VII. Among architects who did not favour competition were some at the top of the profession enjoying a lucrative practice who did not wish to waste time on a speculation. Thus Smirke refused to compete, Wyatville to enter an open competition, and Wilkins was critical of though ultimately taking part in the Parliament competition. See *The Times*, 7 Feb. 1835 ('Scrutator'); 6 June 1836 (review of Wilkins' pamphlet *An apology for the Designs . . . marked Phil-Archimedes*).

45. Collins, *Architectural Judgement*, 148. For contemporary horror stories about competitions, see *Architectural Mag.*, i (1834), 352; ii (1835), 12, 197, 329, 374, 376, 481, 484; iii (1836), 190; *Athenaeum*, 1836, 358–63 (cp. Sir G. G. Scott, *Personal and Professional Recollections* (1879), 73). An important recent competition in which the awards had been set aside was that for a new London Bridge.

46. *Morn. Chronicle*, 14 Feb.; *Morn. Herald*, 18 Feb. 1835. For French practice see *Morn. Chronicle*, 17 Feb. 1836, report of IBA meeting; *PP* 1836 (568) ix, Cockerell's evidence, q.2228; *Morn. Herald*, 31 Mar. 1836, anon. letter.

47. Cf. A. Alison, *Essay on Taste* (1808)—a widely read book, as pointed out by C. Hussey, *English Country Houses: Late Georgian*, 22; also E. Burke, *A philosophical enquiry into the origin of our ideas of the Sublime and the Beautiful*, ed. J. T. Boulton (1958), p. lxxxiii; G. L. Hersey, *High Victorian Gothic* (1972).

48. [A. Alison] 'The British School of Architecture', *Blackwood's Edinburgh Mag.*, xl (1836), 238; J. Pennethorne, description of own design in *Catalogue*, 14; Col. J. R. Jackson, *Observations on a letter from W. R. Hamilton, Esq., to the Earl of Elgin* (1837). Cp. A. W. N. Pugin, *An Apology for the Revival of Christian Architecture* (1843), 37, 45.

49. *Quarterly Review*, xlv (1831), 473.

50. Alison, 'The British School'; Jackson, *op. cit.*; E. Willson, *Specimens of Gothic Architecture* (1821–3), ii, pp. ix–x, cited by S. Lang, 'The Principles of the Gothic Revival in England', *Jnl. Soc. of Architectural Historians*, xix (1960).

51. Jackson, *op. cit.* A. W. N. Pugin, *A letter to A. W. Hakewill, Architect* (1835) also argued for the climatic appropriateness of Gothic.

52. B. Ferrey, *Answer, to 'Thoughts on rebuilding the Houses of Parliament'* (1835).

53. M. Girouard, 'Attitudes to Elizabethan Architecture, 1600–1900', *Concerning Architecture*, ed. J. Summerson (1968), 20–3.

54. *Architectural Mag.*, ii (1835), 382; A. W. N. Pugin, *True Principles*. But the widely-read *GM*, 1833, ii, 50–2, declared, 'We luxuriate in the idea of Elizabethan architecture', 'so national in its character, and so suitable to the climate'.

55. *Quarterly Review*, lxv (1831), 484.

56. *Spectator*, 20 June 1835, 586. W. J. Rorabaugh, 'Politics and the Architectural Competi-

tion for the Houses of Parliament 1834–1837', *Victorian Studies* Dec. 1973, 155–175, attempts to identify stylistic preferences with political attitudes, but a wider survey of contemporary material might have led him to other conclusions.

57. F. Jenkins, *Architect and Patron* (1961), 180. For a contrary view, see Cockerell's evidence to Committee on Arts and Manufactures, *PP* 1836 (568) ix, qq.2208–12.

58. 'W.E.H.', 'Mr Barry's design for the New Houses of Parliament', *Westminster Review*, 1836, 409–24.

59. W. R. Hamilton, *Letter from W. R. Hamilton Esq. to the Earl of Elgin on the new Houses of Parliament* (1836); and *Second Letter from W. R. Hamilton Esq to the Earl of Elgin on the propriety of adopting the Greek style of architecture in the construction of the New Houses of Parliament* (1836).

60. W. R. Hamilton, *Second Letter*, 52; and *Third Letter from W. R. Hamilton Esq to the Earl of Elgin, on the propriety of adopting the Greek style of architecture in preference to the Gothic, in the construction of the New Houses of Parliament* (1837).

61. *Quarterly Review*, liii (1835), 340, 370–1.

62. *Spectator*, 1835, p. 875.

63. *PP* 1835 (262) xviii; and HL 1835 (73), reports of Rebuilding Committees.

64. *Catalogue of Designs for the New Houses of Parliament* (7th edn. 1836); see also Appendix I.

65. Probably the fullest are those in *Architectural Mag.*, iii (1836), 201 ff. and 293–302; and *GM*, 1836, i, 523 ff. and 633 ff.

66. The quotations that follow are taken from the competitors' own descriptions in the *Catalogue of Designs*.

67. E.g. James Hakewill, Foster & Okely.

68. E.g. Knowles, Inman, Thrupp & Burchell, Lamb.

69. The *Morn. Post* (cited, *Art-Architect*, 103) described the Pugin-Graham design as 'presenting combinations of convenience and picturesque grouping in perfect keeping with the character of the style, which is delightful to contemplate.' *GM*, 1836, i, 525, was less complimentary: 'The exuberance of pinnacles and ornamental detail, is not a fault peculiar to any one design. Mr Graham exhibits this mistake in a very high degree, but the character and ornaments of his design, though foreign, are far handsomer and better selected than the detail of many others. A lofty square tower, with an octagon lantern, is added to St Stephen's Chapel . . . The idea of separating the buildings of the Two Houses is carried to an excess on this design, the plan being in two distinct masses, united merely by a corridor. This building throughout is overdone. It is rich, nay, so profuse in forms as to produce confusion. If ornament constituted the beauty of architecture, Mr Graham would be entitled to the highest praise; but the eye becomes fatigued with looking upon an endless profusion of enrichment.'

70. *PP* 1836 (66) xxxvi, report of Commissioners.

71. *GM*, 1836, i, 523.

72. E.g. Wallace.

73. *Architectural Mag.*, iii (1836), 201.

74. *Ibid.*; *Athenaeum*, 1836, pp. 224–5; *The Times*, 27 Apr. 1836, objected that Gothic was an ecclesiastical style.

75. *Morn. Chronicle*, 21 Mar. 1836.

76. *Architectural Mag.*, iii (1836), 201–3.

77. 21 Mar. 1836.

78. PRO Works 11/1/1, f.38.

79. *PP* 1836 (66) xxxvi.

80. *Ibid.* (245) xxi, report of Rebuilding Committee, qq.20–5.

81. *Spectator*, 1836, p. 151.

82. Nash often used the towered porch, first perhaps at Luscombe (*c.* 1800), where it is a towered *porte-cochère*. At Ravensworth (1808) he introduced a towered gatehouse in the centre of a façade. Dr Priscilla Metcalf points out that perhaps the earliest use of the two-storeyed porch in the Gothic Revival was by Wilkins sen. at Donington Hall (*c.* 1793). By 1810 it had become a common Picturesque adjunct.

83. *GM* 1836, i, 525.

84. *The Times*, 29 Apr. 1836. But some reservations were expressed (by apparently the same correspondent) two days earlier.

85. *Athenaeum*, 1836, p. 360.

86. *Morn. Herald*, 25 Mar. 1836. See also 1, 7, 13 and 25 Apr. 1836.

87. *Morn. Chronicle*, 15 Feb. 1836, 'One of the "Ninety-three"'.

88. *The Times*, 11 July 1836.

89. PRO Works 29/38–48.

90. T. Hopper, *Letter to Lord Duncannon on the rebuilding of the Houses of Parliament*, 5; *The Times*, 29 Apr., 3 May 1836; 'Candidus' (W. H. Leeds), *Architectural Mag.*, iii (1836), 299. Loudon described Buckler's mansion at Costessey (Cossey), Norfolk as 'the richest Gothic building in England', *Encyclopaedia of Cottage, Farm and Villa Architecture* (1832), 960.

91. *PP* 1836 (66) xxxvi.

92. PRO Works 29/49–58.

93. *The Times*, 3 May 1836; *Architectural Mag.*, iii (1836), 295, regards it as more 'Elizabethan' than any of the other entries. Cp. for windows Scone Palace, south elevation (after 1600), illustrated in D. Walker, 'Scone Palace', *The Country Seat*, ed. H. Colvin and J. Harris (1970), 210–14.

94. PRO Works 29/59–74. Duncannon's announcement of the results in the House of Lords was misreported in some papers, and the fourth prize allotted to Kempthorne (*Morn. Herald*, 9 Feb. 1836), an error followed by Eastlake, *History of the Gothic Revival* (1872), 171.

95. *PP* 1836 (66) xxxvi.

96. J. Savage, *Observations on Style in Architecture; with suggestions on the best mode of procuring Designs for Public Buildings, and promoting the Improvement of Architecture, especi-*

ally in reference to a recommendation in the report of the commissioners on the Designs for the New Houses of Parliament.

97. *PP* 1836 (66) xxxvi.
98. *The Times*, 6 June 1836.
99. W. Wilkins, *An Apology.*
100. J. Savage, *Observations.*
101. *Ibid.*
102. T. Hopper, *Hopper versus Cust*, 13; *PP* 1836 (568) ix, q.2201.
103. Savage, *Observations*, 32.
104. Review of pamphlets on the Houses of Parliament rebuilding, *Quarterly Review*, lviii (1837), 61–77. The reviewer is not identified in *Wellesley Index*, but internal evidence suggests he is the same as the reviewer of Hope's *History of Architecture* (*Quarterly Review*, 1835, pp. 338–71), i.e. Vivian.
105. Hopper, *Hopper versus Cust*, 14.
106. Cp. Vivian's review, *Quarterly Review*, lviii (1837), 61–77.
107. Savage, *Observations*, 28, 22.
108. *Catalogue*, 45.
109. Savage, *Observations*, 16; *Mirror of Parl.*, 1836, iii, 2491–2; *Athenaeum*, 1836, p. 359; *PP* 1836 (568) ix, qq.2194–5.
110. *Athenaeum*, 1839, 813.
111. *GM* 1836, i, 523; *Spectator*, 1836, 300.
112. *The Times*, 27 Apr. 1836.
113. Wilkins, *An Apology*, quoted in *The Times*, 27 May 1836; BM Add. MS. 40413, f.134.

Chapter IV. Barry and Pugin: A Collaboration

1. There was much correspondence in the press, but the major documents in this dispute are E. W. Pugin, *Who Was the Art-Architect of the Houses of Parliament?* (1867), and Alfred Barry, *The Architect of the New Palace at Westminster. A Reply to a Pamphlet by E. W. Pugin Esq., entitled 'Who Was the Art-Architect of the Houses of Parliament?'* (1868).
2. This account is paraphrased and quoted from that given by A. Barry, *Life*, 145.
3. MS letter, Pugin to E. J. Willson, 6 Nov. 1834 (Fowler Collection, The Johns Hopkins Univ.).
4. MS letter, Pugin to Willson, 6 Nov. 1834 (Fowler Collection, The Johns Hopkins Univ.). Barry was a subscriber to this work.
5. Pugin's drawings of 1830–1, principally for furniture and metal ornaments, are varied: some show no inspiration from Gothic, being rather Baroque and Jacobean, while others are florid, heavily carved proposals, extemporizations on Gothic themes but more ornate than any medieval objects he might have studied. Moreover, they are rendered in bright blue ink, in a heavy line and a sometimes erroneous perspective.
6. P. B. Stanton, 'Pugin at Twenty-One', *AR*, cx (1951), 187–90.
7. MS letter, Pugin to Willson, 26 Feb. 1833 (Fowler Collection, The Johns Hopkins Univ.).
8. Several of these are now in the V & A. With the exception of the startlingly beautiful 'St Marie's College' (dated 1834) all were produced in 1833.
9. MS letter, Pugin to Willson, 22 Aug. 1834 (Fowler Collection, The Johns Hopkins Univ.).
10. *Ibid.* 17 Sept. 1834.
11. A. Barry, *Life*, 87. I am grateful to Miss V. Chancellor for information from the Holland House Papers (BM) which show that Barry dined there 4 times in 1833 (once with Lord Duncannon), 7 times in 1834 (on three of which Lord Melbourne was present), and 3 times in 1835. Lady Holland wrote from Holland House, 26 Dec. 1836, 'We came here, where in former times we should have been frozen, but thanks to the skill of the great architect, Mr Barry, the house is really as warm as the most chilly could desire.'
12. Hull, whose business premises were at 109 Wardour St, knew Pugin and owned at least one volume of his drawings. In rather confused notes for a memoir of Pugin (now in the V & A), Miss Winifred Wyse stated that 'about 1832' Lord Shrewsbury 'discovered' Pugin 'accidentally when looking for Gothic furniture in Wardour Street'. But the first meeting between the Earl and Pugin was to come some years later. Thomas Wyse and Barry, however, were close friends: it may have been Barry who made the 'discovery'.
13. All references to the Pugin diaries are taken from the originals, now in the V & A. Except for the years 1843, 1846 and 1852, the diary is complete from 1835 to Pugin's death.
14. The RIBA Drawings Collection has four volumes of tracings and drawings collected by James Murray from the files in Barry's office between Dec. 1839 and Dec. 1847 (HLRO has a similar volume compiled by O. Moulton Barrett). RIBA Drawings C 10, a quarto entitled 'Sketches', contains several by Pugin (nos. 86, 88, 89); C 9, a large folio entitled 'Gothic', is composed largely of tracings from Pugin drawings: except nos. 78 and 90, 42–131 are Pugin. 116–31 are from his drawings for the Birmingham school, the others from Houses of Parliament drawings. Pugin appears also to have assisted Barry on other buildings: 142 (Highclere) shows Pugin's hand, as does 148 (finial, Hurstpierpoint Church). In addition to the Murray volumes, RIBA Drawings holds a collection of drawings for the school, referred to below.
HLRO folio entitled 'Gothic Architecture' contains many drawings by Pugin and tracings from his drawings; several are for the school.
15. 1835 diary, V & A. On the first pages, Pugin listed the drawings he prepared for the school, and his prices.
16. A. Barry, *Life*, 242–3.
17. It appears that the school was approximately 167 × 70 ft, the club approximately 53 ft high to the eaves.
18. RIBA Drawings, C 5/5³.

19. In addition to *Art-Architect* and *Reply*, E. W. Pugin, *Notes on Dr Barry's Reply* (1868) contains some useful information and speculation.

20. *Reply*, 17.

21. *Ibid.*, 8–11.

22. *Art-Architect*, 13. W. Osmond said that Graham's drawings were prepared in his house rather than at St Marie's Grange. This seems likely as the Grange was scarcely finished and Pugin himself not fully established there.

23. *Reply*, 27.

24. *Ibid.*, 20–6.

25. *Ibid.*, 7. Bury's statement that Pugin first saw Barry's drawings after Graham's design was completed is clearly nonsense.

26. A. Barry reporting, but not quoting, Charles Barry's diary asserted that his father was not in Salisbury on 1 Nov. 1835 (which the Pugins had never claimed!) and that he was 'in town working (as we know) night and day at his own designs' between 2 and 8 November. But the Barry diary was never made public. See *Reply*, 16.

27. *Ibid.*

28. *Art-Architect*, 12.

29. *Ibid.* 13.

30. This figure has been obtained by adding the sums Pugin noted in his diary as charges for individual drawings the subjects of which can be identified as those for the school.

31. *Reply*, 28. Barry gives the date of payment as 10 February 1836—Pugin's date is presumably that when he cashed the cheque.

32. See the comment on Pugin's Graham design, p. 318, n.69.

33. The explanation put forward here is based on a thorough review of MS sources and drawings, but is in general agreement with J. L. Wolfe's in A. Barry's biography of his father and in response to E. W. Pugin's intemperate accusations.

34. 'I must own that I think you are right in the principle of repetition of bays. All the great town-halls are certainly so . . . You know that I never hold out after I am convinced, and now I can advocate it conscientiously.' Pugin to Barry, 'Basel', 1 Aug. 1845, *Reply*, 54.

Chapter V. Select Committees and Estimates: The Collaboration Continued

1. See *Architectural Mag.*, ii (1835), 371, 552; iii (1836), 9; *Morn. Chronicle*, 'An Old Artist', 2 Feb. 1836.

2. *GM*, 1836, i 288.

3. Cp. T. Hopper, *A Letter to the Rt. Hon. Lord Viscount Duncannon . . . in explanation of the proceedings of the Architects, Competitors for building the new Houses of Parliament, who petitioned for an examination of the propriety of the selection made by the Commissioners &c.* (1837), 5.

4. *CJ*, cxi (1836), 17; *3 Parl. Deb.* xxxi, 503 (17 Feb. 1836). If the judges went by the rumours, they were sadly led astray: e.g. the description of Barry's design having a tower 'which forms the centre of the façade of the River front', *Spectator*, 1836, p. 151.

5. *CJ*, cxi (1836), 48, 63–4; *Mirror of Parl.* 1836, i, 41 (5 Feb.), 184–5 (17 Feb.), 228 (19 Feb.).

6. *CJ*, cxi (1836), 100; *Lords' Jnls.* lxviii (1836), 42, 72. The Lords' committee included Lords Rosslyn, De Grey, Ripon, Farnborough, Melbourne, Holland, and several ministers.

7. *PP* 1836 (245) xxi, Report of Select Committee to consider and report on such plan as may be most fitting and convenient for the permanent accommodation of the Houses of Parliament, qq.10, 12.

8. *Ibid.* qq.15–38, 43–7, 51, 53–8, 72–89 (Hume), 38 (Cust).

9. *Ibid.* qq.119, 108.

10. *Ibid.* qq.37–51, 54–6.

11. *Ibid.* qq.211 *et seq.*

12. *Ibid.* qq.300–3. The effect of the denuded design is shown most clearly in a drawing belonging to the Society of Antiquaries inscribed 'Elevation . . . prepared since the decision of His Majesty's Commissioners'.

13. *PP* 1836 (245) xxi, q.3.

14. Ibid. qq.211–404; *Lords' Jnls.* lxviii (1836), 156.

15. *3 Parl. Deb.* xxxv, 407–13 (Sir John Hobhouse, 21 July 1836); *PP* 1836 (245) xxi, Report, p. iii.

16. *Ibid*

17. *Ibid.* qq.129, 130.

18. PRO Works 11/1/1, ff.49–50.

19. *PP* 1844 (448) vi, q.485.

20. Sir E. Cust, *Thoughts on the expedience of a better system of control and supervision over buildings erected at the public expense; and on the subject of rebuilding the Houses of Parliament* (1837).

21. See *King's Works*, vi, 183.

22. *PP* 1836 (245) xxi, (evidence of 22 Apr. 1836).

23. *Mirror of Parl.* 1836, i, 78.

24. *Ibid.* 1836, iii, 2491–2.

25. *Mirror of Parl.* 1836, i, 890 (11 Apr.); *Morn. Chronicle*, 21 Mar. 1836.

26. T. Hopper, *A Letter to . . . Lord Viscount Duncannon* (1837), 6.

27. PRO Works 11/1/1, f.34 (newspaper cutting); T. Hopper, *Hopper versus Cust, on the subject of Rebuilding the Houses of Parliament* (1837), 14.

28. *Morn. Chronicle*, 'One of the "Ninety-three"', 15 Feb. 1836; *Mirror of Parl.* 1836, iii, 2487.

29. *Ibid.* 1836, ii 1986 (21 June).

30. *Ibid.* iii, 2485–7 (21 July); *CJ*, xci (1836), 534 (see also p. 524).

31. *Mirror of Parl.* iii, 2487–9.

32. *The Times*, 8 Aug. 1836.

33. *Ibid.* 9 Aug. 1836.

34. *Architectural Mag.*, iii (1836), 101; *Westminster Review*, 1836, 409–24 ('The infidel portion of the Lower House will no longer be enabled to avoid going to church; every committee-room will be a chapel, furnished, as we understand, with Bibles, prayer-books and useful homilies.' However, its site on 'the very lowest level of the Metropolis' would 'work well for the principle of Annual Parliaments', by killing off 'elderly asmatical gentlemen (who are fortunately all Conservatives), engaged during . . . February and March, in trying to unseat some Liberal representatives of the city of Dublin, in one of Mr Barry's committee-rooms — and the windows occasionally left open at night by the attendants, to air the room, and admit the fog from the river.'); *Morn. Herald*, 30 Apr. 1836; *GM*, 1836, i, 633. Another critic was C. R. Cockerell, who declared that he was weary of vast national buildings 'durably decorated with the barbaric carvings and disgusting monstrosities of Gothic architecture', *PP* 1836 (568) ix, Report on Arts and Manufactures, q.2240.

35. See p. 43 above. *Architectural Mag.*, iii (1836), 249, 299–301 ('Candidus'—W. H. Leeds), 400, 403; *Spectator*, 1836, 300, 393; *The Times*, 27 and 29 Apr. 1836.

36. MS letter, Pugin to Willson, 4 Jan. 1836 (Fowler Collection, The Johns Hopkins Univ.).

37. Barry produced the original *plan*, signed by the commissioners, to a Lords' committee, 29 Apr. 1844 (*PP* 1844 (269) vi, q.128), and it appears to have been before that committee at its meeting on 26 Apr. also (q.85). On 5 Aug. 1845 the Office of Woods applied to Barry for 'the volume of original plans [*?sc.* drawings] signed by the Commissioners of Selection, which were at your solicitation lent you by this Board' (PRO Works 1/28, p. 281). What happened thereafter is unknown. E. M. Barry stated that the prize drawings were not among those bequeathed him by Sir Charles (*PP* 1867 (451) viii, q.5). It may be that the competition drawings were so damaged by use that they were copied and then destroyed, which seems improbable (the more so as they were bound into a volume), or that in the fracas in 1860 between Sir Charles Barry and E. W. Pugin and his stepmother—the prelude to the pitched battle of 1867—Barry himself set out to destroy every trace of Pugin's participation in the design of the Houses of Parliament. By then, however, the volumes of tracings and some drawings now in RIBA Drawings and HLRO had, fortunately, been removed from Barry's office. But Pugin drawings for the throne, panelling, metalwork, glass and furniture remained in the possession of Edward Barry's family and have recently been deposited on loan in the RIBA Drawings Collection by his great-granddaughter, Mrs Stanley-Evans.

38. *The Times*, 29 Apr. 1836. That this observer failed to perceive that Graham's design, too, was autographical and by the same hand as Barry's

does not destroy the theory that Pugin drew all the drawings for Barry's save the plans. Further corroboration was supplied by W. Osmond who, in 1867, remembered that when he and his son went to the exhibition they recognized several of Pugin's drawings in 'Mr Barry's set', *Art-Architect*, 13.

39. PRO Works 29/3204 and 3205 (corresponding plans are 29/81–3). See *King's Works*, vi, 580.

40. *Reply*, 36.

41. *Art-Architect*, 23–4. See also *Reply*, 35 for A. Barry's refutation.

42. *Art-Architect*, 26.

43. The diary here specifies eight: 'porch hall/central lobby/stairs/witness room/Kings tower 2/entrance hall 2'.

44. *Art-Architect*, 28–9.

45. MS diary, V & A.

46. *PP* 1836 (245) xxi, q.397; PRO Works 11/10/1, on which the rest of this paragraph is based.

47. *Art-Architect*, 31.

48. Pugin did not specify in his 1836 and 1837 diaries the payments made by Barry, but lumped his two major clients together in casual lists that do not include and describe all the jobs appearing in the daily entries. A. Barry, however, cited specific payments by his father to Pugin amounting to £248 between Dec. 1836 and 1838, of which £18.14s. were for Dr Jeune's furniture. Thus Barry paid £229.6s by cheque on account of the Houses of Parliament estimates drawings. Cash payments need not have been recorded, and A. Barry could have withheld information (*Reply*, 28). That Pugin was not paid by the day (which implied a lower professional status than payment by drawing), as A. Barry suggested, is shown by the charges in guineas for specific drawings recorded by Pugin; Graham also paid so much per drawing.

49. With but a few exceptions, Pugin was also responsible for all the drawings from which Murray's tracings in the 'Gothic' folio, RIBA Drawings, were taken. Some date from 1844–7 (when Murray left Barry's office), when Pugin was back at work on the Houses.

The Moulton Barrett folio volume in HLRO includes tracings of some of Pugin's drawings of 1836–7: they may be identified because of the scale, an inch to ten feet, because the copyist traced Pugin's handwriting, and because their subjects correspond to those listed in Pugin's diary.

50. *Annual Register*, 1860, App. to Chronicle, 387; *Ecclesiologist*, xiii (1852), 49–50; K. Clark, *The Gothic Revival* (new edn. 1950), 163.

51. C. L. V. Meeks, 'Picturesque Eclecticism', *Art Bulletin*, xxxiii (1950), 226–35.

52. B. Ferrey, *Recollections of A. W. N. Pugin* (1861), 248.

53. C. Hussey, *The Picturesque* (1927), 187.

54. Meeks, *op. cit.*, 233.

55. Cf. *Civil Engineer*, vii (1844), 183; *Westminster Review*, xlix (1848), 466.

56. A. Barry, *Life*, 49–53, 59, 121–2, 130, 242–3.
57. *B*, xviii (1860), 344.
58. *Reply*, 54.
59. *Art Jnl.* 1855, p. 315; *The Times*, 25 Oct. 1855. Even Barry by 1857 thought that he should have chosen an earlier period of Gothic. He said that had there been an open choice, 'I should have adopted Gothic; I do not say that I should have adopted Tudor' (*PP* 1857–8 (417) xi, select committee on reconstruction of the Foreign Office, q.1583). But the *Athenaeum*, 1856, p. 110, asked, 'Is not this the work of a great man who expresses the great thought of a great nation?' And cp. *Athenaeum*, 1860, p. 684.
60. A model of the prize design was shown to the king (*PP* 1844 (448) vi, q.487), but no more was heard of it.

Chapter VI. Problems of Building in the 1840s

1. PRO T.1/4068, f.16677/38; *PP* 1839 (574) xxx; *B*, xviii (1860), 342.
2. Cp. *Civil Engineer*, ii (1839), 331, 372, 419; C. H. Smith, 'On Stone for Building', *IBA Trans*, 30 May 1853, 6; A. Clifton Taylor, *The Pattern of English Building* (2nd. edn. 1965), 110.
3. *PP* 1861 (504) xxxv, Report of committee on decay of stone of New Palace, on which this paragraph and part of the next are based. The statement that 'Bolsover stone' was 'used at the commencement' (*PP* 1926 [Cmd. 2752] xxiii) is misleading. It refers to the Mansfield Woodhouse stone that workmen at Westminster used to call 'Bolsover' (*PP* 1861 (504) xxxv, qq.1900–3, 1949). Bolsover Moor stone had indeed only been used locally for 'trifling matters such as doorsteps', and C. H. Smith had had grave doubts about the practicability of working the thin, contorted beds.
4. Broadlands MS, WFC/HH/18/2, by permission of the Broadlands Trustees.
5. *PP* 1926 [Cmd. 2752] xxiii, with photographs of the decaying stone work.
6. PRO Works 11/6/1, ff. 12, 28; 11/9/7, ff. 3, 4; 29/2487. For the contemporary vogue for Caen stone, see H. Hobhouse, *Thomas Cubitt* (1971) 400–1. Care was taken to secure the best bricks, too, the internal parts being exclusively of hard burnt Cowley stocks manufactured by Mr Westbrook of Heston, agreed to be the best made for the London market, *B*, v (1847), 177.
7. *PP* 1844 (381) vi, report of 1843 Lords' committee on progress of the building.
8. *PP* 1844 (448) vi, report of committee to inquire into the present state of the building, q. 101, and evidence of 1843 committee. The cofferdam accommodated workshops, PRO Works 11/5/17, f.36. Barry complained of the want of space for storage of materials and for workmen in August 1843 (Works 11/6/1, f.27); and two years later he was complaining that

hands would have to be discharged from Thames Bank workshops to make room for storing finished work (Works 11/9/3, f.16, 30 Sept. 1845). Cp. Works 1/24, p. 100 (6 Feb. 1840) for delays caused by difficulties in clearing the site.
9. PRO Works 11/5/17, f.22. The contract drawings are Works 29/3112–20.
10. PRO Works 11/5/17; 11/5/18; 1/23, pp. 372, 483. Extracts from Barry's specifications for the tenders are printed by P. W. Kingsford, *Builders and Building Workers* (1973), 45–50.
11. PRO Works 11/6/1.
12. *Ibid.* ff. 6, 11–13, 28.
13. *PP* 1861 (504) xxxv, q.519.
14. PRO Works 11/6/2, ff.1–2. Prof. F. M. L. Thompson is incorrect in stating that at the Houses of Parliament 'the major part of the building work proper was contracted for ... under a contract in gross', *Chartered Surveyors* (1968), 90.
15. M. D. Wyatt in *B*, xviii (1860), 342; A. Barry, *Life*, 160.
16. PRO Works 11/6/1, f.24; contract drawings in Works 29/1814–56, 1897–1901 and 2009. For a fuller account of the revision of the design, see *King's Works*, vi, 596–8 and Pl. 58.
17. A. Barry, *Life*, 251–2.
18. A Commons' committee under Hawes' chairmanship had recommended that due provision for heating and ventilation be made in the new building from its outset, both to ensure its efficiency and to limit expense, *PP* 1835 (583) xviii.
19. *Ibid.* 1846 (349) xv, second report of committee to consider present state of Westminster Bridge and the New Palace at Westminster, q.258.
20. PRO Works 1/24, pp. 88–9; 11/12, ff.12 (Reid to Duncannon, 5 Oct. 1839), 15, 17 and 19.
21. *PP* 1844 (448) vi, qq.462–6.
22. *PP* 1841 Sess.2 (51) i; 1842 (536) xiv (reports of committees to consider the plan for ventilating, etc.); 1846 (574) xv, third report of committee to consider present state of the Palace, qq.261–2; *3 Parl. Deb.* xcvi, 572–6. Cp. Soc. of Antiquaries' drawing, reproduced *King's Works*, vi, Pl. 61; *Wren Soc.*, i, Pl. XI, XII; xiii, Pl. XIII.
23. The following account is based on cuttings from the *Northern Star* and other papers in BM, Place Collection, 53 E. See also *PP* 1861 (504) xxxv, qq.968–9, 1008, 1037–8, 1099; PRO Works 11/9/7, f.3; *PP* 1844 (448) vi, qq. 504–6. Some source material is printed by P. W. Kingsford, *Builders and Building Workers* (1973), 58–66.
24. Allen had worked for the reputable firm of Messrs Grundy as a mason, preparing stone for Cockerell's works at the Bank of England; and had in 1833 personally selected stone for W. Cubitt's contract for the new Fishmongers' Hall, but Cubitt had discharged him for taking a lead in union agitation.
25. See *Morn. Chronicle*, 8 Nov., *Sun* 8 Nov., *Morn. Advertiser* 9 Nov. 1841. For the implications of Birmingham as seat of the Masons'

Union, see R. Postgate, *The Builders' History* (1923).

26. A. Barry, *Reply*, 80–2.

27. *Art-Architect*, 109.

28. E. M. Barry, who took his brother's place at Westminster in 1847, later identified among the New Palace drawings the hands of George Penrose Kennedy, Robert Kerr, James Murray, Francis Clerihew (employed on measuring and accounts in 1840–1), Louis De Ville, J. W. Walton, F. C. Boughton and one Payne. Examination of the drawings and tracings now in PRO adds to the list F. Earle, J. Bellenger, W. H. Brookes, Maitland Wardrop, W. Field, R. Suter, and one Chilvers; while the correspondence published in the 1867 controversy mentions also Arthur Billing and Richardson (perhaps the same as the quantity surveyor employed in 1837). Those to whom drawings or details were to be referred included Messrs Peckthall, Lamprell and Rome. *Reply*, 82–3, 70–1; *PP* 1861 (504) xxxv, qq.1126–7; drawings in HLRO, Soc. of Antiquaries, RIBA Drawings and PRO Works 29.

29. *Reply*, 42–9; *PP* 1861 (504) xxxv, qq. 776, 788, 811, 1139; PRO Works 11/1/2, ff. 79–82, 107, 191–2, 142–4; *RIBA Trans.*, 1856–7, 156; Wyman's *Architect's, Engineer's & Building Trades' Directory* (1868).

30. *3 Parl. Deb.* xxx, 670 (19 Aug. 1835).

31. *PP* 1844 (381) vi.

32. *Ibid.* (269) and (629) vi, first and second reports of Lords' committee to inquire into progress of the building.

33. Sudeley was so perturbed by Barry's alterations to the plan that he printed his criticisms and suggestions, issued anonymously as *Observations on the plans for the New Houses of Parliament by one of the Commissioners appointed by the Crown in the year 1835, to examine the designs*, etc. [1844].

I am grateful to the present Lord Sudeley for bringing to my attention his own copy of this rare work, which he has presented to HLRO.

34. *B*, i (1843), 206, citing *Morn. Herald*; *PP* 1843 [499] xxix.

35. PRO Works 29/151 and 177; BM Add. MS. 40543, f.365. Cp. *PP* 1844 (448) vi, q.73 and (629) vi, q. 447.

36. Cp. PRO Works 29/400, 399 and 401.

37. *PP* 1843 [499] xxix; 1844 (448) vi, qq.9–13.

38. *Athenaeum*, 1844, p. 460.

39. See *King's Works*, vi, 471 (and references there cited), 567.

40. PRO Works 11/9/7, f.50

41. *PP* 1844 (448) vi.

42. *3 Parl. Deb.* xcv, 1404.

43. *PP* 1844 (448) vi.

44. PRO Works 1/29, pp. 222, 243; M. Bond, *The Table*, xl (1971)

45. *PP* 1844 (448) vi, qq.445, 412.

46. *Ibid.* qq.417, 427.

47. *Ibid.* q.424.

48. *Ibid.* qq.475, 480, 516–18.

49. *Ibid.* pp. iii–iv.

50. *Ibid.* (629) vi.

51. *Civil Engineer*, vii (1844), 217–23; *B*, iii (1845), 301.

52. *ILN*, xii (1848), 95; *The Times*, 27 May, 17 Aug. 1846. See also 3 June 1844; 26 June 1845; 20 Mar., 6 Apr., 27 Apr., 13 June 1846; 15 Feb. 1848. *Punch*, x (1846), 179 'This is the house that Barry (ought to have) built . . .', 218, 263, etc.

53. MS letter, 6 Apr. 1845 (present whereabouts unknown).

54. *PP* 1846 (719) xv.

55. *Ibid.* p. 13.

56. *Ibid.* p. 18 (Gwilt's report, 29 Sept. 1845 is given in full).

57. *B*, iv (1846), 213.

58. *PP* 1846 (177) (349) and (574) xv, first, second and third reports of committee to consider present state of Westminster Bridge and New Palace.

59. PRO Works 1/30, pp. 71–2; 11/12, f.246. See also *King's Works*, vi, 620; *B*, v (1847), 156, 177; vii (1849), 98; viii (1850), 61.

60. *PP* H.L. 1847 (314) and (318); Lord Great Chamberlain's MSS, ser. II, vol. 4, pp. 44, 46.

61. *B*, viii (1850), 61; v (1847), 98.

62. *3 Parl. Deb.* cx, 890 (20 Apr. 1850); *The Times*, 8 July 1850.

63. PRO Works 11/16/3, f.13, 22 Dec. 1849; *3 Parl. Deb.* cxix, 231–4 (6 Feb.), 400–15 (11 Feb. 1852); *PP* 1850 (650) xv.

64. *PP* 1844 (629) vi, qq. 592–4 and pp. 61–5.

65. *PP* 1835 (598) v and 1836 (568) ix, reports of committee 'to inquire into the best Means of extending a knowledge of the Arts and of the Principles of Design among the People (especially the Manufacturing Population . . .)'; 1837–8 (447) xxxvi, on free admission to museums; 1841 (416) vi, on the present state of National Monuments, 'to consider the best means for their Protection and for affording facilities to the Public for the inspection, as a means of moral and intellectual Improvement for the People'; 1841 (423) vi, on the 'Promotion of the Fine Arts of the Country in connexion with the Rebuilding of the Houses of Parliament'; 1850 (655) xvii, on public libraries. Cp. below, pp. 268–9.

66. John Britton was perhaps one: see *Civil Engineer*, vi (1843), 374.

67. *PP* 1844 (629) vi, pp. 61–5; *B* i, 160–2 (6 May 1843), taken from *Morn. Herald*; Tom Taylor (ed.), *Life of Benjamin Robert Haydon . . . from his autobiography and journals* (2nd. edn. 1853), iii, 185 (10 July 1841).

68. PRO Works 1/27, p. 318, 16 Dec. 1844.

69. *Ibid.* p. 434. The extent of Pugin's activity can be judged from an inventory of 1859 which refers to 7499 plaster casts (Works 11/28/16, ff.19 *et seq.*). Apart from a collection from Amiens Cathedral presented by the French government, these were doubtless the fruits of Pugin's activities in 1845–6—by March 1846 there were already more than 2,000 casts at the Thames Bank workshops (Works 11/9/3, f.33).

It included not only carved and linenfold panels, brattishings, pendants, spandrels and bosses, but also buttresses, crowns, finials, animals and inscriptions: a complete assembly of examples for stone as well as wood carvers. Cp. pp. 244, 246 below.

70. *Ibid.* 11/6/5, ff.1–9.
71. PRO Works 11/9/4; MPE 813 and 845.
72. PRO Works 11/9/3; 11/6/5, f.25.
73. *Ibid.* 11/6/5, ff.12 *et seq.*
74. *Ibid.* ff.20, 25–60, 78–84; 1/36, pp. 86–7; M. Bowley, *The British Building Industry* (1966), 336–7, 343.
75. PRO Works 1/28, pp. 48, 163, 233.
76. *Ibid.* 11/7/3 (iron), 11/7/11 (glass), 11/7/14 (metal sashes, estimated at about £17,800, Works 1/28, p. 251; 1/31, p. 362). Cp. list given, Works 1/32, p. 388.
77. *Ibid.* 1/30, pp. 144, 169; 2/5, p. 197; 11/7/6 (painting); 11/7/9 (metalwork).
78. *Ibid.* 11/8/9. See below, chapter XIII, for details of the furniture.

Chapter VII. The Collaboration Resumed: Barry and Pugin, 1844–52

1. *Companion to the Almanac for 1844*, pp. 223–5.
2. Reported, *ILN*, 8 June 1843, p. 363.
3. *B*, ii (1844), 465–6, a verbatim report from *The Times*, 10 Sept.
4. A summary of the committee's report, *PP* 1844 (269, 629) vi, appeared in *B* in August and September 1844.
5. *Reply*, 38.
6. *B*, ii (1844), 69; 'Professor Welby Pugin and His Opinions', *Polytechnic Jnl*, July 1841, 72–80.
7. *Reply*, 53. This letter was endorsed by Barry 16 June 1844, a dating acceptable were it not that Pugin began and ended it with remarks about a debilitating attack of 'English cholera' which had 'prostrated' him from Saturday to the following Thursday when the letter was written. Pugin's diary shows that on those days he was incessantly on the move, travelling from York to Derby, on to Nottingham and Grace Dieu on the day he was 'prostrated', and in the two days following (when he said he 'could hardly hold himself up at all') he visited Mount St Bernard's Abbey and joined Lord Shrewsbury for an inspection of the cathedral at Nottingham. This is not to contradict Barry's dating, however. Pugin also offered to visit Barry 'immediately' upon his return to London on the following Tuesday: he did reach London on that day, but there is no reference in his diary to a meeting with Barry.

It is significant that few of what must have been many meetings with Barry over the work at Westminster were recorded in Pugin's diary.

8. *Art-Architect*, 29. It is possible that between June and September 1844 Pugin did some work for Barry to which 'the discharge of my obligations' may refer.

9. HLRO, Moulton-Barrett vol.
10. PRO Works 1/27, p. 318.
11. *Reply*, 55. Pugin was not near Amiens at any time between those dates. I am assuming that Barry misread the place name and that the letter was written early in 1845.
12. Pugin wrote to E. J. Willson in Lincoln on 24 Feb. 1845, to enquire about the availability of casts and squeezes of the stall finials in the cathedral. A few weeks later he ordered all the casts of crockets, stall details, bosses and finials Willson had found, adding that he also 'wanted some good King's heads from the stalls, some of the Dragon and animals would be very useful indeed', and that details of the Longland Chantry 'would answer admirably as the style was late'.
13. See reports of exhibitions in *B*, 11 and 18 May 1844.
14. *Ibid.* 18 May 1844. Crace may have asked Pugin to design something for him, for Pugin wrote to him in January 1844 that he was 'so constantly occupied that I hardly get through my own works'. The heraldic decoration mentioned in *B* may have been from a design by Pugin.
15. F. Knight Hunt, *The Book of Art. Cartoons, Frescoes, Sculpture and Decorative Art as Applied to the New Houses of Parliament ... with an Historical Notice of the Exhibitions in Westminster Hall and Directions for Painting in Fresco* (1846).
16. 'Pugin's Christian Architecture', *Artizan*, Apr. 1843, pp. 90–1.
17. 'Charles Barry and His Right-Hand Man', *Artizan*, June 1845, p. 137.
18. *Reply*, 56–7.
19. This episode may be followed in *B*, July–Aug. 1845.
20. *B*, iii (2 Aug. 1845), 367; see also p. 416 (30 Aug.).
21. 'Decorations for the New House of Lords', *B*, iii (6 Sept. 1845), 426.
22. *Reply*, 56–7.
23. Crace's design for the decoration of the Lords' Chamber ceiling is V & A, A.52 (E 2746–50–1914).
24. PRO Works 11/7/9, 9 July 1845.
25. Barry diaries, RIBA.
26. *3 Parl. Deb.* lxxxi, 120–2, 203–6 (5 and 9 June 1845), quoted *King's Works*, vi, 225–6.
27. *Art-Architect*, 42–3.
28. Quotations from Stanton transcripts.
29. Barry to Hardman, 21 Dec. 1847.
30. Barry to Hardman, 26 and 3 Feb. 1847.
31. *Art-Architect*, 48.
32. *B*, v (1847), 189. One immediate result of the opening of the House of Lords was a demand for decorations in the Parliament House style. New orders came for the embellishment of large houses such as Bilton Grange and Burton House, while such commissions as Chirk Castle, and Alton Towers continued. These undertakings, managed by Crace, were financially rewarding while they demanded a minimum of design effort,

for the patterns prepared for the Palace were not reserved for use only in that building. Whole interiors could be composed using stock hinges, wallpaper and fabric patterns, though Pugin frequently designed a special paper or supervised a whole composition.

33. Pugin to John Hardman, ?1849 or early 1850.
34. *Reply*, 63. Barry, hard pressed by government for economies, had suggested this reduction, PRO Works 11/11/3, f.162, 18 Feb. 1850.
35. RIBA, Pugin to John Crace, Dec. 1850.
36. *Art-Architect*, 56. See p. 157.

Chapter VIII. Barry's Last Years: The New Palace in the 1850s

1. *3 Parl. Deb.* xcvi, 576–8, 556–7; PRO Works 1/32, p. 167.
2. PRO Works 2/6, pp. 409, 415 (see also 381–415); Works 11/11/3, f.55; *B*, vi (1848), 549, and viii (1850), 61. In 1848 Barry had to provide a Smoking Room and additional offices for the Journal and Library departments of the Commons at an additional cost of some £5,000 (Works 11/8/10, f.5).
3. *3 Parl. Deb.* xcv, 858, 1332 ff., 1401 ff.; xcvi, 290, 543 ff.; xcvii, 138 ff.; *ILN*, xii (1848), 95; PRO Works 11/12, ff.332, 339–41; *King's Works* vi, 232–3.
4. Lord de Grey, MS memoirs, Bedfordshire CRO; *King's Works*, vi, 625. De Grey gives the date of the Commission's resignation as 25 Mar. 1850, but his recollection appears at fault.
5. *3 Parl. Deb.* cxi, 332, 338–9.
6. *PP* 1849 (325) xxx; *3 Parl. Deb.* cxi, 459–60, 1007; cxiii, 739; cxcv, 275.
7. *3 Parl. Deb.* cxi, 959, 1007; *PP* 1850 (650–I) and (650–II) xv.
8. *3 Parl. Deb.* cxiii, 729–30; *PP* 1850 (650–II) xv.
9. *3 Parl. Deb.* cxiii, 735, 727–8, 737–9.
10. *B*, x (1852), 97. For an account of the building at the time of the State Opening, see *ILN*, xx (1852) 113, 117, 120–1, 137, 216.
11. *3 Parl. Deb.* cii, 568; civ, 857–8; *PP* 1850 (709) xxxiii; PRO Works 2/7, pp. 229–34.
12. PRO Works 11/11/3, ff.131–3, 156–8.
13. *Ibid.* f.162 (Barry, 18 Feb. 1850), 171.
14. Marian Bowley, *The British Building Industry* (1966), 356.
15. *King's Works*, vi, 197–8.
16. *Ibid.* p. 238; PRO Works 11/1/2, f.162.
17. *Ibid.* ff.119–23.
18. *Ibid.* ff. 128–30, 135–6.
19. *Ibid.* f.188.
20. *Ibid.* ff.142–4, 151–2; see also *King's Works*, vi, 238–9. Further attempts to ensure that annual expenditure did not exceed the sum voted were made in 1853, *PP* 1852–3 (846) lxxxiii, 247 ff.
21. Cp. Marian Bowley, *The British Building Industry*, 350; W. J. Reader, *Professional Men* (1966), 43, 158–9.

22. *3 Parl. Deb.* cvii, 352–3. On the question of the five per cent commission, see F. Jenkins, *Architect and Patron* (1961).
23. PRO Works 11/1/2, ff.162, 166–75, 180–1.
24. *Ibid.* ff.221–6. See also *PP* 1856 (117) lii.
25. PRO Works 11/1/2, ff.259–63, Treasury Minute, 4 July 1856.
26. *Ibid.* ff.266–7. See also *PP* 1856 (405) lii. For Scott's conduct, see Sir G. G. Scott, *Personal and Professional Recollections* (1879), Chap. iv, and the comment in C. L. Eastlake, *History of the Gothic Revival* (1872), 312.
27. PRO Works 11/1/2, ff.324–5.
28. *Ibid.* ff.343–4, 355–60.
29. PRO Works 1/36, p. 384; 1/37, pp. 16, 54; Works 11/6/5, f.91.
30. *Ibid.* 11/6/6, ff.1, 16; 11/9/7, f.42; Wyman's *Architect's, Engineer's and Building-trades Directory* (1868), 165 (Jay); *PP* 1852–3 (846) lxxxiii, correspondence on supplemental estimates for New Houses of Parliament, Barry's memorandum of 6 May 1853.
31. PRO Works 11/6/6, ff.26–8; 11/6/7, ff.22, 27.
32. *Ibid.* 11/9/7, ff.40, 42.
33. N. Pevsner, *Buildings of England: London I, The Cities of London and Westminster* (1957), 459.
34. *Art-Architect*, 48, 56.
35. PRO Works 11/9/7, ff.36–40; A. Barry, *Life*, 255; *Athenaeum*, 1844, p. 460. Scarisbrick Hall is illustrated, P. Stanton, *Pugin* (1971), 28.
36. *King's Works*, vi, 248–9.
37. *3 Parl. Deb.* cxxix, 1313, 1316.
38. *PP* 1852–3 (846) lxxxiii.
39. Broadlands MS. WFC/DD.1/3.
40. *PP* 1854–5 (333) liii. See also *Civil Engineer*, vii (1844), 183.
41. *PP* 1854 [1715] xxvii, 329.
42. *3 Parl. Deb.* xcvii, 144–5; *PP* 1857–8 (49) xlviii, p. 9.
43. *Ibid.*; *3 Parl. Deb.* cxlvi, 150–2. Cp. the anti-Barry note in the *Observer* (with which Hall had a link), 25 Jan. 1857, p. 5.
44. *PP* 1857–8 (49) xlviii. Cp. Nash's attitude to Buckingham Palace bills, *King's Works*, vi, 160–2, 324.
45. *PP* 1857–8 (49) xlviii, 2–3. For Hall's personal interest in architecture see M. Fraser, 'Young Mr and Mrs Hall', *Nat. Library of Wales Jnl* xiii (1963–4), 37.
46. *PP* 1857–8 (49) xlviii, 18–22; *3 Parl. Deb.* cxlvi, 154.
47. *PP* 1857–8 (49) xlviii, 23.
48. PRO Works 11/7/6, ff.9, 12.
49. *3 Parl. Deb.* cxlvi, 158.
50. *PP* 1857–8 (49) xlviii, 24.
51. *Ibid.* 9, 24.
52. *Ibid.* 25–6 (original papers in PRO Works 11/9/6, ff.17–32). For Nash, see *King's Works*, vi, 160–2.
53. *PP* 1857–8 (297) xlviii, 13; *ibid.* (160), pp. 1–2 (18 Feb. 1858).
54. *Ibid.* (160), p. 2. In 1851 Barry had of his own authority quietly added to Grissell's contract the considerable works of the Commons' private

entrance, for which he was reprimanded by the New Palace Commissioners, Works 11/6/3, ff.34, 36.

55. *PP* 1857–8 (297), 15 Apr. 1858.

56. *Ibid.* (160), 3–5.

57. *Ibid.* (297), 14.

58. *3 Parl. Deb.* cxix, 400; cl, 1203.

59. *Ibid.* civ, 59; cxxxiii, 1285; cxli, 246; cxlvi, 162; cliv, 1342; clvii, 228–30; clviii, 881. *PP* 1861 (504) xxxv, Report of the Committee on the Decay of the Stone of the New Palace at Westminster. See also *PP* 1860 (186), (309) and (475) xl, Accounts and correspondence; 1867–8 (487) lv, report on experiments; and 1870 (142) liv, reports on results of experiments; *The Times* 9 July 1857, p. 12, letter from James Knight.

60. *PP* 1926 [Cmd. 2752] xxiii, 435 ff. (Memorandum based on report by Sir Frank Baines).

61. The story from Barry's point of view is told in A. Barry, *Life*, 171–81. A lively account based on *PP* is given by P. Ferriday, *Lord Grimthorpe* (1957), chaps. 3, 4, 6, and 7. The official correspondence was printed in *PP* 1852 (415), (500) and (500-I) xlii; 1854–5 (436) liii. For parliamentary comments, see, e.g. *3 Parl. Deb.* cxl, 148–9 (4 Feb. 1856); cxli, 245–6; clvii, 103, 336.

62. Ferriday, *Lord Grimthorpe*, 40–1; *The Times*, 22 Oct. 1856. See also M. Fraser, 'Sir Benjamin Hall in Parliament in the 1850s', *Nat. Library of Wales Jnl* xv (1967–8), 389–92, and references there cited. That Hall stood at least 6 ft 4 in made the name particularly appropriate.

63. *Descriptive Account of the Palace of Westminster*, Warrington & Co. (1872), 15. *3 Parl. Deb.* cliv, 1339, 1346.

64. *The Times*, 25 Aug. 1859, given in full by Ferriday, *Grimthorpe*, 205–7.

65. *The Times*, 11 Oct. 1859, quoted by Ferriday, *Grimthorpe*, 50–1.

66. *PP* 1860 (553) xl, Reports on Condition of the Great Bell of New Palace by John Tyndall, John Percy, G. B. Airy and G. Mears.

67. *3 Parl. Deb.* clvii, 218, 1949.

Chapter IX. The Completion of the New Palace, 1860–70

1. *3 Parl. Deb.* clix, 518–9; PRO Works 11/20, 4 Sept. 1860. The Tudor portraits in the Prince's Chamber were executed 'by, or under the direction of' Richard Burchett, head of the Dept. of Science & Art's training school, S. Kensington (*PP* 1860 (320) xl, 691).

2. *PP* 1867 (269) lxviii, 5 June 1860; E. M. Barry, *Lectures on Architecture*, ed. with introductory memoir by A. Barry (1881), 26–8.

3. *PP* 1867 (269) lxviii, 8 June 1860.

4. *Ibid.*, 3–5, 9; *Lectures*, 54.

5. *Lectures*, 431, 63.

6. *Architect*, i (1869), 214–15; *3 Parl. Deb.* cci, 713.

7. *PP* 1867 (269) lxviii, 4; Lady Mount Temple, *Memorials* [of William Cowper Temple] (privately printed, 1890), 50.

8. *Lectures*, 33; *3 Parl. Deb.* clxxvii, 498; clxxix, 247.

9. *Ibid.* clxxxi, 1523; cxcii, 301; PRO Works 11/7/1 *passim*. Works 11/160 contains the specifications for the subway, and E. Barry's designs are Works 29/3131–6; those for the railings are Works 29/2076–83.

Henry Broadhurst (1840–1911), one of the first working-class MPs, worked on this arcade as a 'rougher-out' about 1867, see H. Broadhurst, *Henry Broadhurst, M.P.* (1901), 29. The carving work was contracted to one Herp, and the sculptures executed by Armstead.

10. *Lectures*, 33; PRO Works 11/9/6, ff.30, 67–9; *3 Parl. Deb.* clxxix, 251; cxcvi, 744; cxcvii, 685; cxcix, 236; ccvii, 653, 670.

11. *Ibid.* cxcvii, 679, 683, 1429ff.; cxcviii, 708–20; BM Add. MS. 38997, ff.221–3 (Barry to Layard, 27 Jan. 1870), 236–7; PRO Works 11/248; NRA, Broadlands Mss, E. M. Barry to Cowper, 29 June 1860 (by permission of the Broadlands Trustees). Barry's designs for the roof panels are Works 29/1724–5 (8 Feb. 1869); and Moore's cartoons, in oil on canvas, are Works 29/1732 (cost £126).

12. *The Times*, 28 June 1871.

13. *3 Parl. Deb.* cciii, 915–6; ccxii, 439, 448; ccxv, 447–8, 648; BM Add. MS. 38998, ff.121–2 (30 June 1870), 431–3; PRO Works 11/248.

14. *PP* 1867 (451) viii, Report of Committee on House of Commons (Arrangements); *3 Parl. Deb.* cxcv, 258–67.

15. *Ibid.* 285.

16. R. Jenkins, *Sir Charles Dilke* (1968 edn.), 233. Dilke subsequently secured his seat habitually by attending prayers and slipping a card into the back of the seat. A similar practice in 1774 is referred to by P. D. G. Thomas, *The House of Commons in the Eighteenth Century* (Oxford, 1971), 128–9.

17. *3 Parl. Deb.* clxxxviii, 536–7; cxcv, 301, 258 ff, 299.

18. *Ibid.* cxcii, 301; *PP* 1867 (351) viii, First Report of Committee on the Kitchen and Refreshment Rooms.

19. *PP* 1867 (451) viii, qq.217, 220, 235, 215, 112, 65; and Appendix.

20. These are all printed in the Appendix to the Committee's final report (see next note).

21. *PP* 1867–8 (265) viii, Report of Committee on the House of Commons (Arrangements) [Headlam Committee, 2nd Report].

22. *3 Parl. Deb.* cxcv, 278.

23. *Ibid.* 282, 294–304.

24. *Ibid.* cxcvii, 962–4.

25. *PP* 1868–9 (392) vii, Report from Committee on Plans for New Dining Rooms, &c; 1870 (351) liv, Barry's proposals for new Refreshment Rooms, House of Lords, 27 July 1869; 1870 (374) liv, Correspondence between Barry and First Commissioner of Works relating to plans for new Refreshment Rooms, June 1870; *3 Parl. Deb.* ccii, 1362; cciii, 252, 902–13. Further important changes were made in 1895, *PP* 1895 (i) lxxix.

26. *Ibid.* cxcviii, 4 ff.; *PP* HL 1867–8 (136), Report of Committee of the House of Lords on the Construction of the House.
27. *3 Parl. Deb.* ccvii, 522; cci, 703.
28. *PP* 1870 (154) liv, Correspondence between the First Commissioner of Works and E. M. Barry, Jan.–March 1870.
29. *3 Parl. Deb.* cci, 717.
30. *PP* 1870 (154) liv, 10 Feb. 1870.
31. *Ibid.*
32. *Ibid.*
33. *3 Parl. Deb.* cc, 70, 637, 988.
34. *Ibid.* cci, 670 ff.
35. *The Times*, 8 July 1870. For ownership of architects' plans see F. Jenkins, *Architect and Patron* (1961), 215.
36. By 152 votes to 109. For the debate, see *3 Parl. Deb.* cci, 670–729. Outside Parliament there was almost universal disapproval of Ayrton's behaviour; see, e.g. *Art Jnl*, xvi (1870), 85, 193, 360.
37. *PP* 1871 (199) lvi, Correspondence between First Commissioner of Works and E. M. Barry, March 1870–March 1871.
38. *Ibid.*; *3 Parl. Deb.* ccvii, 524, 648 ff.; PRO Works 11/19/4, f.66.
39. *PP* 1871 (199) lvi, Correspondence between First Commissioner of Works and E. M. Barry, no. 36 (9 Dec. 1870).
40. *3 Parl. Deb.* ccvii, 522–4, 648 ff.
41. See *King's Works*, vi, 182.
42. See M. H. Port, 'The New Law Courts Competition, 1866–7', *Architectural History* xi (1968).
43. *3 Parl. Deb.* ccvii, 522, 653–7; ccxii, 439.
44. *Ibid.* ccxii, 437, 439 ff.
45. *PP* 1894 (268) xii; 1901 (234) vi; *3 Parl. Deb.* ccvii, 672.

Chapter X. The Techniques of the Building

1. PRO Works 11/5/17, Rennie to Chawner (25 June), and Walker to Chawner (19 June 1835). For Walker, see Boase, *Mod. Eng. Biog.* iii.
2. PRO Works 11/5/17, Walker to Chawner, 13 May 1837.
3. E. M. Barry, 'An Account of the New Palace at Westminster, and the progress of building the same', RIBA *Trans*, viii (1858), 80. Sir Charles Barry claimed in 1856 that he had made 'important modifications' in Walker's works, 'upon which I rely mainly for the safety of the embankment and its superstructure', see correspondence in *The Times*, 21, 22, 26 and 28 Feb. 1856.
4. PRO Works 1/22, pp. 302, 307–8; Works 29/3112–20 (contract drawings); *PP* 1847–8 (46-II) lx, p. 14.
5. G. S. Dalrymple, 'A Description of the Coffre Dam at the . . . Houses of Parliament', *Proc. ICE*, ii (1840), 18–19; James Nasmyth, patent no. 9850, 24 July 1848.
6. *CE*, ii (1839), 157.
7. Messrs F. & H. Flowers of Limehouse won the contract for removing the coffer-dam in October 1848 (PRO Works 11/5/17, f.37). The drawing of the piles gave rise to warnings, and it was decided to cut them off (*ibid.* f.48; *B*, vii (1849), 93,520). Underwater cutting was expensive and complicated: two platforms were required, one above the other, attached to the top of the piles. Above, men powered a saw, whilst below one drove the saw into the pile. The apparatus moved from pile to pile, the few left to support it being drawn subsequently without risk to foundations. The additional cost of cutting was £800 (PRO Works 11/5/17, 1 Mar. 1849). See *Encyclopaedia Metropolitana* (1845), viii, 386, *sub* 'Manufactures' (by P. W. Barlow, written 1836).
8. *CE*, i (1837), 33; PRO Works 11/5/18, f.4.
9. Dalrymple, art. cit.
10. *GM*, 1839, i, 535.
11. *CE*, ii (1839), p.v.
12. *Ibid.* i (1837), 34.
13. See J. M. Crook, 'Sir Robert Smirke: A Pioneer of Concrete Construction', *Trans. Newcomen Soc.* xxxviii (1965–6), 5–22.
14. PRO Works 11/5/18, f.4 (8 Nov. 1837). Barry's specification was still being followed in 1869 (Works 11/160).
15. E. Dobson, *Rudimentary Treatise on Foundations and Concrete Works* (1850), 41.
16. E. M. Barry, RIBA *Trans.* viii (1858), 84.
17. *Ibid.*, p. 86; PRO Works 11/6/2, f.12.
18. See *PP* 1831 (329) iv, First and Second Reports on Windsor Castle and Buckingham Palace. See also A. W. Skempton and H. R. Johnson, 'The First Iron Frames', *AR*, cxxxi (1962), 175–86; *King's Works*, vi, 276, 415, 476.
19. E. M. Barry, RIBA *Trans.* viii (1858), 91.
20. J. Weale's *Quarterly Papers on Engineering*, pt. 5 (1844), reprinted in *B*, ii (1844), 581.
21. *PP* 1844 (448) vi, qq. 150–1; and (629) vi.
22. E. M. Barry, RIBA *Trans.* viii (1858), 91.
23. Ryde, *Illustrations* (1849).
24. The top four floors were removed in 1960–1 and replaced by seven new floors; see *Structural Engineer*, March 1961.
25. HLRO file 381/58, memorandum by J. W. Worricker (1962), p. 4.
26. *Ibid.*, p. 3.
27. Holmes, *Illustrations* (1865).
28. *Structural Engineer*, March 1961; PRO Works 11/7/5, f.7.
29. Ryde, *Illustrations* (1849).
30. H. R. Hitchcock, *Early Victorian Architecture* (1954), i, 292; *Architecture of the Nineteenth and Twentieth Centuries* (1971), 335–41.
31. P. Collins, *Changing Ideals in Modern Architecture 1750–1950* (1965), 238.
32. PRO Works 29/3122; 29/1601, dated 27 July 1841.
33. *Ibid.* 29/3052, 29/1603.
34. *Ibid.* 29/1606, 29/1603. See p. 221 below.
35. C. Barry, jr, 'Some Description of the Mechanical Scaffolding used at the new Palace

at Westminster', RIBA *Trans.* (1856–7), 156.

36. T. Grissell, 'Account of the Scaffolding used in erecting the "Nelson Column", Trafalgar Square', *Proc. ICE*, iii (1844), 203–17; *The Times*, 10 Sept. 1844; *ILN*, i (1842), 104.

37. C. Barry, jr, art. cit., on which the following descriptions are based.

38. E. M. Barry, RIBA *Trans.* viii (1858), 86.

39. C. Barry, jr, art. cit., 156.

40. P. Journet, 'Description of the System of Scaffolding, employed at Paris, for the repairs of Public Buildings, Obelisks, &c., and of a Machine for raising Bricks, and other Building Materials', *Proc. ICE*, iii (1844), 218–23. J. Spurgin, 'A New or Improved Ladder or Machinery applicable to the Working of Mines and other useful Purposes', Patent no. 7054, 6 Oct. 1836; *B*, ii (1844), 466.

41. Journet, art, cit., 164.

42. Jabez James, 'On the Process of Raising and Hanging the Bells, in the Clock Tower, at the New Palace, Westminster', *Proc. ICE*, xix (1858–9), 3–20.

43. PRO Works 2/3, ff.545, 556; *PP* 1861 (504) xxxv, q.1909.

44. For the scale of their railway construction force, see J. H. Clapham, *Economic History of Modern Britain*, i (1926), 408.

45. *PP* 1861 (504) xxxv, Report on decay of the stone of the New Palace at Westminster (on which the rest of this paragraph is largely based); PRO Works 11/9/7, f.4.

46. *PP* 1861 (504) xxxv, qq.788, 802.

47. *Ibid.* qq.968 ff., 1895–1932, 1941; *Morn. Chronicle*, 6 Nov. 1841 (letter from Allen); *Northern Star*, 27 Nov. 1841; *The Times*, 10 Sept. 1844.

48. PRO Works 11/9/3, f.2.

49. *Ibid.*; Works 2/4, pp. 341–5, 522–5; H. Hobhouse, *Thomas Cubitt: Master Builder* (1971), Chap. 14.

50. PRO Works 11/8/4 (a description by Barry of Jordan's machine is quoted, *King's Works*, vi, 613n.); 11/6/5, ff.25–6; 11/28/16, ff.9–10.

51. *Ibid.* 11/9/3, ff.15, 16, 18.

52. *Ibid.* 11/11/3, f.175; 11/28/16, ff.9–10; plans: PRO, MPE 813/1 and 845.

53. Barry's grandson presented three plaster-of-paris models of the three great towers to the First Commissioner of Works in 1916, on condition they were placed in the Houses of Parliament 'where they can at times be seen by the public'. Recently re-discovered in the Clock Tower, two were exhibited in the Victoria & Albert Museum in 1973 (*Marble Halls*, p. 33, illustrated), and now may be seen in the Victoria Tower. They were probably the models exhibited by E. M. Barry in his RIBA lecture, 1858.

54. Cf. Thomas Cubitt's joiner's shop, which in 1845 had 'some thirteen to eighteen benches each worth £300'; by 1876 it possessed 'four circular saw benches, a cross-cutting saw bench, and a circular sawing and moulding bench'. His brother's establishment on the Isle of Dogs, again on a large scale, in 1854 had 'one circular

and three vertical sawing machines' and a planing machine: H. Hobhouse, *Thomas Cubitt*, 286, 490 (quoting *B*, xii (1854), 2–4), 491.

55. *PP* 1849 [1123] xxix, Report of Commissioners appointed to inquire into the Application of Iron to Railway Structures, qq. 342, 422.

56. PRO Works 11/7/5, f.1.

Chapter XI. The Building Services

1. See excellent drawings of machinery in Agricola, *De Re Metallica* (Basle, 1556; English language edn. 1950).

2. T. Tredgold, 'On the Principles and Practice of Warming and Ventilating Buildings', *Edinburgh Philosophical Jnl.* xii (1825); C. Hood, *sub* 'Ventilation', *Encyclopaedia Metropolitana* (1845), xxv, 1056.

3. Cresy, *Encyclopaedia of Civil Engineering* (1847), 613.

4. *Phil. Trans. Royal Soc.* 1836.

5. T. Tredgold, *Principles of Warming and Ventilating Public Buildings* (1824), 72; Hood, art. cit. p. 1051; W. Mackenzie, 'On the Mechanical Ventilation and Warming of St George's Hall, Liverpool', *Proc. I. Mech. E.* (1863), 197.

6. See 'Description of the system of ventilation and warming adopted at the model prison, Pentonville', *Mechanic's Mag.* xlix (1848), 26–30.

7. *PP* 1835 (262) xviii.

8. *PP* 1835 (583) xviii.

9. *Ibid.*, Pl. 4.

10. *PP* 1835 (583) xviii, esp. Pl. 4.

11. Hood, op. cit., 1054.

12. PRO Works 11/12/30, 24 Jan. 1840. See above, pp. 102–3.

13. *PP* 1841, sess. 2 (51) i, 8.

14. *Ibid.*, 7, 9, 11.

15. *Ibid.*, 19.

16. *Ibid.*, 3.

17. *PP* 1842 (536) xiv, 3.

18. See above, pp. 115–16. So little had Reid's engineer assistant John Imray to do at this time that he 'was employed to a large extent in making surveys for railways' (*Proc. I. Mech. E.* (1902), 1026).

19. *The Times*, 20 Mar. 1846 and 5 Apr. 1847.

20. 3 *Parl. Deb.* cxix, 400.

21. *Ibid.*, 1147.

22. *Ibid.*, 233.

23. *PP* 1852 (243, 402) xvi, First and Second Reports on Ventilation and Lighting of the House.

24. *PP* 1852 (402) xvi, App. 14. PRO Works 29/2964 (Aug. 1852) shows the iron-framed Lords' boiler house, with five Cornish boilers, supplied and fixed by Messrs Jeakes (Works 11/16/3, 27 Feb. 1850).

25. *PP* 1852 (402) xvi, App. 1, from which the following account is taken.

26. *PP* 1854 (384) ix, Report from Select Com-

mittee of House of Lords on possibility of improving ventilation and lighting.

27. *PP* 1852–3 (570) xxxiv, report from First Commissioner of Works, 9 May 1853.

28. *PP* 1846 (719) xv, pp. 24, 27; (349) xv, p. 3; *The Times*, 27 May 1846.

29. *PP* 1852 (237) xlii, Gurney's first report, April 1852, p. 237.

30. *PP* 1852 (402) xvi, p. 130.

31. *PP* 1854 (384) ix.

32. *PP* 1854 (149) ix, First Report on best means of improving ventilation. Cp. *PP* 1837–8 (358) xxxvi.

33. *PP* 1890–1 (371) xii. Among his experiments, Gurney 'suspended feathers from silken threads' in order to determine the route of draughts in the House; he also improved the humidity of the atmosphere (*PP* 1854 (270) ix).

34. F. Sheppard, *London 1808–1870: The Infernal Wen* (1971), 281–3; Broadlands (Palmerston) MSS, GC/HA 48 (by permission of the Trustees of the Broadlands Archives).

35. *3 Parl. Deb.* cliv, 1339, 15 July 1859.

36. *Ibid.* 1341; clxxix, 252, 12 May 1865.

37. *PP* 1866 (98) lvi, Percy to First Commissioner, 20 Feb. 1866.

38. *PP* 1903 (227) v, First Report of Select Committee on House of Commons (Ventilation), q.61. The evidence of E. G. Rivers, engineer to the Office of Works, q.6, gives a short description and history of the ventilation of the palace, which is supplemented by the evidence of William Jacob Prim, resident engineer at the Palace 1867–97, qq.47 ff.

39. *PP* 1866 (98) lvi, E. M. Barry to A. Austin, 29 Apr. 1865.

40. *PP* (HL) 1867–8 (136), q.194. Apprehensions about the boilers in 1865 resulted in the calling in of the Manchester Association for the Prevention of Boiler Explosions (*PP* 1866 (98) lvi, p. 11).

41. V. C. Joly, *Traité Pratique du Chauffage et de la Ventilation* (Paris, 1869), reprinted in Spon's *Dictionary of Engineering* (1871), iv, 3036.

42. *B*, x (1852), 129; Spon, iv, 3036.

43. *PP* 1852 (402) xvi, p. 539.

44. *Mechanic's Mag.*, xxxi (1839), 96; see also *DNB sub* Gurney.

45. *PP* 1842 (251) xiv, p. 7; and 1852 (481) xlii, p. 163.

46. *PP* 1852 (243) and (402) xvi; *ILN*, 24 Apr. 1852.

47. *PP* 1852–3 (570) xxxiv, Report of Standing Committee on Ventilation and Lighting; 1852–3 (911) lxxxiii, Report of G. Gurney on lighting of Commons; *CJ*, cviii (1852–3), 159, appointment of Standing Committee, 29 Nov. 1852.

48. *PP* 1854 (149), (270) and (403) ix, Reports on best means of improving ventilation; 1854 (384) ix, Report of Lords' Committee on improving ventilation.

49. *PP* 1866 (98) lvi; see also, for expenditure on lighting, 1861, xxxv, p. 533; 1872, xlvii, p. 27.

50. *RIBA Trans.* viii (1858), 81.

51. R. Phillips, *Philosophical Mag.* (1831), 8, quoting C. Babbage, *Reflections on the decline of Science in England*, p. x; *The Times*, 5 Apr. 1847 (see also 17 Aug. 1846). For Reid's self-justification see, in addition to *Parliamentary Papers* already cited, D. B. Reid, *Illustrations of the Theory and Practice of Ventilation* (1844), and *Ventilation. A Reply to mis-statements made by 'The Times' and by 'The Athenaeum' in reference to ships and buildings ventilated by the author* (1845).

52. Support for Reid's 'up cast' principle of ventilating was given in 1906 by Dr John Aitken, FRS, 'Memorandum on the Ventilation of the House of Commons', *PP* 1906 [Cd. 3035] xciv, Report and recommendations of committee . . . on the question of improving the ventilation, App. p. 116.

53. Important aspects of the building services that space does not permit examination of are water-supply and sewerage. Though less controversial than ventilation, the sewerage of the Palace was not without its contentious aspects. The large sewer constructed under Barry's direction in 1839 flowed from north to south, emptying into the Abingdon Street sewer. In 1848 on the advice of John Phillips C.E., the flow was reversed, and the form of invert and gradient were improved: the sewer then emptied into the Bridge Street sewer, five feet lower than that in Abingdon Street, but again above the parliamentary sewer so that pumping was still required. After perennial complaints, a report (*PP* 1884–5, lxii) led to the adoption of the Shone hydro-pneumatic system, powered by Atkinson's differential gas engine (*PP* 1850 (482) xxxiii; and E. Ault, 'The Shone hydro-pneumatic sewerage system', *Trans. Soc. of Engineers*, 4 Apr. 1887). This system, now worked by a steam-engine, is still in use.

Chapter XII. The Palace of History and Art
2. Architectural Sculpture

1. A. Barry, *Life*, 258.

2. *PP* 1843 [499] xxix, Second Report, p. 11.

3. *Ibid.* 1845 [671] xxvii, Fourth Report, p. 10; 1847 [862] xxxiii, Seventh Report, p. 17; 1848 [1009] xxii, Eighth Report, p. 9; R. J. B. Walker, 'Catalogue', pt. III, Sculpture (1961), p. 98, quoting 3 *PD* cxi, 352–3.

4. *PP* 1861 [2806] xxxii, Twelfth Report, p. 13; 1863 [3141] xvi, Thirteenth Report, p. 12; *Art Jnl*, ix (1870), 79; PRO Works 11/22/2, ff.49, 80.

5. A. Barry, *Reply*, 45.

6. *PP* 1843 [499] xxix, Second Report, p. 10.

7. There is a drawing in HLRO, Moulton Barrett vol., f.154.

8. Ryde, *Illustrations* (1849), Pl. VII, commentary; *Guide and Descriptive Account of the Palace of Westminster* (n.d.) [?c. 1912], 15.

9. *PP* 1845 [671] xxvii, Fourth Report, app. 4, p. 12.

10. HLRO, Moulton Barrett vol., ff.55, 64; PRO Works 29/529 and 542.

11. *Ibid.* 11/9/7, ff.3, 5.

12. *Ibid.* ff.24, 26; Ryde, *Illustrations*, Pl. VIII and commentary, Pl. III, commentary; *ILN*, xii, 190 (18 Mar. 1848); xxi, 400 (13 Nov. 1852).

13. PRO Works 11/9/7, f.28; *ILN* xii, 190 (18 Mar. 1848); xxi, 376 (6 Nov. 1852); xxiv, 113 (4 Feb. 1854); xxvi, 136 (10 Feb. 1855); *The Times*, 16 Sept. 1853, p. 8.

14. *PP* 1847 [862] xxxiii, Seventh Report, p. 17; Walker, 'Catalogue', pp. 97–8; *PP* 1858 [2425] xxiv, Eleventh Report, p. 7. The sculptors were J. Thomas (Abp. Langton and E. of Salisbury), J. E. Thomas (Abp. of Dublin and E. of Pembroke), P. M'Dowell (Master of the Temple and E. Warren), H. Timbrell (Clare and Aumale), J. S. Westmacott (Gloucester and Winchester), J. Thornycroft (Hereford and Norfolk), Thrupp (Oxford and Fitzwalter), and A. H. Ritchie (Vesci and Mowbray).

15. PRO Works 11/9/7, f.52; 11/22/2, f.101.

16. See C. Handley-Read, 'Sculpture and Modelling in Victorian Architecture', *Royal Soc. of British Sculptors 1960 Annual Report* (1961), 36–7; C. Eastlake, *Contributions to the Literature of the Fine Arts*, ed. H. Bellenden Ker (1848), vi, 61–94 (originally part of App. 12, Third Report of Fine Arts Commissioners, *PP* 1844 [585] xxxi, pp. 31–44).

17. Unless otherwise indicated, information concerning John Thomas is derived from his obituary, *ILN*, xli, 231–3 (30 Aug. 1862). See also *Art Jnl*, xi (1849), 340; *DNB*; and R. Gunnis, *Dictionary of British Sculptors 1660–1851* (revised edn., n.d.), 388.

18. E. W. Pugin, *Art-Architect*, 32.

19. Walker, 'Catalogue', 95. I was unable to confirm the reference there cited to PRO Works 11.

20. *ILN* obituary (this would make it 1837); PRO Works 1/25, p. 85.

21. *PP* 1850 (709) xxxiii, General statement of expenditure; PRO Works 11/1/2, ff.353–4.

22. *Ibid.* 1/30, p. 221; *PP* 1850 (709) xxxiii, p. 4. See also *Art Jnl*, xi (1849), 340; Ryde, *Illustrations*, Pl. VI commentary; *ILN* obituary; A. Barry, *Life*, 199; PRO Works 11/28/16, ff.23, 24; C. L. Eastlake, *History of the Gothic Revival* (1872), 185.

23. A. Barry, *Reply*, 92, 44, 45, 81.

24. E.g., sketchy—PRO Works 29/316 and 1915; RIBA Drawings, Barry, RAN 2/E/5, 2/I/8. Absent—PRO Works 29/521 and 1745.

25. For coats-of-arms see HLRO, Moulton Barrett vol., ff.150, 154, 155, 157, 159, 161, 163, 165, 167, 169, 171; RIBA Drawings, John Thomas, vol. i, f.26. For bosses, see V & A, Dept. of Prints and Drawings, H.l.a, 8251.1, 8521.2; RIBA Drawings, RAN 2/J/10 (catalogued under Barry). For the royal figures, RIBA Drawings, John Thomas, vol. i, 27–35; ii, 1–3.

26. DoE nos. H.13378–13414, 13427–35. For relevant correspondence, see PRO Works 11/28/16, ff.21–39.

27. PRO Works 29/300, 316, 1687 and 1688; RIBA Drawings, 'Barry' RAN 2/B/11 (1).

28. PRO Works 29/800, 1745 and 1747.

29. *Ibid.* 529 and 2029.

30. *Ibid.* 542.

31. See PRO Works 11/9/4, ff. 7, 33, 39 and 68–101 (catalogue); *Inventory of Plaster Casts in Various Styles ... acquired by the South Kensington Museum* (1874), 10.

32. Walker, 'Catalogue', App. III, 'John Thomas and the Thames Bank Workshop'; H. Hobhouse, *Thomas Cubitt* (1971), 221–2; PRO Works 11/9/3, ff.4, 15, 16.

33. *ILN* xii (1848), 190; H. Broadhurst, *Henry Broadhurst, M.P.* (1901), 29; *Companion to the Almanac, 1842*, ed. C. Knight, 217.

34. PRO Works 11/9/3, ff.1–3; *Athenaeum*, 1856, p. 110; *Northern Star*, 13 Apr. 1842; A. Barry, *Reply*, 91.

35. See, e.g. RIBA Drawings, Rickman E/1/3.3, and E/1/14.

36. See certain Birmingham Grammar School drawings in RIBA Drawings under 'Barry': C 5/1 (1–5), dated 1832; C 5/2 (17); C 5/4 (3), dated January 1835; C 5/5 (6), dated January 1835. This point is confirmed by Gibson in A. Barry, *Reply*, 73.

37. P. B. Stanton, 'Welby Pugin and the Gothic Revival', London Ph.D. thesis (1952), 410, citing *PP* 1841 (423) vi, p. 2; A. Barry, *Reply*, 66.

38. See those in RIBA Drawings, and V & A Print Room. See also Ryde, *Illustrations*, Pl. VI commentary; *Art Jnl* (1849), 340.

39. *Companion to the Almanac, 1842*, ed. C. Knight, 217 (reference by courtesy of Dr Priscilla Metcalf).

40. *ILN* obituary.

41. See E. W. Brayley and J. Britton, *History of the Ancient Palace ... at Westminster* (1836), Pl. xxi (ogee and cusping, window C), xxv (joining of two panels, exterior of cloister buttress), xix and xxxv (quatrefoils and tracery in spandrels).

42. A. Barry, *Life*, 109.

43. See Gunnis, *Dictionary*, for all except Armstead. Gunnis states that Birnie Philip was also employed on ornamental work, but this, it seems clear from Philip's own testimony (A. Barry, *Reply*, 89), related to wood carving.

44. Thomas designed Somerleyton Hall, Suffolk (1844–56) and the Regent's Park Chapel for Sir Morton Peto, until 1846 Grissell's partner as contractor at Westminster. For Barry he did further ornamental sculpture at, e.g., Bridgewater House (1845–54) and Harewood (1848–50). He was employed by Prince Albert on decorative work at Balmoral, Windsor and Buckingham Palace. His sculpture was to be found as far afield as Constantinople. (See *ILN* obituary; T. S. R. Boase, *English Art 1800–1870* (1959), 198; A. Barry, *Life*, 117; W. Ames, *Prince Albert and Victorian Taste* (1967), 104, 109,

110, 114, 115, 133, 165, 218, 220, and Pl. 63, 64, 75.)

Chapter XII
3. Stained Glass

1. Barry, *Life*, 257.

2. *PP* 1843 [499] xxix, Second Report of the Commissioners on the Fine Arts, p. 8.

3. In 1845 Barry considered buying two collections of stained glass (PRO Works 11/9/4, ff.4–6). The following year he had some 2,000 specimens, mainly of carved woodwork but including glass (Works 11/9/4, f.33).

4. Barry, *Life*, 247.

5. A number of Pugin's copies after early windows are in RIBA Drawings.

6. For the notice relating to stained glass, dated 16 June 1843, see the Appendix to the Second Report, of the Fine Arts Commissioners, *PP* 1843 [499] xxix, p. 69. Exhibitors had to submit (a) one and not more than two coloured designs for an entire window, drawn to scale (2 in to 1 ft), and (b) a specimen of stained glass representing part of the same design full scale. Entries had to be 'designed in general accordance with the style of architecture and decoration' of the Palace. Subjects were to be 'either figures or heraldic devices relating to the Royal Families of England . . . and may be accompanied by borders, diapered grounds, legends, and similar enrichments.' The competition was limited to British artists and the work had to be submitted in the first week of March 1844.

7. *PP* 1846 [685] xxiv, Fifth Report of the Commissioners on the Fine Arts, pp. 9–10.

8. *PP* 1846 [749] xxiv, Sixth Report of the Commissioners on the Fine Arts, p. 10.

9. PRO Works 11/9/4, ff.42–3. Barry's defence is the clearest account we have of this confused episode.

10. PRO Works 11/7/12, ff.5–8.

11. He was also prominent in Scots literary circles, publishing several volumes of popular poems and songs. For further details, see *DNB*.

12. HLRO. The drawings, each approximately 15¾ × 8½ in, laid on blue card, are in a maroon morocco folder entitled *Suggestions/regarding the/Stained Glass/for the/Windows of the/House of Lords* in gold lettering. Tipped into this are three printed pages, all of which must have been sent to Eastlake and placed with the drawings at a later date. The first is a title-page (*Suggestions/regarding the/Windows of the House of Lords* (etc.)). The second (which must originally have been placed third) is headed 'Suggestions referred to in the Forgoing Letter': this is the 'explanation' of the scheme to which the letter refers. The third (originally second) page has the letter to Eastlake, addressed from 15 Hanover Street, Edinburgh.

13. *PP* 1844 [585] xxxi, Third Report, p. 19.

14. *A Treatise on Painted Glass, showing its applicability to every style of architecture* (London and Edinburgh, 1845), 47. This was reviewed with illustrations in *ILN*, ix, 107 (15 Aug. 1846).

15. Powell left a graphic description of his arrival at Pugin's house, The Grange, Ramsgate, in his manuscript 'Pugin in his Home', written in 1889 (typescript copy, V & A Library, Box II 72.B).

16. The Birmingham Art Gallery has a large collection of cartoons and sketches for the glass, and a smaller group of preparatory drawings is in HLRO (both given by John Hardman studios in Birmingham, where a pair of cartoons for lancets in the Star Chamber Court may still be seen).

17. HLRO, Moulton-Barrett vol., short page following p. 255. The monarchs are, from L. to R., Matilda, Queen of Henry I (under canopy), the Empress Matilda, King Stephen, and Matilda of Boulogne. The drawings, in pen and watercolour on tracing paper, seem to be records of others supplied by Pugin, as some which follow clearly are (see below, n. 38). The figures are those in the lower tier of the first window on the west side of the Chamber, the specimen window made by Hardman (see below).

18. HLRO Pencil and pen on light blue paper. Inscribed by Pugin 'James II' and 'Mary of Guelders'. Details—'gauntlet', 'ermine', etc.— are also indicated.

19. Some twenty of these studies are at Birmingham, and nine more are in HLRO. The figures are drawn about 1 ft high, full-length, singly or (occasionally) in pairs. Most are in pencil only, but some are touched with brown or mauve wash, and a few are fully developed in watercolour. According to Professor Stanton, all those in HLRO are by Powell, except a medieval King, drawn by Pugin with wash added by Powell, and a Charles II, by another hand altogether. Powell and this third hand appear to be responsible for all the Birmingham group.

20. *Pugin* (1971) 55–9, and *Concerning Architecture*, ed. J. Summerson (1968), 129.

21. Sale of Pugin's engravings, drawings and paintings, Sotheby's, 7 April 1853, lot 85. Hollar's etchings of the two Queens, after portraits by Holbein (Parthey 1342 and 1427), were framed together.

22. Professor Stanton tells me that Stothard was also a source for the armour designed by Pugin for the Grand Talbot at Alton Towers. The inscription of the Catherine of Aragon seems to refer to *Dresses and Decorations*, ii, Pl. 47, 'Margaret, Queen of Henry VI and her Court', taken from a tapestry in St Mary's Hall, Coventry.

23. Significantly, neither volume appeared at the sale of Pugin's library held at Sotheby's on 27–9 Jan. 1853. Both had probably been removed by Powell, as too valuable to part with.

24. Burne-Jones made a number of copies from *Dresses and Decorations* in two sketchbooks in the V & A, dating respectively from *c.* 1859–61 (E.1-1955: 91.D 3/7) and *c.* 1865 (E.4-1955:

91. D. 40). He and Rossetti also borrowed motifs from the book in pictures of this date.

25. Many references to this window occur in Hardman's account books and in the letters he received from Barry. Professor Stanton has been kind enough to show me transcripts of these letters, and the relevant account books were on loan to the V & A in 1972. Other Hardman papers have been given recently to the Birmingham Central Library, but unfortunately were not available for study in time for this article.

26. On 1 Mar. the window was charged to Barry's account at a sum of £200, £130 being for 'reworking and alterations'.

27. *B*, v (1847), 189 (24 Apr.). Confusion as to the relative parts played by Hardman and Ballantine in making the Lords' glass has persisted until the present day, but the reference in *B*, to which Professor Stanton drew my attention, finally reconciles what hitherto seemed conflicting evidence. The presence of studies for so many of the windows among the Hardman material at Birmingham and in HLRO need not disturb us: they were no doubt added to the rest by J. H. Powell after Pugin's death, when he became Hardman's chief designer.

26. *The Houses of Parliament . . . A hand-book guide for visitors*, H. G. Clarke & Co., (n.d.), 24. An engraving which accompanies *B*'s report on 17 Apr. 1847 shows only the third window from the throne on the west or righthand side containing figures. However, the guidebook is more likely to be reliable; and it would certainly be more natural for Hardman to make the first window in the series rather than the third. *B*'s report refers to one of the windows being in place, but the laws of perspective would have made it almost impossible to show glass in the first window, furthest away from the draughtsman's view point.

29. See above, n. 17.

30. PRO Works 11/9/7, f.34, Barry's progress report.

31. A print of the Lords in E. W. Godwin's *Buildings and Monuments, Ancient and Modern* (1850) is misleading here for it shows the windows still not complete by this date. In fact, it is the same engraving that appeared in *B*, 17 Apr. 1847, when only the specimen window had been installed.

32. PRO Works 11/7/12, f.6.

33. 'A novel and happy idea . . . first proposed in our pages', *B* x (1852), 92.

34. These can be seen in a plate in Ryde, *Illustrations*, 1849.

35. See *ILN*, 24 Apr. 1847, 261, and 1 May 1847, 281. Drawings for the Peers' Lobby are in HLRO (sketch by Pugin) and at Birmingham (cartoon).

36. *B*, ix (1851), 461. But according to notes furnished by Roger Watts of Hardmans in 1892 (PRO, Works 11/84, file 2152/1) they were filled with Royal badges.

37. Pugin's drawing for this at Westminster, in Minister's Room 17. See R. J. B. Walker,

'Catalogue', 154, No. 403.

38. Preliminary pencil and pen-over-pencil sketches by Pugin for windows on the Commons' 'polygonal' stair illustrating the life of the Black Prince, and a pencil sketch of a window in the 'Great Octagon' illustrating Saxon, Irish, Scotch and Welsh 'distinguished personalities' with heraldry in alternate lights have recently been loaned to RIBA Drawings (Mrs Stanley-Evans' loan).

Two other pen and ink sketches in HLRO show windows for the Central Octagon and St Stephen's Hall. Both windows of two tiers of five lights, with tracery above, and the main lights contain alternately single figures and heraldry. The figures in St Stephen's Hall include King Edward the Martyr, King Edward the Confessor, St Stephen, and two angels; those in the Central Octagon seem to be royal Saints. Two further figured lights, corresponding to neither of these windows, occur in Moulton-Barrett HLRO vol. (p. 257 and unnumbered preceding page). They show St George and an armed King (device, a swan), and are represented, first, by drawings in pen and watercolour perhaps by Pugin himself, and secondly, by tracings of the same.

39. His watercolour sketch, in reverse, for two of the lights (Queen and Unicorn) is in HLRO. According to Dr Stanton, this is a Pugin design developed by Powell.

40. Powell's sketch for this scene, in reverse, is HLRO. Cartoons for others are at Birmingham.

41. *PP* 1841 [423] vi, Report from the Select Committee on Fine Arts; together with the Minutes of Evidence, p. 59. Barry probably had this objection in mind when he wrote his Report on the decorations two years later. He recommended that the grounds of the windows should be 'of warm yellowish tint . . . in order that so much light *only* may be excluded as may be thought desirable to do away with either a garish or cold effect.'

42. *3 Parl. Deb.*, cxxix, 1316–8.

43. See the long Report of the Select Committee appointed to consider ways of improving the lighting and ventilation in the Commons, *PP* 1852, xvi and also PRO Works 11/7/7, ff.1–10.

44. See PRO Works 11/7/9, ff.8–16 for the Corridors, and 11/22/2, ff.52, 62 and 89 for Central Lobby; *Art Jnl*, v (1859) 80 for move from Commons to St Stephen's Hall. Some idea of the appearance of the windows in the Corridors before 1863 may be gained from the original cartoons now in the Birmingham Art Gallery. They were completely filled with heraldic designs. This glass was restored after the War to its post-1863 condition.

45. *PP* 1842 [412] xxv, First Report of the Commissioners on the Fine Arts, p. 20.

46. *PP* 1843 [499] xxix, Second Report of the Commissioners on the Fine Arts, p. 39.

47. W. Justin O'Driscoll, *A Memoir of Daniel Maclise, R.A.* (1871), 145.

48. See *B*, (1885) 265.

49. For a fuller account of the post-war restoration, see Patrick Feeny, 'The Heraldic Glass in the Houses of Parliament', *Jnl of the British Soc. of Master Glass-Painters*, xii, no. 2 (1956–7) 142–7.

50. See C. Woodforde, *English Stained and Painted Glass*, (Oxford 1954) 61.

51. Compare, for instance, the design of their east window in Bury St Edmunds Cathedral, 1868 (Woodforde, Pl. 67).

52. *Life*, 258.

53. For Willement and his work see Clive Wainwright, 'Davington Priory, Kent' (the artist's country house), *Country Life*, 9 and 16 Dec. 1971.

Chapter XII
4. Metalwork

1. Hardman day book, 1845–9, entries in the name of Barry dated 13, 16 March 1847. Each standard cost £38.10s, executed in iron, with brass panels. A further £3.15s. was added for the cost of packing and transport, thus showing that the day book entries were made after the goods had been completed and despatched. This is the invariable practice and is an invaluable guide to dates of installation.

The Hardman day books, ledgers and all the correspondence surviving in the firm's 'letter boxes', one for each year, together with a separate collection of about 150 letters from Pugin now belong to the Birmingham Reference Library. The relevant day book is hereafter referred to as *H.d.b.*, 1845–9.

2. Most cathedral gasoliers have also disappeared. The only examples traced for the exhibition of Victorian Church Art at the V & A in 1972 were two made in about 1866 by Skidmore's of Coventry for Ely Cathedral (cat. no. F.6)

3. These were installed all over the building. The first were supplied for the swing doors in the West Corridor in the Lords on 16 March 1847. *H.d.b.* 1845–9.

4. The first finger plates appear in an entry dated Mar. 1845. *H.d.b.*, 1845–9.

5. The first entry for these is dated 8 Feb. 1849. In brass, they each cost 13s.9d. *H.d.b.*, 1845–9.

6. First supplied on 26 Apr. 1848 in tinned iron at 18s. each. In brass, they cost 13s.9d. *H.d.b.*, 1845–9.

7. The first eight examples were supplied on 15 May 1851, each costing 7s. *H.d.b.*, 1845–9. A few have survived.

8. The first entry is dated 24 Feb. 1848: 'Plated Date Box, with Ivory Cards, containing sufficient for the Months, Days, & numbers for Days. £16.10s. *H.d.b.*, 1845–9.

9. The first entry is dated 28 Apr. 1848. Made of tinned iron, they each cost 17s. *H.d.b.*, 1845–9.

10. A. W. N. Pugin, *The True Principles of Pointed or Christian Architecture, set forth in two lectures delivered at St. Marie's College, Oscott* (1841), 22, 23, 29, 30; Pl. iv, figs. 6, 7.

11. S. Ayling, *Photographs of Sketches from the Notebooks of Augustus Welby N. Pugin*, 2 vols. (1865). Several of Pugin's sketchbooks are in the V & A.

12. Hardman archives: 1845 letter box. Pugin to Hardman, n.d. Supporting evidence is afforded by a letter from Pugin to Hardman in 1846; this is in a private collection, present whereabouts unknown. I am deeply grateful to Professor Stanton for making her transcripts of this and other letters available to me.

13. See Chapter VII, p. 138.

14. A partnership was formed between the Hardmans, father and son, and G. R. Elkington in 1837 to exploit a gilding process patented by the latter in 1836. S. Bury, *Victorian Electroplate* (1971), 12.

15. Barry preferred fleurs-de-lis to Pugin's crowns when he saw the vanes. Hardman archives: 1845 letter box. Pugin to Hardman, n.d., Alfred Meeson to Hardman, 15 Nov. 1845; *B.*, v (1847), 501; *H.d.b.*, 1845–9, entries dated 21 July, 7 Oct. 1845.

16. PRO Works 11/7/9, ff.1–16. Hardman's tender, 10 May 1845, endorsed by Barry 9 July, accepted 14 July.

17. Hardman archives: 1845 letter box. Pugin to Hardman, 5 letters dating from internal evidence Feb.–Apr. 1845.

18. Hardman archives: 1845 letter box. Pugin to Hardman, n.d. Another letter from Pugin to Hardman, 12 Mar. 1845, Stanton transcript.

19. PRO Works 11/7/9, ff.1–16.

20. Hardman archives: 1847 letter box. Pugin to Hardman, letter postmarked 22/23 Jan. 1847; *H.d.b.*, 1845–9, entries for 22 Dec. 1846, 12, 31 Mar., 12 July 1847. The total cost of the railing was £2006.13s.6d. Similar changes were made in the preparation of the railing for the gallery of the Commons' Chamber in 1849–50: three specimen compartments were submitted to Barry.

21. Hardman archives: 1846 letter box. Barry to Hardman, 13 Nov. 1846. *The Houses of Parliament; a description of the Houses of Lords and Commons in the New Palace of Westminster. A Hand-book for Visitors*, H. & G. Clarke & Co. [c. 1860], 39.

22. Hardman archives: 1846 letter box. Barry to Hardman, 3 and 10 Dec. 1846. Another letter, Pugin to Hardman, n.d. [late 1845], Stanton transcript.

23. *ILN*, xi (1847), 337 (ill.)

24. Hardman archives: 1847 letter box. Pugin to Hardman, n.d. [Dec. 1846, Jan./Feb. 1847, Sept. 1847]; *H.d.b.*, 1845–9, entry dated 30 Mar. 1847: '4 Brass Standards for Lighting Bar End of House of Peers, with Crowns for Wax Lights & Iron Fixing Rods, Tubes etc. 2 Rows of Lights, 13 lights each. No. 1106. £332. 2 Boxes and Packing £2'; entry dated 31 Mar. 1847: '2 Large Brass Standards for Light-

ing Throne end of House of Peers. No. 1198. With Crowns for Wax Lights, and Iron Fixing Rods, Tubes cased with Brass with 3 Rows of Lights, 29 Lights to each, at £297.10s. £595. 5 Boxes & Packing £7.12s.6d. 8 Boxes & Packing & Packing for Crowns £10.10s.' Entry for 9 Nov. 1847: '2 Large Brass Crowns for Great Standing candlesticks No. 1198 altered with New branches etc. etc. & 16 painted Shields with emblems etc. £40.' RIBA Drawings, C. Barry, 'Gothic' Folio, ff.92, 93, 95, tracings made by James Murray of Pugin's sketches for the candelabra and the standards, with details of branches for the former.

25. Pugin to Hardman, 2 letters, n.d. [1846 or early 1847; 1846]; both transcribed by Phoebe Stanton.

26. Ryde, *Illustrations* (1849), Frontispiece, 'The Peers' Lobby'.

27. Holmes, *Illustrations*, (1865), Pl. 8, 'The Commons' Lobby'; Hardman ledger, 1851–3, p. 14: '4 Brass Standards for Commons' Lobby' (the set cost £600).

28. *H.d.b.*, 1845–9, entry dated 31 Mar. 1847; 'A Brass Twisted Railing to go round Throne' £18.10s.; entry for 17 Apr. 1848: 'A Railing for Throne End of House of Peers, consisting of Compartments & Gates of Twisted Bars & Uprights . . .' £148. PRO Works 29/254, drawing of throne area with a small sketch of the outer railing, dated 1845. Does this represent the railing completed in 1848, or is it a later one of iron and brass, entered on 19 June 1850 in *H.d.b.*, 1849–54? The existing railings round the throne appear to be made entirely of brass.

29. John Webb of Old Bond Street was a prominent antiquary, dealer and furnisher with whom Pugin had been acquainted at least since 1844. Webb later became an adviser to the South Kensington Museum, ancestor of the V & A. See *Précis of the Board Minutes of the Science & Art Department, from 8 July 1863 to 23 December 1869* (1870). Webb executed the throne, Prince Albert's chair and the Prince of Wales' chair, as well as the Clerks' table in the chamber. *ILN*, x (1847) p. 293 (*ill.*), 294. The second throne is of much later date.

30. Pugin to Hardman, n.d. [1846]: letter transcribed by Phoebe Stanton; *H.d.b.*, 1845–9. 8 Jan. 1847. 'Mr. Webb, London. A Brass Rose Die, to stamp Leather, at £1.10s. 22 Gilt Enamels, of Lions, with Studs at 9s. each, 22 Oval Crystals in Gilt Mountings, at 7s. each'. (I am indebted to my colleague Clive Wainwright who has pointed out that the chairs in the Prince's Chamber were upholstered with leather stamped with Tudor roses.) Hardman's supplied the two crystals set in enamels for the arms of the throne on 24 Feb. 1847; they cost 26s. each. Quantities of chair nails were also supplied to Webb at about this time.

31. *H.d.b.*, 1845–9, entry dated 22 Feb. 1847 for the banners, costing £10.5s. each; entry dated 31 Mar. 1847 for the shields, costing £13.6s. for the pair; entry dated 2 Feb. 1847

for '8 pieces of Metal, Engraved & inlaid with Colour for Floor of Peers Lobby' at a total cost of £70. See also H. & G. Clarke, *The House of Lords; a Description of that Magnificent Apartment, together with the Peers' Lobby and the Victoria Hall, in the New Palace of Westminster* [*c*.1850], 12.

32. Hardman archives 1845 letter box, Pugin to Hardman, n.d., but written on the day of his visit to Windsor (see Pugin's MS diary for 1845, V & A); Hardman archives, Pugin to Hardman, postmarked 1 Mar. 1845. The engraver might have been Heath, who is cited in other letters as a craftsman working on the firm's memorial brasses.

33. Hardman archives: 1845 letter box, Pugin to Hardman, postmarked 12 Mar. 1845.

34. *Ibid.*, Pugin to Hardman, postmarked 12 June 1845.

35. *H.d.b.*, 1845–9, 24 Feb. 1847: [2] 'Large Wrought Iron Grates with Cast Iron Backs with Arms', each supplied with a 'Pair of ornamented Brass Dogs'. Each grate and set of dogs cost £66. There are other similar entries. See also *The Houses of Parliament*, H. & G. Clarke, [*c*.1860], p. 19.

36. Hardman archives: 1845 letter box, Pugin to Hardman, n.d., but dated to May/June on internal evidence. *H.d.b.*, 1845–9, entry dated 18 Feb. 1847 for 'A Pair of Brass Gates, on Iron Frame with Ornamental panels, Lock & key with Hinges & Plugs to dovetail into wall & Screws etc. £808.2s.'; an entry dated 31 Mar. 1847 shows that the cost of installing the gates was included in a general charge which applied also to the Bar End candle standards.

37. Pugin to Hardman, n.d.: letter transcribed by Phoebe Stanton and dated on internal evidence to mid-June 1845. Hardman's were at work on the gates before the middle of 1846, and Pugin reverted to one of his favourite themes when he wrote to Birmingham about the inscription ('Dieu et mon droit'), which he wanted engraved 'with strong lines' (Pugin to Hardman, ?early 1846, Stanton transcript).

38. *H.d.b.*, 1845–9, entry dated 31 Mar. 1847 and headed: 'Extra Work to Gates'. The charge was included in the cost of the gates.

39. *B*, v (1847), 194 (ill.); *ILN*, x (1847), 261 (ill.); *The House of Lords* [*c*.1850] H. & G. Clarke, 19 (ill.)

40. *H.d.b.*, 1845–9, entry dated 29 Apr. 1847: 'Mr. Thomas Quarm. A Steel Gilt Desk Seal, Initials TQ' (no charge made); 25 Nov. 1847: 'Mr. Thomas Quarm. A Standing Candlestick for 5 Lights on Lions etc, richly wrought' (no charge).

41. Pugin to Hardman, n.d., letter transcribed by Phoebe Stanton and dated to late 1847 on internal evidence. The first of the pierced roundels, made in two sizes, were despatched to the Palace in November 1848; the rest were delivered in the following February. The first hinges, sent off on 30 Dec. 1848, proved unsatisfactory and were returned to have crank

joints fitted. The hinges, lock plates and handles were all completed by the end of January. *H.d.b.*, 1845–9, entries dated 10 Nov., 30 Dec. 1848, 9 Jan., 17 Feb. 1849.

42. J. Harrington, *The Abbey and Palace of Westminster*, (1869), Pl. x. Patrick & Company obtained a contract for oil lamps in the 1860s, which may account for the disappearance of Pugin's light fittings; see also p. 230 above.

43. *ILN*, xxvi (1855), 252 (ill.). There are sketches by Pugin in the Stanley-Evans loan, RIBA Drawings.

44. PRO Works 11/20.

45. *Ibid.*

46. *Abbey and Palace* Pl. iv.

47. The metalwork in this instance was possibly executed by Skidmore's of Coventry.

Chapter XII.
5. Paintings

1. See A. J. Finberg, *Life of Turner* (1939), 351–4.

2. C. R. Leslie, *Memoirs of Constable* (1951), ed. J. Mayne, 237. Sketches by both Turner and Constable are in the lower passage of the Houses of Parliament. For a general account see W. T. Whitley, *Art in England 1821–37* (1930), 292, and Maurice Hastings, 'The House of Commons', *AR*, 1950, p. 161.

3. See Quentin Bell, 'Haydon versus Shee', *Jnl of the Warburg and Courtauld Institutes*, xxii (1959), 347–58.

4. *PP* 1835 (598) v, and 1836 (568) ix, Reports of Select Committee on Arts and Manufactures.

5. The arguments and quotations are summarized from E. Edwards, *The Fine Arts in England*, pt. i, *The Administrative Economy of the Fine Arts* (1840), 181–99. The whole question is treated at greater length in T. S. R. Boase, 'The Decoration of the New Palace of Westminster', *Jnl of the Warburg and Courtauld Institutes*, xvii (1954), 319–58.

6. *PP* 1841 (423) vi, 331 and 408.

7. *Ibid.*

8. See W. Ames, *Prince Albert and Victorian Taste* (1967).

9. The Reports of the Fine Arts Commissioners are to be found in *PP*: 1842 [412] xxv, First Report; 1843 [499] xxix, Second Report; 1844 [585] xxxi, Third Report; 1845 [671] xxvii, Fourth Report; 1846 [685] xxiv, Fifth Report; 1846 [749] xxiv, Sixth Report; 1847 [862] xxxiii, Seventh Report; 1849 [1009] xxii, Eighth Report; 1850 [1180] xxiii, Ninth Report; 1854 [1829] xix, Tenth Report; 1857–8 [2425] xxiv, Eleventh; 1861 [2806] xxxii, Twelfth Report; 1863 [3141] xvi, Thirteenth Report. The early reports were widely disseminated in contemporary periodicals. See also 1854 lxvii, Account of commissions for works of art for the decoration of the New Palace; 1860 (223) xl, Return of

money expended by the Commissioners; 1861 (295) xxxv, Return relating to paintings in fresco. For catalogues and extracts from the earlier reports, see F. K. Hunt, *The Book of Art: cartoons, frescoes, sculpture and decorative art as applied to the New Houses of Parliament: illustrated by engravings on wood* (1846).

10. W. Bell Scott, *Autobiographical Notes*, i 169; see also C. L. Eastlake, *A History of the Gothic Revival* (1872), 185; *Companion to the Almanac for 1844*, p. 223.

11. Some of the cartoons and experiments in fresco work from the later exhibition were stored on deposit from the former Ministry of Works in the V & A, but were transferred in 1960 to the stores of the Ministry of Works. The fullest account of extant paintings in the Palace is to be found in R. J. B. Walker's 'Catalogue' (HLRO) which has very full bibliographical information.

12. Noel Paton's cartoon is reproduced as frontispiece to Hunt's *Book of Art*; Tenniel's in C. Monkhouse, *The Life and Works of Sir John Tenniel (Art Annual 1901)*, 3.

13. C. H. Cope, *Reminiscences of C. W. Cope* (1891), 150.

14. *Ibid.* 158. The dimensions were 8 ft $1\frac{1}{2}$ in × 5 ft $9\frac{1}{2}$ in. Up to 1859 the fresco painters had painting rooms on the North Landing Place (PRO Works 11/28/16, ff.3–4).

15. *3 Parl. Deb.* clxiv, 1546 and 1708.

16. *Ibid.* clxix, 1656.

17. *PP* 1896 [C. 8054] lxvii, memo. IV, V.

18. There is a very full account of these frescoes in T. J. Gullick, *A Descriptive Handbook for the National Pictures in the Westminster Palace* (1865).

19. Herbert exhibited an oil study of his *Lear* in the Academy of 1849 and there are some fine studies for it in the Print Room, V & A. For Watts' *St George* see M. S. Watts, *G. F. Watts* (1912), i, 133. Cope's *Griselda*, to judge from an engraving, was pure melodrama, dominated by a violent bravo, whose foreshortened limbs showed a predilection for more violent movement than the artist could successfully render. The cartoon for his *Death of Lara* ($100 \times 68\frac{3}{4}$ in) is stored in the V & A. Horsley's *Ithuriel* is, in engraving, a feeble period piece, a drifting group of angels passing over a squat and confused group of Adam and Eve. Horsley's own choice of subject had been a combined picture of *Il Pensoroso* and *L'Allegro*, and an oil painting of this, three solemn maidens with a discreet band of dancers in the background, was purchased by the Prince Consort for Osborne. For Armstrong's *Father Thames* see *Art Jnl*, ix (1863) 178.

20. It is reproduced with a long notice in *ILN* xxiv (1854), 421. The *Montrose* is well engraved in T. Archer, *Pictures Illustrative of English History* (1884), i, 180. They are now both in the Peel Gallery, Salford. For Ward generally, see J. Dafforne, *The Life and Works of E. M. Ward* (1879). Ward made replicas in oil of several of the frescoes, as well as the original oil versions; see Dafforne, 40.

21. See *PP* 1861 (295) xxxv, 685; and correspondence about agreements in *PP* 1864 [10231] xix, pt. I, 306.

22. For all questions on Maclise, see W. J. O'Driscoll, *A Memoir of Daniel Maclise* (1871), where there are many extracts from the Commissioners' Reports. See also *Daniel Maclise* (Catalogue of Arts Council Exhibition, 1972), compiled by R. Ormond in collaboration with J. Turpin.

23. It is at present stored away and cannot be seen. The oil sketch for the *Death of Nelson* (31 × 137½ in) is in the Walker Art Gallery, Liverpool.

24. O'Driscoll, 147.

25. See 'Stereochromes, or Water Glass Painting', *Art Jnl* vii (1861), 328, for a full account of Maclise's experiments.

26. It was boarded up again for two years: 'having insufficiently paid an artist, while we received the benefit of his whole time, obtained the prime of his genius and the fruit of his best experience in a noble pair of pictures, we allow one of the two works to be muffled up and do our best to disturb him in completing the other.' *Athenaeum* (1864), 249.

27. There is a reasoned discussion of the payments in *Athenaeum* (1864), 249. See also *An Answer to Report of the Commissioners appointed to consider agreements made . . . in respect to Wall Paintings for the Palace of Westminster* by 'A Silent Member' (1864), and a letter from Maclise, *The Times*, 26 Oct. 1864. For an account of the work on Nelson, see *Art Jnl* ix (1863), 175.

28. *PP* 1860 (223) xl, 637 gives the total expenditure on frescoes and statues as £41,838.15s.6d. (frescoes £19,828.10s.6d., statues £22,010.5s.). In 1864 a new Commission (including Eastlake, A. H. Layard and R. S. Holford) was appointed to review complaints about the contracts.

29. Dyce had been working also on frescoes at All Saints, Margaret Street, work more congenial to him but nonetheless exhausting.

30. Dyce's frescoes were repaired by Cope in 1868 (except for *Hospitality*, only finished in 1864) and again by Church in 1904–5 (*PP* 1895 [C. 7651] lxxix, and 1906 [Cd. 3085] xciv).

31. See F. O. Salisbury, *Sarum Chase* (1953), 21–3.

32. *The British Empire Panels*, Borough of Swansea, 1958.

Chapter XIII. Furniture

1. *PP* 1974 (HL 133), *Furniture in the House of Lords. A Report by the Victoria & Albert Museum.* I am extremely grateful for the help and encouragement of Maurice Bond, John Hardy, Simon Jervis and Peter Thornton.

2. RIBA Drawings, Pugin-Crace letters PUG 8/1.

3. C. Wainwright, 'A. W. N. Pugin's Early Furniture', *Connoisseur*, cxci (1976), 3–11.

4. PRO, Works 11/8/9, ff.1–20.

5. *Ibid.*, ff.22, 24, 72.

6. The Gillow records, at Westminster Public Library, consist of 190 vols covering the period 1731–1932. The New Palace furniture is in Estimate Sketch Book 1849–55, entry 5820 ff.

7. The Holland records, at the V & A, consist of 235 vols covering the period 1824–1942. I am indebted to Edward Joy for information concerning this firm and their work at the New Palace. His forthcoming book on the firm will include a discussion of their considerable business in supplying furniture to government offices.

8. PRO, Works 11/8/9, ff.1–20, 8 May and 25 June 1851.

9. F. J. B. Watson, *Wallace Collection Catalogues, Furniture* (1956), 265.

10. *Jnl of Design and Manufactures* (1849), 60 and 111.

11. B. Ferrey, *Recollections of A. N. Welby Pugin* (1861), 243.

12. M. Girouard, *The Victorian Country House* (1971), 86–7. Dr Girouard suggests that Webb only supplied the furniture; it now seems probable that it was all made in his workshops.

13. RIBA Drawings, Pugin-Crace letters, PUG 7/66.

14. A. Wedgwood, *Catalogue of the RIBA Collection of Pugin Family Drawings.* This fascinating and scholarly volume will appear in the autumn of 1976. I am deeply indebted to Alexandra Wedgwood both for allowing me to read this in manuscript and for her many helpful and perceptive suggestions concerning Pugin's work in the New Palace.

15. I am extremely grateful to Shirley Bury for allowing me to use her transcripts of the entries concerning furniture from the Hardman day books.

16. N. Pevsner, *Buildings of England: London* I (1973), 526.

17. PRO, Works 11/8/4, ff.1–18.

18. T. B. Jordan, 'On Carving by Machinery', *Trans. of the Soc. of Arts*, 1852, pp. 124–36. Barry's description of the machine is quoted in *King's Works*, VI, 613, n.9.

19. *B*, v (1847), 147. To 'bost' is an archaic form of to 'boast', which in this context means to carve roughly from the solid.

20. *PP* 1846 (HL 288) xxvi, 131. I am most grateful to Joan Wilson for examining a large number of printed sessional papers for references to furniture.

21. *PP* 1849 (404) xxx, 327.

22. *B*, v (1847), 153.

23. *ILN*, x (1847), 245–7.

24. J. P. Neale and E. W. Brayley, *History and Antiquities of the Abbey Church of St Peter Westminster* (1823), ii, 133–4.

25. J. Carter, *The Ancient Architecture of England* (1794–1808), 62 and Pl. VI.

26. *The Houses of Parliament* [1860], H. G. Clarke & Co., 40.

27. *ILN*, x (1847), 245–7.

28. *Ibid.* 281–2.

29. Ryde, *Illustrations* (1849), Pl. XVI.

30. *The New Palace of Westminster* (1855), Warrington & Co., 42 and 56.

31. *ILN*, xxi (1852), 376–7.

32. A. Wright and P. Smith, *Parliament Past and Present* [1902–3]. I am very grateful to Maurice Bond and to Nicholas Cooper of the National Monuments Record for having prints made for me for Pls 191, 196, 198 and 199 from Wright and Smith's original negatives now in the HLRO.

33. This drawing is the property of the Royal Academy. I should like to thank their library staff for kindly arranging to have it photographed for me. I am also very grateful to Andrew Saint for drawing it to my attention and giving me information concerning Shaw, Nesfield and the New Palace.

34. PRO, Works 11/21, 12 Mar. 1869. Edward Barry had sent a design for the throne with an estimate of £760 to the Office of Works on 8 Nov. 1866 (*ibid.*); Works 29/268 is probably the drawing then sent.

35. Works 29/2560 is a figured design for this bed (not precisely as executed).

36. *PP* 1974 (HL 133), *Furniture in the House of Lords.*

37. Pevsner, *London*, I, 529.

38. E. M. Barry, 'An Account of the New Palace of Westminster', *RIBA Trans.* 1857–8, p. 94.

Chapter XIV. Mother of Parliaments? Architectural Influences from the New Palace

1. *Works of John Ruskin*, ed. Cook & Wedderburn, 1903–12, quotations indexed under 'London'. James Fergusson, *History of the Modern Styles of Architecture* (1862) 325.

2. Sir Nikolaus Pevsner is dealing with this in *A History of Building Types* (1976) which I have not seen.

3. For illustrated periodicals that made these sets of drawings influential see J. Summerson, *Victorian Architecture* (1970) 124 ff.

4. Melbourne Parliament House: *B*, 1860 xviii, 577; Fergusson, (1902 edn.) 172; A. Garran, *Picturesque Atlas of Australasia* (1886–8) vol. ii; J. M. Freeland, *Architecture in Australia, a History* (1968).

5. Sydney design: *B*, 1862 xx, 66; 1869 xxvii, 647. Lynn: *B*, 1915 cix, 206, 219. Old parliament house: *Glimpses of Australia* (1897) vol. i; also Freeland as n.4.

6. H. L. White, ed., *Canberra, A Nation's Capital* (1954).

7. Ottawa Houses of Parliament: *B*, 1859 xvii, 808–9; *BN*, 1861 vii, 196, 205; Hitchcock, *Architecture: Nineteenth and Twentieth Centuries* (1958) 195, 168, 169; Alan Gowans, *Building Canada* . . . (1966) 156–9, 191–3.

8. Towered porches, e.g. Wilkins at Pentillie,

Barry at Walton House, Teulon at Enbrook; and J. T. Knowles's entry in *Catalogue of the Designs* . . . (1836) 43–4 (last reference kindness of Professor Stanton). Cp. above, p. 41.

9. *B*, 1859 xvii, 808.

10. *B*, 1855 xiii, 319. Ruskin in 1859, *Works*, vol. xvi.

11. Summerson, *Victorian Architecture*, 84.

12. *PP* 1868 (265) viii, Report of Select Committee on House of Commons (Arrangements), appendix, plans submitted for comparison by E. M. Barry in March.

13. *ILN*, 18 March 1911, p. 377.

14. Murray's *Handbook to India*, 1898: architect F. W. Stevens C.I.E.; illustration in *AR*, December 1971, p. 331. One feature of the Houses of Parliament copied in W. L. Granville's Calcutta High Court building was the iron roofs, *B*, 1869 xxvii.

15. Lutyens and Voysey drawings in RIBA Drawings Collection. John Brandon Jones, *C. F. A. Voysey, a Memoir*, reprint from *Architectural Association Jnl*, May 1957, p. 238.

16. Works 11/10/3, f.1, request May 1848 from Prussian government for plan; f.9, Barry's charge for plans, 25 guineas; f.17, similar request from Swiss government. The Federal Palace at Berne had been built in the 1850s in a Florentine Renaissance style.

17. Berlin Houses of Parliament: *PP* 1868 (265) viii, 64; *BN*, 1872 xxii, 8; *B*, 1872 xxx, 587. Scott's design: *B*, 1875 xxxiii, 774, 820; *BN*, 1875 xxix, 166, 196, 224. William Emerson published his own design with German text in an undated pamphlet, *Erläuterungsbericht* . . . (RIBA Library), featuring a low dome surmounted by a tall Gothic open lantern. On a domed Romanesque design of 1845 by Semper, see N. Pevsner, *Some Architectural Writers of the Nineteenth Century* (1972), 255–7.

18. *B*, 1875 xxxiii, 774.

19. Hitchcock in *Concerning Architecture* (ed. J. Summerson, 1968), 202; as completed, *American Architect* 1885 xvii, 54.

20. H. Wagner & P. Wallot, 'Parlamentshäuser und Ständehäuser', in *Handbuch der Architektur* (J. Durm, ed.), part 4 'Entwerfen . . .', 7.Halb-Band [*but* on spine at BM: vol. x] (Darmstadt 1887), 442–5. (One bookseller lists separate publication Stuttgart 1900.)

21. Fergusson, *Modern Architecture* (1873 edn.) 373, expanding remarks of 1862.

22. Leicester Square: *B*, 1851 ix, 803. Sydenham and Whitehall: drawings reprod. in Alfred Barry, *Life*. Washington: unfinished drum, ill. Fergusson 1862, 439, also old and new plans. Fergusson on Barry, 1862, p. 325. Schmidt's design: *B*, 1868 xxvi, 114.

23. Dissemination of E. M. Barry's design: 1867 vols *B*, *BN*, *ILN*; M. H. Port, *Architectural History*, 1968 xi, 75; and articles cited in Summerson, *Victorian Architecture*, 125–6, nn. 23, 35.

24. *BN* 1885 xlviii, 88 and perspective view; Baedeker, *Austria-Hungary*, 1905; plan and

interior in Wagner & Wallot (cited n. 20), 423, 436.

25. Hitchcock, 1958, 198.

26. E.g. Kelham Hall, Preston Town Hall, St Pancras Station Hotel, illustrated with Ypres Cloth Hall (from Fergusson's *Handbook* of 1855) in Summerson, *Victorian Architecture*.

27. Waterhouse's competition perspective of 1859 reprod. in Cecil Stewart, *The Stones of Manchester* (1956), 74.

28. Clock tower and chapel were spared in recent demolition of the house.

29. J. E. O. Wilshere, *Leicester Clock Tower 1868–1968*, pamphlet published by author, 1968. Victoria Street clock tower: *The Times*, 15 Mar. 1892, 12, (reference kindness of Miss Mary Dunbar).

30. Ralph Adams Cram, 'Recent University Architecture in the United States', *RIBA Jnl*, 1912, 3rd ser. xix, 497.

31. John Ritter, 'World Parliament, the League of Nations Competition, 1926', *AR*, July 1964, 17.

32. I am grateful to Sir John Summerson for reading a draft of this essay.

Index